Recording Historic Structures

Recording Historic Structures

HISTORIC AMERICAN BUILDINGS SURVEY/
HISTORIC AMERICAN ENGINEERING RECORD

EDITED BY JOHN A. BURNS
AND
THE STAFF OF HABS/HAER
NATIONAL PARK SERVICE
U.S. DEPARTMENT OF THE INTERIOR

THE AMERICAN INSTITUTE OF ARCHITECTS PRESS
WASHINGTON, DC

This book is dedicated to the continuum of talented and committed individuals who, over more than a half-century, have developed the standards and guidelines of the Historic American Buildings Survey and the Historic American Engineering Record.

THE AMERICAN INSTITUTE OF ARCHITECTS PRESS
1735 NEW YORK AVENUE, NW
WASHINGTON, DC 20006

PUBLISHED 1989
PRINTED IN CANADA

LIBRARY OF CONGRESS CATALOGING-IN-PUBLICATION DATA

Recording historic structures/Historic American Buildings Survey/
Historic American Engineering Record; edited by John A. Burns and the staff of HABS/HAER, National Park Service, U.S. Department of the Interior.
Bibliography: p.229
Includes index.
ISBN 1-55835-018-7: $29.95.—ISBN 1-55835-021-7 pbk.: $19.95
1. Historic buildings—Conservation and restoration. 2. Historic sites—Conservation and restoration. 3. History—Methodology.
4. Historic buildings—United States—Conservation and restoration.
I. Burns, John A. II. Historic American Buildings Survey/Historic American Engineering Record.
CC 135.R4 1989 89-32439
363.6'9—dc20 CIP

Design by Marty Anderson Design, Washington, DC
Composed in Panache with Veljovic by Harlowe Typography
Printed by D. W. Friesen, Altona, Manitoba, through Four Colour Imports, Ltd.

CONTENTS

CONTRIBUTORS

Editor

John A. Burns, AIA

Principal architect of the Historic American Building Survey/Historic American Engineering Record, John A. Burns's areas of specialization are historic building and construction technologies, late nineteenth- and twentieth-century architecture, and documentation technology. He has lectured and written extensively on these topics since 1972, when he first joined the HABS/HAER program. Mr. Burns graduated from the Pennsylvania State University with a bachelor of architecture degree and a bachelor of arts degree in art history. A registered architect, he is a member of the American Institute of Architects' Committee on Historic Resources.

The Staff of HABS/HAER

Sally Kress Tompkins, deputy chief of HABS/HAER, has more than ten years of experience conducting historic structures surveys throughout the United States. She has written numerous articles and lectured widely on historic structures survey methodology. Ms. Tompkins developed the prototypical survey methodology for use by federal agencies.

Alison K. Hoagland has been a historian with HABS since 1979. She has a master of arts degree in American studies from George Washington University and a bachelor of arts degree in American civilization from Brown University. She has researched historic buildings from Washington, D.C., to Alaska.

G. Gray Fitzsimons serves as engineering historian for HAER. He has been with HABS/HAER since 1986, completing his bachelor of science degree in civil engineering at the University of Maryland in 1979 and subsequently working as a structural engineer. Mr. Fitzsimons has conducted inventory and documentation projects on historic bridges, hydroelectric works, and steel mills throughout the United States.

William L. Lebovich is an architectural historian for HAER and has worked for the Department of the Interior since 1974. He has been the curator for two traveling exhibitions, worked in the Office of the Governor of Massachusetts for the Boston Redevelopment Authority, and has published articles and photographs in numerous academic and exhibition publications.

Richard K. Anderson, Jr., has been a staff architect with HAER since 1978, specializing in the documentation of historic industrial sites and ships. He is the author of the HAER Guidelines for Recording Historic Ships (1988) and a co-author of the HAER Field Instructions Manual (1981).

Paul D. Dolinsky is Principal Architect for HABS, where he has more than ten years' experience in developing and conducting historic structure and landscape projects. He has authored many articles and delivered numerous lectures on the subject.

FOREWORD

I am glad to have the opportunity to tell you readers a bit about the history of HABS, which I helped found. It all began with a long, detailed memorandum dated November 13, 1933, which served as the charter for the Historic American Buildings Survey. HABS, as it became known, was quickly implemented by the National Park Service and first staffed by architects Thomas T. Waterman, called back from a study visit to Britain, and John P. O'Neil, an architectural graduate of Notre Dame University with some archeological experience in Latin America. Work proceeded with such speed that within weeks it was possible to have a showing of fine measured drawings from across the country at the National Museum in Washington.

Waterman was mainly responsible for the architectural standards of the recording work. He had a solid background, having made field records of the Cathedral at Palma in the Balearics for Ralph Adams Cram. While working with Perry, Shaw and Hepburn in Williamsburg, he had published (with John A. Barrows) a landmark volume, *The Domestic Colonial Architecture of Tidewater Virginia* (New York and London, 1932), which featured measured drawings with exquisite attention to details of work in brick and wood.

Quite apart from whatever value measured drawings may have as a historical record, the process of measuring and drawing careful records to scale is the most effective way to gain an understanding of a building's fabric. Someone has aptly called it "graphic analysis."

In schools of architecture today, students are taught to "talk architecture" and even make pretty pictures or models of things which could—or could not—be built. But there is no way to appreciate an existing, working structure—its virtues and its failures—like making a careful drawing of it. The man who doesn't get his hands dirty on the job will never know enough.

The high quality of architectural delineation in HABS work of the 1930s was due to the skill of the draftsmen recruited with the help of the HABS National Advisory Board and the American Institute of Architects. The early employees were all architects. There wasn't a building full of people; the administrative staff was small, and the architects had the historical training necessary to do the work. Standards of presentation were achieved by circulating memoranda to field parties. These were compiled in the haste and battle smoke of the emergency campaign to relieve professional unemployment—the overriding problem of the period.

World War II understandably closed down HABS (though Waterman continued to make drawings surreptitiously in a Bureau of Yards and Docks drafting room). When the war ended, the Park Service resumed making HABS records of its own historic buildings while preparing for restoration plans. But new questions arose when substantial funds under the Park Service Mission 66

Program became available with the mandate to record structures outside of government management. The innovation of summer programs employing architectural students brought new problems in directing field parties of beginners, often in remote places.

At this time, we started using the 1930s instructions to guide the work. But the need for an overall handy reference volume became apparent and it was decided to produce one. Who had the field experience—working under Park Service rules and regulations—to tackle the job?

Among the outstanding leaders I had recruited to run the teams in the East was Professor Harley J. McKee of Syracuse University. I had met him during the first Society of Architectural Historians summer field trip, which toured Nantucket Island and Martha's Vineyard in August 1951. McKee had a sharp eye, a clear, discriminating mind, and a long-term interest in American buildings. He had run student teams through several successful seasons, the last one being at Charleston, South Carolina. McKee was the man for the job.

Professor McKee spent two entire summers in our Philadelphia office compiling a set of instructions to the field. The only complete set of circulars from the WPA days was a collection lately inherited from Earl H. Reed, FAIA, of Chicago, one of the original HABS district officers, who had later served as national advisor to the program. I worked very closely with McKee, and it was a pleasure. As the various parts of the new book were drafted, they were mimeographed and sent to the field for comment and recommendations. At the end of the 1961 recording season we had a measured drawings manual of 109 pages, which seemed to serve the purpose.

In 1970 architect James C. Massey, originally a student recruited from the University of Pennsylvania who eventually served as national head of HABS in Washington, directed a handsome production of McKee's work, *Recording Historic Buildings,* through the U.S. Government Printing Office. For that he deserves great credit.

We are now to have a new version for a new generation of readers and users. I wish you well.

Charles E. Peterson, FAIA
Former Supervising Architect for Historic Structures
Eastern Office of Design and Construction
National Park Service

Philadelphia
June 1988

PREFACE

America has a long, rich architectural and engineering heritage, as evidenced by our built environment. The study of historic structures provides insight into the ways in which earlier generations lived and worked. Through the techniques discussed in *Recording Historic Structures,* that heritage is being documented so that many future generations can understand and appreciate their rich heritage.

Recording Historic Structures will assist individuals in preparing documentation (usually measured drawings, large-format photographs, and histories) for inclusion in the Historic American Buildings Survey/Historic American Engineering Record (HABS/HAER) collections maintained by the Library of Congress. *Recording Historic Structures* is the principal handbook, the Bible, so to speak, of the HABS/HAER programs for those who are interested in America's historic architecture, engineering, and industry and who wish to see that heritage documented for subsequent generations. The book is thus indispensable for the student architect, photographer, or historian working on a HABS/HAER summer recording team, as well as for the professional who has been hired to document, to HABS/HAER standards, historic structures that are about to be demolished or substantially altered as a result of federal action.

The book is also intended for another group of individuals: those interested in the general principles of architectural, engineering, and industrial documentation used to prepare drawings, photographs, and data pages to archival standards, and in the general requirements of documenting historic structures. *Recording Historic Structures* is not only a handbook directed specifically to the preparation of HABS/HAER documentation; it also covers the broader principles applicable to the field.

The gestation of the book began after the "Secretary of the Interior's Standards and Guidelines for Architectural and Engineering Documentation" were published in 1983. Harley J. McKee's predecessor to this volume, *Recording Historic Buildings,* had gone out of print. Diane Maddex of Preservation Press had approached HABS/HAER about reprinting McKee's book as a classic work in preservation literature, prompting discussions within HABS/HAER over whether to reprint, revise, or replace *Recording Historic Buildings,* a text which had over the previous decade-and-a-half become a familiar sight on the bookshelves of persons interested in preserving and documenting historic structures. A committee of HABS/HAER staff members, chaired by Deputy Chief Sally Kress Tompkins, was formed to discuss the options. Ultimately a consensus emerged from the committee that a new handbook was needed. It was decided that senior staff members would author chapters in their areas of expertise.

I selected John Burns to be the overall editor based on his knowledge of the HABS/HAER recording process, his knowledge of architecture and photography, and his excellent writing ability. Sometimes John and I would meet daily for weeks on end to iron out problems. In the end, it was John who made this book work.

At one time or another, virtually the entire staff of HABS/HAER has worked on the preparation of the manuscript, whether researching, writing, typing, gathering illustrations, or providing peer review. Their years of accumulated field experience plus thousands of measured drawings, photographs, and pages of historical and descriptive data are synthesized in the pages of this volume.

Since the founding of HABS in 1933, more than 3,000 men and women have worked with the Historic American Buildings Survey/Historic American Engineering Record to "preserve" approximately 22,000 historic structures throughout the United States, using documentation processes described in this book. At least one-third of these structures have been lost to us forever. But the historical documentation sits safely in the Library of Congress.

Through written studies, measured drawings, and photographs stored in the Library of Congress collections, a permanent record now exists that is accessible to the public. In fact, these records represent the most widely used of all the special collections of the library. This architectural and engineering documentation will continue to provide future generations with information on our precious built heritage long after the structures themselves have disappeared.

We hope that the methods explained here and the structures already documented will inspire students, professionals, and others interested in architecture, engineering, history, photography, and landscape to continue this important quest.

Robert J. Kapsch, Chief
Historic American Buildings Survey/
Historic American Engineering Record

ACKNOWLEDGMENTS

Recording Historic Structures draws heavily on the accumulated knowledge and writings of former HABS and HAER employees who produced the early "Bulletins," "Circulars," and "Specifications," and the more recent "Field Instructions" and "Procedures Manuals." It also owes a special debt to the National Park Service people involved with *Recording Historic Buildings,* the predecessor to this volume. Charles E. Peterson, then Supervising Architect for Historic Structures, identified the need for a handbook students could use and hired the late Harley J. McKee to produce the text. McKee, working under Peterson's supervision and with the assistance of HABS architect James C. Massey, wrote the "Manual of the Historic American Buildings Survey" in several parts, issued starting in 1961. In 1968 it was under Massey's supervision as Chief of HABS that the parts were first published collectively under the title "Recording Historic Buildings." That offset edition of 1968 was further refined and ultimately became the book *Recording Historic Buildings* in 1970.

Recording Historic Structures owes its existence to a large number of people. The other authors and I would like to acknowledge and thank these people for their contributions.

The entire staff of HABS/HAER offered continuing support from the inception of the project to its completion. Without their assistance, the book would not have been possible. Chief of HABS/HAER Robert J. Kapsch directed the effort, pushing for its completion, encouraging, advising, and making sure we were all headed in the same direction. Sally Kress Tompkins chaired the committee of HABS/HAER staff who developed the concept for the book: Richard K. Anderson, Jr.; Jack E. Boucher; John A. Burns; S. Allen Chambers, Jr.; Eric N. DeLony; Paul D. Dolinsky; Alison K. Hoagland; Jet Lowe; Susan McCown; Ellen B. Minnich; and Denys P. Myers. Other staff members who contributed their time and talents include Frances P. Alexander; Kenneth L. Anderson, Jr.; R. Marlene Bergstrom; Holly K. Chamberlain; Judy R. Davis; Robyn M. Elliott; Frederick C. Engle; Doreen E. Keyes; Robie S. Lange; Catherine C. Lavoie; Tammy D. Washington; and Jean P. Yearby.

For the introduction, James C. Massey, Robert Vogel, and Neal Fitzsimons shared their personal knowledge of the establishment of HAER. Carol Shull and Beth Savage of the National Register reviewed and commented on the survey chapter. Former HABS staffer S. Allen Chambers, Jr., helped with the first draft of the history chapter. William H. Pierson, Jr., as well as staff photographers Jack E. Boucher and Jet Lowe, offered suggestions on the photography chapter. The measured drawings chapter benefited from the generously shared teaching experience of Professors K. Edward Lay of the University of Virginia; F. Blair Reeves,

FAIA, of the University of Florida; David G. Woodcock, AIA, of Texas A&M University; and John S. Garner and Walter L. Creese of the University of Illinois. Within HABS/HAER, Kenneth L. Anderson, Jr., AIA; Richard K. Anderson, Jr.; Eric N. DeLony; and Paul D. Dolinsky contributed ideas based on their extensive field experience with measured drawings. J. T. Smith of the Royal Commission on Historical Monuments sent information about English philosophies and practices for measured drawings. The case study on landscapes was strengthened by Marion Schlefer's historical research and editorial suggestions by Frances P. Alexander.

At the Library of Congress, Mary M. Ison, Joyce Nalewajk, C. Ford Peatross, and Elisabeth Betz Parker shared their extensive knowledge of HABS and HAER garnered through their important work of making the collections accessible to the public. They graciously endured seemingly endless requests to borrow drawings and photographs to be used as illustrations. Thanks also to the HABS/HAER staff who retrieved the material from the library: Jean P. Yearby, Catherine C. Lavoie, Ellen B. Minnich, and Holly K. Chamberlain.

Five outside reviewers, Orlando Ridout V; William H. Pierson, Jr.; Jeff Dean; Tomas H. Spiers, Jr., AIA; and Larry Lankton, agreed to review and comment on the manuscript. Their thoughtful and valuable suggestions for improving the text are deeply appreciated.

John Ray Hoke, Jr., AIA, and his staff and consultants at the AIA Press were all an author could hope for: enthusiastic, supportive, and patient. Our thanks to Marty Anderson, Kathleen Hughes, Claudia Ringel, Janet Rumbarger, Alexander Shaw, and Cynthia Ware.

Finally, I would like to thank my wife, Deborah Stephens Burns, herself an alumna architectural historian from HABS. Debbie's knowledge of HABS/HAER practices, people, and activities made her an invaluable sounding board and insightful reviewer.

John A. Burns, AIA
Principal Architect, HABS/HAER

CHAPTER 1

John A. Burns

Recording Historic Structures is the basic guide for creating architectural and engineering documentation to the standards of the Historic American Buildings Survey (HABS) and the Historic American Engineering Record (HAER) of the National Park Service. While the primary focus of this book is the production of HABS and HAER documentation, researchers will find its contents useful for compiling architectural and engineering documentation for other purposes as well. The recording methods and techniques described in the book are fundamental tools for examining any existing structure. The word "structure" will be used in this book to mean building, site, structure, or object, without making a distinction between architecture (HABS) and engineering (HAER).

What Is Architectural and Engineering Documentation?

Architectural and engineering documentation is a compilation of both graphic and written records that explain and illustrate the significant characteristics of a historic building, site, structure, or object. Graphic records are most commonly photographs and drawings. Photographic records can consist of contemporary and historic photographs and photographic copies of historic documents or illustrations. Drawings may be historic drawings or measured drawings. Measured drawings are produced from measurements taken from the structure being documented. Written records are both historical and descriptive. Written historical records are based on research performed to determine the chronology and context of the structure being documented. Descriptive records are based on inspection of the physical fabric of the building, site, structure, or object being documented.

With the help of architectural and engineering documentation one can study a building, site, structure, or object without necessarily visiting it. The purpose of documentation is to explain and illustrate. While the goal of this book is to encourage the creation of architectural and engineering documentation for inclusion in the archival collections of the Historic American Buildings Survey and Historic American Engineering Record, the techniques and methods are applicable to any type of documentation.

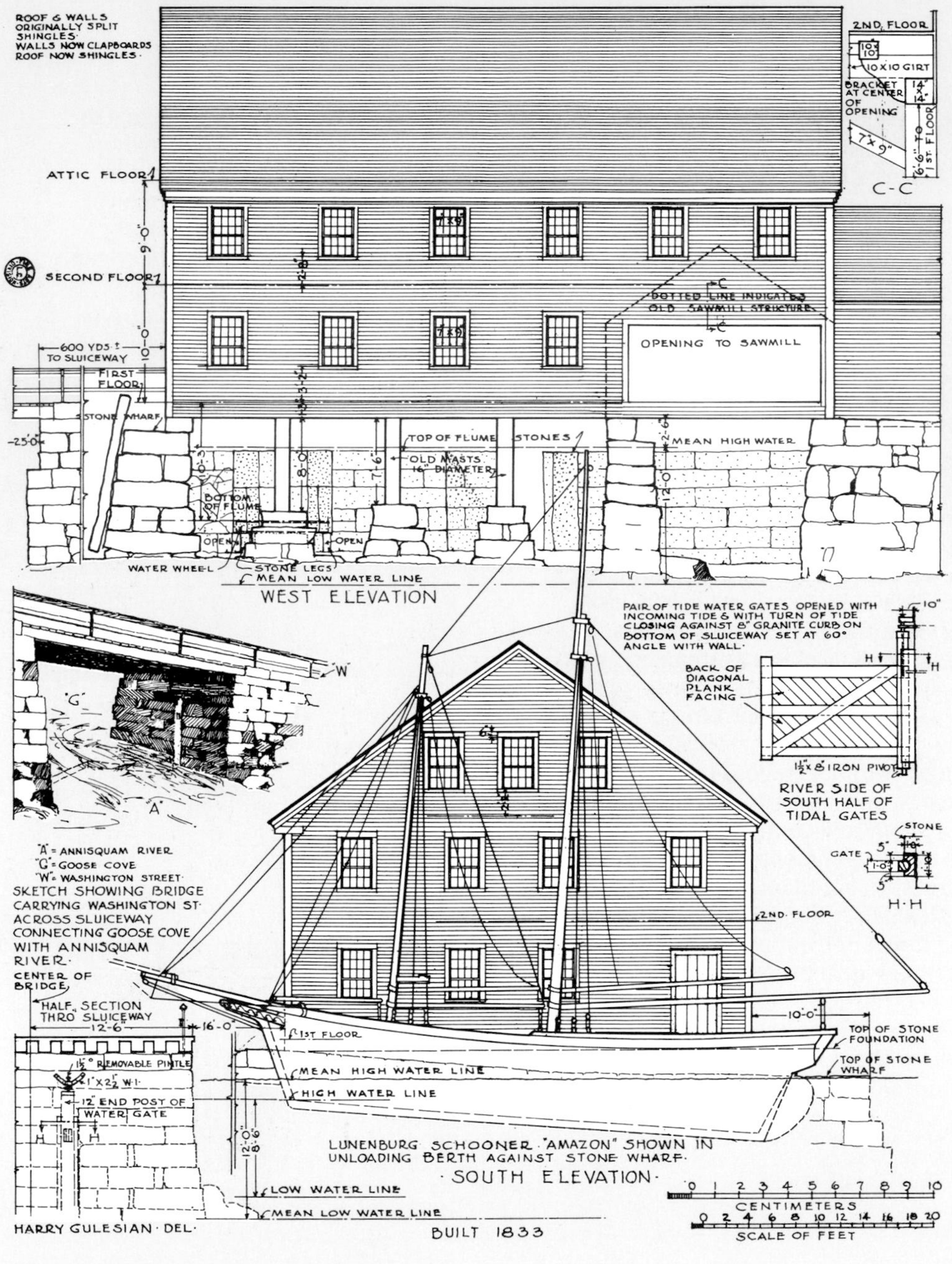

Background of HABS/HAER

HABS/HAER records are a particular form of architectural and engineering documentation that has evolved since the founding of HABS in 1933. The memorandum from Charles E. Peterson to his superiors in the National Park Service proposing the establishment of HABS also determined its initial direction:

The plan I propose is to enlist a qualified group of architects and draftsmen to study, measure and draw up the plans, elevations and details of the important antique buildings of the United States. Our architectural heritage of buildings from the last four centuries diminishes daily at an alarming rate. The ravages of fire and the natural elements together with the demolition and alterations caused by real estate "improvements" form an inexorable tide of destruction destined to wipe out the great majority of the buildings which knew the beginning and first flourish of the nation. The comparatively few structures which can be saved by extraordinary effort and presented as exhibition houses and museums or altered and used for residences or minor commercial uses comprise only a minor percentage of the interesting and important architectural specimens which remain from the old days. It is the responsibility of the American people that if the great number of our antique buildings must disappear through economic causes, they should not pass into unrecorded oblivion . . .

The list of building types . . . should include public buildings, churches, residences, bridges, forts, barns, mills, shops, rural outbuildings, and any other kind of structure of which there are good specimens extant . . . Other structures which would not engage the especial interest of an architectural connoisseur are the great number of plain structures which by fate or accident are identified with historic events.

Figure 1.1

An early HABS drawing recording architecture, industry, and a sailing vessel.

Peterson's memorandum included a recommendation that the survey should not document structures built after 1860. Aside from being a logical end point, the date determined the type and style of buildings that would dominate the early recording efforts of HABS. The recommendation implied that buildings should be at least seventy-three years old to be considered historic and eliminated from consideration the huge number of buildings constructed in the last part of the nineteenth century.

Given these limitations, the body of buildings to be studied was relatively small and included a limited number of building types and materials of construction. Before 1860, materials of construction were predominantly brick, stone, and wood. The format designed for the documentation was correspondingly simple and straightforward. The drawing sheet size was roughly 60′ x 80′ at the common scale of ¼″ = 1′-0″, which accommodated most pre-1860 buildings. The drawing format was horizontal; the need to document tall buildings was outside the scope of early HABS work.

Another influence on early recordings was the fact that HABS was designed as relief employment for unemployed architects. The funds were targeted for salaries, not materials or equipment. The labor-intensive measured drawings were the dominant means of recording. These drawings, at the time, defined HABS. The program is still known primarily as a measured drawings collection (see fig. 1.1). By contrast, the accompanying early photographs and histories seem inadequate by current standards.

More than fifty years later, one now finds a different set of circumstances. The labor-intensive nature of hand measuring and drafting, ideal for relief employment, is expensive. Students

Figure 1.2

HABS has begun to record buildings younger than itself, in this case the Walter Gropius house of 1937 in Lincoln, Massachusetts.

have been substituted for the professionals employed in the early days. Following National Register criteria, buildings come of age historically in just fifty years, which means that HABS is documenting buildings younger than itself (see fig. 1.2).

After 1860, manufactured building materials began to dominate construction. Structural systems changed as well, from simple bearing wall or post-and-beam construction to balloon and platform frame, steel skeleton, and reinforced concrete (see fig. 1.3). Composite materials and systems became common. Building systems—including heating, plumbing, gas, electrical and vertical movement—developed as an integral part of almost every building.

Figure 1.3

A recent HABS initiative to record state capitols resulted in this section drawing through the sheet metal dome of the Texas State Capitol in Austin.

Paralleling these developments in the building industry were even broader changes in engineering and industry (see fig. 1.4). By the 1960s there was growing interest in America's technological heritage. Gail Hathaway, past president of the American Society of Civil Engineers (ASCE) and chairman of ASCE's History and Heritage Committee, approached the National Park Service with the idea of setting up a companion program to HABS that would record historic engineering and industrial sites. The Historic American Engineering Record (HAER) was established in 1969. The first recording efforts of the fledgling program were managed by HABS until congressional funding could be secured.

The founding of HAER reflected the growing interest in all aspects of the built environment and the changing scope and emphasis on documentary recording (see fig. 1.5). Changes such as these have forced reassessment and adjustment in HABS/HAER's methodology for documentation and will continue to do so. The changes will be governed by (1) the resources available to produce documentation, (2) the actual structures that will be considered historic and significant, and (3) the available research materials on those structures.

Given the greatly increased universe of structures HABS/HAER is mandated to survey, and the limited resources available, HABS/HAER will, of necessity, become more selective in recording historic structures.

FIGURE 1.4

A shaft of light illuminates the work area as molten metal is poured from a furnace into molds at the American Brass Company in Buffalo. Industrial photography presents challenges to the photographer to explain and interpret a production process, often under difficult lighting conditions.

FIGURE 1.5

HAER's long-standing interest in the iron and steel industry is being realized with congressionally mandated funds in cooperation with the National Park Service's America's Industrial Heritage Project. The Cambria Iron Company in Johnstown, Pennsylvania, was one of the major early iron producers in the United States. The foundry building was recorded through the use of hand measuring and documentary records from Bethlehem Steel Corporation.

A

B

C

D

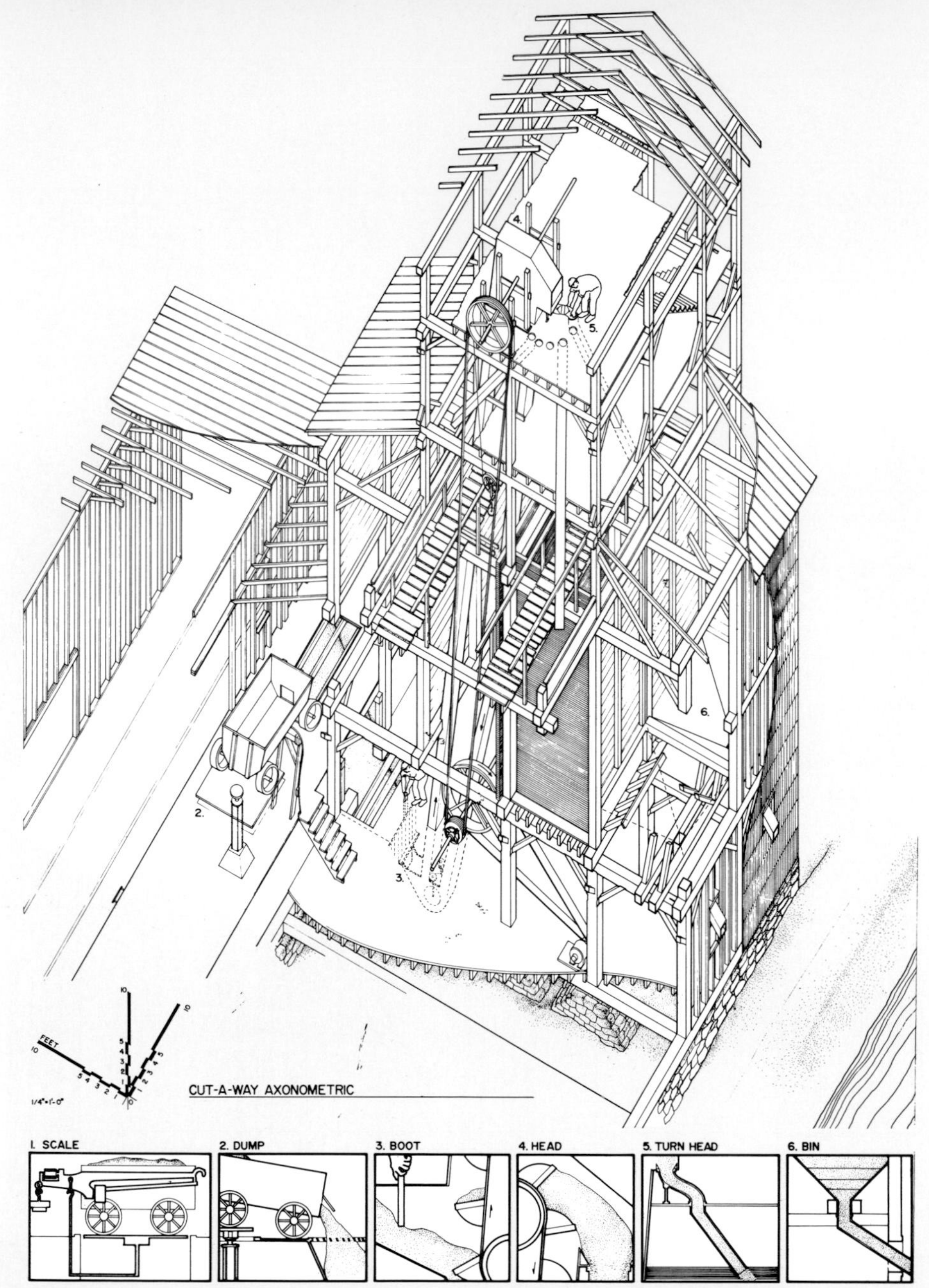

FIGURE 1.6

This 1861 grain elevator in Illinois continues to be used to store grain, while the method of transport has changed from horse-drawn wagons and canal boats to railroad cars to trucks. A portion of the elevator was graphically cut away to depict the movement and storage of the grain and to reveal the structural system of the bins.

HABS/HAER Standards

Since its inception the Historic American Buildings Survey and, since 1969, the Historic American Engineering Record have had consistent standards concerning the size and format of documentation as well as its reproducibility. The uniform format and reproducibility are what set the HABS/HAER collections apart from most other collections of architectural and engineering documentation. Those two characteristics make the HABS/HAER collections easily accessible to users.

The National Historic Preservation Act, as amended in 1980, directed the secretary of the interior to develop "a uniform process and standards for documenting historic properties by public agencies and private parties for purposes of incorporation into, or complementing, the national historical architectural and engineering records within the Library of Congress." These standards derived from existing HABS and HAER standards. "The Secretary of the Interior's Standards and Guidelines for Architectural and Engineering Documentation" (hereafter referred to as HABS/HAER standards) were published in 1983 as part of "Archeology and Historic Preservation; Secretary of the Interior's Standards and Guidelines" (*Federal Register*, 29 Sept. 1983; see Appendix A).

There are four HABS/HAER standards. Standard I includes content and requires documentation to adequately explicate and illustrate what is significant or valuable about the historic building, site, structure, or object being documented. Standard II covers the quality of the documentation, stating that it must be prepared accurately from reliable sources with limitations clearly stated to permit independent verification of the information. Materials are described in Standard III, which requires that documentation be prepared on materials that are readily reproducible, durable, and in standard sizes. Standard IV says that documentation shall be clearly and concisely produced.

FIGURE 1.7

A richly detailed section drawing of the home of the wealthy industrialist Asa Packer in Jim Thorpe, Pennsylvania.

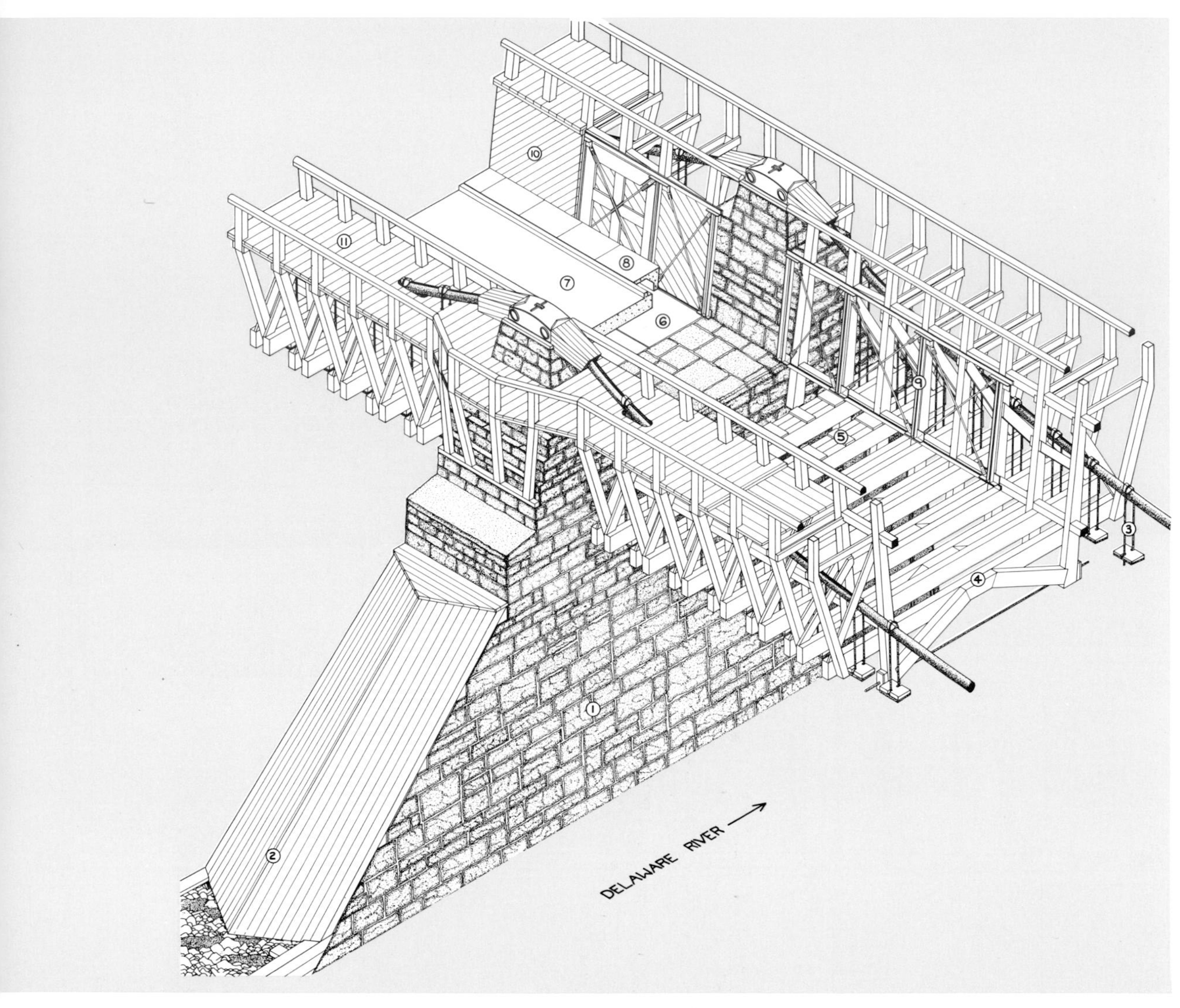

FIGURE 1.8

Work on the Delaware Aqueduct to convert it to an interpretive structure demonstrating its use as a canal aqueduct and as a modern highway bridge brought HAER back in 1988 to produce additional drawings to supplement HAER drawings done nineteen years earlier (see also fig. 5.28).

Why Document?

Architectural and engineering documentation broadens our experience of American history. Historic structures are frequently the only tangible evidence of history. They can open new doors to understanding the past. They can be significant for their characteristics and features, as well as for their association with people and events. As artifacts, they can provide insights into past cultures and activities, events and people.

If a structure is significant, whether for its history, design, sentiment, or some other evaluation criteria, some means of preservation can usually be found. Continued use is the most common and best form of preservation, ideal for structures that have not lost their functional usefulness (see fig. 1.6). Other historic structures have been adapted to new uses or turned into museums (see fig. 1.7). A major problem with preserving historic structures is that they are large objects. The vast majority of historic structures must be preserved in place, being too large to move (see fig. 1.8).

One important purpose for architectural and engineering documentation is for academic study. The records can provide a way to investigate artifacts from the past that may otherwise be too scattered or too difficult to visit, or that have subsequently disappeared. Some artifacts may exist only in documentation, any physical remains being gone.

Architectural and engineering documentation can be used to record historic structures that cannot be saved or are too big for curation in museums. Structures are destroyed in many ways and for many reasons: new development, technical or functional obsolescence, neglect, fire, natural disaster, and war. Some of the causes can be mitigated, with precautions taken against others. Architectural and engineering documentation can provide future generations with information on structures long since vanished. Documentation can also serve as a form of insurance for a significant structure so that if there were to be a catastrophic loss, the structure could be rebuilt.

A fundamental principle of architectural and engineering documentation is that historic structures cannot be recorded and explained adequately by words alone. The graphic content is integral to recording the history of the built environment (see figs. 1.9 and 1.10).

The advantages of HABS/HAER as a repository of historical information are in the quality of the documentation, standardization of methodology, durability of archival materials, archival storage methods, and accessibility to the public. Unlike some preservation agencies that lose interest in historical documentation once a building is demolished, HABS/HAER retains all material that is accessioned into its collection. The HABS and HAER collections are in the public domain and are available at the Library of Congress.

The permanency of the written material in the collections is accomplished not only by its retention but also by the fact that it is typed or photocopied xerographically onto archival paper. The permanency of the

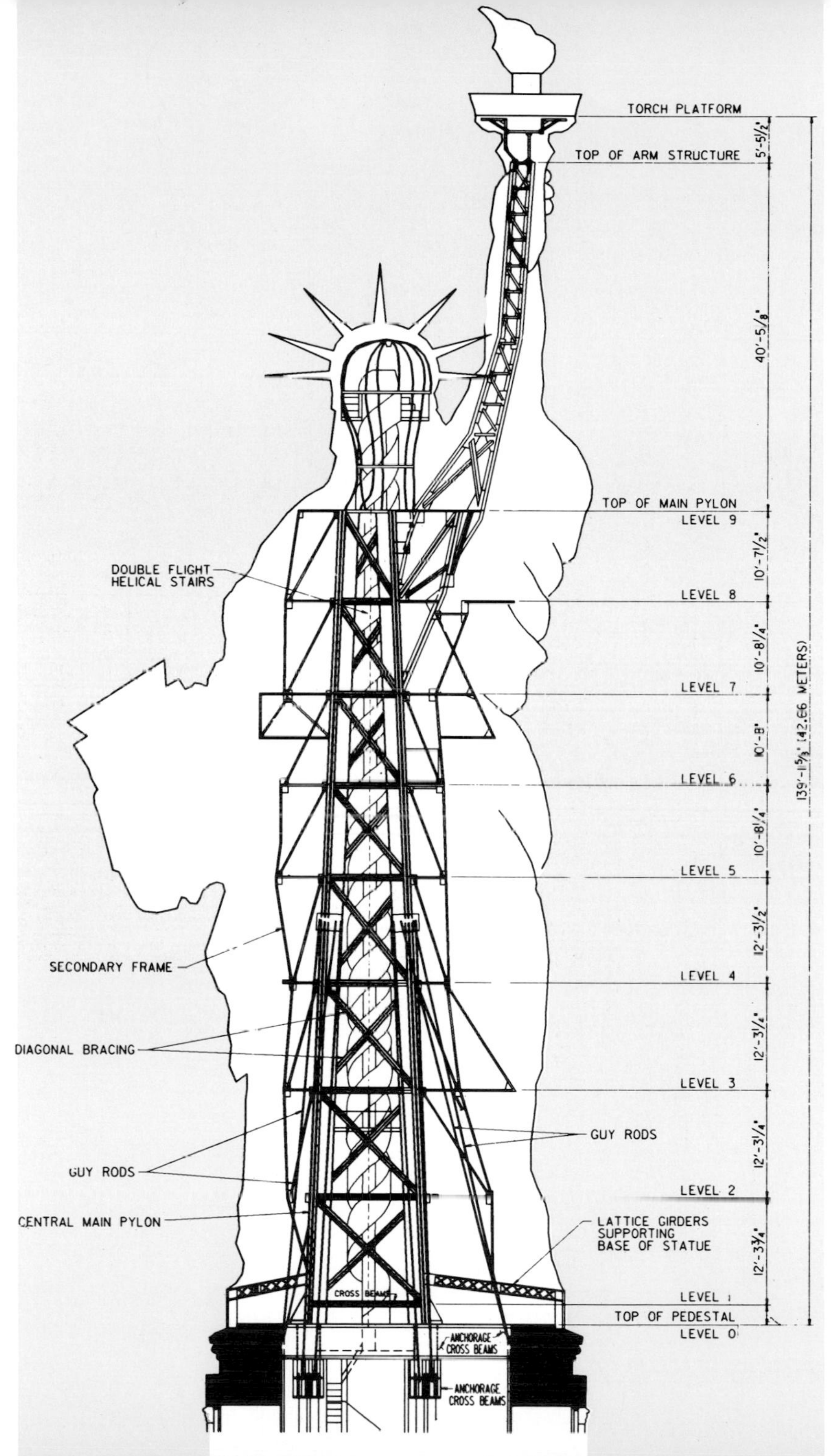

FIGURE 1.9

A diagrammatic drawing produced by a computer of the armature for the Statue of Liberty. The drawing was one of a set produced for the restoration of the statue and was among the first computer-generated HAER drawings.

Figure 1.10

The Walker Family Farm in Great Smokey Mountain National Park, photographed in 1962 with two daughters of the original builder.

HABS/HAER collections also provides an advantage for primary material that may be unprotected. Rare documents can be photocopied xerographically onto archival paper and included with the HABS/HAER reports. Unprotected graphic material can, likewise, be photographed or photocopied for the HABS/HAER collection, barring copyright problems for either.

The permanence and accessibility of the photographs are ensured by careful archival processing of the negatives and prints and careful handling and storage. The original large-format negatives are retained and used for making prints so that there is no degradation of the image from the original.

Reproducible copies of the measured drawings are made so that additional copies can be made without damage to the originals. The original drawings are produced with archival ink on polyester sheets for archival permanence.

In the HABS/HAER collections, the written material is filed along with the large-format photographs and measured drawings, all of which constitute the formal HABS/HAER documentation. The important relationship between the written information and the graphic material is fostered by HABS/HAER's careful guardianship. The compiled package, in a permanent and accessible repository, makes an important addition to our store of historical knowledge.

How HABS/HAER Documentation Is Produced

The majority of HABS/HAER documentation is produced during the summer months by undergraduate and graduate students who work in teams under professional supervision. A typical team is led by a supervisor, usually a professor with credentials in the subject area being studied. Architecture students do the measuring and drafting. A historian, again with credentials in the area being studied, provides the historical research. Teams are tailored to the needs of each particular project, taking into account the significance of the site, existing records, site conditions, and the ultimate purpose of the documentation. A team will work in the field for approximately twelve weeks, producing completed measured drawings and written historical and descriptive data. The formal photographs are usually taken by a HABS/HAER photographer.

HABS and HAER have always given priority to recording structures threatened with destruction. Although the federal government has taken steps to ensure that its activities do not adversely affect historic structures, when there is no reasonable alternative to demolition or substantial alteration, HABS/HAER documentation can mitigate the loss by providing graphic and written records (see fig. 1.11).

FIGURE 1.11

A private developer produced HABS documentation of the City of Paris Dry Goods Company Building in San Francisco before it was demolished. The rotunda, with its stained glass skylight shown here, was dismantled and reconstructed in a new department store on the same site.

The National Historic Preservation Act, as amended in 1980, stipulates that "each Federal agency shall initiate measures to assure that where, as a result of Federal action or assistance carried out by such agency, an historic property is to be substantially altered or demolished, timely steps are taken to make or have made appropriate records, and that such records then be deposited . . . in the Library of Congress . . . for future use and reference."

The mitigative documentation produced in compliance with this law adds hundreds of structures a year to the HABS and HAER collections (see fig. 1.12). Several states and local jurisdictions have laws that produce similar results. New Jersey, for instance, has a law protecting its coastal areas that also provides protection for historic structures along the shoreline. Several historic hotels have been documented under this law.

Architecture schools have been using HABS documentation as part of their curricula for decades. Producing HABS/HAER documentation provides training in research, inspection, analysis, measuring, and drafting and results in an invaluable record of a historic structure, not to mention drawings for the student's portfolio (see fig. 1.13). Faculty and students who work with HABS/HAER material in their course work are an important source for HABS/HAER summer employees.

The Charles E. Peterson Prize, established by HABS in conjunction with The Athenaeum of Philadelphia, is an annual award that recognizes the best sets of measured drawings of a historic structure produced by students and donated to the HABS (see fig. 1.14). The prize honors Charles E. Peterson, FAIA, founder of the HABS program, and is intended to increase awareness and knowledge of historic buildings throughout the United States. The cash awards are endowed by a private fund held by The Athenaeum of Philadelphia. The students who participate in the competition learn about historic construction materials and techniques, while gaining hands-on experience in the process of measuring and producing measured drawings of a historic structure. HABS, in turn, gains hundreds of measured drawings for its collection.

From the beginning, HABS and HAER have relied on the generosity of organizations and individuals as a major source for documentation. Donated records continue to be a significant part of the collections. Preservation professionals working with historic structures are another source for HABS/HAER documentation. Measured drawings and historical research are integral aspects of planned work. Architects, engineers, historians, photographers, and others who work with historic structures are encouraged to produce their documentation to HABS/HAER standards for inclusion in the HABS/HAER collections (see fig. 1.15).

Copies of documentation can be donated to the HABS/HAER collections for safekeeping. HABS/HAER records are stored under conditions in which temperature and humidity are controlled to ensure longevity. Needless to say, records stored at a site or in office files are not likely to receive the same level of care. Furthermore, having a structure documented in the HABS/HAER collections graces it with additional prestige and makes it accessible to a wide variety of scholars and researchers.

The Administrative Organization of HABS/HAER

The Historic American Buildings Survey/ Historic American Engineering Record is part of the National Park Service of the Department of the Interior. HABS operates under congressional authorization from the Historic Sites Act of 1935. Under a tripartite agreement among the Department of the Interior, the Library of Congress, and the American Institute of Architects, HABS is operated by the National Park Service; the records are housed and made available to the public through the Library of Congress Prints and Photographs Division. The American Institute of Architects provides technical advice and assistance through its Committee on Historic Resources.

HAER was founded in 1969 under another tripartite agreement among the Department of the Interior, the Library of Congress, and the American Society of Civil Engineers. HAER is operated by the National Park Service, the records are housed and made available to the public through the Library of Congress Prints and Photographs Division, and the American Society of Civil Engineers provides technical advice and assistance. A protocol signed in 1987 adds the support of other engineering societies—the American Society of Mechanical Engineers; the Institute of Electrical and Electronics Engineers; the American Institute of Chemical Engineers; and the American Institute of Mining, Metallurgical, and Petroleum Engineers—to the HAER program.

Figure 1.12

This photograph of an 1875 cast-iron commercial building in Connecticut was made for HABS by a local redevelopment agency. Agencies receiving federal funding for a project are required to document historic structures to HABS/HAER standards before demolishing them.

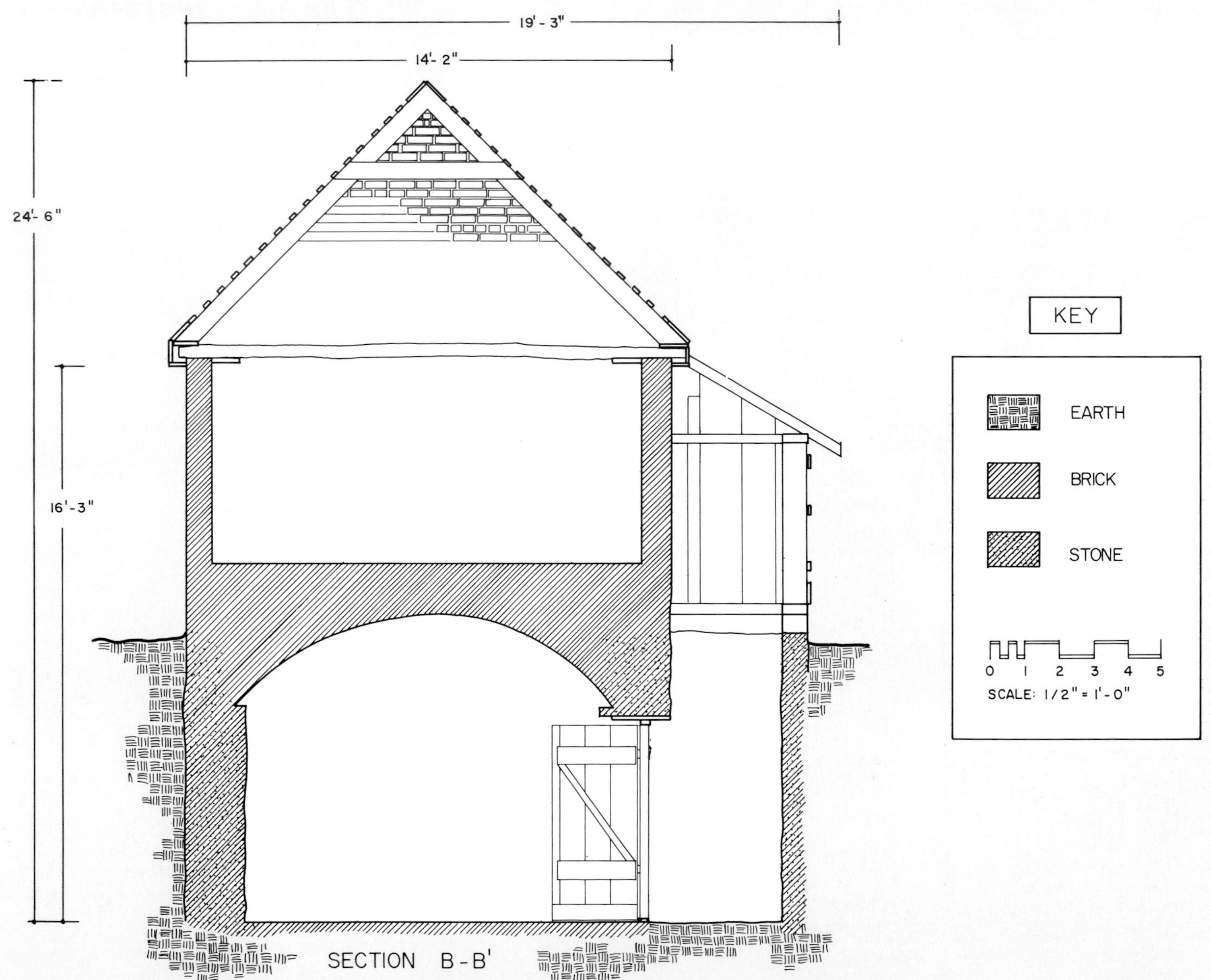

FIGURE 1.13

Students at the University of Delaware measured and drew seven smokehouses throughout the state as part of a study of vanishing agricultural building types. The completed measured drawings and written data were donated to HABS. This particular smokehouse had a root cellar underneath it.

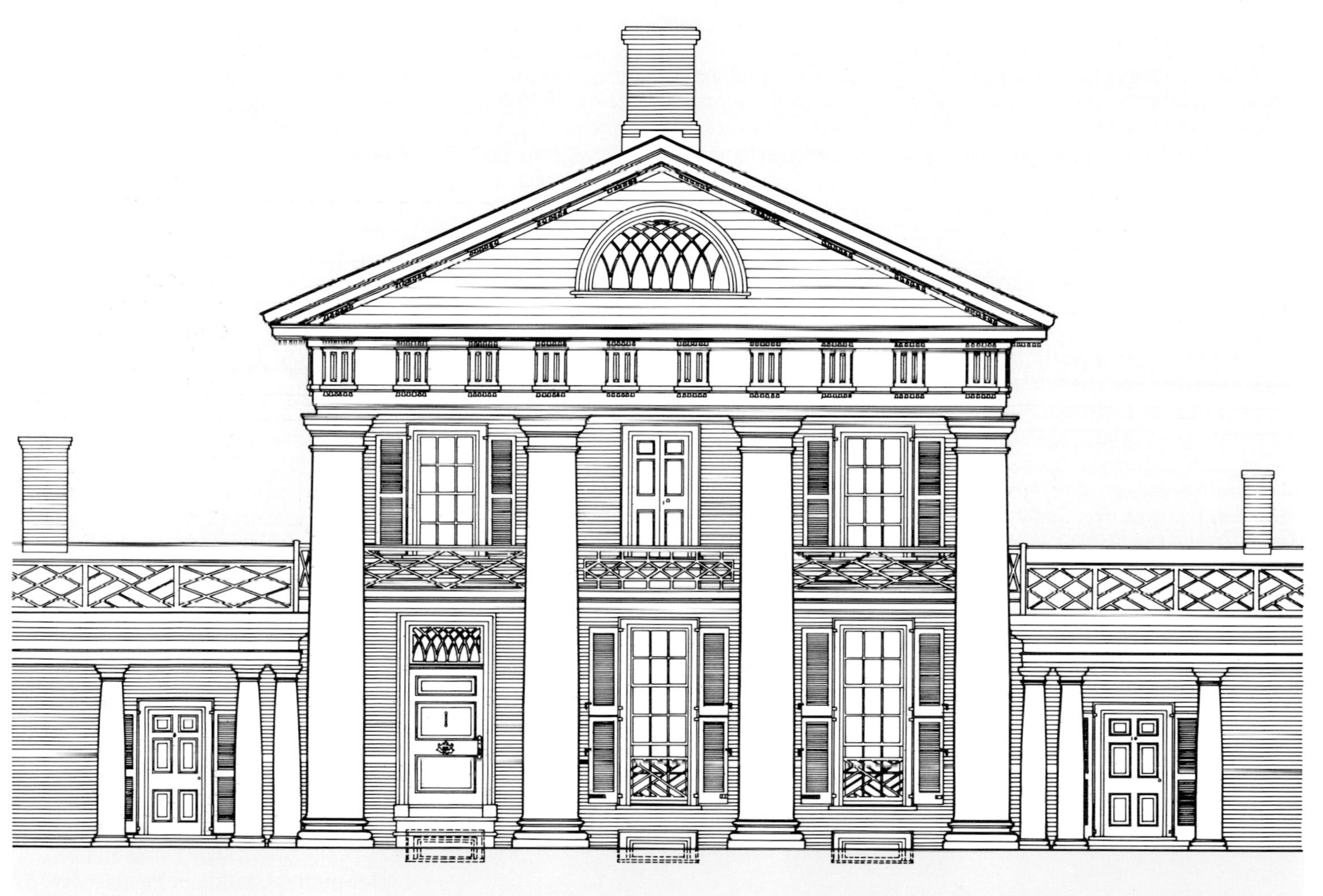

Figure 1.14

Measured drawings of Pavilion IV at the University of Virginia won first place in the 1984 competition for the Charles E. Peterson Prize.

About This Book

In chapter 2, Sally Kress Tompkins describes how HABS/HAER conducts surveys to identify structures worthy of further documentation, a fact that readers of this chapter should keep in mind. An inventory of a historic neighborhood uses building dates; type, size, and opulence of the structures; and comparisons of original, subsequent, and contemporary uses to show how a neighborhood and its economy developed and changed.

In chapter 3, Alison K. Hoagland and Gray Fitzsimons describe how historical research provides context, chronology, description, interpretation, and assessment for architectural and engineering documentation. Research forms the basis for identifying significant structures, the initial step in the documentation process. Historians then investigate and assemble information on selected structures, analyze the structure and the historical data, and distill the information into a cogent history and description. The authors describe a methodology for research, discuss what questions should be asked, and offer guidelines for describing architectural and technological sites. The chapter concludes with a section on the reporting formats used by HABS and HAER.

In chapter 4, William L. Lebovich describes techniques for producing photographs that record, reveal, and interpret historic structures. Photography is a universally accepted medium for conveying graphic information. Documentary photography is specialized, demanding more of the photographer than merely technical ability and artistic skill. For a photograph to convey the necessary information, the photographer must have an understanding of the subject matter as well. Nevertheless, the best documentary photographs not only record and interpret, they also exhibit more familiar attributes of high-quality photography, such as lighting and composition. The suggestions in this chapter can improve both the technical quality and informational content of documentary photography. All but the most specialized techniques are usable in any format.

In chapter 5, John A. Burns explains what measured drawings are and how to plan and execute them. Measured drawings can vary from simple line drawings that show room relationships or the arrangement of machine tools in a shop, to elaborately detailed drawings of a pin connection in a bridge or moldings in a mantelpiece. Decisions on what to draw, how to obtain the measurements, levels of accuracy, types of drawings, and appropriate scales are discussed. The last part of the chapter describes the special characteristics of HABS and HAER measured drawings.

In the final chapter, four case studies of HABS and HAER documentation are presented. Each study shows how the nature of a resource dictates the manner in which it should be documented. The Auditorium Building, for instance, is significant in many ways and, therefore, requires multiple recording techniques. Picatinny Arsenal was the United States Army's first smokeless powder production line, so recording the industrial process was a major focus of the documentation. The Schooner *Wawona* is HAER's first documented historic ship, featuring the specialized techniques required to record a historic vessel. Meridian Hill Park was recorded in a manner that accommodates the ephemeral nature of landscapes and interprets the changing visual appearance of the park.

The following chapters will guide those interested in the production of architectural and engineering documentation for any purpose, but ideally for inclusion in either the HABS or HAER collections. Regardless of the changing focus and form of recording, HABS/HAER provides a unique opportunity to expand the horizon of our understanding of America's cultural heritage. The continued growth of these collections will ensure an even better understanding of the past for future generations.

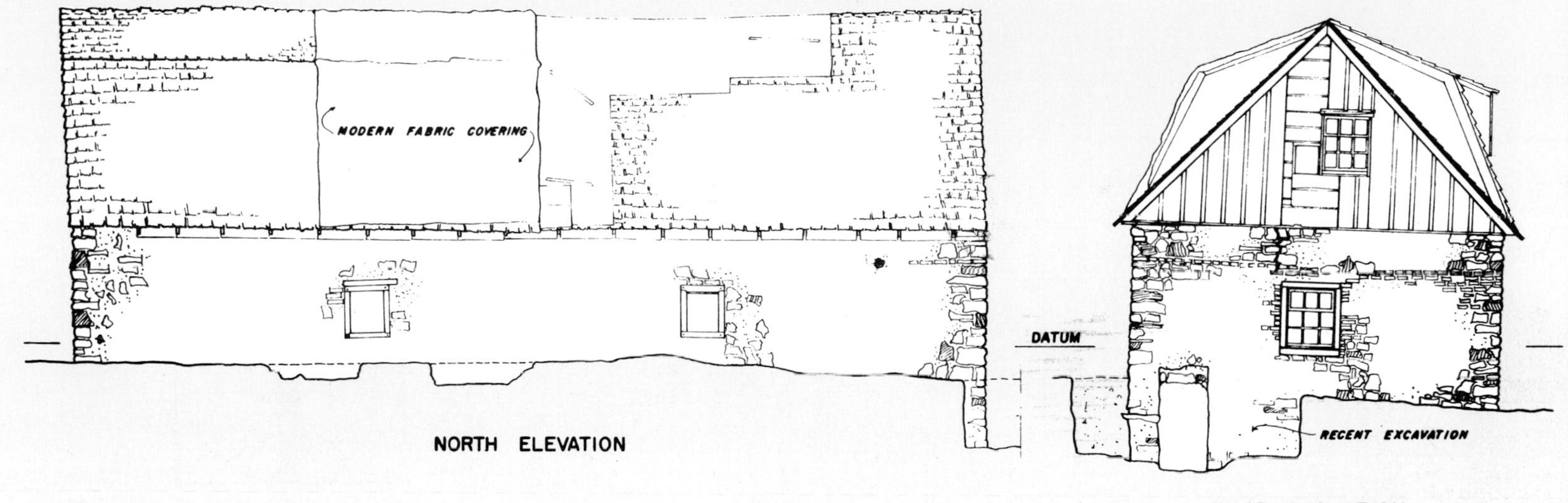

Figure 1.15

Existing conditions drawings of the Caleb Pusey House in Upland, Pennsylvania, were produced on HABS sheets by the restoration architect as a historical record prior to beginning work on the house. The measured drawings, large-format photographs, and historical data were then donated to HABS by The Friends of Caleb Pusey House, Inc.

CHAPTER 2

Sally Kress Tompkins

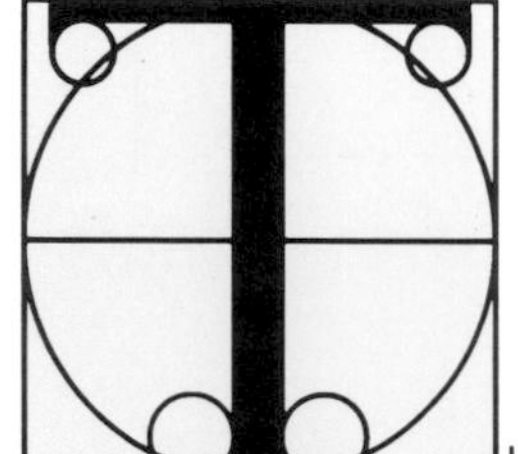

The Historic American Buildings Survey (HABS) and the Historic American Engineering Record (HAER) have conducted many surveys throughout the continental United States, Alaska, Hawaii, and Puerto Rico. They have surveyed resources as diverse as a state's historic bridges, a steel plant's buildings and machinery, the log structures in an area about to be flooded by a dam, the buildings of a nineteenth-century army post, and the storefronts along the main street of a small town in the Southwest.

The focus of this chapter is on historic structure surveys undertaken primarily for identifying structures meriting HABS/HAER documentation. The philosophy and rationale, the objectives set forth, and the various approaches of such surveys are discussed. Steps are set forth for conducting surveys drawing on past HABS/HAER surveys for examples. For the most part, architectural and technological or industrial surveys are similar, and they are treated together. Where there are distinctive differences, these are noted. The following chapter focuses on historical documentation and details methods of recording individual structures beyond the survey level. It contains, however, information that surveyors will find helpful and should, therefore, be used in conjunction with the information in this chapter.

What Is a HABS/HAER Survey?

A HABS/HAER survey is a systematic examination and analysis of individual historic resources reinforced by a literature search. It provides the basis for compiling an inventory of historic structures. Most simply, the survey is the process by which we arrive at an inventory. The focus is always the artifact, in this case the structure or the complex. While a site with no physical remains may have historical value, it is not a subject for HABS or HAER recording.

"The Secretary of the Interior's Standards and Guidelines for Identification" ("Archeology and Historic Preservation; Secretary of the Interior's Standards and Guidelines, Archeology and Historic Preservation," in the *Federal Register*, 29 Sept. 1983) state that a survey of an area, district, or region is normally undertaken for the purpose of identifying those resources that have historic value. The survey methodology described in this chapter is a refinement of those guidelines for historic preservation set forth by the Secretary of the Interior (see chapter 1 and appendix A). A HABS/HAER survey focuses on both the identification of significant historic resources and on those characteristics that contribute to their significance. This joint focus helps the surveyor to decide which resources warrant further investigation and what type and level of additional documentation is needed. Ideally, all recording begins with a thorough survey.

The reasons behind the survey may vary considerably. Resources may be scheduled for destruction; an area with diverse resources may require data for future planning; a federal agency may need a survey to comply with federal preservation legislation. In all cases, there is a need to know more about a group of resources, how they relate to one another, and which need further study.

The HABS/HAER survey has three major objectives:

1. The survey results in a record of large numbers of historic structures that form either a historic district, a definable region, or a related grouping, such as an industrial complex. Because they collect less detailed information, surveys are able to record larger numbers of buildings and structures than more labor-intensive documentation projects.

2. The survey identifies structures that warrant more extensive documentation for inclusion in the HABS/HAER collection at the Library of Congress. Selection of buildings and structures to be documented is based on the characteristics of the structure, HABS/HAER standards, and the needs of the HABS/HAER collection.

3. The survey develops information needed by others. A survey develops data for planners, government officials, and other decision makers. The wide range of buildings covered by the survey provides the kind of data needed to plan for preservation as a part of future development and growth.

A survey is the first step in the HABS/HAER recording process. For some resources of limited architectural, industrial, or technological importance it may also be the last step. In this case, the collection of data during the survey is the only recording to be done. HABS/HAER standards define four levels of documentation. Level IV, the least extensive, is for structures that require only survey-level data.

One important factor in evaluating the benefits of a survey is that although the level of information collected on a single resource is minimal, information on a group of resources related by use, geography, and the like can be extremely helpful, not only in guiding the direction of future work but also in analyzing differences and similarities among individual resources. By computerizing the survey, an increasingly viable option discussed later in this chapter, the uses of the information are further enhanced.

It is often desirable to organize material collected during the survey in a way that facilitates its use by others

FIGURE 2.1

This massive sand-sorting house, part of the Ottawa Silica Company Mill C Complex, was identified as an important industrial structure during a survey of the Illinois and Michigan Canal Corridor in 1985. The following summer it was recorded with large-format photography, measured drawings, and a written history.

EXAMPLE: THE ILLINOIS AND MICHIGAN CANAL SURVEY

The HABS/HAER survey of the Illinois and Michigan (I & M) Canal National Heritage Corridor is an excellent example of how a survey can meet the three HABS/HAER objectives, namely: to record a large number of historic buildings and structures in a definable region; to identify which of the buildings and structures warrant more extensive documentation for inclusion in the HABS/HAER collections at the Library of Congress; and to develop information needed by planners, decision makers, and others.

The corridor covers almost a hundred miles along the trace of the I & M Canal, running southwest from Chicago to the LaSalle/Peru area. It includes the canal itself, the early canal towns, and several industrial sites. The legislation establishing the corridor called for the area to be developed for mixed industrial, commercial, recreational, and cultural uses. At the time of the survey, many general and partial studies of the area had already been completed, but a comprehensive inventory of properties of architectural, industrial, and engineering importance was needed to assist the I & M Canal National Heritage Corridor commissioners in making the decisions that were facing them. So while HABS/HAER needed to identify important structures that should be documented, the Heritage Corridor commissioners needed to know what their important historic structures were, where they were, what made them important, and which structures were more important than others (see fig. 2.1).

HABS/HAER researched and developed historical contexts for the canal and each of the canal towns. The chronological periods in the history of the canal and recurrent historical themes were identified and weighted according to their relative importance. Surveyed structures were placed in one of five categories based on their historical, architectural, technological, or industrial importance. Integrity and setting were also considered in the categorization process. Statements of significance tied individual resources into previously identified historical periods and themes. The result was a comprehensive inventory of historic resources which was then computerized to allow for comparative analysis and put into priority order to provide guidance to commission members and to allow HABS/HAER to plan for future documentation projects.

or to analyze it to assist the property owners with future preservation planning. Depending on what type of information has been collected and how it is to be used, the inventory may be recorded on traditional inventory cards or in a computer data base. Some examples of ways in which surveys can be expanded to serve other uses are:

1. By applying National Register criteria to surveyed properties and developing a list of structures that are potentially eligible for nomination to the National Register. This information plus that gathered on each resource can be used as a basis for a National Register nomination by the state historic preservation office staff or others qualified for this task.

2. By categorizing resources based on historical, architectural, industrial, and technological importance. This technique is particularly helpful to planners and decision makers in allocating scarce funding.

3. By expanding the part of the survey that identifies those features of a historic structure that contribute to its importance. This is helpful for preservation planning and maintenance.

4. By recording usable interior space to assist in developing potential uses for a property. This is particularly helpful when economic development is one of the survey's goals.

A HABS/HAER survey has four major components: planning, field work, analysis, and report writing.

Planning

The planning component comprises two major phases: (1) preliminary data gathering, consisting of an initial literature search and a reconnaissance of the area; and (2) the formulation of a survey methodology, which includes development of a research design, survey parameters, a field form, and a plan for handling survey logistics. Whether the survey will be computerized or recorded on inventory cards must be decided during the planning stage. All of the above tasks must be addressed before the field work begins.

Literature Search

A literature search is undertaken to identify written data on an area or on an individual resource and is generally expanded to include photographs, drawings, and other material of a nonverbal nature. While the literature search is usually ongoing throughout the project, it can be divided into two parts. The initial literature search identifies the location of repositories of data and reviews what general sources are available. For instance, if the inventory is in Nantucket, but the relevant maps and numerous historical photographs are at the Library of Congress in Washington, D.C., the necessary time and funds for travel and research must be accounted for in the planning stage. The second part of the literature search, discussed later in this chapter under the topic of field work, explores a sufficient amount of data to develop a context for evaluation of the resource. This stage is usually concentrated on an individual structure and is usually accomplished in local repositories.

The initial literature search is the first step in planning the survey. What is learned from it will help the surveyor define the survey and develop a methodology. As in any research project,

Figure 2.2

Henry T. Gordon of Mendocino, California, built this redwood cottage in 1886. A modest version of a Gothic Revival cottage, it was selected during a reconnaissance survey of the Mendocino Historic District for further documentation. Sanborn fire insurance maps assisted surveyors in dating the structure.

general source works should be consulted first before moving to the specific.

It makes sense to start with resources that are easily accessible. If the project area and major repositories of information are not in the same place as the surveyor, the surveyor should first consult the resources that are nearest and obtain other information by telephone and written request. Plans can then be made to visit repositories located at a distance from the surveyors. This will, of course, include the archives and the historic preservation office of the state in which the survey is to be done and may also include the National Archives and Library of Congress. An effort should be made at this point to determine which, if any, properties in the survey area have been listed on previous inventories. County and state historic inventories, the National Register of Historic Places, National Historic Landmarks, and HABS/ HAER (the last three operating under the auspices of the National Park Service) need to be checked.

The importance of contacting the state historic preservation office in the state in which the survey area is located cannot be overstressed. The earlier this is done in the planning stage, the better. This office either directs or is aware of the historic surveys that have been conducted in the state and generally keeps files of federal program listings. In addition to pooling of information, the state historic preservation office can be helpful to the survey planner in other ways, for example, sharing human resources.

Some professional societies maintain landmark programs of their own. Depending on the type of structure being researched, surveyors may write or call the American Institute of Architects, the Society of Architectural Historians, the Society for Industrial Archeology, the American Society of Civil Engineers, the American Society of Mechanical Engineers, and the Institute of Electrical and Electronics Engineers, all of which may have information on historic properties (for addresses, see Appendix B).

At the end of the initial literature search, survey planners should have at least a general understanding of the project area and should know what properties, if any, within the area have been listed in or determined eligible for the National Register of Historic Places, designated a National Historic Landmark, documented by HABS/HAER, or listed on a state or local register. Most important, it will have established where repositories of information, including historic maps and photographs, are located and what knowledgeable personnel need to be contacted. The planning process can then proceed.

Reconnaissance

A reconnaissance, or an inspection of the project area prior to surveying, is the second step in the data-gathering phase and a necessary step in intelligent survey planning. A reconnaissance allows the surveyor to examine the area first-hand and to talk, if only briefly, to local people who know about the area. Surveyors can proceed without this step, but the information gained through firsthand observation is invaluable in survey planning (see fig. 2.2).

Having first obtained a good map, a drive-through or walk-through of the area can help the survey planner ascertain several important facts, such as prevailing structural types, repetitive or unusual features, uses of buildings, layout of complexes of buildings, general condition of building structures, and remaining machinery. Early knowledge of the existence of machinery in a building or of a historic bridge in the project area will alert the survey planners that special types of expertise will be required to conduct the survey properly. A visit to the project area also provides necessary information for logistical planning, such as how to get surveyors in and out of the area, availability of housing if required, and so on. An effective reconnaissance involves visits to local libraries and historical societies to talk with residents who may be knowledgeable

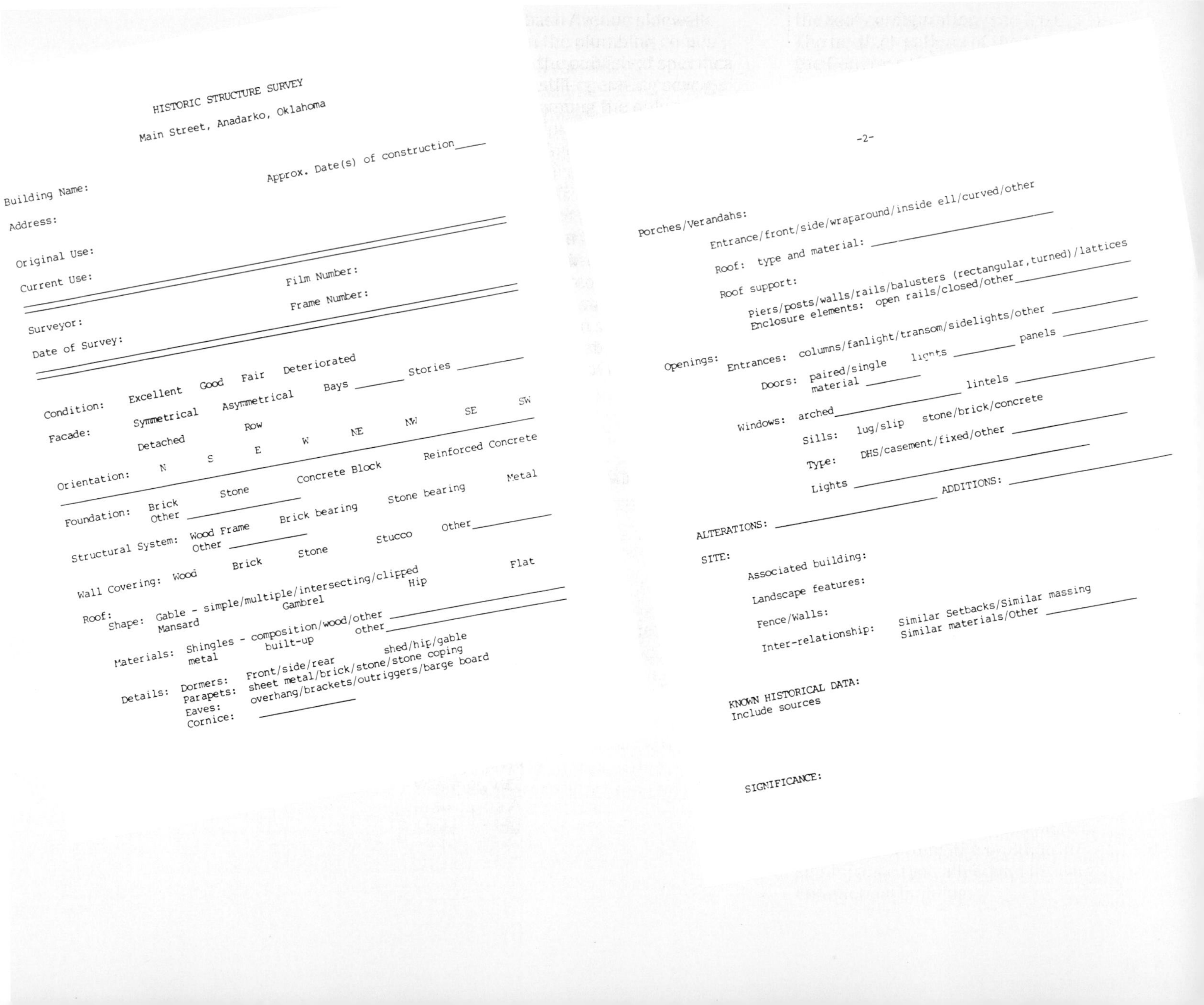

HISTORIC STRUCTURE SURVEY

Main Street, Anadarko, Oklahoma

Building Name: Approx. Date(s) of construction____

Address:

Original Use:

Current Use:

Surveyor: Film Number:

Date of Survey: Frame Number:

Condition: Excellent Good Fair Deteriorated

Facade: Symmetrical Asymmetrical Bays ____ Stories ____

Detached Row

Orientation: N S E W NE NW SE SW

Foundation: Brick Stone Concrete Block Reinforced Concrete

Other ____

Structural System: Wood Frame Brick bearing Stone bearing Metal

Other ____

Wall Covering: Wood Brick Stone Stucco Other____

Roof:

Shape: Gable - simple/multiple/intersecting/clipped Flat

Mansard Gambrel Hip

Materials: Shingles - composition/wood/other ____

metal built-up other____

Details: Dormers: Front/side/rear shed/hip/gable

Parapets: sheet metal/brick/stone/stone coping

Eaves: overhang/brackets/outriggers/barge board

Cornice: ____

-2-

Porches/Verandahs:

Entrance/front/side/wraparound/inside ell/curved/other

Roof: type and material: ____

Roof support:

Piers/posts/walls/rails/balusters (rectangular,turned)/lattices

Enclosure elements: open rails/closed/other ____

Openings: Entrances: columns/fanlight/transom/sidelights/other ____

Doors: paired/single lights ____ panels ____

material ____

Windows: arched____ lintels ____

Sills: lug/slip stone/brick/concrete

Type: DHS/casement/fixed/other ____

Lights ____

ALTERATIONS: ____ ADDITIONS: ____

SITE:

Associated building:

Landscape features:

Fence/Walls:

Inter-relationship: Similar Setbacks/Similar massing

Similar materials/Other ____

KNOWN HISTORICAL DATA:

Include sources

SIGNIFICANCE:

FIGURES 2.3 AND 2.4

A good field form speeds up the visual survey and keeps the surveyor, often distracted by outside conditions, from forgetting to record certain items. The Anadarko field form reproduced here is an example of a basic field form, which need not be elaborate to be effective.

about the survey area. An effective reconnaissance can be the most important part of the planning effort.

In the following two examples, reconnaissance efforts yielded different kinds of information but proved equally valuable to survey planners.

In Anadarko, Oklahoma, a team of architecture students conducting a reconnaissance of Main Street made a list of features that recurred in individual buildings, both commercial and residential, and of questions concerning style, structure type, and materials. When they met again to put together a field form, knowledge of nomenclature was pooled, uniform use of stylistic terms was agreed upon, and an excellent field form was developed, which proved invaluable to the field surveyor. See figures 2.3 and 2.4 for a copy of the Anadarko field form.

A reconnaissance of Picatinny Arsenal, an army manufacturing site in northern New Jersey, provided a wealth of information to survey planners. They discovered a large amount of intact machinery and buildings whose form, construction, and materials reflected the highly specialized functions concerned with the manufacture of smokeless powder. Based on data provided by the reconnaissance, the surveyors realized that a highly specialized knowledge of early explosive manufacture would be required to describe and evaluate properly the remaining machinery at the arsenal.

A reconnaissance can also be used to create an initial inventory from which a selection of structures for a more in-depth survey can be made. This method can produce an inventory that lists all buildings by name and address along with a photograph. From this preliminary listing decisions can be made as to both unique and representative structures, producing a selected inventory of structures for the survey itself.

Methodology

The second phase of the planning component is the development of a survey methodology. The purpose of a survey methodology is to ensure completion of the work in an organized fashion. An acceptable methodology should (1) demonstrate that all buildings and structures within the parameter of the survey area have been surveyed, (2) allow results to be verified, (3) ensure that needed information is collected, (4) establish a uniform level of information to be collected for surveyed structures, and (5) provide a means for evaluating resources.

The survey methodology comprises the following elements:

1. Developing a research design. A research design can be defined as a work plan to guide future data collection, in this case, the field work. It should state the goals of the project and identify the information needed to meet those goals. The research design will be based on the type of structures to be surveyed, the extant features of those structures, and the type of information required to meet the survey's objectives. Once in place, the research design will provide the overall framework of the survey.

The research design will address those questions that the data resulting from the project should answer. This will in turn define both type and level of information to be sought and the professional expertise required on the project. Since the survey is a first step in recording a structure, the research design at this stage must usually be general in nature. At the completion of the survey, a list of research questions of a more specific nature connected with documentation projects can be developed to guide future work.

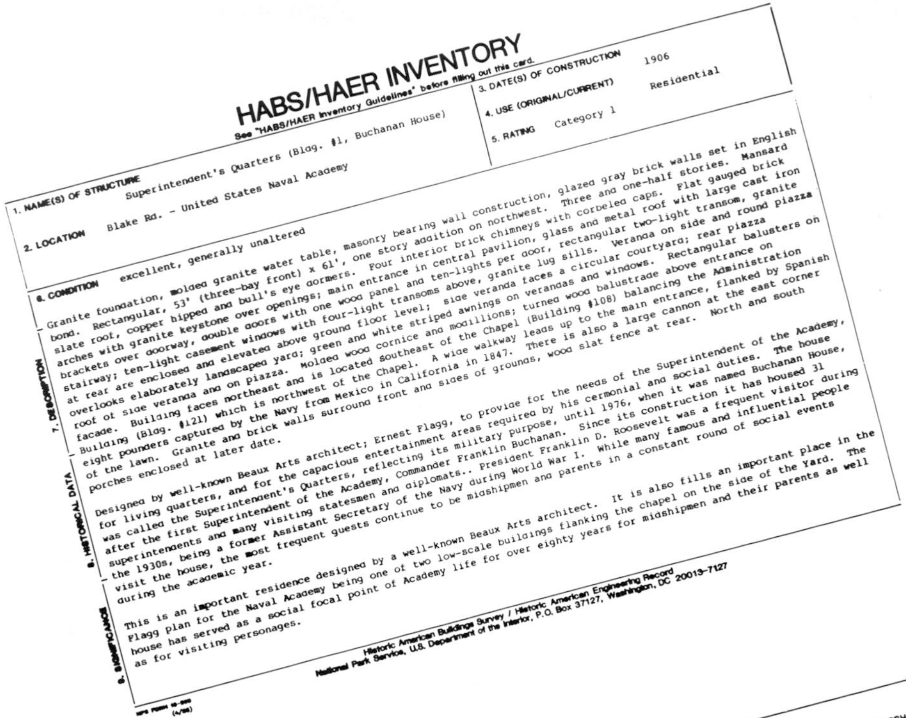

HABS/HAER INVENTORY

See "HABS/HAER Inventory Guidelines" before filling out this card.

1. NAME(S) OF STRUCTURE Superintendent's Quarters (Bldg. #1, Buchanan House)

2. LOCATION Blake Rd. - United States Naval Academy

3. DATE(S) OF CONSTRUCTION 1906

4. USE (ORIGINAL/CURRENT) Residential

5. RATING Category 1

6. CONDITION excellent, generally unaltered

7. DESCRIPTION Granite foundation, molded granite water table, masonry bearing wall construction, glazed gray brick walls set in English bond. Rectangular, 53' (three-bay front) x 61', one story addition on northwest. Three and one-half stories. Mansard slate roof, copper hipped and bull's eye dormers. Four interior brick chimneys with corbeled caps. Flat gauged brick arches with granite keystone over openings; main entrance in central pavilion, glass and metal roof with large cast iron brackets over doorway, double doors with one wood panel and ten-lights per door, rectangular two-light transom, granite stairway; ten-light casement windows with four-light transoms above, granite lug sills. Veranda on side and round piazza at rear are enclosed and elevated above ground floor level; side veranda faces a circular courtyard; rear piazza overlooks elaborately landscaped yard; green and white striped awnings on verandas and windows. Rectangular balusters on roof of side veranda and on piazza. Molded wood cornice and modillions; turned wood balustrade above entrance on facade. Building faces northeast and is located southeast of the Chapel (Building #108) balancing the Administration Building (Bldg. #121) which is northwest of the Chapel. A wide walkway leads up to the main entrance, flanked by Spanish eight pounders captured by the Navy from Mexico in California in 1847. There is also a large cannon at the east corner of the lawn. Granite and brick walls surround front and sides of grounds, wood slat fence at rear. North and south porches enclosed at later date.

8. HISTORICAL DATA Designed by well-known Beaux Arts architect; Ernest Flagg, to provide for the needs of the Superintendent of the Academy, for living quarters, and for the capacious entertainment areas required by his cermonial and social duties. The house was called the Superintendent's Quarters, reflecting its military purpose, until 1976, when it was named Buchanan House, after the first Superintendent of the Academy, Commander Franklin Buchanan. Since its construction it has housed 31 superintendents and many visiting statesmen and diplomats.. President Franklin D. Roosevelt was a frequent visitor during the 1930s, being a former Assistant Secretary of the Navy during World War I. While many famous and influential people visit the house, the most frequent guests continue to be midshipmen and parents in a constant round of social events during the academic year.

9. SIGNIFICANCE This is an important residence designed by a well-known Beaux Arts architect. It is also fills an important place in the Flagg plan for the Naval Academy being one of two low-scale buildings flanking the chapel on the side of the Yard. The house has served as a social focal point of Academy life for over eighty years for midshipmen and their parents as well as for visiting personages.

Historic American Buildings Survey / Historic American Engineering Record
National Park Service, U.S. Department of the Interior, P.O. Box 37127, Washington, DC 20013-7127

10. NAME(S) OF STRUCTURE

11. PHOTOS (W/ FILM ROLL & FRAME NO.) AND SKETCH MAP OF LOCATION

12. SOURCES Real estate records
Public Works Office
U.S. Naval Academy
Annapolis, MD 21402

13. INVENTORIED BY: Sally K. Tompkins

AFFILIATION HABS/HAER

DATE JUNE 1980

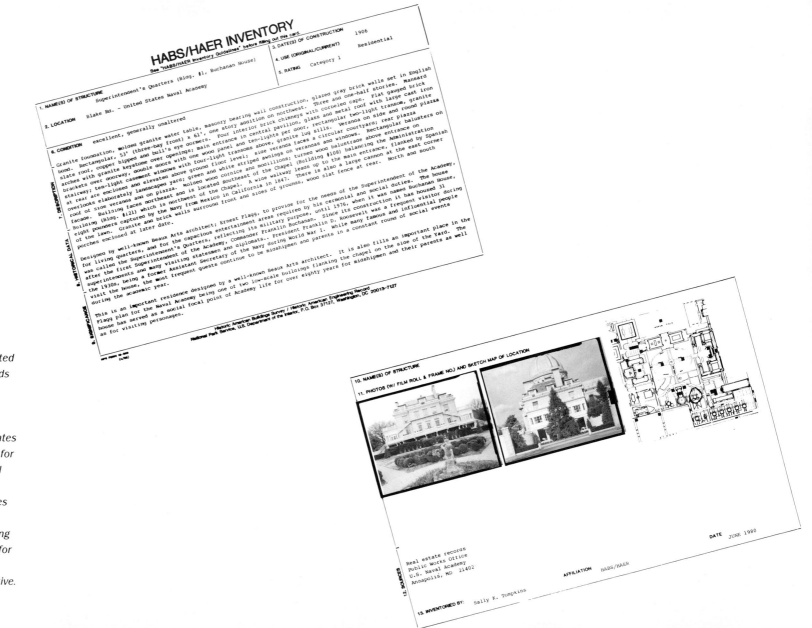

***Figure* 2.5**
***Figure* 2.6**
***Figure* 2.7**
***Figure* 2.8**

These examples of completed HABS/HAER inventory cards cover a cement company, significant as a historic industrial property, and a residence at the United States Naval Academy, important for historical and architectural reasons. The cards shown here are excellent resources for planners, but are time-intensive. If the person using the inventory has no need for the cards, a computerized inventory offers an alternative.

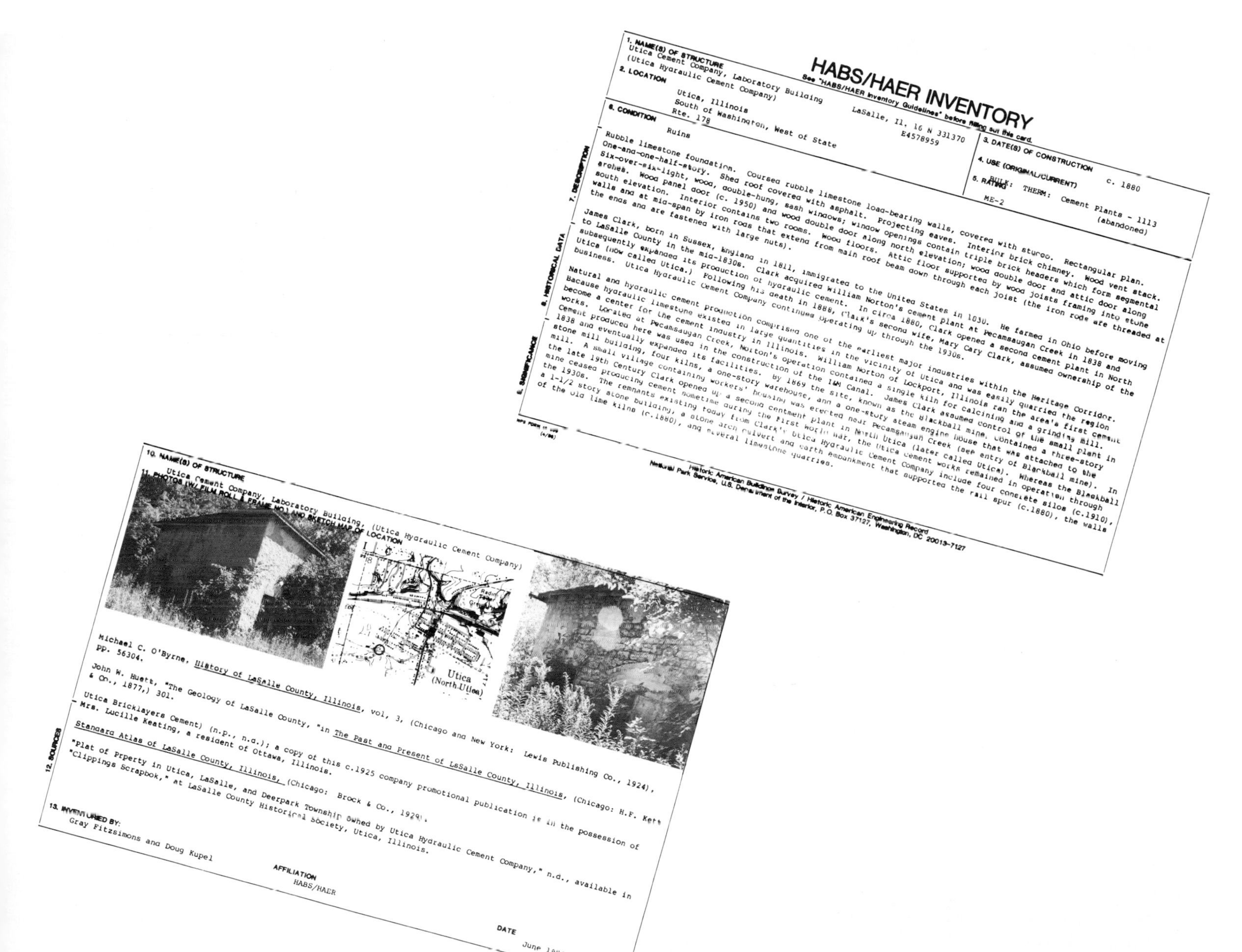

HABS/HAER INVENTORY

See "HABS/HAER Inventory Guidelines" before filling out this card.

1. NAME(S) OF STRUCTURE
Utica Cement Company, Laboratory Building
(Utica Hydraulic Cement Company)

2. LOCATION
Utica, Illinois
South of Washington, West of State
Rte. 178

LaSalle, Il. 16 N 331370
E4578959

3. DATE(S) OF CONSTRUCTION
c. 1880

4. USE (ORIGINAL/CURRENT)
BULK: THERM: Cement Plants - 1113
(abandoned)

5. RATING
ME-2

6. CONDITION
Ruins

7. DESCRIPTION
Rubble limestone foundation. Coursed rubble limestone load-bearing walls, covered with stucco. Rectangular plan. One-and-one-half-story. Shed roof covered with asphalt. Projecting eaves. Interior brick chimney. Wood vent stack. Six-over-six-light, wood, double-hung, sash windows; window openings contain triple brick headers which form segmental arches. Wood panel door (c. 1950) and wood double door along north elevation; wood double door and attic door along south elevation. Interior contains two rooms. Wood floors. Attic floor supported by wood joists framing into stone walls and at mid-span by iron rods that extend from main roof beam down through each joist (the iron rods are threaded at the ends and are fastened with large nuts).

8. HISTORICAL DATA
James Clark, born in Sussex, England in 1811, immigrated to the United States in 1830. He farmed in Ohio before moving to LaSalle County in the mid-1830s. Clark acquired William Norton's cement plant at Pecamsaugan Creek in 1838 and subsequently expanded its production of hydraulic cement. In circa 1880, Clark opened a second cement plant in North Utica (now called Utica.) Following his death in 1888, Clark's second wife, Mary Cary Clark, assumed ownership of the business. Utica Hydraulic Cement Company continued operating up through the 1930s.

9. SIGNIFICANCE
Natural and hydraulic cement production comprised one of the earliest major industries within the Heritage Corridor. Because hydraulic limestone existed in large quantities in the vicinity of Utica and was easily quarried the region become a center for the cement industry in Illinois. William Norton of Lockport, Illinois ran the area's first cement works. Located at Pecamsaugan Creek, Norton's operation contained a single kiln for calcining and a grinding mill. Cement produced here was used in the construction of the I&M Canal. James Clark assumed control of the small plant in 1838 and eventually expanded its facilities. By 1869 the site, known as the Blackball mine, contained a three-story stone mill building, four kilns, a one-story warehouse, and a one-story steam engine house that was attached to the mill. A small village containing workers' housing was erected near Pecamsaugan Creek (see entry of Blackball mine). In the late 19th Century Clark opened up a second centment plant in North Utica (later called Utica). Whereas the Blackball mine ceased producing cement sometime during the First World War, the Utica cement works remained in operation through the 1930s. The remnants existing today from Clark's Utica Hydraulic Cement Company include four concrete silos (c.1910), a 1-1/2 story stone building, a stone arch culvert and earth embankment that supported the rail spur (c.1880), the walls of the old lime kilns (c.1880), and several limestone quarries.

NPS FORM 10-* (4/86)

Historic American Buildings Survey / Historic American Engineering Record
National Park Service, U.S. Department of the Interior, P.O. Box 37127, Washington, DC 20013-7127

10. NAME(S) OF STRUCTURE
Utica Cement Company, Laboratory Building, (Utica Hydraulic Cement Company)

11. PHOTOS (W/ FILM ROLL & FRAME NO.) AND SKETCH MAP OF LOCATION

12. SOURCES
Michael C. O'Byrne, History of LaSalle County, Illinois, vol, 3, (Chicago and New York: Lewis Publishing Co., 1924), pp. 56304.

John W. Huett, "The Geology of LaSalle County," in The Past and Present of LsSalle County, Illinois, (Chicago: H.F. Kett & Co., 1877,) 301.

Utica Bricklayers Cement) (n.p., n.d.); a copy of this c.1925 company promotional publication is in the possession of Mrs. Lucille Keating, a resident of Ottawa, Illinois.

Standard Atlas of LaSalle County, Illinois, (Chicago: Brock & Co., 1929).

"Plat of Prperty in Utica, LaSalle, and Deerpark Township Owned by Utica Hydraulic Cement Company," n.d., available in "Clippings Scrapbok," at LaSalle County Historical Society, Utica, Illinois.

13. INVENTORIED BY:
Gray Fitzsimons and Doug Kupel

AFFILIATION
HABS/HAER

DATE
June 1980

HABS SURVEY
Ottawa, Illinois
1987

Name:
Address: 909 Congress St.
Date: 1915 ca   Original Use: RS
Exterior Material: stucco
Structural System: wood frame
Architect:

Area: E
Block: U1
Present Use: RS

Surveyor: JCL

20/12

Name:
Address: 912 Congress St.
Date: 1920 ca   Original Use: RS
Exterior Material: stucco
Structural System: wood frame
Architect:

Area: E
Block: U2
Present Use: RS

Surveyor: MKS

6/35

Name: Oscar Kroehnke House
Address: 913 Congress St.
Date: 1913   Original Use: RS
Exterior Material: aluminum
Structural Material: wood frame
Architect: Kesson White & John Hanifen

Area: E
Block: U1
Present Use: RS

Surveyor: MKS

20/13

Name:
Address: 915 Congress St.
Date: 1920 ca   Original Use: RS
Exterior Material: aluminum
Structural Material: wood frame
Architect:

Area: E
Block: U1
Present Use: RS

Surveyor: MKS

20/14

FIGURE 2.9

This is an example of how a computerized inventory can be printed out. The example shown uses a limited number of data elements. Data elements can be increased or decreased as desired.

2. Defining the parameters. The parameters of a survey are those conditions and factors that in some way place limitations on the extent of the survey and thus determine its form. In some cases they are constraints from circumstances not controlled by survey planners. In other cases the surveyors themselves set parameters to guide and provide focus for the survey.

Time limitations, funding sources, what is already known about the structures in the area from the preliminary data gathering, and the survey's objectives are the main determinants of the survey parameters. In the HABS/HAER survey of Picatinny Arsenal, for example, the determinants of the parameters were: (1) Picatinny Arsenal had used important historic chemical processes up to and through the 1930s; (2) the HABS/HAER collection had no documentation on chemical processes; (3) the installation had over fifteen hundred buildings, some of which contained machinery; (4) the project was limited to the twelve weeks during the summer when a HABS/HAER team operates; and (5) it was not known during the planning stage which buildings and structures contributed to the historic processes.

Weighing all these factors, the following parameters were set: (1) The survey would include all structures within the boundaries of the installation. (2) The year 1940 was set as the chronological cut-off: thus, all pre-1940 buildings, of which there were eight hundred, were to be surveyed. This insured that all structures relating to pre-World War II chemical processes would be identified. (3) Data were to be collected on any remaining machinery so the interiors of the buildings and structures were to be surveyed and separate research was to be conducted into all historic industrial processes that took place at Picatinny. (4) Later, during the analysis phase of the survey, it was decided that the production of smokeless powder at Picatinny was an important historic process that should be the subject of more intensive documentation.

Another example of setting parameters is offered by the survey of Morris, Illinois. The survey encompassed all structures within the town boundaries; and again, all pre-1940 structures were to be surveyed. Census data collected early in the project, however, revealed approximately seventeen hundred pre-1940 properties. Since funding limited the size of the team and the amount of time available, more realistic geographical boundaries had to be set.

It is not always necessary to cut back on geographical boundaries or chronological period because of funding or time limitations. The amount of information recorded can be adjusted also.

The general determinants of the amount and type of data sought during the course of the survey are the stated objectives of the survey. These in turn influence the form and scope of the research design. The current HABS/HAER inventory card suggests basic data requirements. Its format designates special areas for historical data, descriptive data, and analysis of significance. The actual information recorded on the card, however, may vary from survey to survey. Computerizing the data from the survey provides even greater flexibility for the surveyor in type and amount of data recorded. Figures 2.5 through 2.9 provide examples of HABS/HAER inventory cards and computer survey entries.

The amount of information collected should be sufficient to allow for evaluation of the structure and for reviewers to determine what future work needs to be done. In some cases, the information level can be adjusted downward without compromising these requirements. Acceptable shortcuts can be taken, for example, by omitting locational maps where street addresses exist and a good overall project map appears in the overview, or by grouping similar properties on one card, using a master card to describe in detail a recurrent property type or a common history (as in the case of a steel mill) then referencing the master card rather than repeating the description or history each time it occurs.

3. Determining the chronology. It is extremely helpful in evaluating a structure to know its date of completion. In many cases, however, when records have been lost or are confusing, the time spent establishing a date for a particular property may prove to be excessive for survey-level work. Guidelines for establishing dates should be set in the planning stage but may be revised if necessary when it is known what records, maps, and so on exist for dating properties, the accessibility of the records, and the length of time required for research. Estimated dates based on map work, analysis of the structure, and oral interviews can be substituted at this stage for more precise dating, which is often a time-consuming activity that is more appropriate as part of the extensive historical documentation process discussed later in this volume.

4. Handling the logistics. Assembling the project team, transporting them, housing them, providing office space and equipment, and arranging for film development and clerical support are logistical problems. They should be addressed in the planning stage. There will be problems that must be dealt with when the team is in the field, but good planning should minimize last-minute crises.

5. Preparing a field form. On the basis of the initial literature search and reconnaissance and the parameters set for the survey, it is possible to develop a good field form.

At a minimum, the field form should provide a checklist for surveyors to ensure that all required information is recorded. At best, it can speed up field work by listing commonly found features so that they can be circled or checked rather than written in. A good field form can aid in analysis by anticipating the values that will be used to decide historical, architectural, or technological importance.

The format of the field form will vary according to the type of structures being surveyed and the preferences of the surveyors. The information can be divided into three categories: (1) identification (name, location, organization conducting the survey, date, etc.), (2) history (information usually gained through research: date of construction, architect or engineer, values associated with an important historic figure or event, etc.), and (3) description (information gained through analysis of the structure, such as roof shape, extant machinery, type of construction, etc.). These categories can be reflected in the form. The form can also be arranged to facilitate the transfer of information from the field form to the HABS/HAER inventory card or to the computer. Descriptions should proceed logically from foundation to roof and from exterior features to interior features, including in-place machinery. The following checklist suggests the basic information that should be recorded on the field form. This may, of course, be adjusted up or down, depending on the objectives of the inventory. It should be noted that checklists or fill-in-the-blank types of field forms are more compatible with a computerized survey.

Computerized Inventory. Early in the planning stage, the surveyor must decide whether to organize the information in the narrative form called for by the HABS/HAER inventory card or in a form compatible with a computer program. Computerization has the advantage of being able to sort vast amounts of data. The computer can take what would have been a large file of inventory cards and provide answers almost instantly as to such questions as what were the uses of the recorded resources, how many are there of various types, and so on. These answers can help the researcher to spot trends and anomalies and establish the significance of individual buildings.

A research design is as necessary for a computerized survey as it is for any other survey. As mentioned earlier, it is wise to start with the research questions, or what the user will want to know at the end of the survey. If the question is, "How many hop barns are there in this county?," then a use field that provides for hop barns should be a part of the program. If the question is, "how many nineteenth-century churches survive in this city?," then a date-of-completion field should be incorporated with a use field that provides for churches. If, for example, churches are the subject of the survey, then more specific fields, such as one that records denominations, might be included.

There are two basic approaches that can be taken with computerized surveys: (1) reducing the information required to defined fields, which requires careful planning, or (2) computerizing only the types of information

that might be searched, and retaining additional information in another form.

With the first approach, the information that is being collected through the survey should be carefully reviewed and refined into specific fields. This nearly always necessitates a careful look at the structures to be surveyed before determining which fields are appropriate, and is especially compatible with checklist or fill-in-the-blank survey field forms. If this method is used, *all* of the information that is collected should fit into the program; it may be difficult to cope with complex sites or unusual cases that have not been foreseen.

With the second approach the kind of information that is computerized should be that which can be efficiently researched through the computer, such as architects' names or dates of completion. Complex descriptive information that is unlikely to form the subject of an inquiry is best left to another form of retention, for instance in a narrative description that accompanies the computerized form, or in a file folder available only to interested researchers.

This second approach is particularly suitable to surveys that are conducted on two levels, the first level being a general reconnaissance, as described earlier, in which basic information on a

FIELD FORM CHECKLIST

General Data

- Name of surveyor
- Film number/Frame number

Historical Data

- Names of building or structure *(current and historic)*
- Location *(street, city, county, state)*
- Present function, including industrial processes
- Original and interim functions, including industrial processes
- Date of completion
- Architect, designer, or manufacturer
- Major modifications with dates
- Sources of information
- Unexplored sources

VISUAL SURVEY DATA Building or Structure Description

- Foundation material(s)
- Wall material(s)
- Structural and mechanical systems
- Bays
- Stories
- Measurements
- Shape and orientation
- Roof *(shape, material, other features such as chimneys, dormers, cupolas, etc).*
- Openings *(doors, windows)*
- Porches, verandas, balconies
- Exterior trim

Notable Interior Features *(if interior is examined)*

- Plan, decorative features, finishes
- Machinery in place

Setting

- Integrity of site
- Associated buildings
- Interrelationships *(include water and transportation features if relevant)*
- Notable landscaping
- Has structure been relocated?

Condition

- Present condition
- Is this building being adversely affected? By what?
- Other (specify)

large number of structures is recorded in the computer, and the second, a more limited inventory selected from the structures identified during the reconnaissance, in which the information would be in prose form. Using this approach the selection of those structures to be researched in greater depth for the second level is a crucial one. Criteria should be explicit, but will vary widely according to the objectives of the survey.

In a kind of compromise approach, the computer can be used to record narrative data, which can be retrieved with the help of a computerized thesaurus. This has the advantage of avoiding the use of codes, sets, and subsets, which characterize many computer programs and which are not as easily used by the general reader.

Each year new programs and methodologies are developed for using computers in preservation efforts. One of the more popular programs for survey work has been dBase III Plus, used by HABS/HAER, which is run on a personal computer. Applications of computer programs will continue to evolve, but probably no one approach will emerge as ideal for overall use. Instead, different applications will continue to be used for different kinds of surveys.

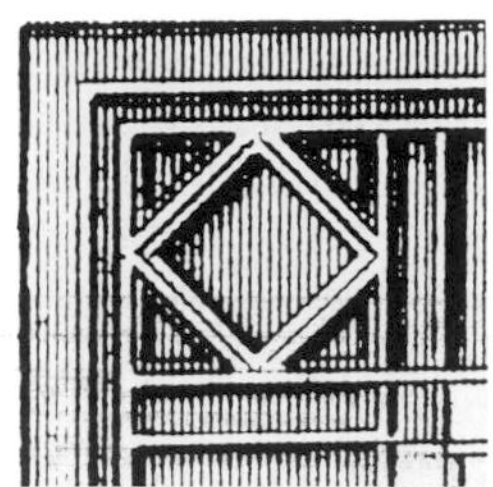

SOURCES OF USE TO THE SURVEYOR

Local and regional histories: Available from local libraries/archives or on interlibrary loan through a local library.

Maps and atlases: Including plat maps, bird's-eye views, fire insurance maps. Available through local libraries/archives; municipal/county government; private collections. Fire insurance maps for cities only may be available from major repositories in larger cities or the Library of Congress in Washington, D.C.

Tax records: Available from the municipal/county assessor's office, tax records provide the full legal description of a property, current owner, Sidwell mapping number used for identification and filing purposes. Current tax record maps also note date(s) of construction/alterations, but these dates have not been found to be accurate, especially for pre-1900 structures. While the time involved in this type of research may be prohibitive, historic tax assessment books can be immensely useful.

Newspapers: Local newspapers dating to the historical periods of interest to the surveyor may be available on microfilm and may be indexed by the local library or historical society. Old newspapers may also be found in the files of the newspaper itself if it is still in existence. These records can be useful in providing dates and uses for commercial and industrial structures.

Gazetteers and directories: Available from local, regional, or state libraries or archives. Especially useful in linking a business to a particular building.

Brochures, unpublished material, clippings: In private collections and vertical files of libraries/archives.

Photographic sources: Housed in libraries, archives, private collections.

Genealogical information: Published genealogies are available from local historical societies and libraries and are useful in establishing historical associations and significance.

Building permits: A useful tool in many localities, available from the municipal or county government.

Deeds: In view of the time-consuming nature of deed research, it is recommended that this not be undertaken as part of the inventory unless special circumstances warrant it.

Property managers or owners: A likely resource for existing drawings, photographs, and so on.

Field Work

Field work is the second of the four components constituting a HABS/HAER survey. In this phase, the second part of the literature search is accomplished and architectural analysis is undertaken. Here the surveyor examines the structure, fills out the field form, and, using 35mm black-and-white film, photographs it.

Literature Search

The literature search for surveys begins with secondary sources. It is conducted simultaneously with the visual survey of the structure itself, which is, of course, the fundamental source. Among the secondary sources that are most helpful are architectural and technological references, which are particularly important in establishing and maintaining consistency in terminology. These include architectural dictionaries and style handbooks, including works concentrating on vernacular architecture and regional studies. Primary works useful to the surveyor include tax records, building permits and deeds, historic photographs, and newspaper files.

General source works and guides to industrial archeology and the history of technology are not nearly as extensive in this area as they are in architecture. However, the literature in the field is growing rapidly. The best sources

Figure 2.10

This six-column beam steam engine and flywheel are part of a cane mill complex in Nianato, Puerto Rico. While in this case the engine could hardly be missed, careful scrutiny of the interiors of industrial buildings and of adjacent areas to identify remaining machinery is a crucial part of a HABS/HAER inventory.

remain *Industrial Archeology*, the annual journal of the Society for Industrial Archeology since 1975, and the society's newsletter since 1972, which carries an excellent "Publications of Interest" supplement. Because of the great diversity of structures important to the history of technology and industrial archeology, it is advisable to seek out the available literature on specific structure types (bridges, mills, windmills, structures related to the steel industry, etc.) through available bibliographies. See the bibliography of this book for an annotated list of secondary sources in architecture, industrial archeology, and history of technology.

While the time and funding constraints of most surveys force a reliance on secondary sources, primary sources can be investigated as time allows. It is up to the surveyor to decide which primary resources are necessary and appropriate to the survey and which primary sources, once identified, are best simply noted for possible future work.

Visual Survey

The purpose of the visual survey is to obtain a description of the building or structure, ascertain its general condition, and determine style, construction type, and defining features. At this time, repetitious photographs are taken to provide an additional record of the property (see fig. 2.10).

Because of the large number of structures usually included and the limited scope of the HABS/HAER survey, the visual survey can often be limited to the exterior of the structure, and the rear and side of the structure, not readily visible from the street, need not be recorded. The problem of gaining access to interiors or back areas of most properties is great and adds considerably to the cost and time of the survey as well as increasing the risk of injury to the surveyor. Unless the characteristics of the resource or the demands of the research design require that these areas be visually inspected, they should not be included in the survey.

This shortcut cannot be used in surveying technological resources and industrial sites that require a more specialized approach. In these cases, all sides of the structure, as well as the interiors, should be examined for building configuration, remaining machinery, and related or attached structures. The evidence of the visual survey must join with that found in records to explain the site, how it worked, and how it changed over time. Proximity to water sources and transportation, if relevant to the process that took place there, needs to be noted, and a site plan drawn up. The interior of industrial structures must be examined not only for remaining machinery, but for any features that assist the surveyor in analyzing the interior space as a workplace.

Photography. Photographs of the main facades of surveyed structures should be taken with a 35mm camera, ideally with a perspective-correcting lens. It is also helpful to have photographs of architectural details and streetscapes when appropriate. Photographs can be recorded on photo identification sheets (See fig. 2.11), as well as on the field form itself, to ensure that the photograph is matched with the right structure.

Related Structures. In any historic district, there are similar features that tie the structures together. Streetscapes often share function, setbacks, scale, and building materials. Industrial buildings are related and grouped by function and often possess similar styles and building materials. Locations of individual buildings within a grouping may demonstrate how the buildings relate to one another.

Related facilities can also be important to interpretation. Noting and

National Park Service
Photo Identification Sheet

PHOTOGRAPHER

Location	Building	Date	HABS #
		Field Film #	HAER #
		Elevation/View	

WASO-29

GPO 942 4[illegible]

interpreting such interrelationships are an important aspect of the survey. For example, an industrial complex such as a deep-shaft copper mine might include the mine proper, hoist houses, machine shops, blacksmith shops, shaft houses, pumphouses, mills that pulverized rock and concentrated the mineral, smelters, and transportation facilities. Each of the structures must be identified individually and their relationship to one another established in order to permit the tracing of the process that occurred at the site. While an in-depth technological analysis of the processes that took place must await the more extensive research discussed in the following chapter, the surveyor should, at this point, establish the function and the reason for the location of the individual structures.

Similarly, a farm complex with main house, summer kitchen, springhouse, barn, and so on, must be examined both individually and as a series of interrelated structures. A sketched site plan is an ideal way to quickly show the locations of the structures in such a way as to assist in interpreting and demonstrating interrelationships.

In large complexes, where ages and types of structures vary considerably, the most important structures are recorded on individual HABS/HAER inventory cards, with secondary or auxiliary structures recorded briefly in the history and description section of the card. This situation is most likely to arise in the case of large industrial complexes, where major buildings may have a host of auxiliary structures.

Aerial photography is an excellent way to demonstrate interrelationships among structures on a site. It is generally helpful at any time during the survey; but, to allow the information it contributes to be properly considered, it should be completed before the end of the field work (see fig. 2.12).

FIGURE 2.11

This photo identification sheet is used by HABS/HAER to record photographs taken in the field during the course of a survey. It provides a back-up method of photo control. Photo numbers are also recorded on individual field forms to ensure accuracy.

***Figure* 2.12**

This aerial of Fort Jay, located on Governors Island, New York, and completed in 1809, was taken during a HABS/HAER survey of the island in 1983. Fort Jay was one of the largest fortifications in the defense system that protected New York City and its harbor during the War of 1812. The aerial photograph allows the surveyor to analyze the siting of this large structure and to determine interrelationships with other structures built inside the fort.

Analysis

The third of the four components constituting a HABS/HAER survey is analysis of data. Once all the data have been collected, someone must determine the historic, architectural, industrial, and engineering values of the resources and how these values relate to existing structures, fitting each resource in the context required to evaluate it properly, deciding what is significant, and recommending what further work needs to be done. While analysis is ongoing throughout the project, there are two distinct tasks that must be accomplished when the data collection is complete: evaluation of resources and recommendations for future work.

Evaluation for purposes of a HABS/HAER survey is best accomplished in two steps. The first is to determine whether or not a property is significant by National Register of Historic Places criteria. While identification of National Register properties may not be the primary goal of the survey, surveyors should not overlook the importance of National Register nomination or determination of eligibility in providing protection to a property. The second phase of the evaluation can be called categorization or classification. This is done to supply additional guidance to planners and other decision makers by differentiating between degrees of historic, architectural, industrial, and engineering importance. It also determines

Figure 2.13

The area of the U.S. Military Academy's campus known as the Plain, shown in the upper middle of this view, is depicted early in the Academy's history (circa 1830). The fortifications from the pre-Academy days are visible to the left toward the river. Early buildings, some of which still exist, are shown to the right. This view, showing an early definition of the Plain and reinforcing its importance as a central historic open space, alerted surveyors to the unique impact of the Plain on the development of the Academy and served as an early milestone in comparing historic photographs with document changes.

which properties should be documented further.

The National Register of Historic Places criteria are as follows:

> The quality of significance in American history, architecture, archeology, engineering, and culture is present in districts, sites, buildings, structures, and objects that possess integrity of location, design, setting, materials, workmanship, feeling, and association, and (A) that are associated with events that have made a significant contribution to the broad patterns of our history; (B) that are associated with the lives of persons significant in our past; (C) that embody the distinctive characteristics of a type, period, or method of construction, or that represent the work of a master, or that possess high artistic values, or that represent a significant and distinguishable entity whose components may lack individual distinction; or (D) that have yielded, or may be likely to yield, information important in prehistory or history.

Guidance for applying these criteria can be found in "How to Apply the National Register Criteria for Evaluation" (National Park Service, Department of the Interior, Washington, D.C., 1982).

All properties that appear, on the basis of survey-level information, to meet these criteria should be noted. As a rule, the amount of information gathered in the course of a survey is not sufficient to nominate a property to the National Register. A list of those properties that, in the best judgment of the surveyor, appear to qualify for the National Register of Historic Places should be given to the state historic preservation office or qualified local preservation organization for additional assessment and, if they appear to be eligible, for completion of nomination forms.

Categorization ensures that the most important resources will be recognized and that resources of minor importance will not be neglected simply because they do not meet National Register criteria. While there are no gradations of eligibility in relation to the National Register (that is, a property meets National Register eligibility criteria or it does not), categorization of resources provides as many alternatives as necessary for fine-tuning a preservation plan.

HABS/HAER has worked with various types of categorization systems. A very simple one categorizes structures according to national, regional, or local importance. It does not address the level of importance within the three categories. Although this system ties closely to National Register criteria, not all the buildings and structures classified as having national, regional, or local importance in a HAER survey would necessarily be eligible for listing in the register. This is particularly true since HAER recognizes no cut-off dates, although most inventoried resources are approaching or are more than fifty years old.

Another type of categorization system is one in which structures are graded by level of importance. While national, regional, or local importance form a part of the criteria, other aspects are also addressed.

In this system, the surveyors can have as many categories as are required to address all the levels of importance of the surveyed structures. HABS/HAER has found that five categories usually provide sufficient flexibility without becoming too cumbersome. Category 1 is the highest, including structures of major importance in history, architectural history, industrial history, and history of engineering. For these structures, restoration, or at the very least, special historic structure maintenance plans, are recommended. Category 2 includes structures of importance or structures of major importance to which unsympathetic modifications resulting in some loss of integrity have been made. Category 3 embraces structures of minor importance, but that contribute to the grouping of which they are a part, or more important structures to which unfortunate modifications of a major nature resulting in a significant loss of integrity have been made. Category 4 is used for structures of little or no historic importance. Category 5 is for intrusions. These category definitions are purposely general so that they can be tailored to the historical, architectural, industrial, or engineering values established for a particular grouping of structures.

Categorization systems can vary depending on the type, number, range, and complexity of resources. They can employ simple statements of historical, architectural, and technological values designated as being of primary or secondary importance to the district or grouping, or they can involve a more complex numerical scoring system. The numerical scoring system is particularly well adapted to surveys of large numbers of structures with multiple areas of importance. Criteria such as historical value, architectural merit, integrity, setting, and visual value are assigned numerical values. While the range for historical value might be from plus 1 to plus 3, the range for integrity might be from minus 1 to plus 1 allowing the evaluator to subtract points for damaged integrity. The structures with the highest number of points would be placed in Category 1, with lower scores assigned to the lesser categories. Such systems require some testing and adjusting, but once in place, surveyors should attempt to live with the results. The goals of any system should be ease of use, consistency, and appropriateness of categorization.

The second major task in the analysis phase is development of recommendations for future work. These should focus on the appropriate level of HABS/HAER documentation, but, depending on the purpose of the survey, can also include proposed National Register nominations, historical studies, repositories needing further investigation, planning for future use, preferred preservation treatment, and so on.

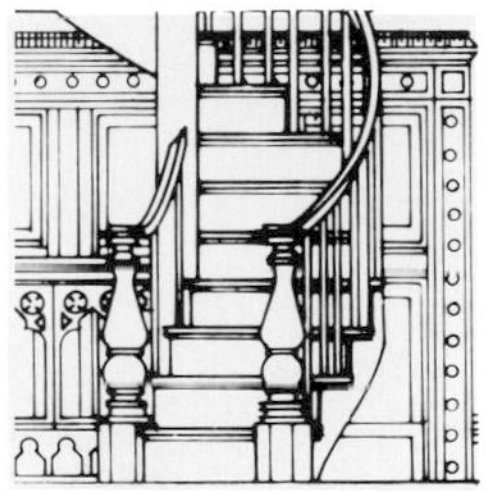

***Figure* 2.14**

The Plain's importance made it the frequent subject of paintings and photographs of the U.S. Military Academy, allowing surveyors to monitor changes in the adjacent buildings. This 1881 photograph of engineering training taking place on the Plain shows the old West Point Hotel, with its laundry building, at center. The hotel had been torn down, but surveyors were able to identify a building currently used as a residence as the laundry building.

Figure 2.15

This 1933 aerial photograph of the Plain at West Point shows its survival as the central feature of the Academy into the twentieth century. The photograph allowed surveyors to quickly identify changes which had occurred between the date of earlier photographs and 1933 and between 1933 and the time of the survey in 1982. The prominence of the railroad tracks and related buildings along the waterfront was just one of the features that assisted surveyors in establishing historical values and evaluating the Academy's structures.

Report Writing

The fourth and last component of a HABS/HAER survey is report writing. A basic survey report contains the following parts: methodology, historical overview, bibliography, and inventory.

1. Methodology. This is a statement of how the survey was conducted based on the methodology outlined in this chapter, but pointing out specific aspects of the particular survey in question, such as inaccessibility of certain records or how construction dates were ascertained. The methodology section should include the reason for the survey, who conducted the survey, the parameters of the survey, and how these parameters were set.

2. Historical Overview. The overview is the main statement of the historical, architectural, industrial, and engineering values established for the survey area. The overview should bring together directed historical research with information about individual structures gained during the survey to provide a context or framework for the evaluation of the resources. It should be specific to the site, locale, or town being investigated.

The overview section should sum up known data, evaluate past work, identify data gaps, and provide a framework for future research. It should include (1) significant historic events and people associated with any surveyed structure; (2) patterns of historic property types, including locations, density, distribution, and diversity; (3) relationship of structures to national, regional, or local architectural styles or structural types; (4) relationship of any identified industrial processes to the history of that industry and the region, including any modifications that have occurred in the process which are demonstrated by the site; and (5) construction technology.

The following chapter on historical documentation contains additional information that will be helpful to surveyors in completing the historical overview.

An excellent example of how an overview can do this is drawn from the Historic Structures Inventory of the United States Military Academy at West Point, New York. The academic area at West Point centers on an open space known as the Plain. The following passage from that report describes it:

> The academic area is located on a point of land which juts out from the west shore of the Hudson River. It is this topographical situation which led to the use of the term, West Point. The utilization of this site has historically been dependent upon the availability of flat open space in an otherwise hilly area. As the largest and most historic area at West Point, the academic area's importance goes back to the Revolutionary War, when it contained Fort Clinton, the Great Chain, and numerous redoubts. The level ground nearest this point, historically known as the Plain, is bordered on the north and the east by the Hudson River. A steep slope, which leads down to the area identified as the Post Services area, creates the northwest border. The southwest border is formed by a rocky ridge, and the southern border is marked by the beginning of the South End Officers' Quarters area. The academic area at West Point occupies one of the most commanding sites along the Hudson River.
>
> Having served as a parade ground, cadet summer camp, and cavalry and artillery drill ground, the Plain presently contains a parade ground and several athletic fields. Historically and presently, the academic area has contained those buildings directly related to the

teaching mission of the Academy, including: Cadet Barracks, Academic and Administration Buildings, Library, Gymnasium, Chapel, and Mess Hall.

The architecture of these buildings has, over the years, varied in style, but the buildings have continued to define sharply and preserve the openness of the Plain. In most cases, later additions strengthened rather than lessened its visual impact. It remains the most historic of all areas at the Academy, as central to Academy life now as it was in the early 19th century.

The conclusion reached about the important historic role of the Plain and the surrounding buildings grew out of exhaustive research and visual investigation. A number of historic photographs from 1828 to aerials taken in the 1930s graphically display the Plain's character during numerous periods in the Academy's history and demonstrate how the surveyor can use historic photographs as a rich data source (see figs. 2.13 through 2.15).

The use of historic photographs proved an excellent research tool to assist in developing historic values at the Academy. Establishing the paramount importance of this central open area provided a major focus for the categorization process. The overview is the format in which these values are stated and defined.

The character of each overview will differ depending on the resources, the available data, and the identified historical values or themes. The subheadings utilized in an overview as part of a HABS/HAER survey of Morris, Illinois, are typical: Location, Physical Setting, Early Settlement, Site Selection, Platting, Industrial Development, Commercial Development, Residential Development, Education and Religion, and Political Development.

In the Morris survey, one of the most fruitful areas of research proved to be platting activities in Morris, which were closely examined during the research phase. Using the available data, a series of maps were drawn detailing platting activities over an eighty-four-year period. This exercise helped in dating buildings and areas within the town as well as tracing building activity and growth, thus providing an excellent context for evaluation.

3. Recommendations for Future Work. Based on the results of the analysis component, recommendations for future work should be enumerated as part of the report. Determining what type of future documentation is appropriate is the main goal of HABS/HAER surveys. But if the purpose of the survey is to determine preservation planning, or treatment, the report should include these recommendations. The resources should be addressed here both as a group and individually.

4. Bibliography. This should identify persons interviewed, as well as secondary and primary sources consulted.

5. Inventory. If the surveyor has used the HABS/HAER inventory cards to record information about a structure, these are included in the report. If the information about a specific structure has been computerized, the printouts will be included. Statements of significance for individual structures should refer to those values established in the historic overview. Whatever rating has been assigned to the structures should be noted, as should recommendations for future work when appropriate.

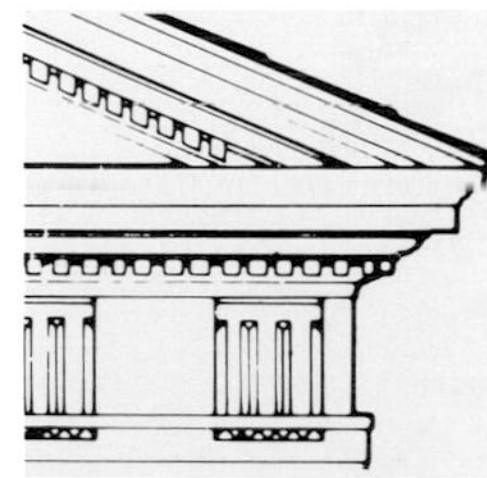

CHAPTER 3

Alison K. Hoagland
Gray Fitzsimons

Historical research plays a central role in recording historic structures. Historians examine both physical remains and written documentation to acquire a greater understanding of a historic structure or site. In the HABS/HAER program, the products of the historian's work appear in three forms: written documentation, measured drawings, and selection of and captions for large-format photographs. While the focus of this chapter is on how to produce written documentation, a historian's work often involves close interaction with architects, for many of the questions posed by the historian are answered in graphic form in the architect's drawings. Conversely, many of the architect's questions about a site or structure are answered by the historian.

In producing written documentation for historic structures or sites, the historian should seek to impart information that explains why a specific historic structure or site is significant.

Written documentation involves collecting historical information, analyzing the structure or site in question, investigating graphic documentation, and then synthesizing these elements to provide a better understanding of its historical importance.

Because written documentation is more than mere fact-collecting, it has been HABS/HAER's experience that professional historians are generally better suited to this task. Historians are trained to direct their inquiries in a logical and systematic fashion, to research and evaluate a wide range of source materials, and, finally, to present the research findings and analysis in a cogent form. Because scholars of American history represent diverse fields of study—ranging, for example, from political, to social, to economic history—this chapter is designed to aid historians trained not only in material culture or technological history, but also in more general fields. Moreover, this chapter is intended to remind both architectural and technology historians of the need to place specific structures or sites in a more general historical context.

Technological history, seemingly a very specialized field, actually embraces a wide range of human activities and historical subjects. Such disciplines as the history of science, economic history, labor history, social history, political history, and intellectual history, to name but a few, are often addressed when examining a specific topic in the history of technology. Many of the historian's traditional approaches—primarily the reliance on written documentation to provide factual evidence and substantiate historical theses—are also a requisite for the historian of technology. While the field of technological history draws heavily on these "mainstream" disciplines and traditional approaches, however, it also requires an ability to understand and analyze topics in science, mathematics, and engineering and an ability to understand and evaluate mechanical objects and engineering structures. By using traditional historical methods to approach the subject—identifying the important avenues of inquiry, undertaking the research in a carefully thought-out and well-organized fashion, and presenting the findings in a clear and cogent form—a historian can produce a successful technological history.

This chapter outlines a general methodology for producing written historical documentation and underscores the major contributions that historians can provide in recording historic structures. Although the material presented largely constitutes the approach to historical documentation taken by the Historic American Buildings Survey (HABS) and the Historic American Engineering Record (HAER), this approach is also applicable to many other kinds of historical investigations into the nation's architectural and engineering heritage. This chapter contains five parts: historical information, description, significance, sources and methodology, and presentation, relating an approximately chronological approach to documenting a historic structure. While overlap exists in the fields of architectural history and the history of technology, differences are apparent in the kinds of questions asked and in the answers sought. Accordingly, while this chapter generally discusses documenting architecture, separate sections that address engineering and industrial structures are included.

Figure 3.1

The McLachlen Building (1910–11, J. H. de Sibour), in Washington, D.C., has been little changed since construction, except for alterations at the first floor. From this 1923 photograph the original storefronts can be determined. The photograph appeared in a promotional publication of the architect's works.

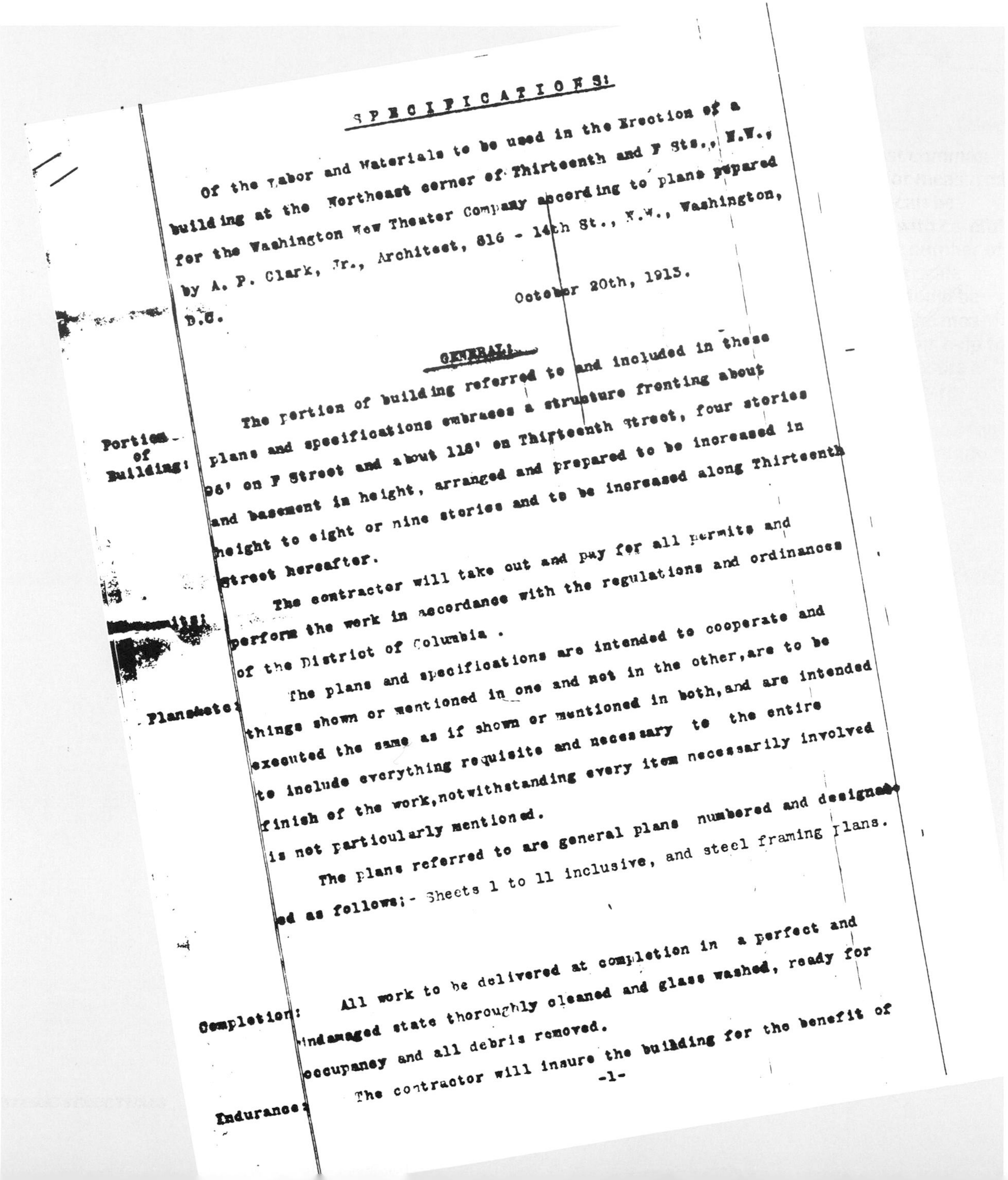

SPECIFICATIONS:

Of the Labor and Materials to be used in the Erection of a building at the Northeast corner of Thirteenth and F Sts., N.W., for the Washington New Theater Company according to plans prepared by A. P. Clark, Jr., Architect, 816 - 14th St., N.W., Washington, D.C. October 20th, 1913.

GENERAL:

Portion of Building: The portion of building referred to and included in these plans and specifications embraces a structure fronting about 96' on F Street and about 118' on Thirteenth Street, four stories and basement in height, arranged and prepared to be increased in height to eight or nine stories and to be increased along Thirteenth Street hereafter.

Permits: The contractor will take out and pay for all permits and perform the work in accordance with the regulations and ordinances of the District of Columbia .

Plans etc: The plans and specifications are intended to cooperate and things shown or mentioned in one and not in the other, are to be executed the same as if shown or mentioned in both, and are intended to include everything requisite and necessary to the entire finish of the work, notwithstanding every item necessarily involved is not particularly mentioned.

The plans referred to are general plans numbered and designated as follows;- Sheets 1 to 11 inclusive, and steel framing Plans.

Completion: All work to be delivered at completion in a perfect and undamaged state thoroughly cleaned and glass washed, ready for occupancy and all debris removed.

Insurance: The contractor will insure the building for the benefit of

-1-

Figure 3.2

Specifications for construction can be highly informative. In this example from the Homer Building (1913–14, Appleton P. Clark, Jr.), the second paragraph specifies that the building will be four stories, but "arranged and prepared to be increased in height . . . along Thirteenth Street hereafter." The extra height was never added, but the building was doubled in size with an addition to the north.

Historical Information

The historian should begin with an understanding of the significance of the structure under study. Some areas of significance will have been previously established through the initial survey, discussed in chapter 2. The research that is undertaken through documentation, though, will expand and in some cases redefine the previously documented historical and architectural significance.

The preliminary assessment of significance will determine the basic research. If a building is identified as being an example of French Colonial construction, for instance, then the research should concentrate on the manner in which it was built. Not only should historians explore the building date, original owner, and possible builders, they should also interpret the construction by identifying it, for example, as *pôteaux sur solle* (posts on sill), and by placing that fact in the context of French Colonial settlement. If a house has been identified as the home of a signer of the Declaration of Independence, then his relation to the house and what the house can tell us about that time period should be early avenues of investigation.

This initial assessment of significance is frequently modified after more research. Sometimes the context will change. For example, a theater may have been identified as significant to its city because it was the last remaining example of a once-common building type. It may even turn out that it was the work of an architect known nationwide for designing theaters. The documentation should address both of these aspects of the theater's history. Similarly, a building identified as significant for stylistic reasons may, upon further investigation, be found to have unusual structural features not readily apparent to the casual viewer. Archival resources, too, may point the researcher in directions not anticipated.

The ultimate purpose of the investigation is to develop a better understanding of the significance of a structure or site. Setting the structure into context is essential—how does it compare with what was going on around it? Such declarations as "first," "only," and "most" are extremely difficult to make, but very effective when proven.

In addition, the product—the reason for which the documentation is being produced—should guide the historian. If the basic question is when the roof was put on, then the research should be directed to sources which might answer that question: the building itself, contemporary drawings and photographs, contemporary descriptions, building permits, and so on. Time and money constraints will further define the task at hand. At a minimum, though, basic research questions of who, what, where, when, and why should be answered and the significance of the building should be addressed.

Questions

Writing history is a process of answering questions, and good research is a product of good questions. For every structure, there will be some basic questions, common to all. The particular characteristics of the site should provoke additional questions that will demand other avenues of inquiry.

When documenting a structure, specific questions relevant to that structure must be answered. Even if the structure is more significant for the people associated with it than for its architecture, the structure should still be explained and identified. The structure is, after all, the object of the documentation. Basic questions that should occur to a researcher include the following:

1. Who designed it, built it, used it?
2. When was it built, altered, demolished?
3. What was it originally, is it now, was it meant to be?
4. Why was it built, does it look the way it does?
5. How was it built, has it been altered, did it function?
6. Where was it, is it?

To explain or define the significance of the site, additional questions may have to be asked. These questions derive from the nature and significance of the resource. Generally they involve setting the resource in a larger context, as well as focusing on particular features or elements. For example, a bank has been identified as significant to the business district because of its design. The researcher will first want to answer the basic questions of who designed it and when, how it was built, the arrangement of banking functions on the interior, how long it was used as a bank, why it was located there, and so on. To set it in context, the researcher will probably also want to look first at other banks in the city, their designs and locations, and secondly at other downtown buildings in the same style. An interesting item may have been turned up in the process of answering these questions—say, the architectural commission was awarded through a competition. This provokes other questions, all relevant to the significance of the design: why a competition, who competed, why was this firm selected, what program were they given, how did this design compare to the others, who selected it?

Engineering and Industrial Structures

Histories of engineering structures—dams, bridges, or buildings, for example—emphasize design innovations, construction methods, and structural performance, while histories of industrial sites often focus on the process—how the system operated, how the goods were produced, or how the resource was extracted. To set an engineering structure or industrial complex in context, the research requires additional questions which address the following kinds of specific engineering or technological issues: What were the precedents for the development of the technology? Was the technology unusual or common for its time? What impact did the technology have over time?

In the case of an industrial complex or factory where historic machinery exists, HAER often directs its questions along descriptive and analytical lines. For example, the study of a woolen mill in Missouri sought to answer several basic questions for each piece of machinery. The descriptive questions included the following: What was the historic name of the machine? Who manufactured it? When was it manufactured? How did it operate? What changes were made to the machine? What is its current condition? The analytical query focused on the significance of each piece of machinery: Was the machine technologically unique or was it a common "garden-variety" type? Did it reflect national technological advancement or was it a local adaptation of a national type?

Answering Questions

The many questions confronting the historian require a multitude of primary and secondary sources. For structures of technological historical interest, some

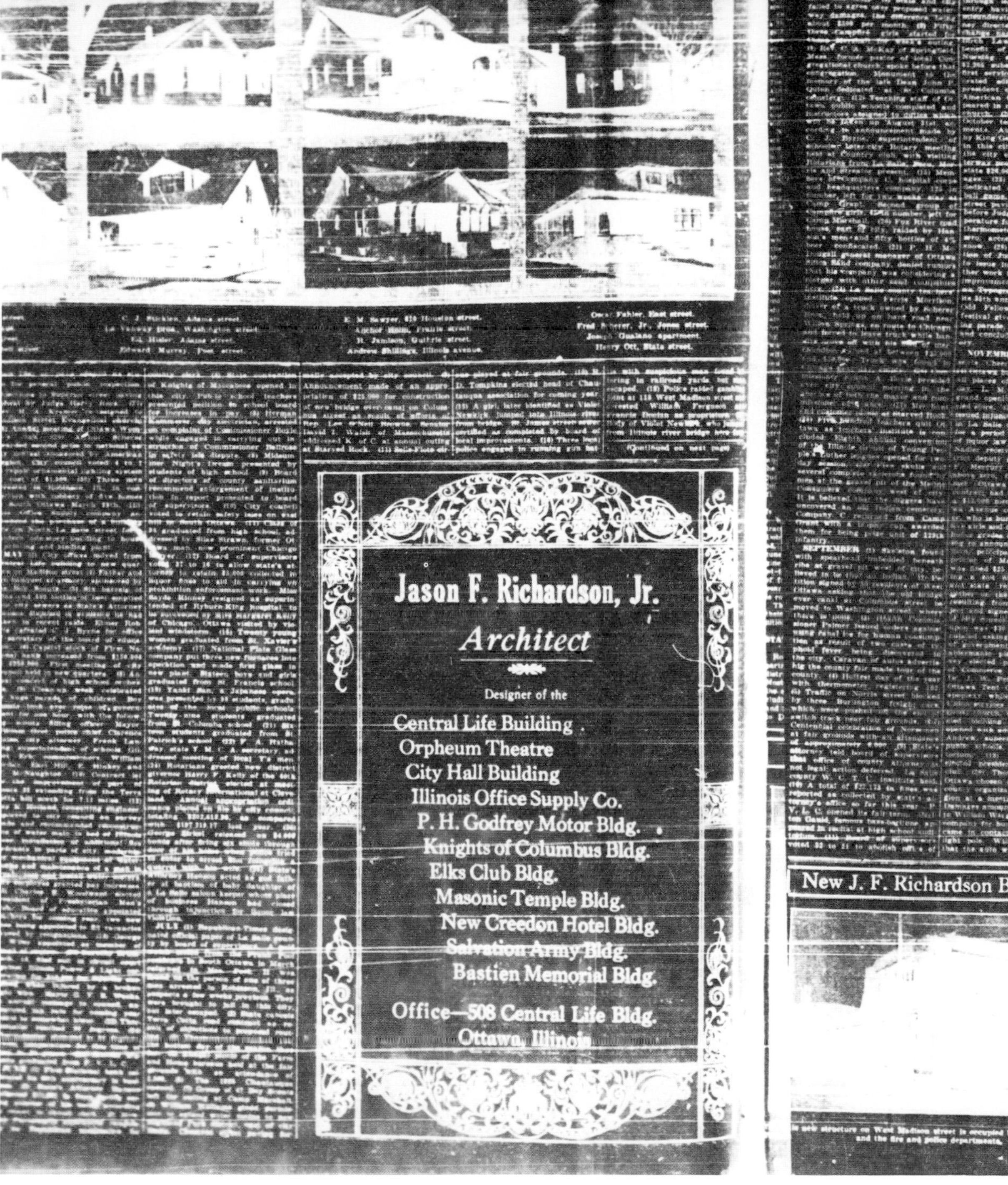

Jason F. Richardson, Jr.

Architect

Designer of the

Central Life Building
Orpheum Theatre
City Hall Building
Illinois Office Supply Co.
P. H. Godfrey Motor Bldg.
Knights of Columbus Bldg.
Elks Club Bldg.
Masonic Temple Bldg.
New Creedon Hotel Bldg.
Salvation Army Bldg.
Bastien Memorial Bldg.

Office—508 Central Life Bldg.
Ottawa, Illinois

New J. F. Richardson Bui

Figure 3.3

An advertisement from the Ottawa Republican-Times of 31 December 1925 lists the buildings of which architect Jason F. Richardson, Jr., was most proud. The historian found it on microfilm, as indicated by the white-on-black print.

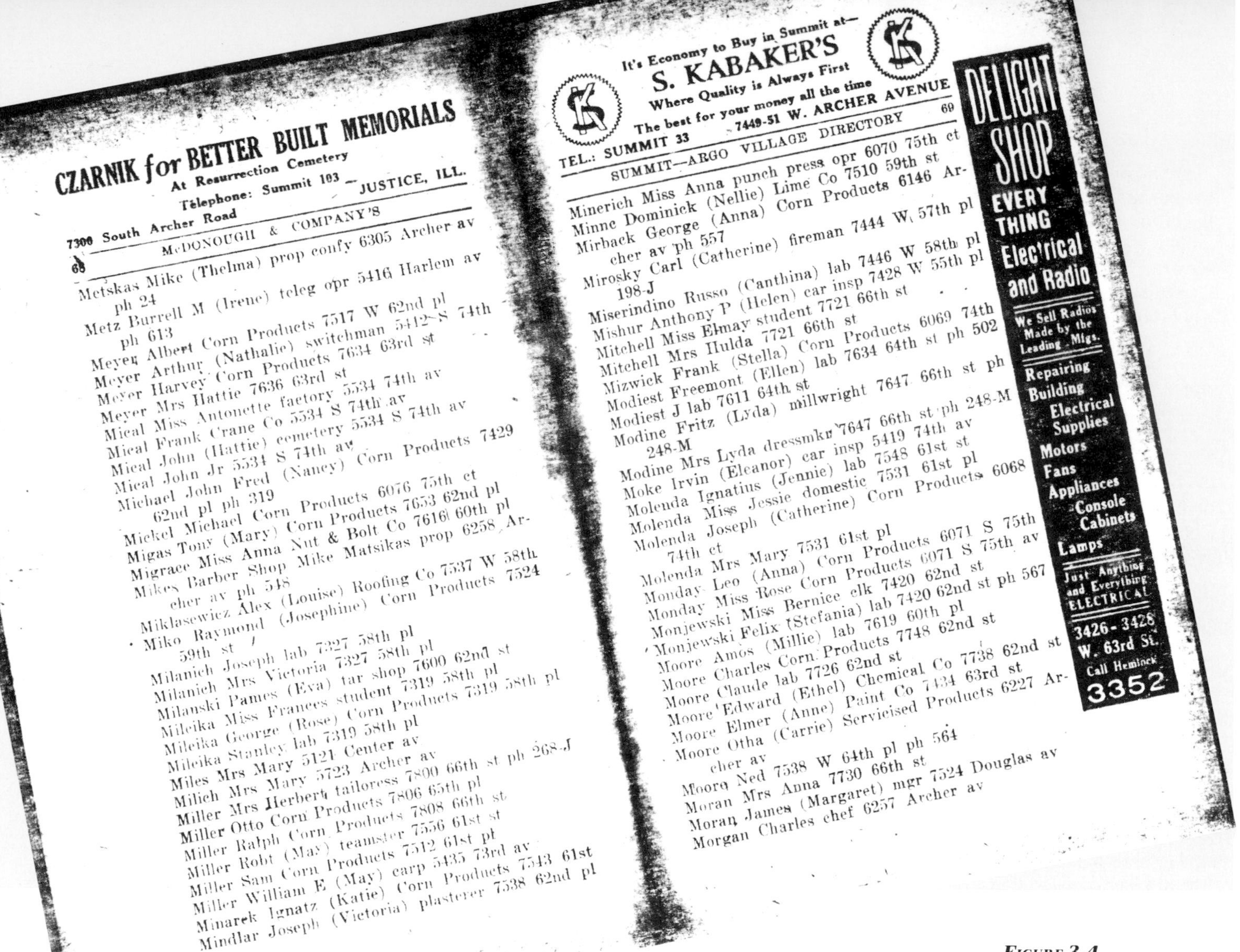

CZARNIK for BETTER BUILT MEMORIALS
At Resurrection Cemetery
Telephone: Summit 103 — JUSTICE, ILL.
7300 South Archer Road

68 McDONOUGH & COMPANY'S

Metskas Mike (Thelma) prop confy 6305 Archer av
ph 24
Metz Burrell M (Irene) teleg opr 5416 Harlem av
ph 613
Meyer Albert Corn Products 7517 W 62nd pl
Meyer Arthur (Nathalie) switchman 5412 S 74th
Meyer Harvey Corn Products 7634 63rd st
Meyer Mrs Hattie 7636 63rd st
Mical Miss Antonette factory 5534 74th av
Mical Frank Crane Co 5534 S 74th av
Mical John (Hattie) cemetery 5534 S 74th av
Mical John Jr 5534 S 74th av
Michael John Fred (Nancy) Corn Products 7429
62nd pl ph 319
Mickel Michael Corn Products 6076 75th ct
Migas Tony (Mary) Corn Products 7653 62nd pl
Migrace Miss Anna Nut & Bolt Co 7616 60th pl
Mikes Barber Shop Mike Matsikas prop 6258 Ar-
cher av ph 548
Miklasewicz Alex (Louise) Roofing Co 7537 W 58th
Miko Raymond (Josephine) Corn Products 7524
59th st
Milanich Joseph lab 7327 58th pl
Milanich Mrs Victoria 7327 58th pl
Milanski Pames (Eva) tar shop 7600 62nd st
Mileika Miss Frances student 7319 58th pl
Mileika George (Rose) Corn Products 7319 58th pl
Mileika Stanley lab 7319 58th pl
Miles Mrs Mary 5121 Center av
Milich Mrs Mary 5723 Archer av
Miller Mrs Herbert tailoress 7800 66th st ph 268-J
Miller Otto Corn Products 7806 65th pl
Miller Ralph Corn Products 7808 66th st
Miller Robt (May) teamster 7556 61st st
Miller Sam Corn Products 7512 61st pl
Miller William E (May) carp 5435 73rd av
Minarek Ignatz (Katie) Corn Products 7543 61st
Mindlar Joseph (Victoria) plasterer 7538 62nd pl

It's Economy to Buy in Summit at—
S. KABAKER'S
Where Quality is Always First
The best for your money all the time
7449-51 W. ARCHER AVENUE
TEL.: SUMMIT 33

SUMMIT—ARGO VILLAGE DIRECTORY 69

Minerich Miss Anna punch press opr 6070 75th ct
Minne Dominick (Nellie) Lime Co 7510 59th st
Mirback George (Anna) Corn Products 6146 Ar-
cher av ph 557
Mirosky Carl (Catherine) fireman 7444 W 57th pl
198-J
Miserindino Russo (Canthina) lab 7446 W 58th pl
Mishur Anthony P (Helen) car insp 7428 W 55th pl
Mitchell Miss Elmay student 7721 66th st
Mitchell Mrs Hulda 7721 66th st
Mizwick Frank (Stella) Corn Products 6069 74th
Modiest Freemont (Ellen) lab 7634 64th st ph 502
Modiest J lab 7611 64th st
Modine Fritz (Lyda) millwright 7647 66th st ph
248-M
Modine Mrs Lyda dressmkr 7647 66th st ph 248-M
Moke Irvin (Eleanor) car insp 5419 74th av
Molenda Ignatius (Jennie) lab 7548 61st st
Molenda Miss Jessie domestic 7531 61st pl
Molenda Joseph (Catherine) Corn Products 6068
74th ct
Molenda Mrs Mary 7531 61st pl
Monday Leo (Anna) Corn Products 6071 S 75th
Monday Miss Rose Corn Products 6071 S 75th av
Monjewski Miss Bernice clk 7420 62nd st
Monjewski Felix (Stefania) lab 7420 62nd st ph 567
Moore Amos (Millie) lab 7619 60th pl
Moore Charles Corn Products 7748 62nd st
Moore Claude lab 7726 62nd st
Moore Edward (Ethel) Chemical Co 7738 62nd st
Moore Elmer (Anne) Paint Co 7434 63rd st
Moore Otha (Carrie) Serviciscd Products 6227 Ar-
cher av
Moore Ned 7538 W 64th pl ph 564
Moran Mrs Anna 7730 66th st
Moran James (Margaret) mgr 7524 Douglas av
Morgan Charles chef 6257 Archer av

DELIGHT SHOP
EVERY THING
Electrical and Radio
We Sell Radios Made by the Leading Mfgs.
Repairing
Building
Electrical Supplies
Motors
Fans
Appliances
Console Cabinets
Lamps
Just Anything and Everything ELECTRICAL
3426-3428 W. 63rd St.
Call Hemlock
3352

Figure 3.4

A page from the 1929 city directory of Summit, Illinois, indicates the blue-collar nature of the town. Corn Products is easily identifiable as the town's major employer.

of the reference works cited in the bibliography will be helpful in setting the technological context. For buildings of local historical interest, often little secondary source material exists, and primary research is the only course. The sources vary from place to place and no list could ever be exhaustive. Many local historical societies or other organizations have published guides on researching in their locality.

The effectiveness of the primary sources will depend on the questions that are being asked. It is important to evaluate progress constantly so that the researcher does not get sidetracked or fail to pursue something that could be significant. This evaluation could consist of writing down research questions at the start and reviewing them periodically, or of writing an outline or a first draft of the final product before the research is complete.

The historian should also evaluate the quality of sources to determine accuracy and reliability. When was the data produced—contemporaneously with the resource itself (a primary source) or later (a secondary source)? Did the recorder have first-hand knowledge, or was it hearsay? What was the motivation and funding for producing the data? What were the recorder's biases? Keeping these questions in mind can prevent too much credence being given to unreliable sources (see fig. 3.1).

The researcher usually starts with secondary sources, such as published architectural guides and histories and technological reference works. Unpublished surveys also deserve investigation. The researcher will probably have to come back to secondary sources after learning more about the structure through primary research; but, as a starting point, secondary sources can save a lot of time. By identifying basic facts, such as year of construction, secondary sources can point the researcher to the best primary sources, such as the right tax books. In addition, a careful reading of a secondary source's bibliography can reveal important sources the researcher might otherwise have missed.

Some secondary sources can change the thrust of the research approach. If, for example, it is found during the initial research that a definitive study of the architect in question has been written, then the research might shift from investigating that architect's entire work to merely fitting the building into it. Such a definitive study could be referenced in the work, rather than recounted. But it is important that basic facts about the structure not be accepted from a secondary source without verification. Construction dates and attributions in secondary sources have been known to be wrong, and if an error is accepted as a premise, the research will obviously be faulty.

Legal records are one of the best primary sources. A chain of title, which establishes ownership of the property, can be constructed from deeds. Variations in the price of the property, or in some cases in the description of the

Figure 3.5

Correspondence concerning building suppliers can provide valuable information, particularly for restoration work. In this example, found in the collection of Scotty's Castle in Death Valley, California, the locations intended for each piece of metalwork are given.

Aztec Forged Hardware Co.

MIDLAND 5306

MANUFACTURERS OF
FORGED IRON AND BRASS HARDWARE
2369 EAST FIFTY-FIRST STREET
LOS ANGELES

March 21, 1929

FOLLOWING ARTICLES SHIPPED TO
DEATH VALLEY RANCH

Three Only Hinges for Solarium (Top, Center & Bottom).
Three Pair #2065 Hinges. (Music Room) Circle Top Door.
One Only Center Hinge for Mrs. Johnson's Bed Room.
Three Pair Hinges (Music Room) French Door.
One Plate Latch --- One Pr. Half Surface Hinges for Cupboard in Mr. Johnson's Lavatory
#206 4 Plate Latch Complete (Music Room) Circle Top Doors.
Two Only Complete Latch Sets for Two South Gallery Doors.
Eighteen Only Shutter Hinges. (new)
One Only #2078 Latch Complete (Music Room) French Doors.
One Only #2064 Plate Latch Complete (Music Room) Square Top Doors
One Transom Ornament (Music Room)
One Only #1849 Latch Handle for Mr. Scott's Apartment.
Three Hinge Straps and Three False Hinges for Tower Door (Music Room)
Sixty-Two Studs for Hinges in Music Room.
Two Pr. 2½" Half Surface Hinges #2375 (Linen Closet in Gallery).
Twenty-Four Slide Bolts for Shutters.
Two Only #861 Tips
Two Only Handles --- (Note:-) One of these Handles goes on Power Room door. Put the other Handle on the door that has the same Hinges as the Power Room.

Mr. Thompson:
Mr. Brown:

Dear Sirs:

Mr. Earle has discontinued his business here in Los Angeles and I have taken over the shop and am going to make the same hardware.

If, by any chance, there are any missing screws, lags or studs write us in care of the Aztec Hardware Company (this is the name we are doing business under) and we will mail missing items.

Hoping to see you gentlemen in the near future, I remain

Yours very truly

AZTEC HARDWARE COMPANY

MH:NG H

P.S. Please mail me the thickness of the shutters.

FIGURE 3.6

The Washington Public Library (1899–1903, Ackerman and Ross) was designed through a competition, as were many Carnegie libraries. The program provides insights into the Library Board's original intentions, as well as some of the constraints the architects faced.

Programme of Competition

FOR THE

Washington

Public Library Building

Washington, D. C.

Washington, D.C. Public Library Commission

To be erected with funds donated by Mr. Andrew Carnegie

MAY, 1899

[illegible] of library substations in the [illegible] located, and another entrance for the [illegible] and workmen, supplies, etc.

The book-stack should begin at the first floor and extend to the roof with decks at intervals of seven feet, and it may be practicable to extend it one tier into the basement, but space must be saved for the warming and ventilating apparatus of the stack.

SCHEDULE OF ROOMS.

The rooms suggested for the first floor, if practicable, with their approximate areas, are as follows:

Book room .... 6,000 sq. ft., or less

There should be present provision for at least 225,000 volumes and a much larger ultimate capacity. As far as the symmetry of the building and the limitation upon its cost will permit the Commission desires a book room covering a considerable ground area and shelving as many books as possible in stack tiers included within the first story of the building. Designs are, however, admissible which place the stack tiers in numerous stories, one above another, to the full height of the building, with a corresponding reduction of the ground area occupied. Full statement should be made of the reasons which determine the architects' suggestions concerning the shape and size of the book stack.

Lending department .... 2,200 sq. ft., or more

Delivery counter, seats for persons waiting, suitable shelving, card catalogue space.

Public reading room .... 3,000 sq. ft.

Reference library, suitable shelving.

Cataloguers' room .... 800 sq. ft.

Shelving.

Accessions room .... 500 sq. ft.

Shelving.

Open shelf room .... 1,500 sq. ft., or more

Shelving.

This room is for the display of new books and selected classes of other books on shelves to which the public is to have unobstructed access.

Children's room .... 1,500 sq. ft., or more

Shelving.

Librarian's room .... 300 sq. ft.

With safe or vault.

Reception room.

Cloak rooms.

Lavatories, etc.

On the second floor might be placed:

Periodicals and newspaper room . 3,000 sq. ft., or less

Shelving.

Class or lecture room .... 3,000 sq. ft.

Shelving; wall space for maps, plans, etc.

Trustees' room .... 500 sq. ft.

Four special reading rooms, 400 sq. ft. each .... 1,600 sq. ft.

Shelving.

Book room—

If continued through this story.

Among the rooms in the basement should be a packing and delivery room, a lunch room, a binding and repair room, two or three stock and store rooms, including scrubwomen's room, engineer's department, boilers and mechanical apparatus, bicycle room and fuel rooms, either in basement or in vault outside underground. The boiler chimney should be incorporated in the building.

It is expected that the greatest development of the library will be in its lending department. It is desired, also, to give special attention to the open shelf facilities, to the children's room, in short, to all departments which will increase the usefulness of the property, can indicate major construction or alterations. The effectiveness of chains of title varies from place to place, but for rural areas they are often the only key to ownership. Other legal records include tax records, which indicate ownership and changes in assessment; building permits, which are invaluable, but which are usually available only in cities; and probate records, which often include explicit inventories of real and personal property.

Contemporary publications and accounts are another important source (see fig. 3.2). Newspapers are helpful; but as they are often unindexed, the pertinent articles may be hard to find (see fig. 3.3). City directories can identify occupants and uses of the structure, and are also helpful in determining construction dates (see fig. 3.4). Promotional publications such as real estate brochures and souvenir booklets can be helpful, but their self-serving nature should be taken into account (see fig. 3.1). Letters, diaries, and corporate records, although difficult to locate, can be extremely rich resources (see figs. 3.5 and 3.6). The manuscript version of the U.S. Census, which contains detailed information on building occupants, is available, but only for censuses taken more than seventy-two years ago. Real estate insurance maps give site plans, number of floors, and construction materials and often include information on power supply and machinery for industrial sites (see fig. 3.7). Issued every few years, they can help pinpoint construction dates and show alterations. Although these maps generally are limited to urban areas, they also focus on industrial sites outside the city limits which pose a fire hazard and are likely to be insured.

Because a structure is the focus of the research, architectural and engineering records should not be overlooked. Original architectural drawings are most likely to be found in the possession of the original architectural firm or its successor firm. They may also be in the building itself, in the company archives, or in the owner's papers. "The National Union Index to Architectural Records" can be found in the Library of Congress and the *Avery*

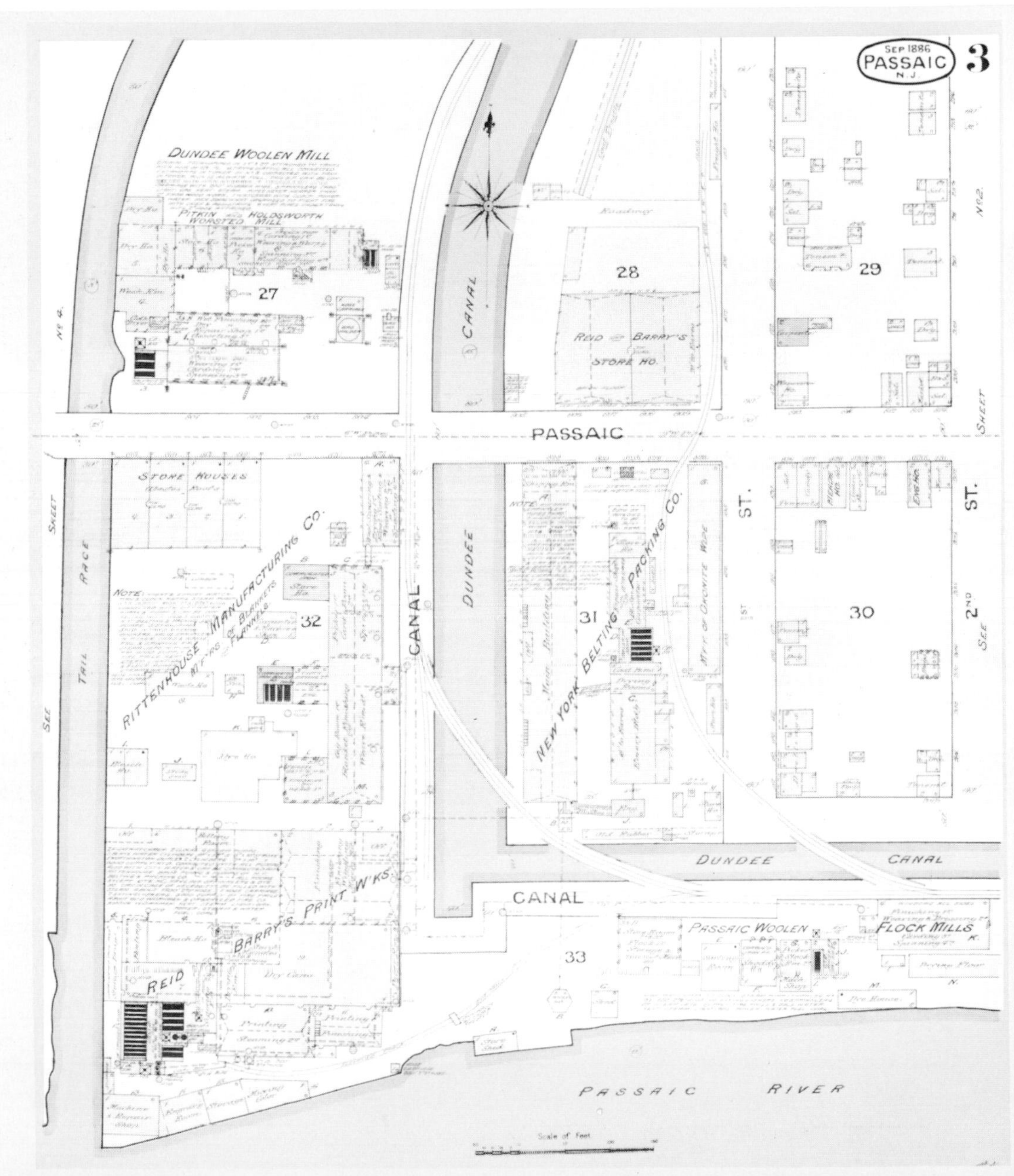

FIGURE 3.7

An 1886 Sanborn Map of Passaic, New Jersey, showing both industrial and residential areas along the canal and Passaic River.

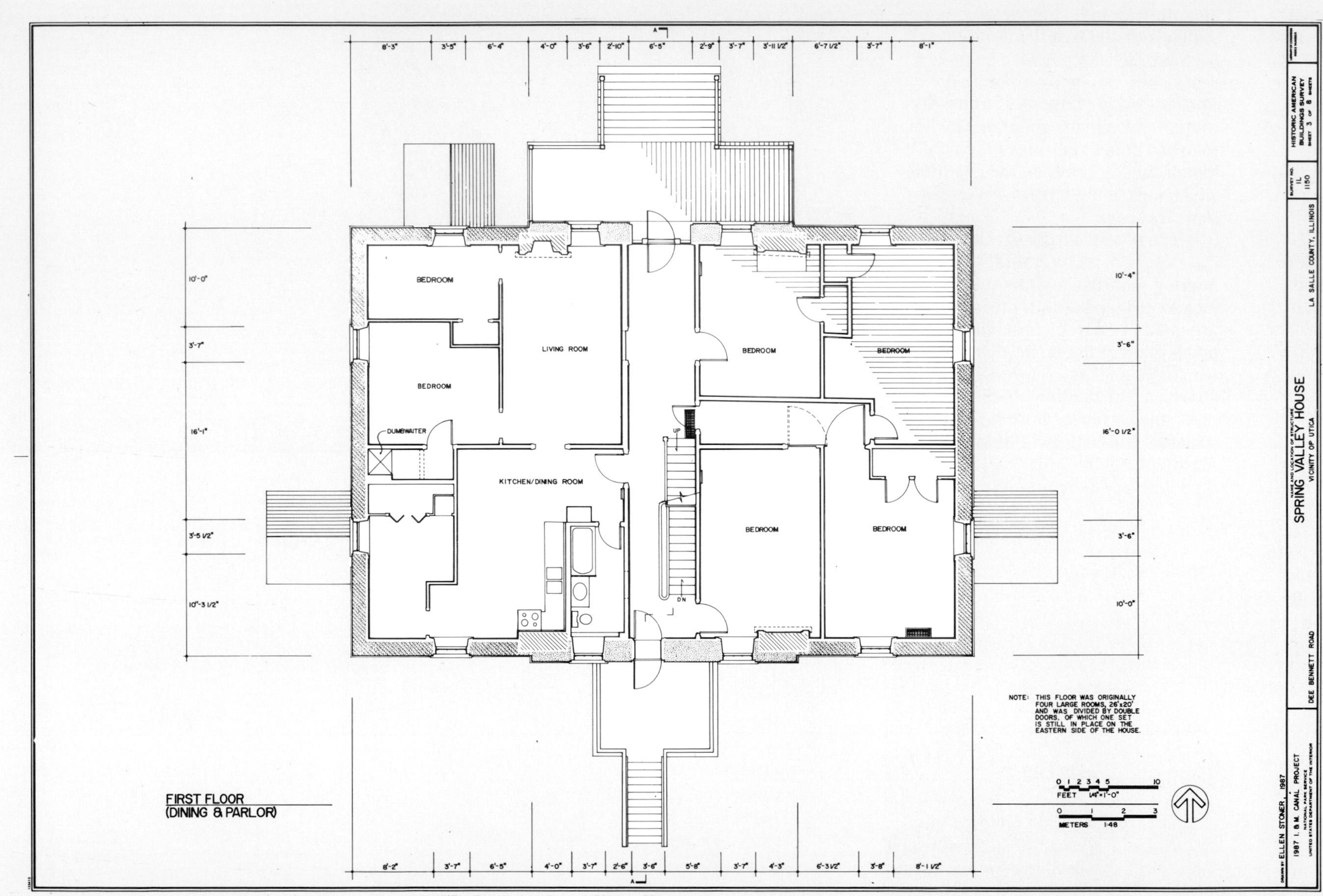

Figure 3.8

Measured drawings are excellent research tools. The partitions that have been added to the interior of this building might be confusing to someone on site, but the partitions are distinct from the original walls in this HABS drawing. The first floor of the 1850s Spring Valley House near Utica, Illinois, was originally divided into four large rooms with a central hall.

Index to Architectural Periodicals may provide good leads (see fig. 3.8).

Other graphic sources should also be investigated. Historic photographs can be extremely helpful, not only in identifying original appearance and subsequent alterations but also in identifying occupants and uses (see fig. 3.9). Published compilations of historic photographs, which usually concentrate on a specific area, are a good place to start. Otherwise, a local historical society and local newspaper files are probably the best source. Postcards, manufacturers' catalogs, and other promotional illustrations can also be important graphic sources. Bird's-eye views and elaborated maps can be helpful, but are not always entirely accurate because of their promotional nature (see fig. 3.10).

The historian should include copies of important graphic records with the written documentation. A careful selection should be made, depending on the preservation and accessibility of the records in their current repository. If the records are well preserved and well known, it is less important to include them with the documentation; a reference to their existence and location might suffice. A second consideration is the importance of the graphic records to the significance of the building. For example, if a photograph is found that illustrates the building before major alterations, it will be important to include it with the documentation. Even if copied, a citation to the location of the original photograph is absolutely necessary, and copyright restrictions must be observed. Graphic material can be copied either by photography or photocopier; a photograph is more easily reproducible for the next researcher. The archival stability of any type of copy should be consistent with the standard of the rest of the documentation.

People connected with the structure should be consulted, not only for their knowledge of the structure, but also for their help in identifying other possible sources. While oral tradition is often suspect, it can provide good leads. For more recent structures with few archival materials, oral histories can be a good source. The researcher who asks the informants how they happened to remember these facts may get an indication of their reliability. Data from oral tradition must be credited as such.

The structure itself is, of course, the most important resource. This would include not only archival materials stored there, such as company records or correspondence, but also the very structure that reveals its alterations and uses. While the information for the description is being gathered, the historian should also regard the structure as a document. On the exterior, interruptions in symmetrical fenestration patterns may indicate alterations, just as changes in moldings on the interior may indicate an altered room arrangement. Basements and attics, traditionally unfinished spaces, can be a rich source of structural information. The building, too, can leave incidental clues, such as the dates of newspapers used for insulation. It is also important to keep consulting the structure as information is turned up elsewhere that, for example, indicates alterations—are they visible on the structure? Do not take the structure itself for granted, but question every aspect of it.

Engineering and Industrial Structures. Among the most useful and readily available sources to the technological historian are the professional engineering and scientific journals, as well as the industrial and engineering trade journals. The earliest of the indexes that provide a comprehensive listing of citations in the trade journals is the *Engineering Index*. This annual index was first published in 1896 and groups the citations by subject, such as railroads, wastewater treatment, steel works, and so on. The *Industrial Arts Index*, published from 1913 to 1957, is an outstanding tool for researching the trade journals and, unlike the *Engineering Index*, its citations are listed by both geographic region and corporate name. American trade and professional journals of the nineteenth century exist; however,

Figure 3.9

Three historic photographs of the Leland Stanford House (1857, Seth Babson) in Sacramento, California, reveal the extensive alterations that had occurred to this building. The lithograph was printed in the California Farmer *of July 4, 1862, and showed the building shortly after construction. The pre-1870 photograph, from a book about Leland Stanford, likewise showed the original house. The 1902 photograph from the collection of the California Society of Pioneers pictures the building after the changes of 1871 when it was raised and a mansard roof and wings added.*

THE
STANFORD-LATHROP
MEMORIAL HOME
For FRIENDLESS CHILDREN.

Figure 3.10

Bird's-eye view of Cambria Iron Works in Johnstown, Pennsylvania.

these tend to be indexed at best in the *Readers' Guide to Periodical Literature* or at the very least in the individual journals.

Engineering and industrial texts and treatises are often a neglected resource. These frequently provide the historian with an understanding of the period's state-of-the-art technology, and occasionally permit a glimpse of society's attitudes toward the technology. For example, J. A. L. Waddell's *Bridge Engineering*, published in 1916, is an excellent reference for late nineteenth- and early twentieth-century bridge design and construction, and even aesthetics (see fig. 3.11). For a historian studying a mid-nineteenth-century flour mill, an indispensable work is Oliver Evans's *The Young Mill-Wright and Miller's Guide*, first published in 1834 with several other editions issued throughout the late nineteenth century (see fig. 3.12). One frequently used reference from the late nineteenth century is *Appleton's Cyclopaedia of Applied Mechanics* (1880). This two-volume set provides a fine overview of the major engineering works and mechanical equipment dating from the mid- to late nineteenth century.

An often neglected resource, patent records are frequently useful in helping understand how a mechanism or structure was intended to function. Researching patent records has been greatly facilitated by the development of the Classification and Search Support Information System (CASSIS), available at select libraries in each state.

Description

A description of the structure that is the object of research is always necessary. Too often, historians take it for granted that the reader is as familiar with the object as the writer, or that drawings or photographs will suffice to "describe" the structure. The present appearance of a structure, though, should always be documented in the written history. A description should not only relate what a structure looks like, but also qualify that appearance.

Important characteristics of a building should be identified and defined. These would include qualities such as massing, shape, scale, rhythm, and texture, which are particularly concerned with the three-dimensional character of a building—qualities that are not always effectively portrayed in drawings or photographs. While each of these qualities can be interpreted literally, such as "four stories," the scale of the building has more to do with how these four stories are perceived. Similarly, describing the massing of a building is more than explaining the plan and bulk, but rather the impression that the bulk leaves on the viewer. In a way, these qualities are a means of interpreting the designer's intentions: for example, in selecting a particular fenestration pattern, what rhythm did the designer create? Examining these qualities helps the researcher and the reader to comprehend a building.

A description of a building should include its size, shape, materials, and fenestration, as well as the shape and materials of the roof. The actual structural system should be noted in addition to the exterior material. On the interior, plan and materials are important. Any significant features should receive special attention. The site is also important, especially for relating the building to others around it or to landscape features that bear on it, such as a mill's relation to a stream.

The issue of architectural style categorization has come under increasing debate in recent years. In some cases, style assignation has reached absurdity, with styles that the designer had never conceived being assigned to buildings that bear little resemblance to the historical style. On the other hand, styles are of great importance to buildings that were conceived to represent that style, such as the Greek Revival-style U.S. Patent Office in Washington, D.C. Not to label the Patent

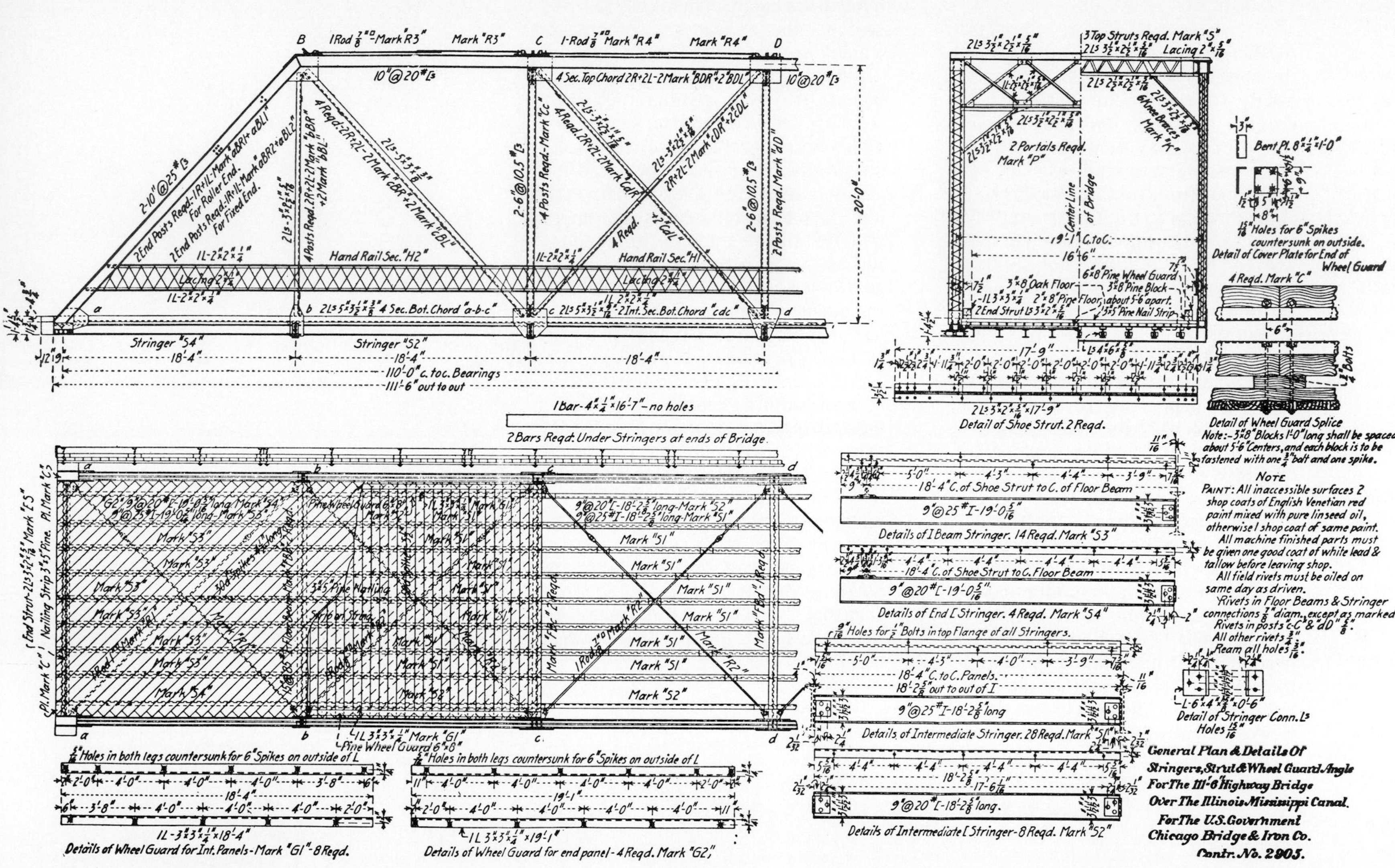

FIGURE 3.11

Drawing from Milo S. Ketchum's Design of Highway Bridges.

Office "Greek Revival" in any description of it would show a severe misunderstanding of the significance of that building. In addition, style can provide a shorthand description to someone who speaks the language. For example, terming a country house "Georgian Revival" conveys a great deal about the appearance of the building, the era in which it was constructed, and the aspirations of its owner. Style names should be used when they serve a purpose and are accurate, but should not be created to fill in a blank, to sound erudite, or when a building does not fit the style that is being assigned.

Attention should also be paid to vernacular building types, without attempting to convert the type to a style by creating a new name. A "three-bay row house" conveys an instant picture of an attached dwelling three bays wide, probably two or three stories tall, and, more than likely, having a side hall entrance. With vernacular buildings, the historian should pay increased attention to structure, material, form, and plan.

A description can be augmented through research. For example, a structural system may be determined through a building permit or construction photographs, rather than destructive testing. Similarly, the origin of an element, such as a mantelpiece adapted from a pattern book, should be included in the description if it is known.

Making interpretive statements, such as defining the important characteristic features, identifying style, and employing research, should never be confused with, or take the place of, actual description. A description of present appearance should be clearly limited to what can actually be seen. When interpretation or guesswork is involved, it should be explicitly labeled as such.

Relation of description to graphic material that will accompany it is crucial. Because a physical object is the subject of investigation, some graphic representation is always desirable. Before referring to the graphics, or letting them take the place of description, make sure that they actually will accompany the written material. Also, the quality of the graphic material is important—a 35mm contact print will need to be amplified by far more verbal description than would an 8" x 10" print of a large-format negative. If the written information is to be complemented by good graphic documentation, then the description should concentrate on things that need to be emphasized or that the graphics represent poorly. If black-and-white photographs are the only graphic documentation, then particular attention in the written description should be given to such features as color, materials, structural system, and plan. Details that will appear in the graphic material but not be explained might also be emphasized, such as quoins, modillions, and inscriptions.

Interpreting drawings is also important. For example, when the written material is accompanied by floor plans, a convoluted description of spatial relationships is unnecessary. In fact, that type of description is rarely helpful. If a plan is complicated and there are no measured drawings, then the written description should be complemented by a sketch plan. A characterization of the floor plan, such as "center passage plan," is sufficient.

A description can be extremely detailed, and it is sometimes difficult to know where to stop. Infinitely detailed descriptions are rarely necessary, for if the specifics are that important, they should be illustrated. Instead, a written description should interpret the structure broadly. It should record the appearance of features that graphic materials do not record, and it should interpret specific features of significance. If, for example, an auditorium is significant for its acoustics, then the acoustic features should be described in detail. While the latter will be illustrated in the graphic material, its effectiveness will not be obvious to uninformed readers. Finally, a written description may be the best or only documentation of a structure. Do not overlook the obvious.

Engineering and Industrial Structures

Engineering and industrial structures generally fall into two categories: the first is structural, namely bridges, dams, and buildings; and the second, which encompasses a larger range of objects, is mechanical, including, for example, textile machinery, steel-making contrivances, hydroelectric equipment, chemical processing and industrial apparatuses, and so on. Resources included in the structural category are often easier to describe than those in the mechanical. For example, the description of a metal truss bridge should include such basic information as the truss type, age, span length, and supporting structures (piers or abutments). Often the description of the truss type should include a discussion of the truss members (what they consist of) and any changes made to the trussing as well as to the rest of the bridge. The historian should organize the description so that readers can better understand the form and function of the site or structure.

The descriptive information on sites or structures included in the mechanical category is often more involved. However, whether it is a complex array of machinery in a textile mill or an intricate network of electronic components in an early computer, the historian's description should always proceed from the general to the specific, relating the physical description to the way in which the machinery or equipment operated. Such basic information as the manufacturer (or inventor) of the machine should be noted, as well as its date of manufacture and installation, and its production capabilities or output. Attention should also be given to the physical relationship of one machine to another, that is, how did an individual machine function as part of a larger industrial process? Relating the physical layout of the machinery or equipment to the people who used it is central to the description.

The historian can provide greater insight into the drawings of the structure through the description. For instance, a truss bridge may be drawn showing details of the various truss members; it is the description that makes sense of them by explaining their composition (their materials and the way in which they were fabricated) and their function (the way in which they behave under loads). When the description and analysis are well integrated with the drawings, each becomes a far more useful tool.

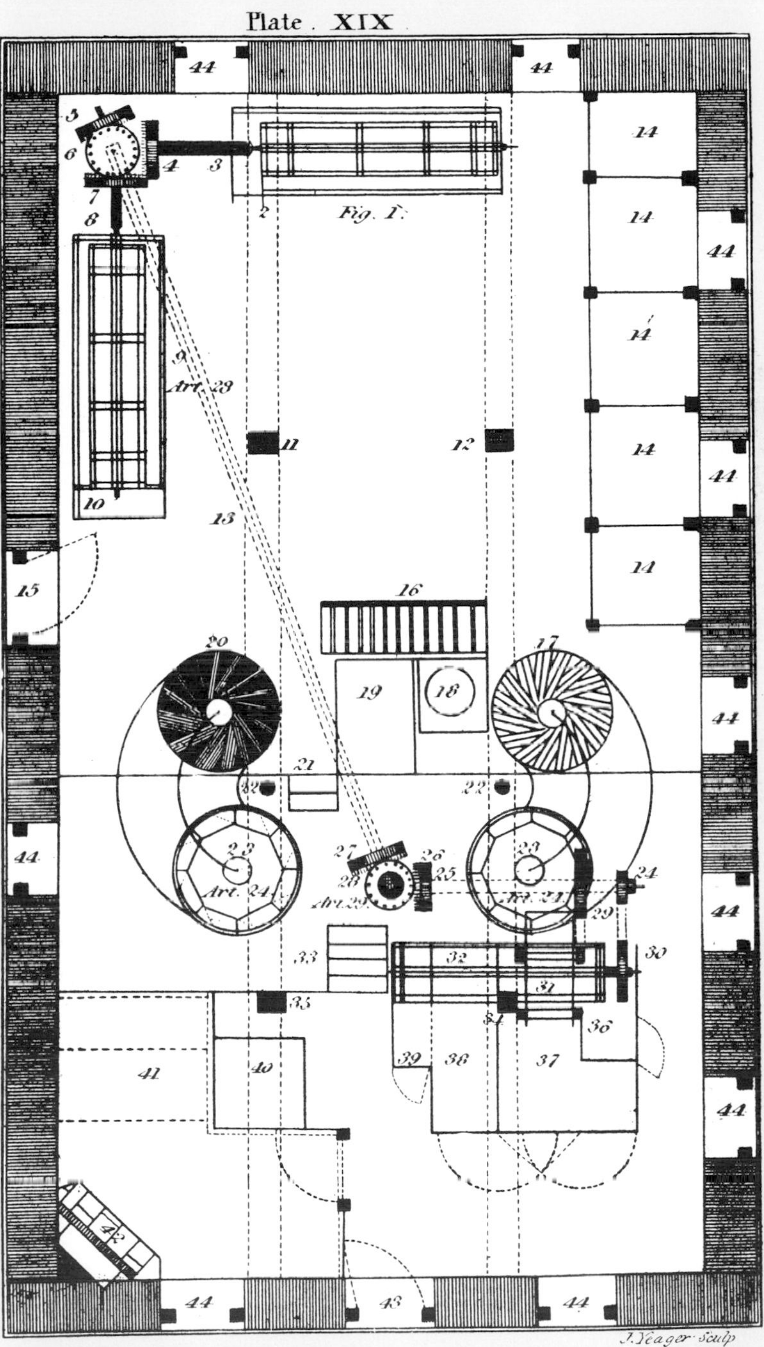

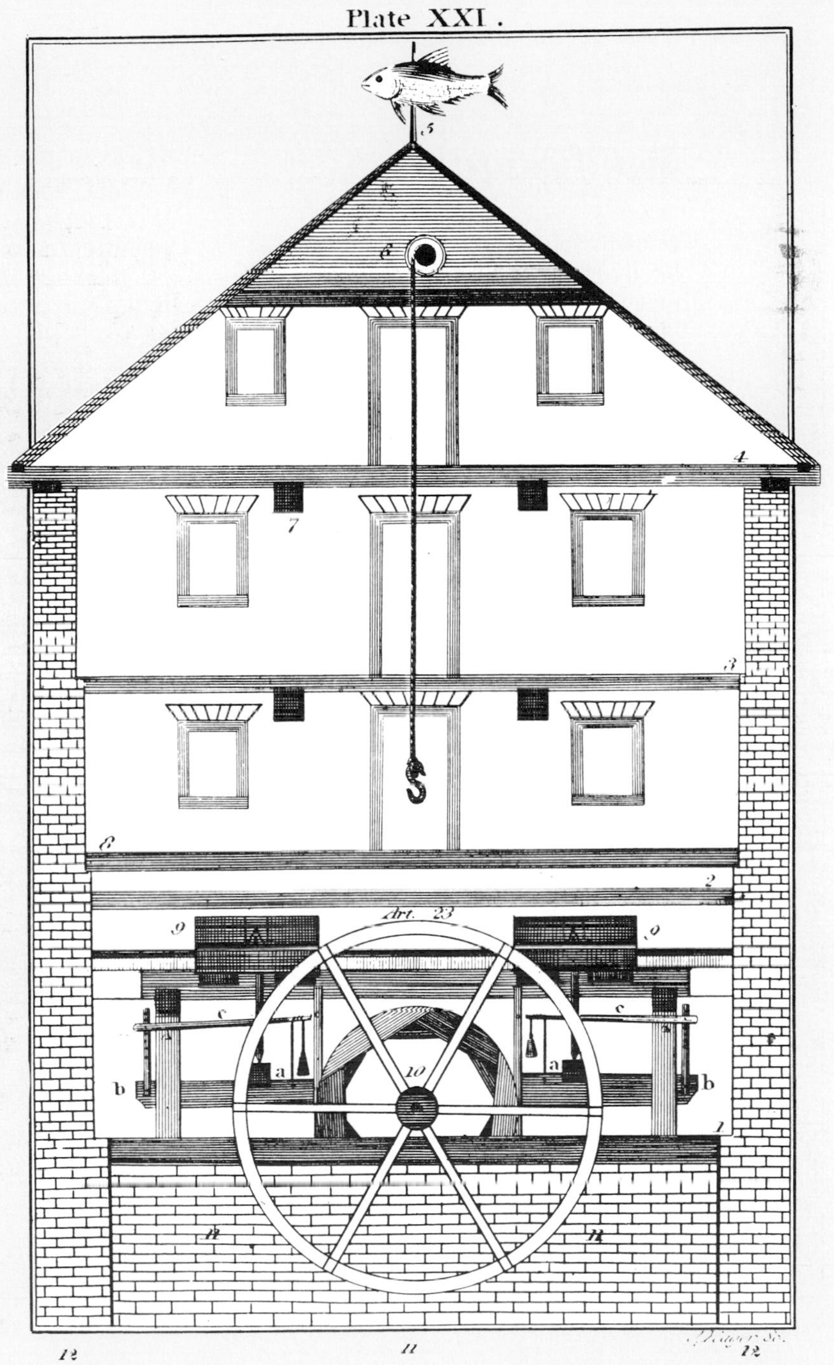

***Figure* 3.12**

Engravings from Oliver Evans's Young Mill-wright and Miller's Guide.

Significance

Once the history of a structure has been researched and its present appearance has been assessed, this information should be analyzed and synthesized. Only then can a statement of significance be written. The significance should be derived from the history and design of the structure. While it is often easy to focus on a person or event associated with the structure, the structure itself should be related to that person or event; for instance, does it look the way it did when that person lived there? It may be that after research, the significance is less than had been assumed in the preliminary assessment. There is nothing wrong with this; a structure's significance should not be exaggerated. Everything that is asserted in the significance statement should have been proven and amplified in the historical and descriptive sections.

A well-written significance statement should be clear, pithy, and supported by the evidence. As a rule, the more significant the building, the shorter the significance statement.

Sources and Methodology

No research work is complete without the inclusion of the sources consulted and the whys and hows of documentation. A list of sources consulted permits the research to be verified by another historian and gives appropriate credit to original thoughts. Standard scholarly procedure demands that sources be credited and that quotations be referenced.

Information about the documentation project helps readers evaluate the research. For complicated projects, particularly where judgments have been made in the selection or evaluation of the buildings, a statement of methodology should be included to state the assumptions and show how the work was approached and undertaken. For simpler projects, a project information statement should be included that tells who did the work, when, and for whom. This latter statement, which can be the affiliation of the researcher or the organization that funded the work, implies the reasons behind the project, the constraints it may have faced, and the direction it took.

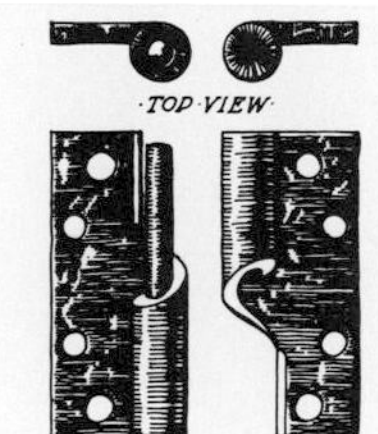

Presentation

Many possible formats exist for presenting research. Some are closely prescribed, such as National Register nomination forms, which are preprinted and are accompanied by specific instructions for their use. Others, like the standard HABS outline format, divide the information into specific categories. Still others are not even written, such as oral presentations to boards and commissions. All of them, with the possible exception of scholarly articles, should be presented so that they can be understood by an inexpert but interested audience. Avoid overly technical language whenever possible, and use the active voice, particularly in the description of industrial processes.

Report findings selectively; do not include everything that was learned. For example, the historian researching a rural site may have had to trace a chain of title from the present back to 1810 to determine the original owner. There is no need to repeat the entire chain in the report if it is not informative. Instead, the specific deeds pertaining to the original owner should be cited and, in the list of sources consulted, the deed books with their location should be noted. Likewise, although every occupant of a building may have been determined through city directory research, making generalities about these occupants, rather than listing them individually, is often sufficient.

Nevertheless, a problem more common than reporting too much of the research is that of omitting important aspects of the building or site from the investigation. For this reason, HABS uses an outline format wherein each heading serves to remind the writer of items to be covered. In addition, the reader can find answers quickly by going directly to the relevant section. A paragraph or more of information follows each heading. The "HABS Historian's Procedures Manual" discusses this issue in greater detail and should be consulted before writing information for submission to HABS/HAER. HAER, it should be noted, does not use this outline.

HABS Outline

For each of the headings in the Historical Information section of the HABS outline, a direct answer should be given first, then expanded upon. For example: "Date of erection: 1917–18. The foundation was laid in June 1917, according to the building permit (Permit #7548, June 8, 1917). The building was formally opened on September 9, 1918 (*Daily Planet*, September 10, 1918, p. 4 c.1)." The section entitled "original plans and construction" is designed to permit discussion of the importance of the original design. The second part of this section, "historical context," is where the building should be set in context, geographically, chronologically, stylistically, technologically, or whichever way is appropriate. In addition, people and events associated with the structure should be discussed here.

The "architectural information" section is self-explanatory. In this format, the description proceeds logically from foundation to roof, and then to the interior, concluding with a description of the site.

HABS OUTLINE

Building Name and HABS Number
Location
Present Owner
Present Use
Significance

Part I. Historical Information

- A. Physical History
  1. Date of erection
  2. Architect
  3. Original and subsequent owners
  4. Builder, contractor, suppliers
  5. Original plans and construction
  6. Alterations and additions
- B. Historical Context

Part II. Architectural Information

- A. General Statement
  1. Architectural character
  2. Condition of fabric
- B. Description of Exterior
  1. Overall dimensions
  2. Foundations
  3. Walls
  4. Structural system
  5. Porches
  6. Chimneys
  7. Openings
     - a. Doorways and doors
     - b. Windows and shutters
  8. Roof
     - a. Roof shape, covering
     - b. Cornice, eaves
     - c. Dormers, cupolas, towers
- C. Description of Interior
  1. Floor plans
  2. Stairways
  3. Flooring
  4. Wall and ceiling finish
  5. Openings
     - a. Doorways and doors
     - b. Windows
  6. Decorative features and trim
  7. Hardware
  8. Mechanical equipment
     - a. Heating, air conditioning, ventilation
     - b. Lighting
     - c. Plumbing
- D. Site
  1. General setting and orientation
  2. Historic landscape design
  3. Outbuildings

Part III. Sources of Information

- A. Original Architectural Drawings
- B. Early Views
- C. Interviews
- D. Bibliography
  1. Primary and unpublished sources
  2. Secondary and published sources
- E. Likely Sources Not Yet Investigated
- F. Supplemental Material

Part IV. Project Information

The "sources of information" section encourages the use of sources other than published material, such as original architectural drawings, early views (photographs and drawings), and interviews, as well as a bibliography. Each source, and its location if obscure, should be fully described. The concluding section, "project information," is a free-form description of the project, its goals and constraints, the people and organizations involved, and the date.

The disadvantage of the outline format is that writers feel constrained by it and limit their inquiry strictly to the categories that appear on the outline. Despite entreaties to add or delete categories as necessary, most writers adhere to the rigid format instead of using it as a springboard. HABS therefore accepts written information in other formats.

HAER, and sometimes HABS, manuscripts appear in a narrative style with headings tailored by the historian for the individual structure or complex. For example, a HAER historian used a chronological approach in the history of a grist mill, with chapters on the following: Alexander's Mill (1855–1894), Wilson's Mill (1900–1940), and The Mill in 1940. Alternatively, when relating the history of a neighborhood, one historian divided the manuscript into the general HABS headings of history and description. Subheadings in the historical information section were street railway, parks, water, gas and electricity, and paving. The architectural information included discussion of the buildings' floor plans, heating and lighting, and exterior and interior ornamention.

HAER and HABS have also developed a one-page architectural and engineering data form appropriate for cases in which there is minimal information, or for structures of less-than-national significance. Not all of the blanks need to be filled in to make the form meaningful. Even limited information, if it is accurate, is better than none.

The complexity of the structure that is being recorded will determine which format is most appropriate. Regardless of the format, the written documentation should complement and illuminate the measured drawings and photographs. When the documentation is complete, an understanding of the structure will emerge.

Photography

CHAPTER 4

William L. Lebovich

At the professional as well as the amateur level, photography is the most popular means of documenting structures. Photography is the least expensive, fastest, and easiest method of documentation. But photographs are also taken when measured drawings and histories are prepared. In such situations, photographs complement the other work. Photographs are more easily understood and can convey information not normally included in the other forms of documentation (see figs. 4.1, 4.2, and 4.3).

A photograph can convey three-dimensional qualities, spatial relationships, current conditions, texture, and context. The size of an engine or the degree to which the main pavilion of a house projects beyond flanking side wings is more quickly comprehended in a photograph than through a lengthy written description or by a measured drawing (see fig. 4.4). Texture of materials is difficult to depict by drawing or writing. Certain aspects of current conditions, such as minor cracks, spalling, or peeling paint, would be too small or too time-consuming to draw (see figs. 4.5 and 4.6). A single photograph, taken from the right vantage point, establishes the environmental setting for a building or structure to be studied (see fig. 4.7). To achieve the same result with a history or drawing would require expending too much effort on a secondary aspect of the subject being documented. In making decisions about documenting a resource, it is critical to understand what aspects of a building or structure are best depicted by photographs, a history, or drawings.

Despite photography's popularity and demonstrated usefulness, few documentary photographs display the technical and aesthetic qualities of the large-format photographs produced by the Historic American Buildings Survey (HABS) and the Historic American Engineering Record (HAER).

Figures 4.1, 4.2

It is easier to read the projections of the entrance and flanking wings in this photograph than in the measured drawing of the Maurice Bathhouse in Hot Springs National Park, Arkansas. The wings and mosaic panels between the second-story windows are also more apparent, but the height of the roof is shortened and the tower is not visible in the photograph. Notice the flagpole, which was not included in the measured drawing.

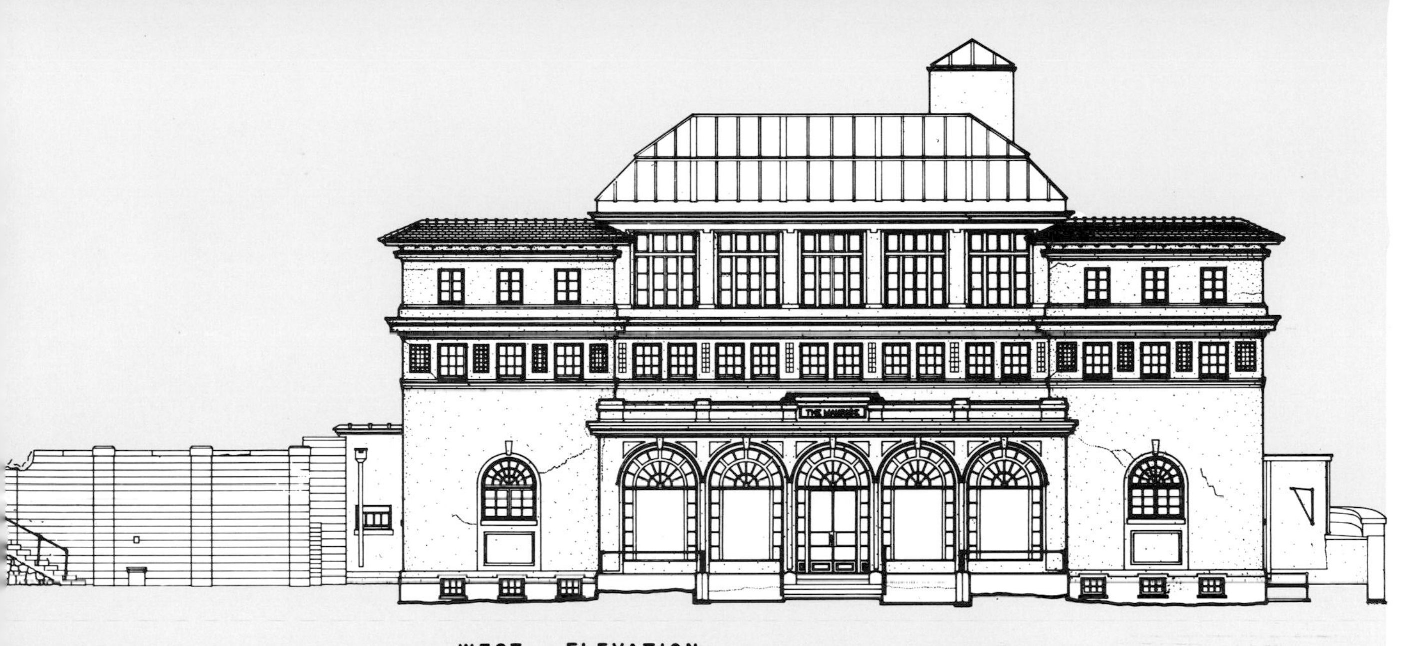

FIGURE 4.3

This perspective photograph most clearly shows the depth of the entrance bay and flanking wings of the Maurice Bathhouse. It also shows the round-headed window in the wings which is obstructed by a tree in Figure 4.2. And in this photograph, the gate post with eagle is obvious. It had been deleted from the west elevation drawing (but is included in another drawing) and is not apparent in the west elevation photograph.

FIGURE 4.4

Worker gives scale to the photograph, making it possible to estimate size of the horizontal Corliss engine.

FIGURE 4.5

Notice the rivet holes in the statue's face. Rivets are used to attach the saddle holding the wrought-iron strap that supports the copper skin. Also notice the damage at the tip of the nose. Note the need for safety precautions (hard hat, etc.).

The HABS/HAER Approach

HABS/HAER has been doing large-format photography for more than fifty years and has developed approaches that can improve anyone's photographs of architecture or industrial/engineering structures. This chapter explains those approaches and demonstrates, through words and photographs, what constitutes good documentary photography. These approaches are applicable to nearly all formats of photography. The strengths and weaknesses of 35mm, medium-size, and large formats will be discussed to aid readers in picking the one best suited to their needs.

HABS/HAER uses large format for official HABS/HAER photographic documentation of a building or structure. This formal photography is deposited in the Library of Congress as part of the permanent, archivally stable HABS/HAER collection. HABS/HAER defines large format as cameras producing 4″ x 5″, 5″ x 7″, or 8″ x 10″ negatives. HABS and HAER staff photographers use 5″ x 7″, which seems to have been the most popular format since the founding of HABS in 1933. HABS/HAER staff architects and historians use smaller-format cameras to photograph the buildings and structures they are researching, measuring, and drawing. The resulting prints are incorporated in the documentation. This informal photography, consisting primarily of 35mm negatives and contact sheets or small prints, is transmitted to the Library of Congress as field records. Informal photography should ideally meet the archival standards of the formal photographic documentation, though it is not required to.

Formal HABS/HAER photographic documentation is done with black-and-white film. The negatives and contact prints are archivally treated. The contact paper is fiber-based rather than resin-coated (RC) and the paper and negatives have had sufficiently long washings in water to remove all processing chemicals. Archivally stable negatives and contact prints will last at least a hundred years.

HABS/HAER photographers, architects, and historians also use color transparency film in large-format and 35mm sizes. The 35mm slides are used primarily for lectures, and the large-format transparencies are used for publications and exhibitions. Because color film fades and its colors change, the transparencies are not currently part of the formal HABS/HAER collections at the Library of Congress.

Why does HABS/HAER use one format for formal photography and another for informal photography? HABS/HAER photographers, along with most other professional architectural photographers, use large format because of its large negative size and extensive range of camera movements (see fig. 4.8). All other factors being

***Figure* 4.6**

Texture and tone are easily conveyed in black-and-white photographs.

equal, the larger the negative, the better the prints made from it. HABS/HAER sends contact prints rather than black-and-white enlargements to the Library of Congress. It is much easier to see details on the large-format contact than it would be on the smaller 35mm or medium-format contact print. From the point of view of the Library of Congress, large-format negatives are considerably easier to handle and less likely to be damaged than the medium-format or 35mm strips of negatives.

On the large-format monorail camera, the front standard, which holds the lens, and the rear standard, which holds the film, can be raised, lowered,

Figure 4.7

Tree-lined approach to Gunston Hall.

tilted, swung, and shifted laterally. These movements enable the photographer to eliminate the perspective distortion common in photographing tall buildings or structures. Perspective distortion is often apparent in photographs where the camera must be inclined in order to include the entire subject in the field of view. In the resulting image, the structure appears trapezoidal.

On the other type of large-format camera, the flatbed or field camera, there are fewer movements possible. Most important, the rear standard, which holds the film, does not move on the field camera, leaving less opportunity for perspective correction.

HABS/HAER does not do informal photography in large format for several reasons. First, the architects and historians who are working in the field often use their personal equipment, which is seldom larger than a 35mm camera (see fig. 4.9). Such cameras are usually equipped with a perspective correction wide-angle lens, which gives results similar to those achieved with large format, except that the negatives are smaller. In addition, 35mm equipment is more portable; less expensive; offers a wider selection of lenses, film, and accessories; and is easier to operate. These advantages are compelling for those who do not need or cannot afford the highest quality images that can be produced with large-format equipment.

In addition to the structures themselves, HABS and HAER photographers are also called upon to shoot old photographs, drawings, or lithographs (see fig. 3.7). This is done only with the owner's permission and waiver of any copyright restrictions. As these collections are usually too numerous to copy in their entirety, the most informative representative examples should be selected. As HABS and HAER have been recording more post–Civil War structures, historic drawings and construction photographs have become more important. The earliest American architectural photographs date to the 1840s. To obtain the best results, historic drawings, photographs, and historic views should be sent to a graphic reproduction service, which has the appropriate copy lenses, filters, special films, lighting, and horizontally mounted cameras. But often such historic documents cannot be removed from the site. In that case, documents must be photographed in the field, a less than ideal situation, but one that is sometimes unavoidable.

There are several specialized types of photography that HABS/HAER does not commonly employ: rectification, stereophotogrammetry, x-ray photography, infrared photography, and the computer enhancement of photographs. These techniques are discussed later in this chapter.

Figure 4.8

HABS photographer Jack E. Boucher loading film holder in rear of his thirty-pound 5" x 7" monorail camera supported by twenty-two-pound tripod.

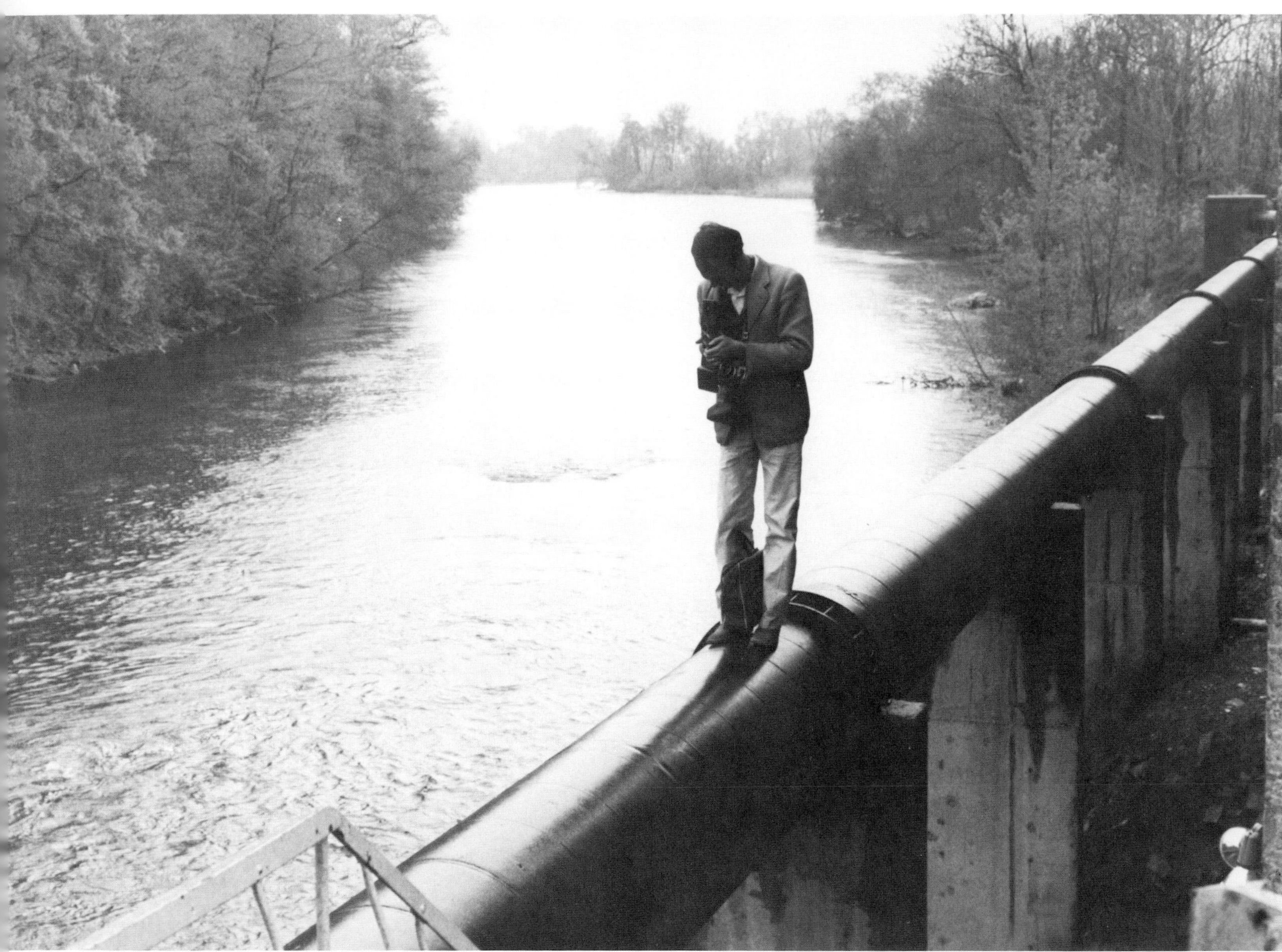

Figure 4.9

HAER architect Eric DeLony (now Chief of HAER) standing on a water pipe doing field photography with a hand-held 2¼" x 2¼" twin-lens reflex camera, weighing less than five pounds. Dangling below it is a 35mm single-lens reflex camera, which weighs even less. Field photography is usually done by architects to aid themselves in their drawings. Small- (and medium-) format negatives and contact sheets are sent to the Library of Congress as field records.

Principles of Architectural Photography

Photographers often seem more concerned with camera equipment than with subject matter. Perhaps an unconscious assumption is made that composition comes naturally if one has the right equipment. Every photographer needs a certain amount of equipment and a certain level of expertise to take good photographs, but much more is needed to produce high-quality documentary photographs.

Photographers must understand the subject and have a clear concept of what they are trying to accomplish. They must know why a certain residence, for example, or a blast furnace is worth documenting. They must understand the historical context and key elements of the particular building or structure being photographed (see fig. 4.10). They then distill that knowledge to decide what to photograph, and from what vantage point, so that the resulting images convey the importance of the structure. If the photographer lacks such understanding, a historian or other person knowledgeable about the subject can assist.

To appreciate the importance of understanding the subject matter, look at the photographs in the HABS collection. Many of the photographs from the 1930s and 1940s are still

Figure 4.10

This photograph illustrates the simple detailing of a bungalow. Good coverage would require having a close-up of the timber roof showing how it is finished and how it is joined to the other structural elements.

***Figure* 4.11**

Simple photographic documentation of an architectural detail resulting in a crisp, pleasing, and informative image.

***Figure* 4.12**

Notice the absence of harsh, distracting shadows common to many contemporary photographs. Instead, the photographer created an image in which the details are not obscured by shadows cast by lighting, and there is a natural look to the photograph.

striking images because the photographer understood the building, understood composition, and understood the effective use of natural lighting to create a dramatic evocation of the building. Remember that all of these early images were shot with lenses, films, and cameras that can only be considered primitive in comparison with present-day equipment (see figs. 4.11 and 4.12).

Assuming the photographer has the prerequisite knowledge of architecture, engineering, or industrial history, and has the necessary photographic equipment, as well as the skill to use it, what are the specific components of a high-quality documentary photograph? Put simply, a good documentary photograph is an accurate, informative record of the building, structure, or site. The photograph should not have a distortion of straight lines caused by tilting the camera (see fig. 4.13). To ensure that the images are sharp and suitable for enlarging, tripods are used, and the camera is carefully leveled (using one or more spirit levels) and focused on the image. The lens is then stopped down to ensure a sharp focus.

Whenever possible, the angle of the sun and camera position are chosen to avoid casting details into deep shadows, thus obscuring them. Artificial lighting can be used to lighten shadows cast on the exterior of a building. Another means is to lower the contrast of the image when processing or printing the negative, although this

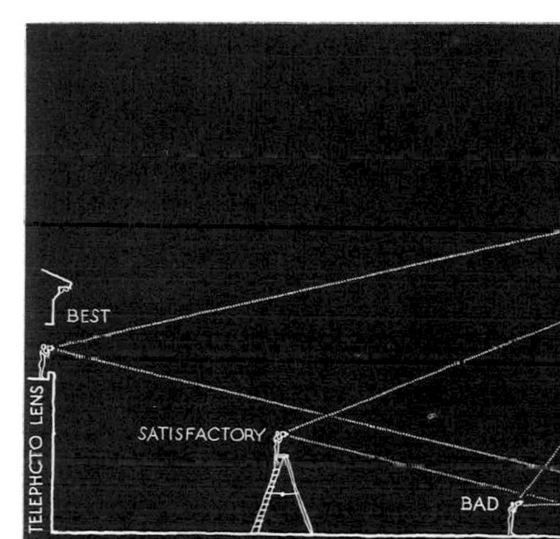

Figure 4.13

Diagram showing how to minimize distortion in photographs.

Figure 4.14

A demonstration of the effective use of artificial lighting to simulate natural lighting.

Figure 4.15

Notice how the scale stick gives a sense of scale, enabling the viewer to gauge the approximate size of the vessel's features.

Figure 4.16

Photograph of an incline skip, which carries raw materials to the top of the blast furnace and then unloads them so that steel can be produced. This photograph is an excellent example of a technically perfect illustration. The most important element, the incline skip, occupies a prominent location, yet it is clear how it relates to the surrounding machinery. The exposure of the negative and its printing are proper, so that no detail is too dark.

may be more difficult to control. Building interiors are illuminated so as to avoid creating harsh shadows and to simulate natural lighting (see fig. 4.14). An additional benefit of using artificial lighting to open up shadows is that the negative will yield a higher quality enlargement. There are a few excellent architectural photographers working in black-and-white who do not use artificial lighting because they do not like the look of artificially lit photographs or do not want to carry the additional equipment. Professional architectural photographers shooting in color almost always use artificial lighting because color film is more sensitive to changes in light levels. If color film is being used, then the natural lighting coming in through the windows or open doors, the ambient lighting from lamps and light fixtures, and the artificial lighting are color balanced to match the film for accurate color reproduction.

To get accurate exposures, a light meter is essential. Large-format cameras do not have built-in light meters, so a photographer must use a hand-held light meter. Some professional photographers use a separate light meter even when using 35mm or medium-format cameras with meters. HABS and HAER photographers use one high-quality light meter, which can be used to measure either reflected or incident light and has an accessory spot metering attachment. Some photographers carry as many as three meters: one for reading incident light (the light striking the subject), a spot meter (which reads a small angle of light reflected off the subject), and an electronic flash meter (for measuring the light produced by the flash).

To enable the viewer to sense the scale and size of the subject being photographed, scale sticks can be placed in the field of view. As these sticks are painted in alternating blocks of black-and-white, each one foot in height, they are easy to read and give a quick approximation of the size of the

Figure 4.17

Notice how the elevated camera position gives an unobstructed overall view of the building. The cropping of the top of the building actually occurred in the printing of the negative, rather than in the taking of the photograph, but is illustrative of what can happen when equipment will not cover the entire building. The spandrel detail is a strongly composed and dramatically lit photograph. It would have been better from a documentary viewpoint if it had been taken straight on from an elevated position with fill flash to provide greater shadow detail.

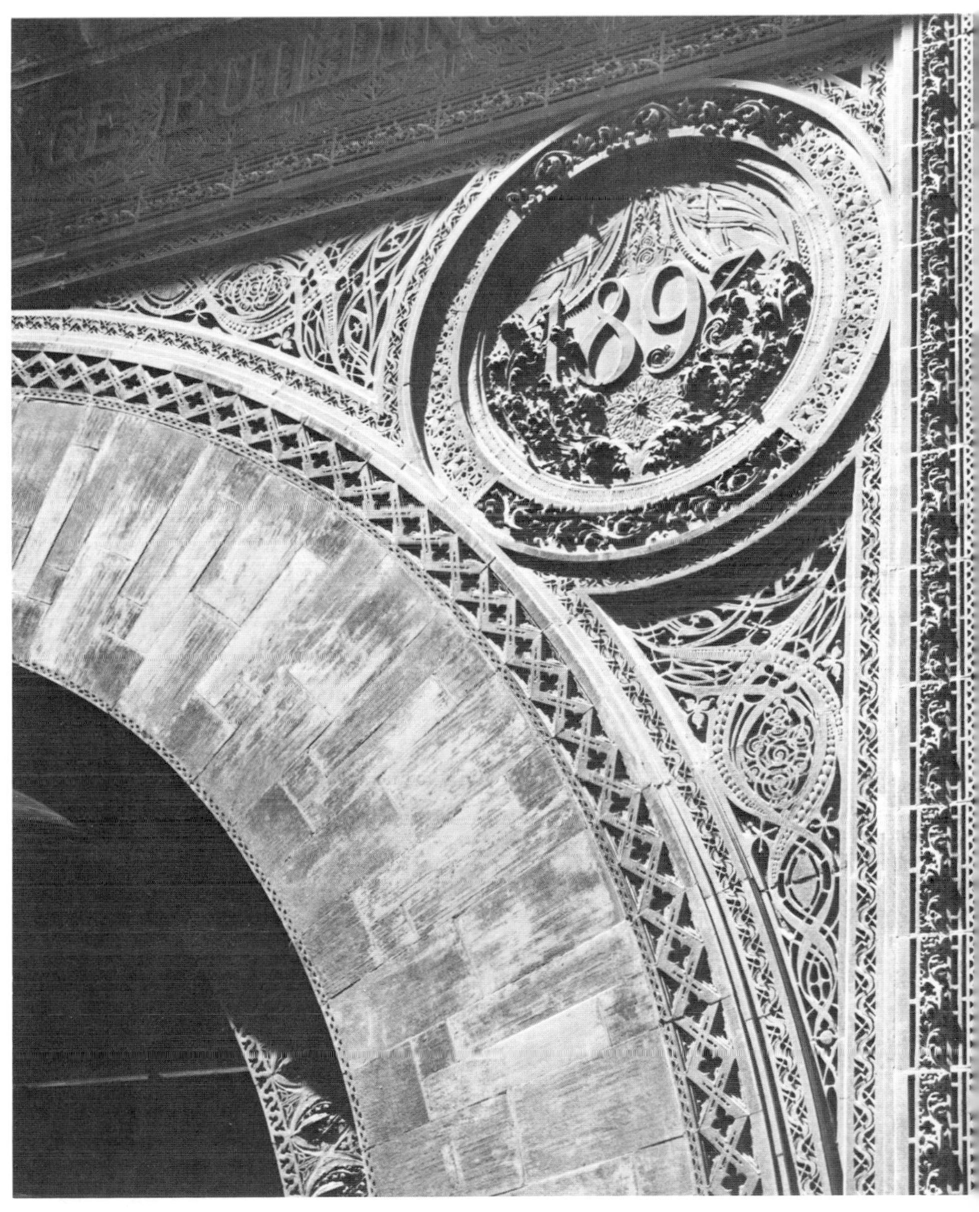

object they are placed against (see fig. 4.15). The HABS/HAER standards require that when photographing a Level I structure (the most important resources), the photographer take two shots of each view, with one of them displaying the scale stick. For photography of Levels II and III structures, at least one photograph showing the scale stick, usually of the principal facade, should be made. Field photographs often have a scale stick in every view.

If the photograph is of high technical quality, the viewer will concentrate on the subject matter, not on the photographic medium (see fig. 4.16). The photographer can enhance the potential impact of the image by paying attention to technical considerations such as leveling the camera, using the proper exposure, lighting, and film; and filtering properly. A checklist can help eliminate technical mistakes.

As mentioned above, in addition to technical skills, a photographer must have an understanding of the structure being photographed and the purpose of the photography. Misunderstanding the subject can lead to glaring errors in a photograph, such as cutting off part of

FIGURE 4.18

South elevation of conservatory of Borough House in Stateburg, South Carolina, taken with a wide-angle lens (121mm lens on 5" x 7" camera).

Figure 4.19

Subject in Figure 4.18 shot from twice as far away with normal lens (210mm lens on 5" x 7" camera). Not only do more details of the walls flanking the conservatory become apparent, but, most important, the roof and upper section of the main house are visible. This photograph suggests a reality very different from that which Figure 4.18 projects.

Figure 4.20

Shot from same camera station as Figure 4.19, but using the wide-angle lens used in Figure 4.18. No other details about the house are visible and the relationship/ perspective between the conservatory and the main house is unchanged. The wider lens at this camera station provides a better sense of the environment of the Borough House.

the structure. This is not restricted to cutting off the tops of skyscrapers (see fig. 4.17). In some photographs of bridges, for example, the abutments and approaches, elements that are integral to understanding the bridge and its design, are cut off. Only slightly less embarrassing are the numerous instances when the photographer has not gone to the trouble of finding a camera position that will provide an unobstructed view of the facade, interior space, or detail being photographed. Not only have some photographers failed to change the camera position or shift the lens (or front standard) to

FIGURE 4.21

Roughing stands for the eighty-four-inch strip mill of the Corrigan, McKinney Steel Company in Cleveland. This machinery is used to remove extraneous materials from steel slabs processed in the bar mill. Photographer used flash to supplement existing light.

avoid cars and trees, but many interior or detail shots have columns, pipes, or shadows obstructing important elements of the subject. Nothing is more distracting than a column in the center foreground of a photograph of an interior, a flaw that can usually be avoided.

A more subtle problem occurs when the photographer uses an extremely wide-angle lens and then moves in too close to the subject. The result is either distortion of the edges or obstruction of parts of the building. If a house is photographed from too close, for example, the eave blocks any view of the roof. When photographers do not have an adequate understanding of the resource, it is unlikely that they will photograph all of the important aspects of the building or take photographs from positions that emphasize these aspects (see figs. 4.18, 4.19, and 4.20).

Someone who is not familiar with steel production would not recognize the key machines, operations, and buildings in a large plant or which position would best show the way the machines work (see fig. 4.21). Likewise someone unfamiliar with architectural history would not know the importance of photographing the simple but important rustic detailing of a bungalow-style house.

In addition to technical knowledge of photography and scholarly knowledge of the subject, high-quality documentary photography requires an eye for

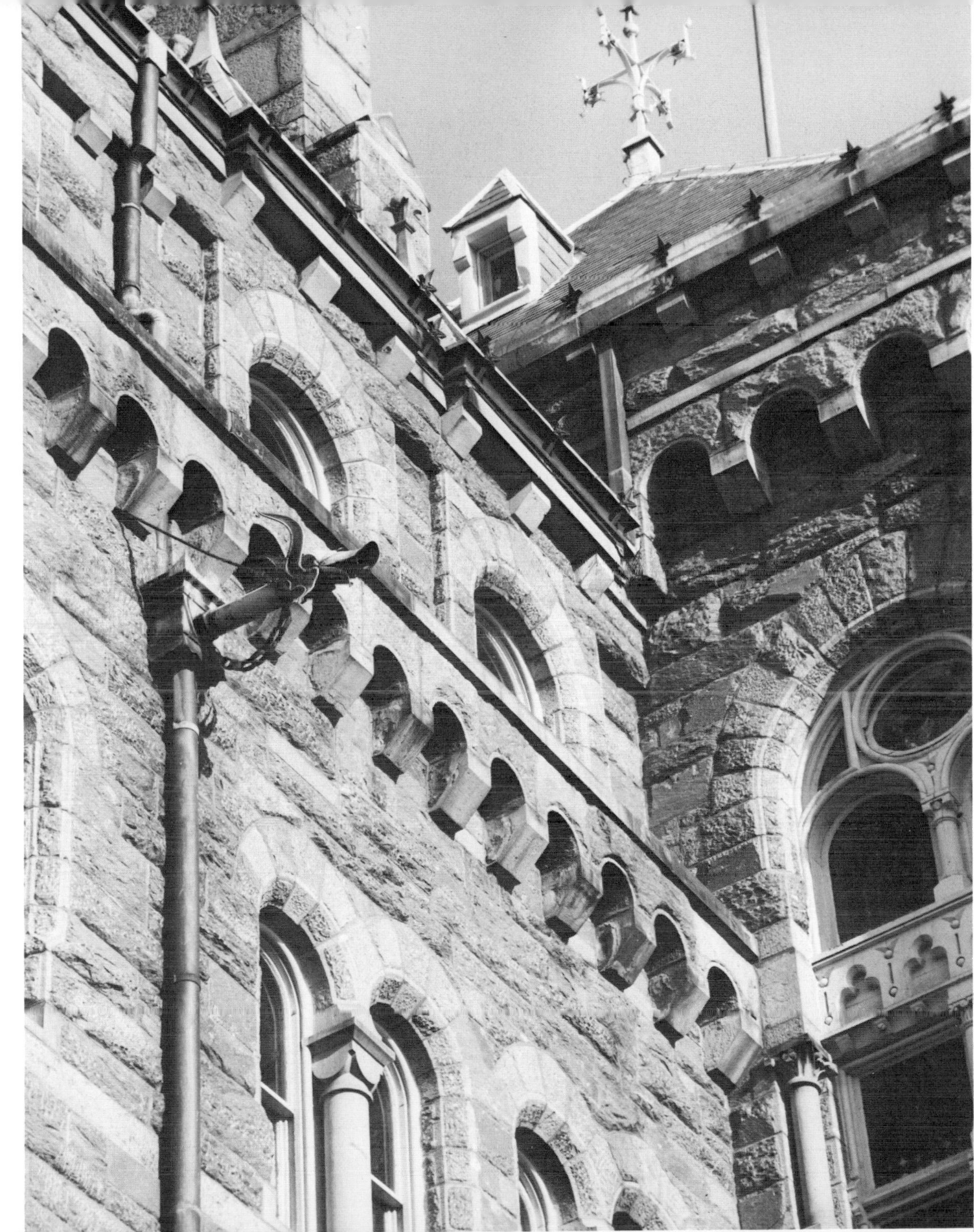

Figure 4.22

The photographer selected a camera station, lens length, and angle to tilt the camera that assured that the viewer would be drawn in. This strong composition is not at the expense of the subject; a great deal of information about the building is conveyed by the photograph.

aesthetics. As HABS photographer Jack E. Boucher has written, "Follow standard elements of composition—for example, have structures photographed from a perspective positioned off center, so they (the viewers of the photograph) 'look in' to the photograph, not out! Eliminate or minimize distracting foreground, such as pavement in favor of sky" (see fig. 4.22).

Aesthetic considerations, meaning strong composition, are important because they make the photograph more compelling and, therefore, more likely to hold the viewer's attention. When looking at a weak photograph, a viewer unconsciously assumes that it is uninteresting because the subject is uninteresting, not that it is weak because it is technically or aesthetically inept. No matter how important a bridge or house is, those qualities that make the structure significant will not be apparent unless the photograph is compelling enough to hold the viewer's attention long enough to study the photograph (see fig. 4.23).

Figure 4.23

An aesthetically pleasing photograph which also captures the structural system of the windmill. The worn stairs suggest the great age of the structure.

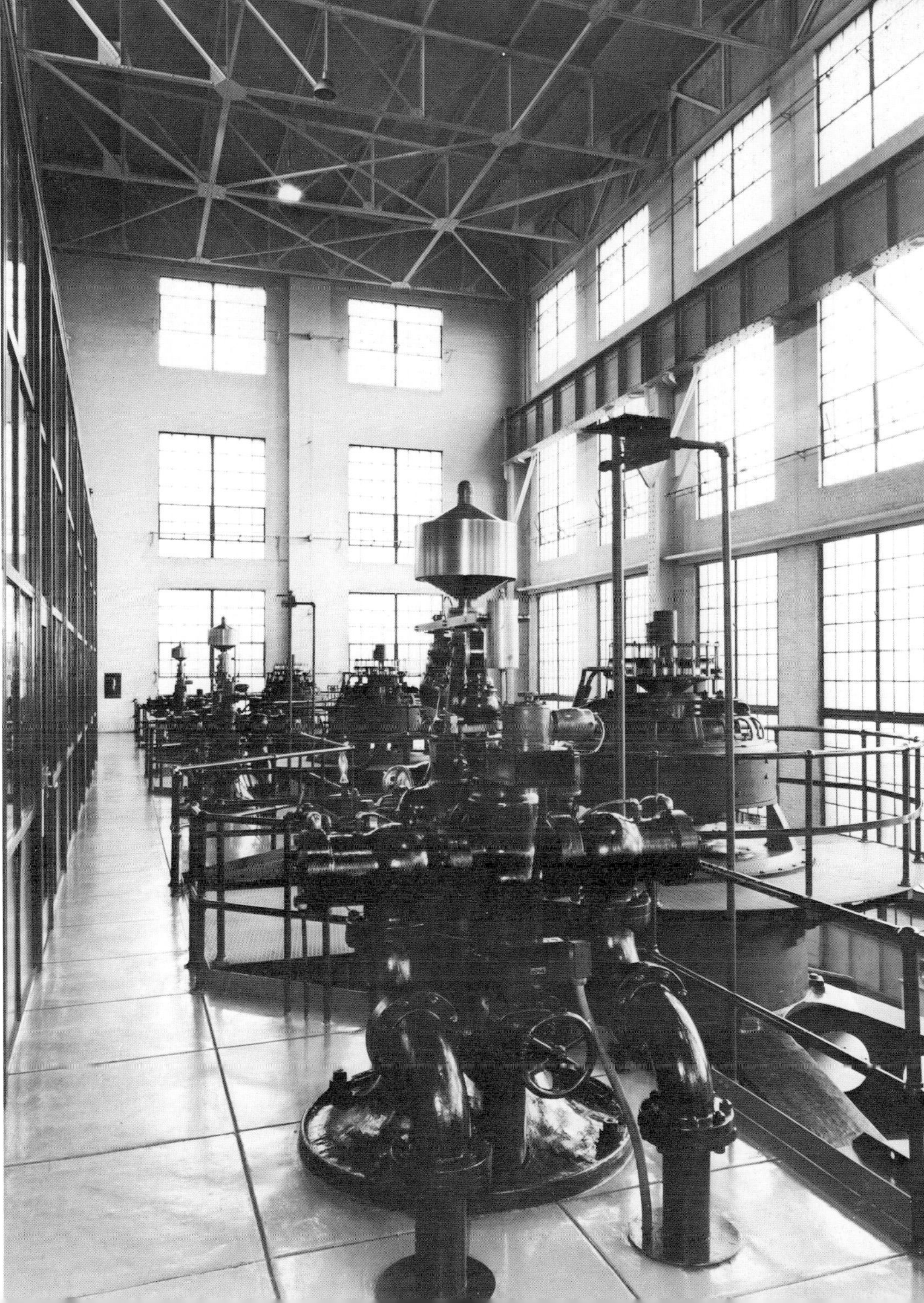

Historians and architects know that their depiction of a building or structure is an interpretation, but they assume that the photographer's illustration is impartial. Yet, a photographer can exaggerate, distort, or conceal spatial relationships and prominence of features, thereby influencing whether a viewer even finds the subject attractive or worthy of documentation.

A photographer, therefore, has a two-part obligation: first, to provide technically good and aesthetically pleasing photographs—properly exposed, properly focused, well lit, effectively composed, undistorted, and rich in detail (see fig. 4.24)—and second, to provide photographs that convey the importance of the structure and give enough information for viewers to make their own analysis of the resource (see figs. 4.17 and 4.25).

Figure 4.24

Built into the Lake Lynn Dam near Morgantown, West Virginia, in two stages, 1913–1914 and 1925–1926, the power plant's generators provide electricity for a number of towns in the region.

Figure 4.25

Photographer Jack Boucher's camera equipment and the van he uses to haul it. This photographer prefers to drive rather than fly because of the amount of equipment he requires.

Planning and Producing Photographic Documentation

How much equipment?

Some HABS photographers feel strongly about not wanting to miss a shot because they are not carrying the necessary equipment. The difficulty with this approach is that it can be physically demanding and time-consuming for photographers who work alone to get all of their equipment to the site (see fig. 4.25). When documenting Buffalo Bill Dam in Cody, Wyoming, the HABS photographer had to lower his equipment by rope and then climb down to get a certain vantage point.

In general, the amount of equipment to be carried should be based on how important the resource is, how comprehensive the documentation will be, and how the photography will be used. One slide of a relatively insignificant structure, to be used for a lecture, should require much less equipment than images of a National Historic Landmark structure intended for publication.

Which format?

As discussed above, HABS/HAER standards require large-format (4" x 5", 5" x 7", or 8" x 10") negatives for formal HABS/HAER documentation.

If the intended use of the photography is not HABS/HAER documentation, but lecturing, then 35mm would be the obvious choice because 35mm slide projectors are widely available and 35mm cameras and lenses are less cumbersome in the field. If the documentation is to be used in a publication, then the medium-format (120/220mm) negative is preferable.

Often photographers will shift to smaller formats if their subject is extremely isolated and inaccessible. In Alaska, the HAER photographer used a 4" x 5" camera rather than the bulkier 5" x 7" equipment he usually uses (see fig. 4.26).

Which film?

The only suitable film for permanent documentation purposes is black-and-white, which is archivally stable. Of the panchromatic, continuous-tone black-and-white films available, the slower the film (lower ASA/ISO designation), the less grainy it is; and the less grain,

Figure 4.26

This Pennsylvania through-truss bridge carried the Copper River and Northwestern Railroad between two glaciers; one span collapsed during the Alaska earthquake of 1964. Shot with a 4" x 5" camera and 300mm lens.

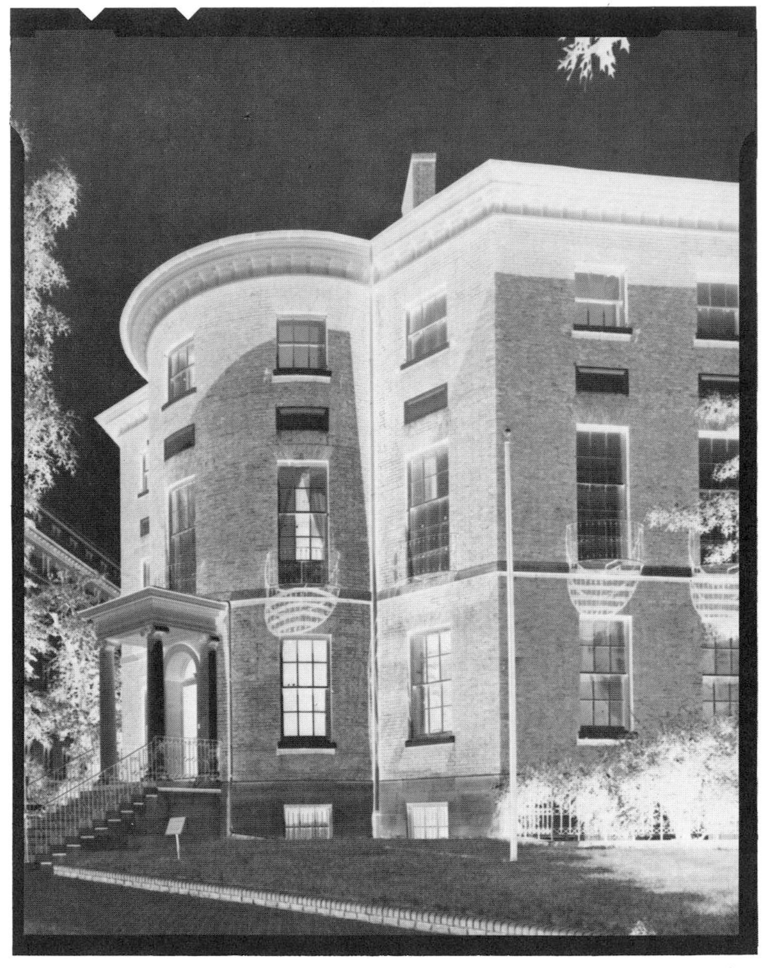

Figure 4.27

Diagram comparing sizes of negatives.

the more the negative can be satisfactorily enlarged. Grain in a negative consists of clumps of silver particles that make up the image. Faster films have bigger clumps, and when the negative is enlarged the grain becomes visible. This is especially distracting in continuous-tone areas such as the sky or blank walls, where the grain is clearly visible as a salt-and-pepper pattern. Grain is not a serious consideration with large-format equipment, as the negative is already so much larger, and the grain, therefore, finer. HABS and HAER photographers have favored 5″ x 7″, 400 ASA black-and-white film, which makes tremendous enlargements possible. The same speed film in 35mm cannot be enlarged much beyond 8″ x 10″ before the image becomes unacceptably grainy. To appreciate this, consider that enlarging a 4″ x 5″ image to an 8″ x 10″ print requires projection at a scale of slightly more than 2 to 1 linearly (4 to 1 by area), while enlarging a 35mm image to an 8″ x 10″ print requires projection at a scale of 8.5 to 1 linearly (60 to 1 by area) (see figs. 4.27 and 4.28).

What about lighting equipment?

If interiors are to be photographed, substantial lighting equipment will be necessary. Continuous lighting and the larger electronic strobes provide a great deal of light but require electricity, and many historic properties—especially those that are unoccupied—will not have enough, if any, electricity. It is possible to generate the needed electricity by using portable gas-powered generators, which are heavy. Truly portable, but less powerful, battery-powered electronic strobes are available and, along with continuous lighting and photoflash bulbs, are used by HABS

Figure 4.28

Two photographs of a building detail—one made with a 35mm camera and the other with a 4″ x 5″.

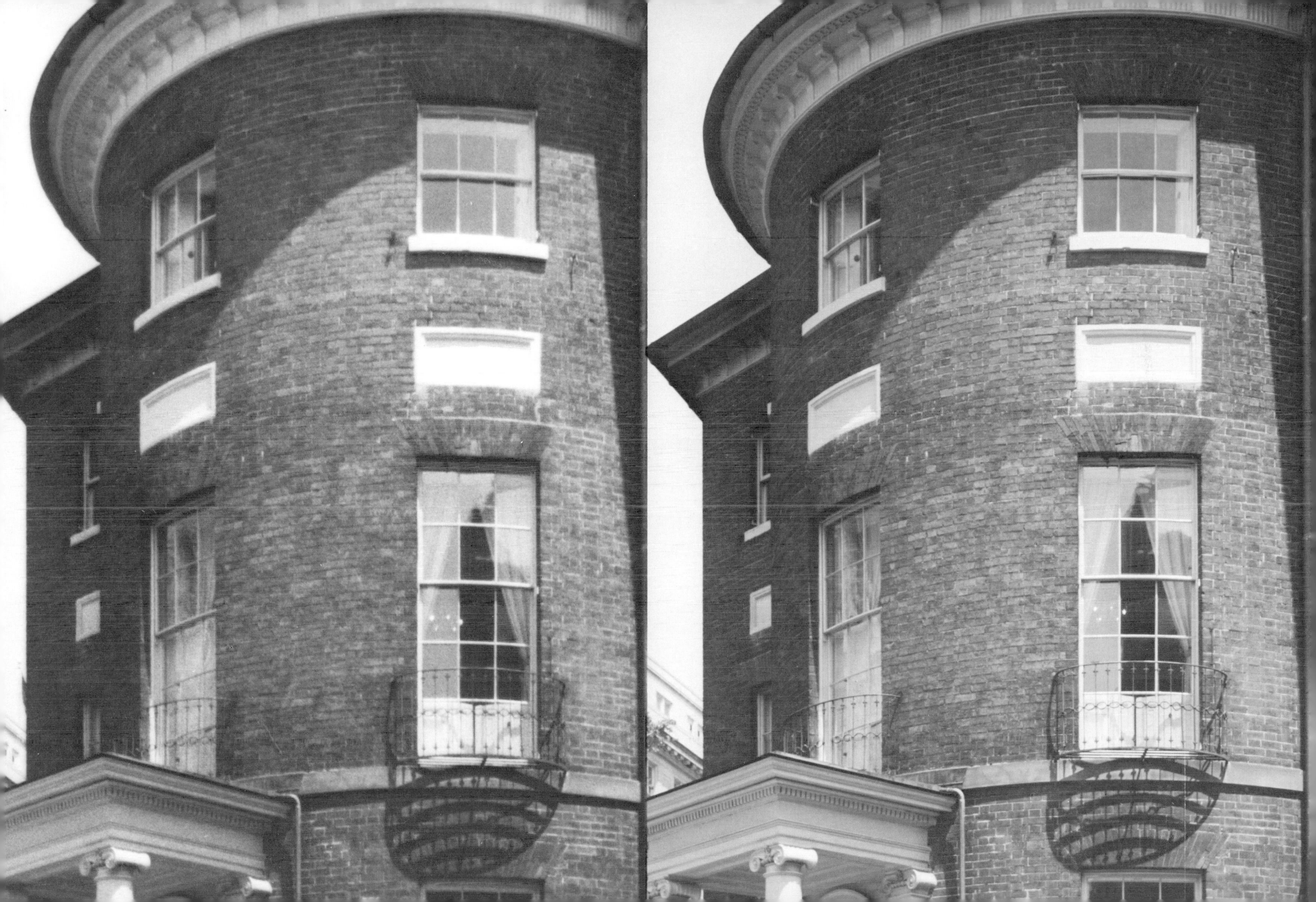

FIGURE 4.29

Inkskip powerhouse generator built in 1910 as part of the Battle Creek hydroelectric project, Tehana County, California. The photographer used strobe to ensure even lighting.

FIGURE 4.30

To light this tunnel, the photographer used a technique called painting with light. He walked down the tunnel firing a total of eight flashbulbs, one at a time, with the lens shutter left open. If the tunnel had not been so dark, he would have had someone cover the lens between firings of the flashbulbs; otherwise the lightest areas of the image would have been overexposed.

and HAER photographers. HABS photographers carry strobe, continuous lighting, and photoflash bulbs. Photoflash bulbs are fragile and do not always fire, but they do produce tremendous illumination and do not require electricity (see figs. 4.29, 4.30, and 4.31). Even when interiors are not to be shot, it is advisable to carry a portable flash to provide "fill" lighting in exterior areas (such as porches, doorways, under eaves), which might otherwise be cast in shadows that would obliterate details. Where there is a risk of explosion, such as in grain elevators and ammunition or chemical plants, any flash might be too dangerous.

What about other equipment?

It is probably impossible to come up with an all-inclusive list, but a fairly complete one would include tripod, light meter, filters (especially a yellow filter for black-and-white photography), extra batteries, powerful flashlight, knife, repair tools, gaffer tape for holding small objects in place, scale stick, compass (essential for captioning photographs), name and telephone numbers of property owners, log for recording information on shots, plenty of film, film holders for large format or extra film backs for medium format, Polaroid back for making test exposures, and changing bag/portable darkroom for loading and unloading film holders (see fig. 4.25).

Figure 4.31

The photographer placed his lighting to accentuate floor wear from the workers' repetitive routine.

STATE | COUNTY | MUNICIPALITY | STRUCTURE | NUMBER

COMP.

☐ HABS
☐ HAER
☐ ________

DEPARTMENT OF THE INTERIOR
NATIONAL PARK SERVICE
HISTORIC AMERICAN BUILDINGS SURVEY/HISTORIC AMERICAN ENGINEERING RECORD
PHOTOGRAPHIC SERVICES REQUEST
(INSTRUCTIONS–PLEASE TYPE. Use a separate sheet for each structure except dependencies.)

STRUCTURE AND EXACT LOCATION:

HABS/HAER Number

DEADLINE

USGS or City Map attached.
____

PRIORITY: ☐ High ☐ Medium ☐ Low

DATE OF REQUEST:

DIRECTION PRINCIPAL ELEVATION FACES:

Number on location map

PHONE NO.: *(Include Area Code)*

FOR ENTRY CONTACT:

Is this structure being measured? ☐ YES ☐ NO

ADDRESS:

EXTERIOR VIEWS REQUESTED: *(Be specific, see instructions, reverse side)*

TOTAL:

USE EXTRA SHEETS, IF NECESSARY

INTERIOR VIEWS REQUESTED: *(Be specific)*

TOTAL:

(phone)

USE EXTRA SHEETS, IF NECESSARY

ORDERED BY:

PROJECT

TITLE:

OFFICE and/or FIELD PROJECT TITLE

ACCOUNT NUMBER

DIVISION APPROVAL:

DATE:

SPECIAL INSTRUCTIONS: (If any)

(date)

SCHEDULE AND DISPOSITION:

(initials) *(date)* *(code)*

PHOTOGRAPHER'S REMARKS:

· · · COMPLETE THIS INFORMATION AREA ONLY · · ·

· · · COMPLETE THIS INFORMATION AREA ONLY++DO NOT WRITE ABOVE OR BELOW HEAVY LINES · · ·

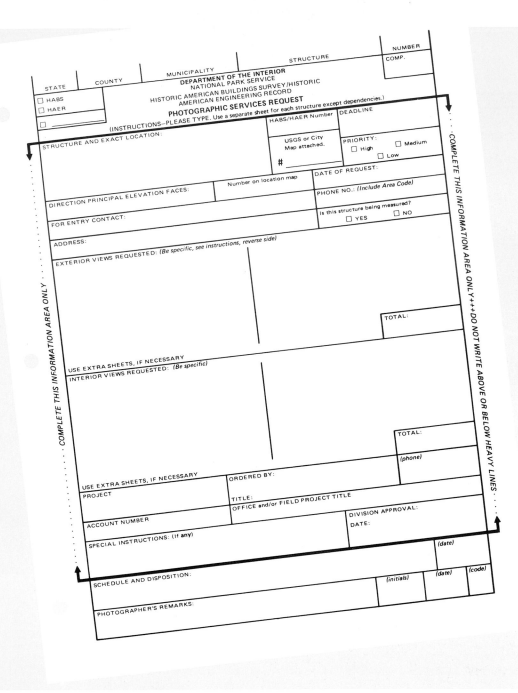

Figure 4.32

This specialized form serves the needs of HABS/HAER photographers. Others might need only a simplified version of this document.

What about background research?

HAER photographer Jet Lowe says he tries to learn everything he can about a project before he goes out to photograph it. He sees this preparation as a way of "narrowing" the assumptions he is going to be making. In addition to the photographic request form filled out by the project historian or leader and discussions with the project historian, the HAER photographer also reads general texts on the subject (see fig. 4.32). For example, Jet Lowe has tried to become knowledgeable in the fields of bridge construction and steel fabrication to aid in his photographing of bridges and steel plants (see fig. 4.33). HABS photographer Jack E. Boucher has over the last thirty years read extensively in and acquired an extensive personal library on local and architectural history (see fig. 4.34).

Most photographers do not prepare to the degree that HABS/HAER photographers do for an assignment, but all photographers do make assumptions about the subject they are about to photograph. These assumptions concern how important the subject is and what condition it is in. Based on these assumptions, the photographers make "working" estimates as to approximately how many shots will be made and approximately how long it will take. This process all takes place before the photographers see the property being photographed.

Once on site, photographers need to make a visual reconnaissance—to walk around and through the site. This inspection can correct erroneous assumptions about the significance and

FIGURE 4.33

Close-up of Egyptian revival detailing on diagonals of the Reading-Halls Station Bridge in Lycoming County, Pennsylvania.

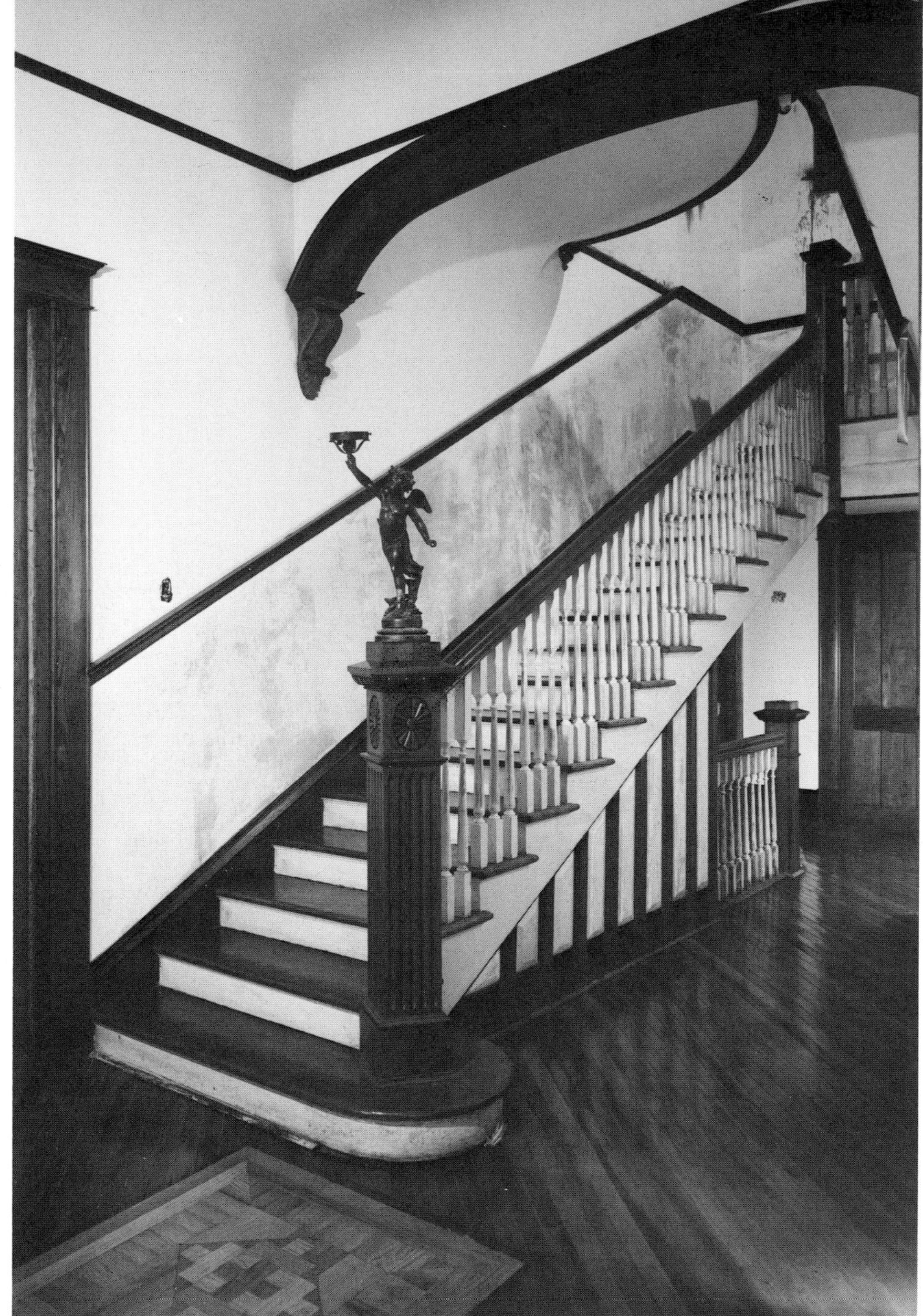

***Figure* 4.34**

Well-composed image of a stairwell, properly lit to suggest even, natural lighting and to highlight the grain in the wood.

PHOTOGRAPHIC STABILITY

The issue of archival stability is not a simple one. There are too many variables affecting negatives and prints for experts to do more than speak about general time periods. Knowledgeable people talk about stability in terms of short lifetime (ten years), medium lifetime (between ten and a hundred years), and long lifetime (more than a hundred years). Ilford, Eastman Kodak, Fuji, and Polaroid, as manufacturers of color negative materials or color prints, provide information on the stability of their products. In general, each manufacturer believes its products are becoming more stable and that the major causes of fading or color changes are high temperature, high humidity, strong lighting, atmospheric pollution, and careless handling. For specific information, it is recommended that one consult the publications of the American National Standards Institute (New York City) and the Society of American Archivists (Chicago). Professional users extend the life of color negatives, transparencies, and prints by using cold storage (with low humidity) or by making three black-and-white separations (negatives) from color images. The process of making three separations, which can be recombined at any point to produce a color image, is expensive, as is having special cold storage facilities.

condition of the subject, and about the number of shots and amount of time required.

Some architectural photographers always take certain shots of a building. Such standard shots are not always worth taking, especially when they are taken in lieu of shots that would convey more information about the particular property being photographed. The visual inspection often reveals uncommon, unanticipated "targets of opportunity" such as exposed structural systems. If a photographer does not expect to see such features and does not search them out, they will not be photographed. In summary, whether photographers are shooting their hundredth bridge or hundredth house, each bridge and each house needs to be approached afresh; otherwise the photographer unconsciously starts shooting by rote, photographing each bridge and each house

Figure 4.35

The photographer could take this photograph only on one of the few days of the year when sunlight illuminates the north side of the White House. He photographed the White House again in 1987 and 1988, when the paint had been removed, revealing the original stone surfaces.

7

MASSACHUSETT NO.

HABS / HAER / NR / OT — 88 YEAR — MA STATE — E/NE ORIENT.

DEADLINE — PRIORITY: HIGH / LOW / MEDIUM

PROJECT:

STRUCTURE: Higgins Armory — CITY: WORCESTER

ADDRESS: 100 BARBER AVE — PHONE 617 / 853-6015

ENTRY CONTACT: PHYLLIS STODDARD — DESCRIPTION 1930's — MEASURED? NO

APPOINTMENT: Kathy LEBOEUF

REMARKS — DISPOSITION — PS: # — DATE: — PHOTOGRAPHER Jack E. Boucher — DATE: 4 VISITS, LAST ON 30 APR 88 — EXT. 9 — INT. 5 — C — S — COMP.

HISTORIC STRUCTURE FIELD PHOTO RECORD

USDI—HERITAGE CONSERVATION AND RECREATION SERVICE

GPO 933 593

FHR-8-245 (August 1978)

Figure 4.36

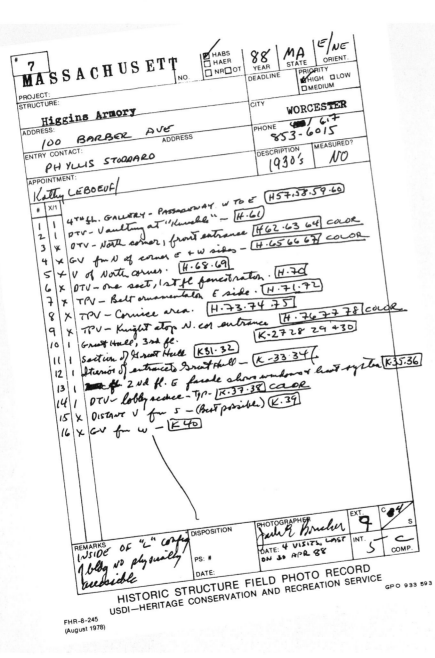

Jack Boucher's shooting log for the Higgins Armory, stating address, compass orientation, number and description of shots, whether a filter was used, and date of photographs. Notice that each image has a letter and number in a box. This code corresponds to a number he exposes on the film before going into the field. The same number is written on the film holder. This numbering procedure is necessary because sheet film (for large format) unlike roll film (for 35mm and medium format) does not come from the factory with sequential numbering in the margin.

from the same angles, with the same views.

The high cost of producing large-format photographs forces photographers to plan shots carefully, avoiding those that are redundant or insignificant. With 35mm photography, which allows much more mobility at a much lower cost, photographers are much freer to experiment and shoot lots of film, but they still need to know what the key or essential shots are.

The visual reconnaissance serves another purpose beyond assuring that a photographer will not miss an important shot. A walk around and through the site reveals environmental limitations imposed on the photographer.

COLOR PHOTOGRAPHY

HABS and HAER have been increasingly shooting large-format color transparencies, in addition to the usual black-and-white photography, even though color photography does not meet the HABS/HAER standards for formal documentation because it is not considered archivally stable. There has been increased demand for color images for publications and the reproduction of the colors is becoming more accurate. Once color photography is considered archivally stable, it will be included as part of the formal HABS/HAER photographic documentation.

The two most common are foliage and the compass orientation of the structure. In the summer it is virtually impossible to get unobstructed photographs of residences, whether rural or urban, because of foliage. This is not a problem with industrial structures, such as steel mills, but can be a problem with other engineering structures, such as bridges whose abutments are concealed by vegetation. The northern facade of any structure is almost always in shadow, making it difficult to get a photograph with sufficient contrast. It is, therefore, often necessary to shoot in the early morning or late afternoon light, when a northern facade is illuminated (see fig. 4.35). Commercial architectural photographers sometimes shoot the north fronts of buildings at night, using street lights and the building's lights to illuminate and add interest to the photograph. This approach is most effective in photographing storefronts and small office buildings.

Other constraints on the photographer are (1) adjacent buildings that block unobstructed shots of the elevations; (2) operating machinery; or (3) abandoned, decayed buildings, which can pose safety hazards. In shooting bridges or other potentially hazardous structures, the photographer should use safety devices such as a hard hat and a harness to minimize risks (see fig. 4.5).

The most common and probably most cumbersome constraint is that of time—very rarely do photographers get to spend as much time at a site as they would like.

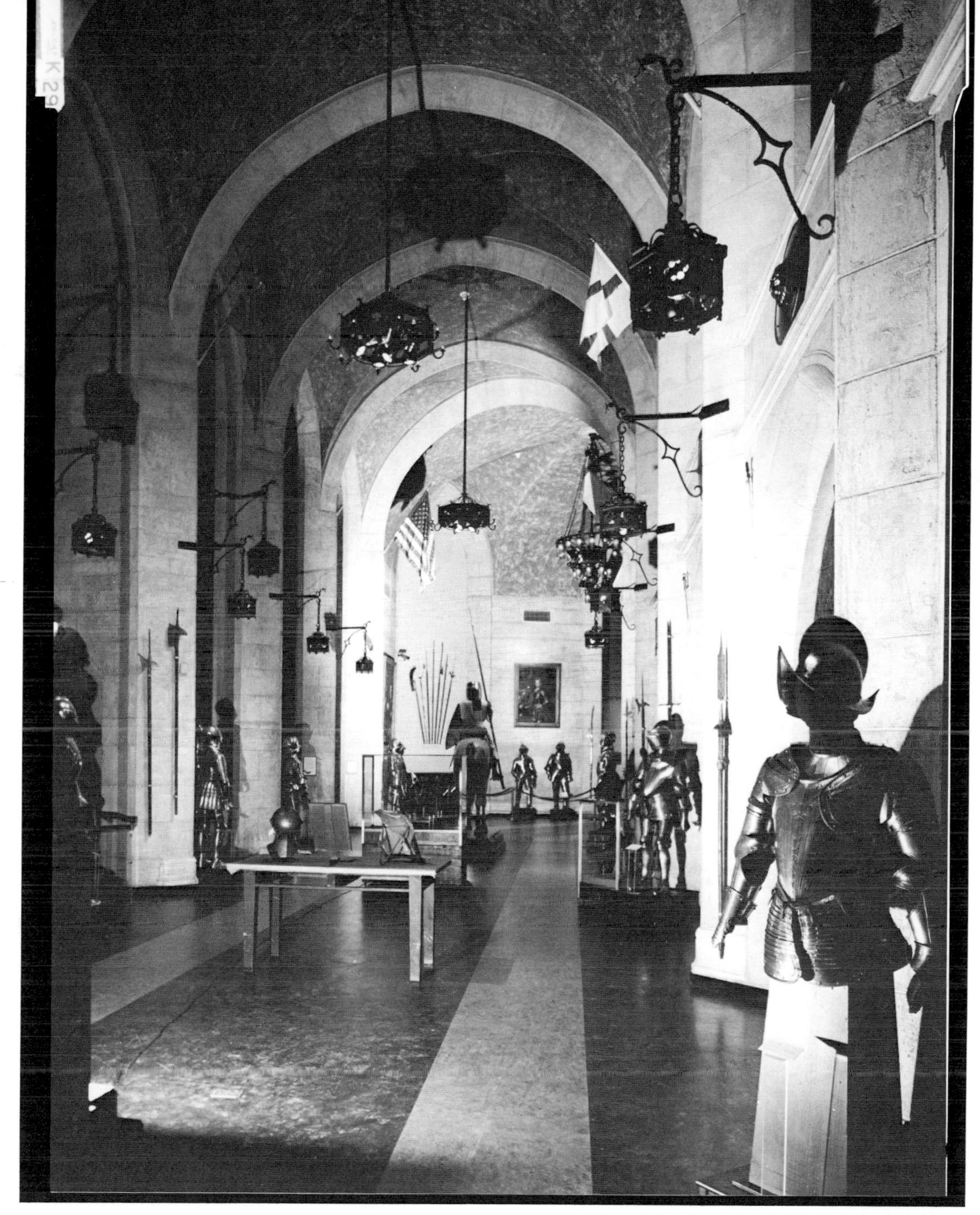

FIGURE 4.37

Notice number K 29 in the upper left corner, identifying this image as "Great Hall, 3rd fl." on photo log (figure 4.36).

Figure 4.38

Sample HABS photograph showing large-format negative, archival negative sleeve, and photograph in archival mount card.

Processing the Film

There are two key aspects to the processing phase: proper darkroom procedures and systematic and complete labeling.

The processing of exposed film into a negative and the subsequent making of a print from that negative are two distinct darkroom procedures, but the same standards must be applied to both. A conscientious darkroom worker always uses clean containers and trays to avoid chemical contamination. All chemicals must be fresh and kept at the proper temperature, and the manufacturer's recommendations for processing must be followed. It cannot be overemphasized that negatives must be handled properly. Any other part of processing—contact prints or enlargements—can be redone in the darkroom, but damage to the negative, ranging from scratching to dried dust to chemical stains, is permanent and can rarely be concealed.

HABS/HAER standards for archival processing of prints and negatives require that chemicals used to develop and fix the image will have been completely removed. The presence of these chemicals on the negative or print will cause discoloration and, eventually, deterioration. After they have been treated with hypo remover (a chemical that facilitates washing)—one of the last steps in darkroom processing—the negatives and prints are washed for a long period to remove any remaining traces of hypo or other chemicals. (Adding a small amount of selenium toner to the hypo remover increases archival stability.) Once processed, the negatives must be stored in archival sleeves. An archivally permanent print has all chemicals removed and is made on fiber-based rather than resin-coated paper, which is considered chemically active and is, therefore, expected to deteriorate over time.

Once processed, negatives and prints must be given accurate and adequate identification. The following information should be provided: (1) name and location of structure, (2) the elevation or detail covered in the particular photograph, (3) the name of the photographer, and (4) the time and date the photograph was taken (see figs. 4.36 and 4.37). Too often photographers rely on their memories to identify photographs taken weeks or even months earlier—a system that simply does not work. It is too hard to remember enough about the subject, to recall specific details, to identify a particular image. It cannot be stressed strongly enough how important it is to take the time in the field to keep a good photographic log.

If the photographs are to be included in the HABS or HAER collection at the Library of Congress, the following procedures are followed. The negatives, archival sleeves, archival contact prints, and archival photo mount cards are all

LENS COVERING POWER

The advantages of a large-format camera for photographing large structures are limited by two factors: (1) the characteristics of the camera and (2) the characteristics of the lens being used. A large-format field or flatbed camera is less able to cover a tall building than a large-format monorail camera. The reason is that most field cameras have no vertical fall with their rear film standards and relatively limited rise on their front lens standard. For example, the Calumet field camera permits 45mm of front rise, while the Calumet monorail camera has a total of 95mm rise (total of rising front and falling rear). Even within the monorail camera type, manufacturers vary as to the amount of total rise offered. The Toyo G permits a 115mm total rise while the Horseman permits a total rise of 60mm (rising front and falling rear).

Even more important than the amount of rise and fall built into the camera is the coverage of the lens. Lens coverage is simply how large an area of film a particular lens will cover. When a camera is raised, lowered, or shifted too much for the particular lens being used, the corners of the image are darkened, creating a less than pleasing image. Such an effect is called vignetting (see fig. 4.46). The covering power of a lens should not be confused with angle of view of a lens. The latter indicates how wide a view of the subject a particular lens projects onto the film plane.

Lens coverage is also independent of the lens's focal length (f). For example, Schneider produces two 90mm lenses, f 5.6 and f 8. The f 5.6 lens has an angle of coverage of 105 degrees and the f 8 lens has an angle of coverage of 100 degrees. Translated into practical terms, the f 8 lens will cover a 4" x 5" piece of film, the f 5.6 lens will cover a 5" x 7" piece of film. Used on a 4" x 5" camera, the f 5.6 lens, therefore, can be raised (lowered/shifted) more than the f 8 lens can before vignetting occurs. Even with the limited total rising and falling of the Horseman (in comparison with the Toyo), it is possible to get an image with vignetting when using the 90mm f 8 lens, when there would not be vignetting with the f 5.6 lens.

One advantage of most medium- and large-format cameras is that they may accept a holder for Polaroid film which enables the photographer to make an exposure on Polaroid film and, in less than a minute, see the image. The photographer uses the Polaroid to test exposure and check composition. With large-format cameras, it is very difficult to see what is happening in the four corners, which appear quite dark. The test exposure enables the photographer to spot and avoid annoying, irrelevant features such as overhead wires.

Figure 4.39

Rectified photograph of Stan Hywet Hall, Akron, Ohio. Note targets placed in field of view.

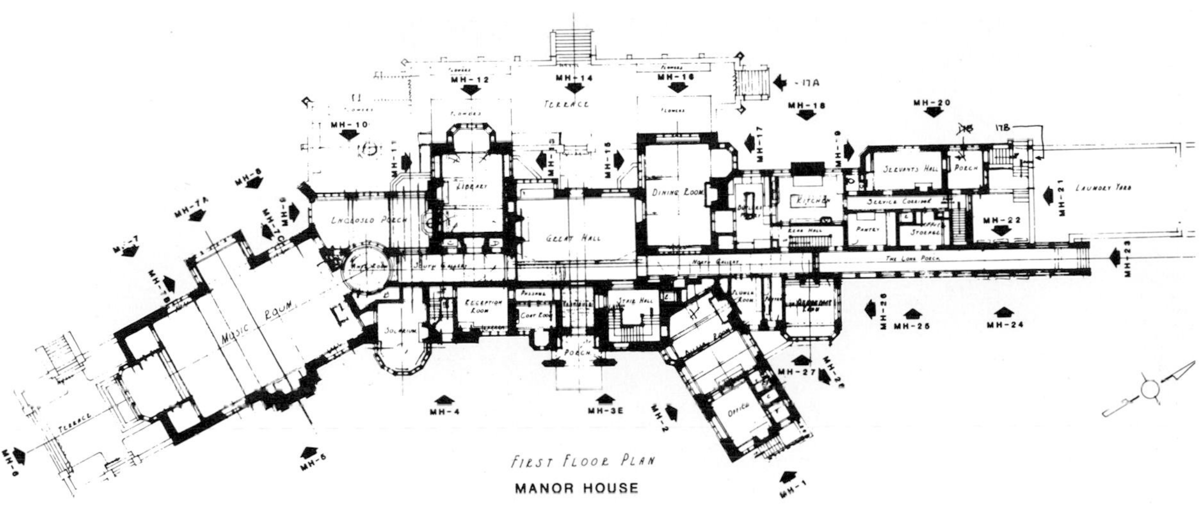

FIGURE 4.40

Partial view of floor plan of Stan Hywet Hall, annotated by Chambers & Chambers to show location of various rectified photographs.

FIGURE 4.41

An unrectified photograph of the same section of Stan Hywet Hall shown in Figure 4.39. A comparison of the rectified and unrectified photographs demonstrates that each serves a different purpose, conveying different information about the subject.

Figure 4.42

Copy photograph of photogrammetric plate of north elevation, Dorchester Heights Monument, Boston. A Wild C-120 stereometric camera was mounted in a cherry picker. It is obvious how difficult and dangerous it would have been to hand measure this 115-foot monument, so photogrammetry was the appropriate technique.

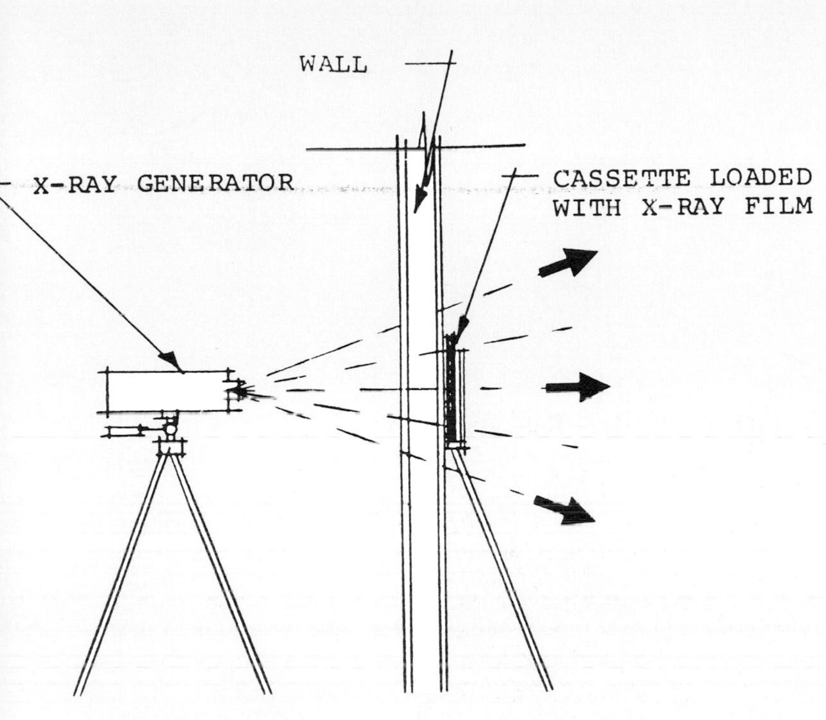

FIGURE 4.43

X-ray generator and film cassette are placed in position for exposure. Generator is activated for approximately five seconds, then the cassette is removed for development of film.

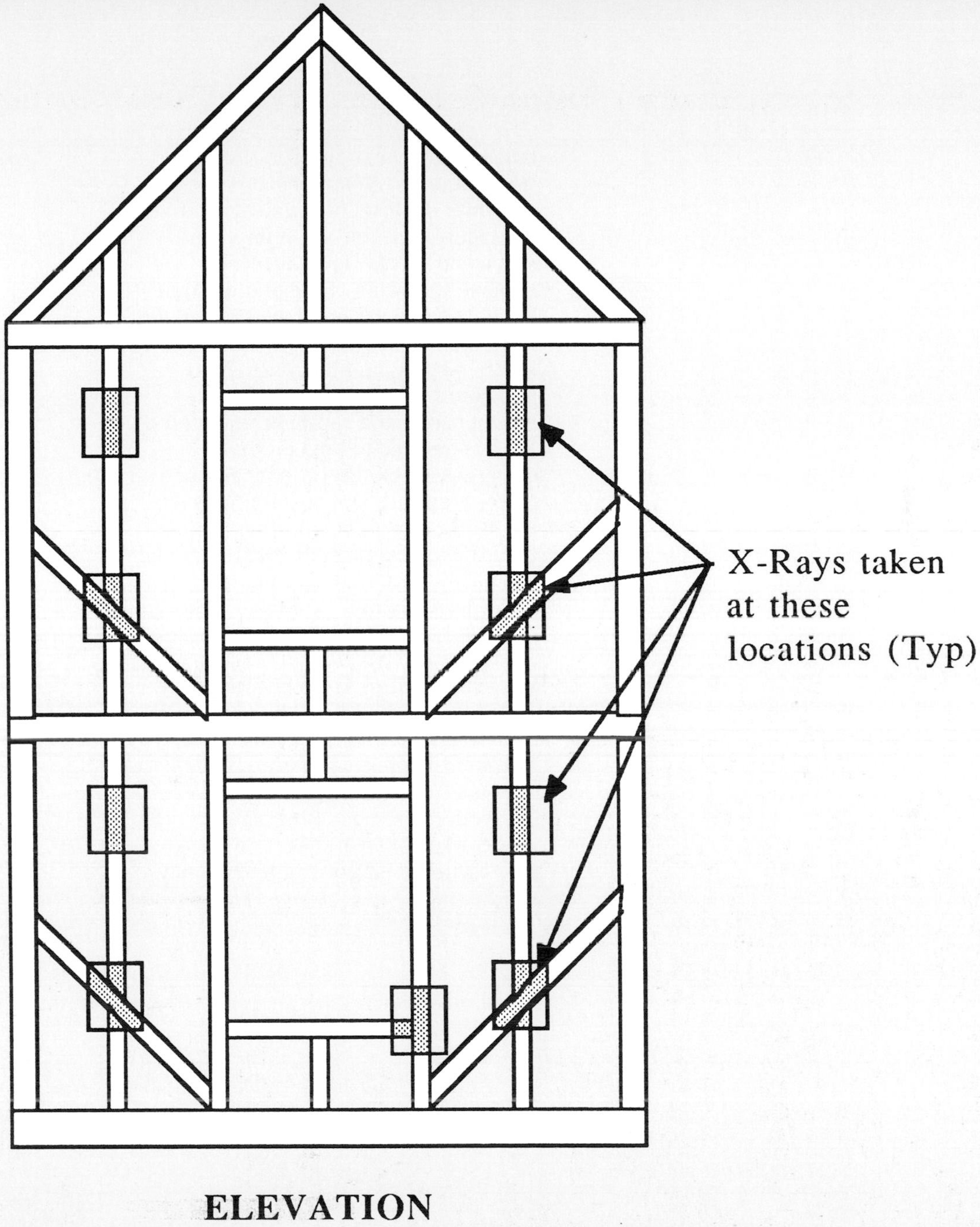

FIGURE 4.44

Radiographs of strategically located small sections of structural components can be used to determine the overall structural system of a wooden-frame building. Radiographs taken at the location of 45-degree wind-braces determined their configuration. The entire structural system was then derived from this small amount of information.

X-Rays taken
at these
locations (Typ)

ELEVATION

labeled with the property's HABS or HAER number. A caption list is prepared for each set of negatives and contact prints. This sheet lists the name and precise location of the subject, the name of the photographer, the date the photograph was taken, the description of each image, and the HABS or HAER number. The negatives in holders, contact prints on photo mount cards, and captions (all archival) are transmitted to the Library of Congress, where they are maintained under archivally stable conditions (see fig. 4.38). Any of the photographs can be retrieved by the staff, and the public can easily find out if a particular building, structure, or site has been recorded by HABS or HAER as long as the name and location are known. These two features—archival stability and easy retrievability—are standards that everyone should try to achieve, whether the photographs are to be deposited in a local library or university, or are to remain as working records in the office of an architect, historian, photographer, or government agency.

LARGE-FORMAT PHOTOGRAPHY

There are two major reasons HABS and HAER continue to use large-format photography. The large negative permits maximum enlargement without the film's grain reducing the sharpness of the image (see fig. 4.28). It is, therefore, possible to make substantial enlargements of small details to understand features that would be too difficult to describe by word or too small to understand in person or on a drawing. The large-format monorail camera allows more movements to correct for perspective than is possible with any other format or type of camera. On a 35mm camera, by comparison, with perspective control lens, it is possible to move the lens up and down and sideways (and on a few lenses it is even possible to tilt it), but the degree of movement is limited to approximately an 11mm shift. Because the large-format camera consists of a lens mounted on a front standard, connected by a flexible bellows to a rear standard which holds the film, it is possible to substantially raise or lower the front and rear standards as well as shift them horizontally and even to tilt them. In comparison with the limited rise possible on a 35mm, some large-format cameras offer the equivalent (front rise and rear drop) of nearly a 100mm rise. The range and extent of movement on a large-format camera permit the photographer to capture tall or wide structures without distortion, to increase depth of field (called the Scheimpflug effect), and to displace obstructions blocking the view of the structure being photographed.

For the photographer using large-format equipment, 4" x 5" is the most popular size, offering the most film types, lenses, and accessories. HABS and

HAER photographers, however, have traditionally used the larger 5" x 7" camera, despite its greater weight and fewer offerings in terms of lenses or films. The larger negative is nearly twice as large, offering an additional fifteen square inches of negative over the 4" x 5". It is easier to see all the details in a 5" x 7" contact print than in a 4" x 5" contact print. This point is especially important because users of the HABS/HAER collection at the Library of Congress are viewing these contact prints, rather than enlargements. Also, because a 5" x 7" negative is less square than a 4" x 5" negative, some photographers consider it a better-proportioned size for photographing architectural and engineering structures.

There are photographers who employ even larger or more specialized equipment than HABS/HAER for documenting architecture and engineering. Although 8" x 10" cameras are considered studio cameras, some photographers use them in the field. A few architectural photographers use panoramic cameras, with moving lenses or camera bodies, which are capable of capturing extremely wide expanses, such as the downtown of a city, and can produce a very distinctive image. A banquet camera was another type of wide-field camera, producing a negative over twice as wide as it is high. Its name comes from the type of photograph it was designed for: banquets and graduating class pictures.

Specialized Techniques

More information can be gleaned from photographs than HABS and HAER normally need. Two techniques that provide more precise information are rectified photography and stereophotogrammetry. Rectification attempts to eliminate the slight distortion that is inevitable even in large-format photography when the camera's film plane is not perfectly parallel to the building. With a rectified photograph, it is possible to make an accurate measured drawing from the photograph of elements in the main subject plane by taking measurements directly from the photograph (see figs. 4.39, 4.40, and 4.41). Stereophotogrammetry takes rectified photography one step further (see fig. 4.42). To further reduce the possibility of imprecision caused by distortion, stereophotogrammetry uses two cameras, rather than one, very precisely placed in relation to each other and the facade being photographed. The resulting glass plate negatives can be plotted to produce accurate measured drawings. And unlike rectified photography, depth can be measured because a stereo image is produced. Because both of these types of photography are used to produce measured drawings, these techniques are discussed in greater detail in the next chapter.

X-ray photography, or radiography; infrared photography; and the computer

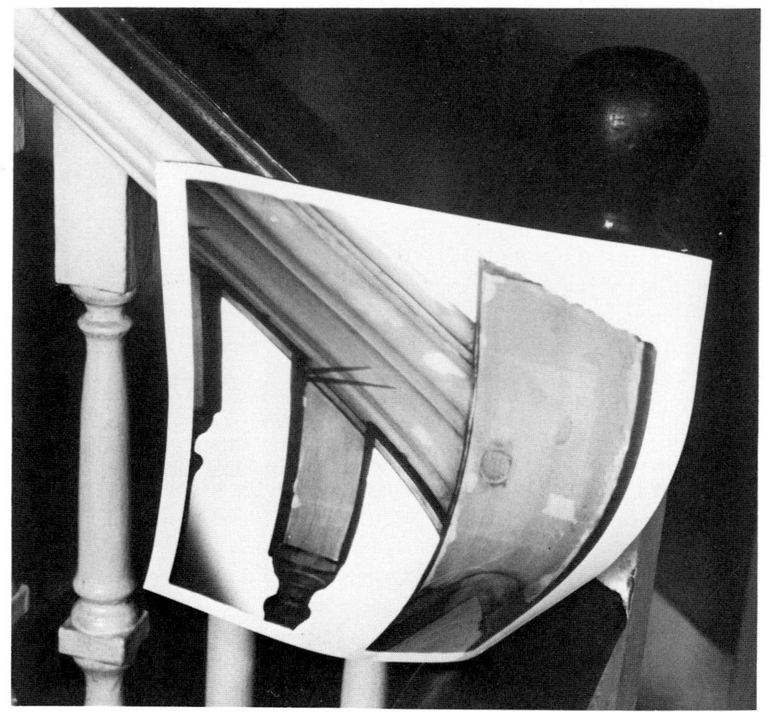

FIGURE **4.45**

Radiographs of finish materials allow dating of components by comparative methods. The wooden peg used to attach the handrail to the newel post is evidence of early construction. The use of hand-wrought nails to attach the balusters to the rail confirms the stylistically established late eighteenth-century dating of the assembly.

enhancement of photographs are three highly specialized techniques of great value in the right circumstances. Restoration architects have used portable x-ray equipment to uncover what was inside a wall without destroying the interior or exterior finishes (see figs. 4.43, 4.44, and 4.45). David M. Hart, AIA, a restoration architect and expert in the use of radiography, has written:

> Historic buildings containing the usual building materials such as plaster and lath, wood and steel or iron can usually be easily examined non-destructively by the use of portable x-ray machines. Masonry walls and partitions composed of brick or stone, thick cementitious plasters or stucco, and earth-type structures are not easily examined by x-rays.
>
> Radioactive isotopes have also been used, but safety issues are a factor which preclude widespread use of this method.
>
> The examination of buildings can reveal information in the following categories:
>
> **1.** Structural systems, to illustrate the location, size, configuration and joints of components. Structural conditions of components can also be determined.
>
> **2.** Construction details of finish materials for historical and dating purposes. The configuration and ages of components can be determined by comparative methods. Changes and alterations within the building fabric can also be ascertained by the same method.

In infrared photography, a special film with corrective filters is used. The resulting images—whether in color or black-and-white— have tones or colors different from those produced with normal film. The unusual pattern of tone and/or colors in infrared film reveals characteristics not visible on normal film or to the eye. One of the most effective uses has been in aerial photography, where the infrared photography reveals below-ground structures that otherwise would not be apparent without conducting an archeological dig.

The computer enhancement of photographs is a technique developed by the National Aeronautics and Space Administration (NASA) to improve the clarity of photographs sent back from space. The same technique can be used to make historic photographs less fuzzy and, therefore, more informative.

When done carefully, photography justifies its popularity. Photographs of buildings, bridges, or almost any structure can be aesthetically pleasing and informative. Photography is not a substitute for drawings, histories, or actually seeing a structure, but it does offer a unique viewpoint.

Figure 4.46

Note vignetting in upper corners. Sometimes it is impossible to avoid vignetting in documentary photography, especially with tall structures, like this abandoned iron furnace in a congested industrial complex.

CHAPTER 5

John A. Burns

Measured drawings constitute a third type of formal HABS/HAER documentation, which complements the format photographs and written documentation discussed in the preceding chapters. This chapter will explain what measured drawings are and how to plan and execute a set of measured drawings. Decisions on what to draw, the types of drawings to use, how to obtain the measurements, the levels of accuracy required, and the appropriate scales for the drawings will be discussed.

Measured drawings are one of the most expensive forms of architectural and engineering documentation because of the length of time they take to produce. But they are produced for many reasons. They can be used as the basis for planning restoration or rehabilitation work, to record a structure facing imminent demolition, to aid in the normal maintenance of a structure, as protection against catastrophic loss, or as a scholarly study. The types of subjects recorded with measured drawings are widely varied. The HABS and HAER measured drawings collections represent an encyclopedic range of the built environment, from mansions to doll houses, corn cribs to skyscrapers, windmills to steel mills, and from ships and canals to missile test facilities.

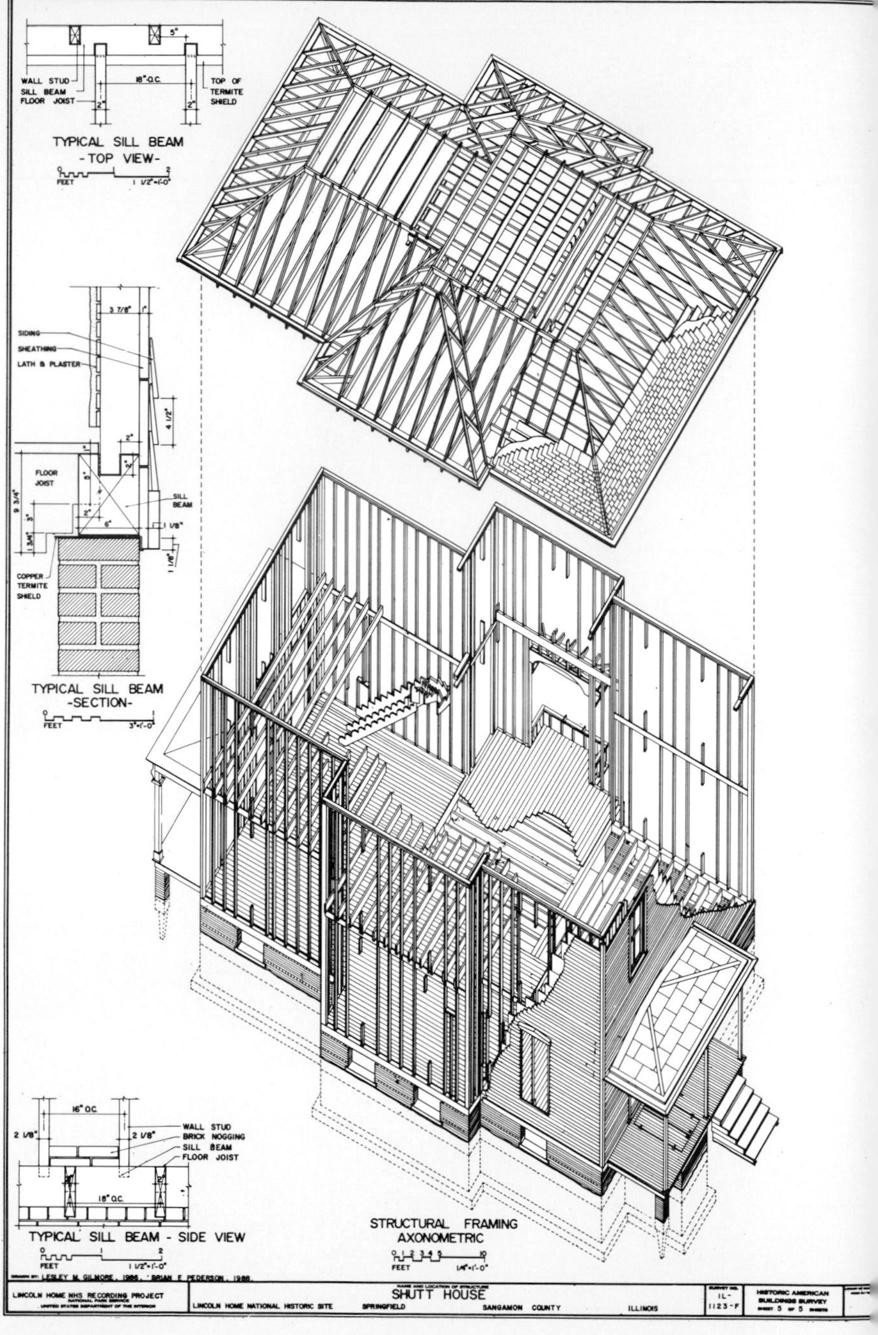

FIGURE 5.1

Structural framing axonometric.

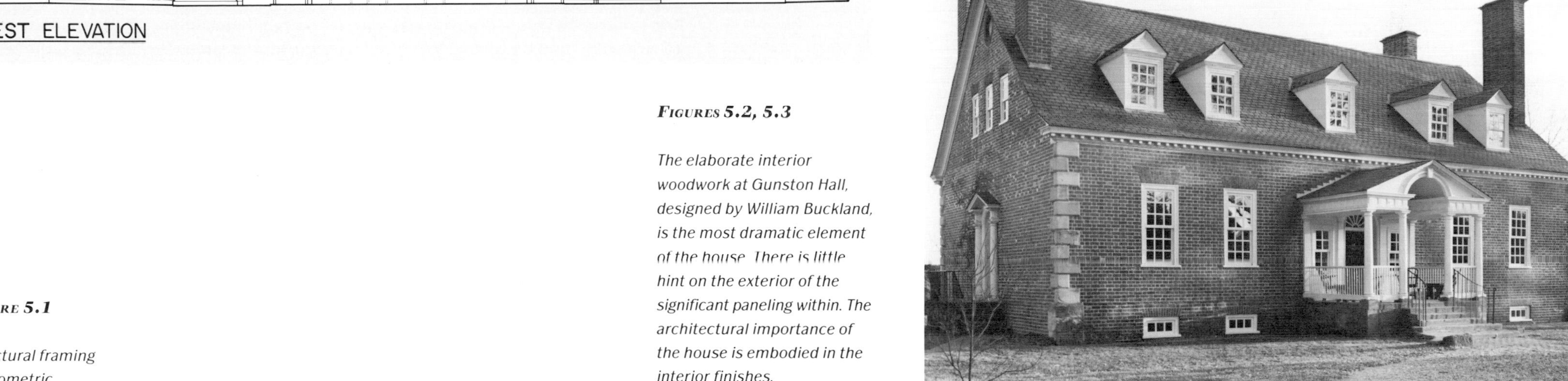

FIGURES 5.2, 5.3

The elaborate interior woodwork at Gunston Hall, designed by William Buckland, is the most dramatic element of the house. There is little hint on the exterior of the significant paneling within. The architectural importance of the house is embodied in the interior finishes.

What Are Measured Drawings?

Measured drawings are line drawings that follow standard drafting conventions to portray in two dimensions a three-dimensional structure. Measured drawings are similar to as-built architectural drawings, except that they are generally produced years after a structure is built, not immediately after construction. Measured drawings portray conditions at the time of documentation, including the accretions, alterations, and deletions that have occurred on the original. Hidden elements, exploded views, sequences of construction, and functional processes are easily portrayed in a drawing. HABS/HAER drawings are produced as a documentary record of a given structure, although they often serve another purpose, as, for example, an easement document, the basis for restoration work, catastrophic loss protection, or interpretive drawings that explain how something works.

HABS/HAER measured drawings are accurate, detailed, scaled drawings that portray or interpret the significant features of the recorded structure on a standardized format of archival stability. HABS/HAER drawing sheets come in two sizes, 19" x 24" and 24" x 36", with preprinted title block and borders that reduce the actual drawing areas to 15¾" x 20⅛" and 21¾" x 31¾", respectively.

The principal medium for HABS/HAER drawings is ink on polyester film, referred to by the trade name Mylar. The ink is archival quality, and designated for use on plastic drawing films. HABS/HAER Mylar is four mils thick (a mil is equal to a thousandth of an inch) with a drawing surface on both sides. Rag paper and vellum with ink and pencil have been used in the past. The key test of these materials is the archival stability of the medium. Ink-on-Mylar drawings should meet a performance standard of five hundred years.

The extent and level of detail of HABS/HAER measured drawings are related to the nature and significance of the subject being recorded. For instance, drawings of a balloon-frame house should include not only the expected plans, elevations, sections, and details but also information on the walls and how they were constructed (see fig. 5.1). Measured drawings of a building with highly significant interiors should emphasize large-scale detail drawings of room elevations and interior decorative finishes (see figs. 5.2 and 5.3). Drawings of a significant machine shop should concentrate on the machinery and process of work (see fig. 5.4). Measured drawings can be heavily annotated and dimensioned for restoration work or unadorned for publication purposes.

Measured drawings are based primarily on physical evidence, but may rely on other sources of information. Documentary sources can provide evidence of former conditions and may help to interpret physical fabric. Historic views, whether drawn or photographed, can be invaluable. Key features in any HABS/HAER measured drawing are citations to the sources for the measurements. Such sources include hand measurements, photographs, original drawings, and restoration drawings.

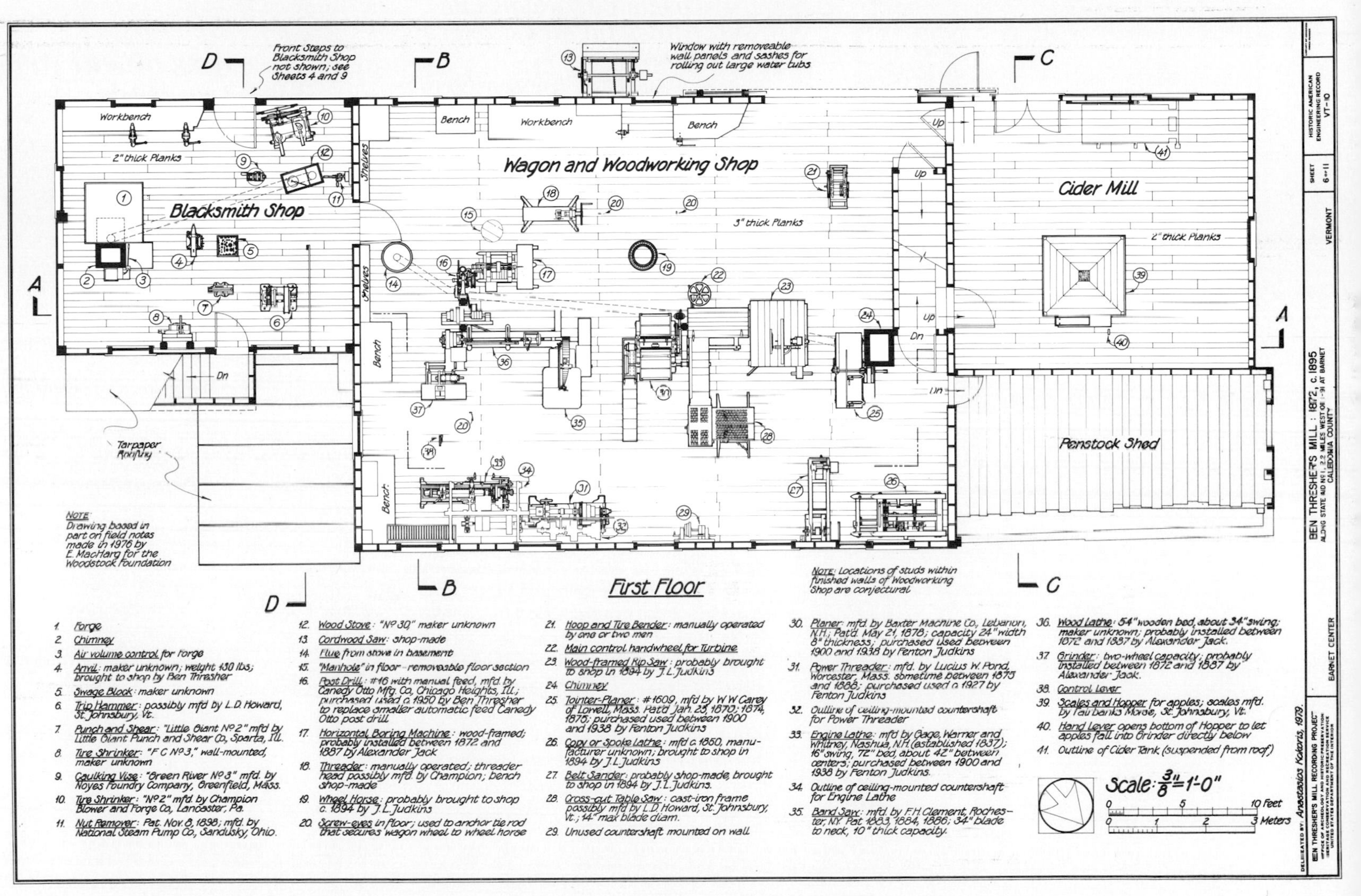

Figure 5.4

This HAER drawing was intended to capture the overall machine layout of Ben Thresher's Mill in Barnet Center, Vermont. Each machine is identified and a brief description given. Note that the architectural features of the structure are minimized, without given dimensions or annotations. Annotations relate only to the machinery and function of the mill.

Can Original Drawings Be Substituted for Measured Drawings?

A basic assumption in producing measured drawings is that other sources for drawings do not meet the needs of the project being undertaken. The discovery of original drawings for a structure about to be hand-measured is usually a great relief. However, the term "original drawings" can refer to many drawing types (see sidebar). Also, the oldest buildings only had rudimentary sketches developed to guide the craftsmen, while more recent structures may have dozens or even hundreds of detailed drawings. The drawings should be studied carefully to make sure they are reliable, accurate, and can fulfill the same needs as a measured drawing. Original drawings of one house that HABS planned to document revealed, upon close inspection, that the dimensions were for the structural elements of the house. The elaborate interior finishes were not included in these drawings because they were contracted separately. HABS hand-measured the interior details to complement the basic measurements of the house obtained from the structural drawings in order to produce the measured

TYPES OF ARCHITECTURAL AND ENGINEERING DRAWINGS

Architects and engineers use drawings to portray buildings and structures as they move from conceptualization to completion. These drawings can be useful in preparing HABS/HAER measured drawings. The types of drawings you may encounter are outlined below.

- *Conceptual drawings are intended to depict how an object is to work, be used, or to appear. Also called schematics, they are diagrammatic drawings of the essential elements of a design. Conceptual drawings are small-scale, single-line drawings (walls drawn as a single line) with little detail or dimensions. They most closely resemble sketches in appearance.*

- *Preliminary drawings, sometimes called preliminaries, work out the arrangement of spaces, circulation, and massing. They are double line drawings (walls drawn as two parallel lines) drawn at a larger scale than conceptual drawings. They include plans, elevations, and sections. Preliminaries fix and describe the size and character of the entire design.*

- *Design and bid drawings work out the details, aesthetics, dimensions, and costs for construction or manufacture. They include detail drawings of design features.*

- *Construction, working, and shop drawings are the drawings actually used in construction or manufacturing. They are dimensioned completely and accurately and include annotations.*

- *As-built drawings are produced after completion and show the structure as it was actually built, incorporating changes that were made as construction progressed. As-built drawings are usually produced by modifying a reproducible copy of the construction drawings.*

Collectively, these drawings show how a structure was conceived, designed, and produced. They are commonly called "original drawings," because they are important records of the original designs and conditions at a site. They could be used to build another identical structure. Note that they may not show a structure as it was finally built. They do not include information on later changes, either, whether major or minor, as do the following types of drawings.

- *Alteration drawings are generally very specific, dealing only with that portion of the structure being altered or added to. They are less informative about the overall structure, but are nevertheless useful as a historical record.*

- *Existing condition drawings are just that. They record the physical fabric and conditions of a structure at a given point in time. They are often produced as the first step in the rehabilitation or restoration of a historic structure. HABS/HAER measured drawings are a specialized subset of existing condition drawings.*

- *Restoration drawings can be highly informative about the historic fabric of a structure because they are frequently adapted from existing condition or HABS/HAER measured drawings. They are somewhat less useful as a historic record because they primarily depict contemporary treatments.*

drawings (see fig. 5.5). In this case, the original drawings, while extremely useful, did not adequately describe or interpret the significance of the site.

As with buildings, original drawings of engineered or industrial structures may preclude the necessity of preparing contemporary measured drawings. Engineering drawings of, for example, a bridge, a steel mill, or a machine may be so dense with dimensions, notations, and other information, however, that they confuse and obscure a basic understanding of the structure. These drawings are intended for construction or manufacture, not for interpretation. Even if original drawings can be copied, interpretive drawings may still be necessary to explain an industrial process, a construction technique, or the function of a machine.

The copying of original and other drawings for HABS/HAER can be accomplished in several ways. In most cases, HABS/HAER copies drawings from other accessible sources by making 8" x 10" copy negatives and contact prints. The reproduction is thus a photograph of the original drawing. HABS/HAER generally does not photographically copy other drawings onto a measured drawing sheet unless there is some reason to do so—for instance, if the drawing is deteriorating or inaccessible to the public. When a drawing is photographically copied onto a HABS/HAER measured drawing sheet, this point must be clearly labeled on the

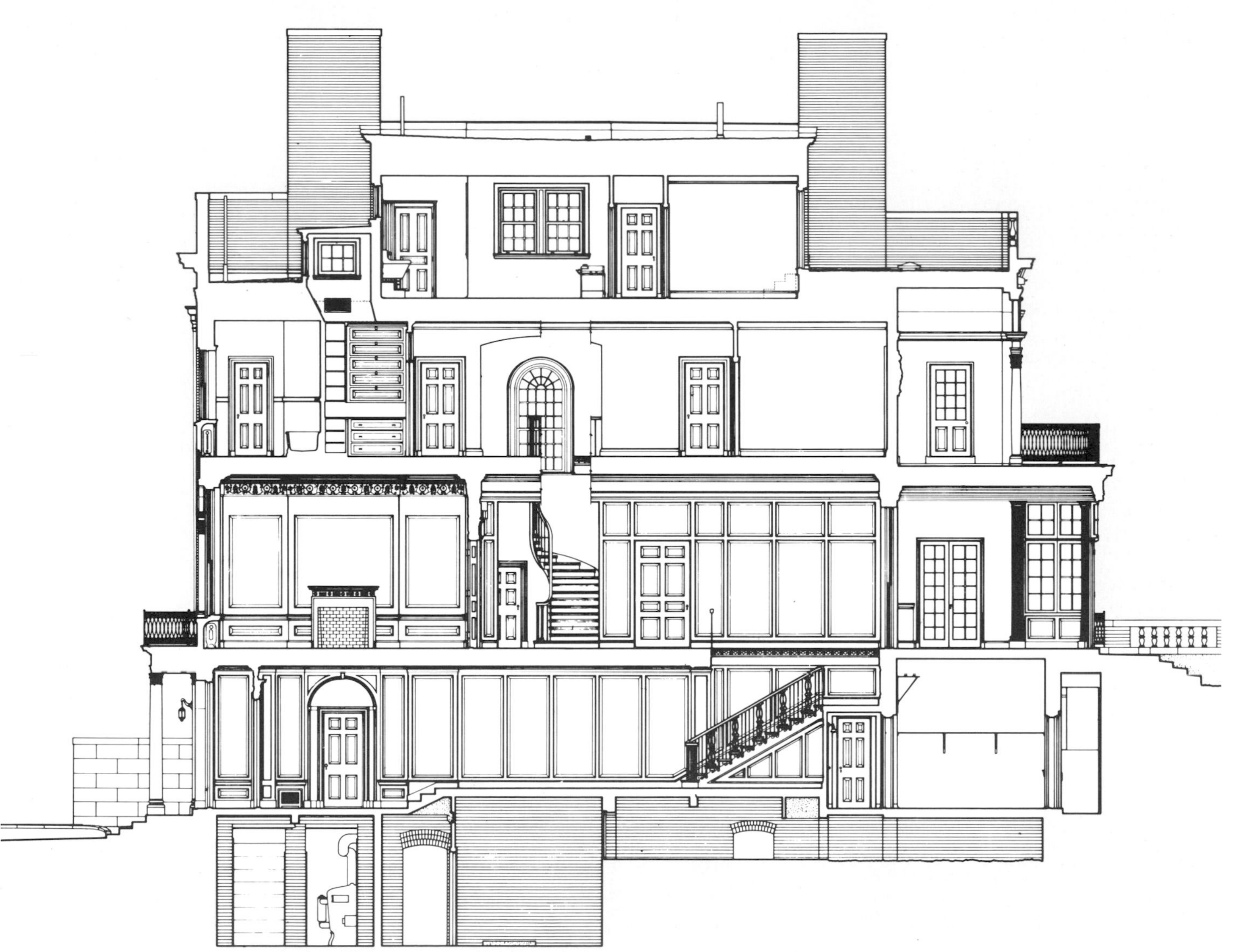

sheet so that there is no confusion regarding its source. HABS/HAER does routinely trace or otherwise adapt drawings to produce measured drawings, again, clearly citing what is copied and what is new. Since all HABS/HAER records are in the public domain, owner permission and copyright restrictions may limit the copying of historic materials for the HABS/HAER collections.

HABS/HAER measured drawings can be produced for any or several of the following reasons:

- when restoration or rehabilitation work is planned, to establish existing conditions,

FIGURE 5.5

The original 1915 drawings were found in a vault in the Woodrow Wilson House in Washington, D.C. They did not include the interior finishes, so were of limited use in preparing this measured drawing of the completed interior. Prints of the drawings were used in taking field measurements and were included in the field records for the house.

- as part of normal conservation and maintenance of a structure,
- for research,
- when demolition is planned to keep a permanent record for future generations,
- as insurance against catastrophic loss, should something happen to the structure, and
- for public information or interpretation.

While measured drawings are utilitarian, HABS/HAER measured drawings must additionally meet all HABS/HAER standards for content, quality, materials, and presentation. A HABS/HAER measured drawing project begins with the assessment of the need for measured drawings, which is based on the significance of the structure to be recorded. Information for a preliminary assessment of significance can be gleaned from written sources such as local guidebooks, company histories, National Register nominations, or preliminary archival research. A site visit to reconnoiter the structure in its context and to inspect it inside and out and from bottom to top is imperative (see chapter 2). The physical fabric of a structure may both provide answers and prompt further questions. What was its period of significance and what remains from that period? Does the structure retain its integrity? Is it threatened by development or neglect? Observations are recorded and compared with the written history uncovered, and rough measurements are taken to prepare for planning the scale and composing the drawings.

Traditionally, associative historical value and architectural importance have been the determinants of significance. For the most part, however, the built environment was not designed by a prominent architect or engineer and was not associated with a famous person or event. Under HABS/HAER standards, an individual structure does not have to be nationally significant to be recorded with measured drawings. For instance, a two-story army barracks with a gable roof and pent eaves is ordinary until you consider that its standardized construction had a considerable impact on the construction industry and that thousands of them were built and still exist. It represents a plan and construction type of national significance (see fig. 5.6).

Once the decision to produce measured drawings has been reached, the type of information essential in the finished drawings must be considered:

1. What drawings will best explain and illustrate the significant features of the site?

2. What kind of detail is required in the finished drawing? This will determine the scale of the drawing. At the common scale of ¼"=1'-0" the smallest distance that can be accurately drawn is approximately one inch.

3. How many dimensions and annotations are necessary?

4. What level of accuracy is needed in the measurements? Dimensions to the nearest inch are perfectly adequate for site plans but inadequate for details, where measurements to the nearest 1/16" or ⅛" are required.

5. What sheet size should be used? For planning purposes, the area inside the borders of a small HABS sheet (15¾" x 20⅛") scales 63'-0" x 80'-6" at ¼"=1'-0". Most domestic and similarly scaled structures will fit comfortably on this sheet size. The area inside the borders of a large HABS or HAER sheet (21¾" x 31¾") scales 87'-0" x 127'-0" at the same scale. Some structures or complexes may require several large sheets to accommodate a single elevation or plan at an appropriate scale. Do not mix sheet sizes in a single set of drawings. Note that HAER does not use the smaller sheets.

Figure 5.6

The simple character and plain appearance of this 63-man barracks belies the significance of the thousands of similar temporary wooden structures built during the mobilization for World War II. The standardized designs, standardized construction techniques, economy of materials, and ease of erection using relatively unskilled labor had significant impact on the post-war construction industry.

Figure 5.7

Independence Hall is one of the most famous and significant structures in the country. Interestingly, given the amount of attention the building has received over the years, the most pristine parts of the building were never recorded in detail. The central hall and stair tower had never been altered or restored, so there had been no need to produce detailed measurements and drawings for those purposes. Also, there was no complete, accurate set of drawings for the entire structure. Rather, there were a series of drawings of varying quality produced over the years for many different purposes. There were several driving forces behind the documentation: maintenance, restoration, interpretation, public requests for drawings, and catastrophic loss protection. Independence Hall's significance is such that if it were damaged or destroyed, in all likelihood it would be rebuilt as faithfully as possible. Accurate, detailed documentation would be imperative for reconstruction.

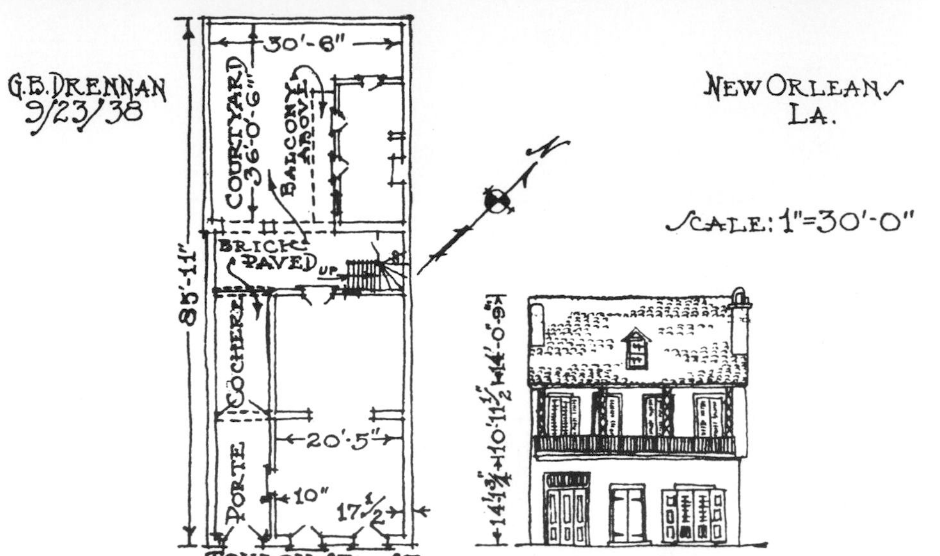

Figure 5.8

This sketch conveys the basic information necessary for understanding the room arrangements and appearance of a town house. It is simple and easily understood. Major dimensions are included along with a north arrow to give orientation. A sketch plan provides highly useful information with a minimum of effort and skill.

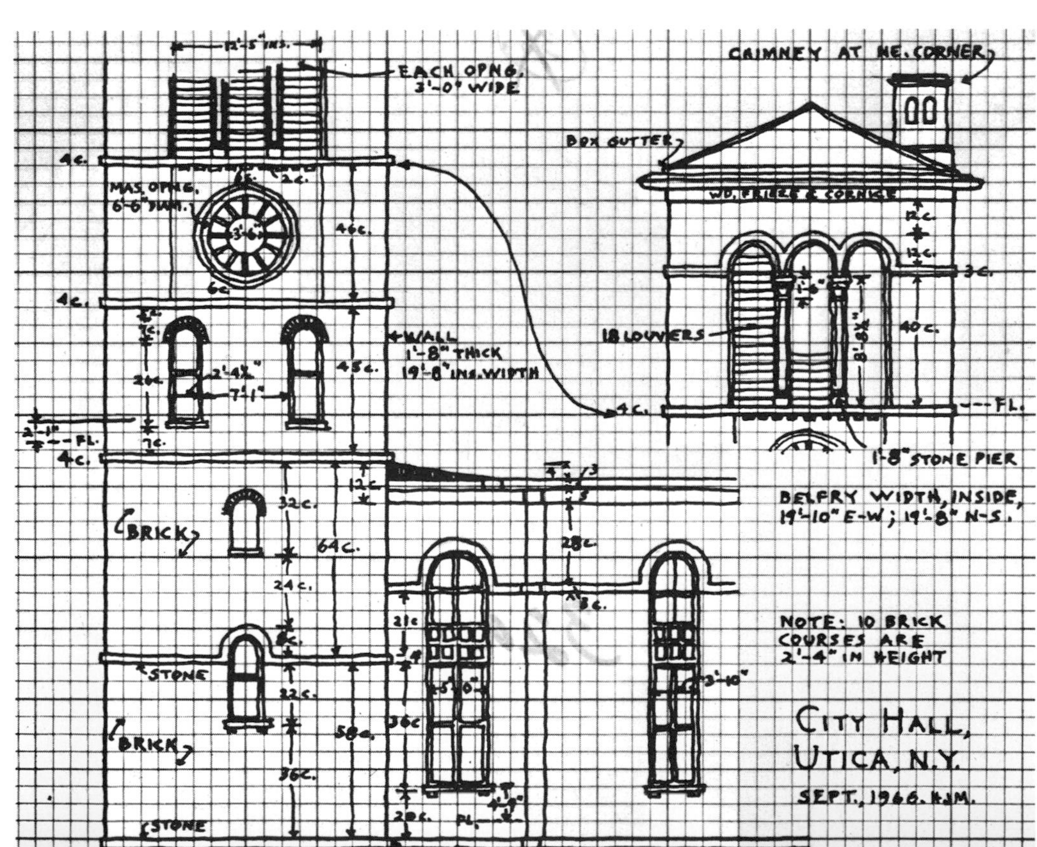

Figure 5.9

Counting repetitive materials is a way to determine measurements that are inaccessible, such as the tower on this city hall. The dimensions of the brick coursing were recorded ("Note: 10 brick courses are 2'-4" in height") so that the dimensions of the tower could be calculated.

After the type of measured drawings required has been decided, the source of the measurements needed to produce those drawings becomes the next consideration. The following questions can help in determining how measurements can best be obtained.

- Do any drawings exist or must they be produced?
- If drawings exist, are they accurate and useful to the current need?
- If measurements must be taken, what tools and expertise are available?
- Does the structure itself (its size, condition, use, and accessibility) dictate the manner in which it can be measured?

Measured drawings require varying levels of detail and annotation depending on their ultimate use. Drawings that are intended to provide the basis for restoration will require extensive dimensions and annotations to record the necessary historical and conditional information, while drawings intended for maintenance purposes may require little more than material indications and dimensions for calculating gross areas needing treatment. Measured drawings produced as mitigation are the "last rites" for a structure slated for demolition, recording for future generations all its salient features. Drawings intended to serve as protection from catastrophic loss must be detailed enough to allow the exact replication of a highly significant structure should that structure be destroyed (see fig. 5.7).

Sketch plans are an alternative to measured drawings when a structure does not warrant measured drawings, or when time or money is not available to produce measured drawings. Sketch plans do not have to be accurately scaled, but they should show elements in proper proportion to each other. They are generally drawn on 8½" x 11" archival paper (see fig. 5.8). HABS/HAER treats these sketches as data pages, including them with the formal written data. Sketches may include the primary and typical floor plans, site plans, and, less frequently, sections and details. Sketches of floor plans can also be used to key locations for photographs. Sketch plans should always include basic dimensions, approximate scale, a north arrow, the name of the delineator, and the date. Elevations are better shown in photographs.

After the decisions have been made about the type and quantity of measured drawings to be made, as well as their level of detail, scales, accuracy, and sheet layout, the field work can begin.

Figure 5.10

Note the mix of general and detail views and the systematic coverage of the entire exterior surface of the springhouse in this contact print of field photographs. The interiors were documented on another roll of film.

Gathering Information

The assembled raw materials for producing measured drawings constitute the field records. Field records are valuable because they contain all the detailed information on methodology, dimensions, and notes made at the time of recording. They are a primary resource and may be consulted by users because of their great detail. Field notes are invariably more comprehensive than the given dimensions and annotations on a finished drawing. For this reason, some people consider the field notes more important than the final drawing. A complete measured drawing cannot be more accurate than the field records from which it was produced.

The quality of the field work has a substantial impact on the quality of the completed documentation. Field work must be thought out in advance in order to organize the recording efficiently and to minimize the chances for mistakes. Field notes must be accurate and comprehensive. They must be carefully annotated and neatly labeled so that others can understand the information. Hasty or sloppy field work invariably includes errors and omissions that cause repeated trips to the site or flaws in the final drawings.

Field records may consist of copies of original drawings annotated to include later alterations, dimensioned sketches, photographs, and whatever

MEASURING TIPS

A few points are important to remember in making hand measurements (see figs. 5.13A and 5.13B):

- *It cannot be assumed that rooms or buildings are square or that floors are level. Taking diagonal measurements and checking levels will allow you to determine if there is any distortion.*
- *Establish datum lines and planes as points of reference for the measurements.*
- *Cumulative measurements are more accurate than consecutive measurements because they use a common zero point and thus do not require that the tape be relocated after each measurement.*
- *Hold the tape taut when making measurements. Temperature, tension, and wind can affect the accuracy of taped measurements by causing the tape to stretch, shrink, or sag.*
- *Know where the zero point is on the tape. It is not always at the end.*
- *Horizontal distances must be measured with the tape held level. Use a plumb line to measure points displaced vertically.*

- *Triangulate to features on inclined or curved surfaces from fixed points.*
- *Remember that the minimum distance from a point to a line is always in a direction perpendicular to the line, so that if you set the end of a tape at the point and swing it near the line, the minimum measurement is the true dimension. Similarly, the distance from a point to a plane follows the same geometric rule.*
- *Use the utmost care in transcribing dimensions. Use a standardized system of notation to reduce the chance of error. For instance, the dimension 1'-8" is similar to 18" both visually and literally.*
- *The use of surveying instruments and other measuring tools can both speed up measuring and increase accuracy.*

Hand measuring can be broken down into a three-step process (see sidebar, page 125). After the principal dimensions have been accurately determined, repeat the process at the next higher level of detail until the entire structure has been measured at the level of detail necessary to produce the planned drawings.

FIGURE 5.11

For structures that are unlikely to be recorded in measured drawings, a scale stick placed in the field of view of the photographs will provide basic dimensional information. Note that the recessed entry and projecting cornice will be distorted in relation to the distance they are displaced from the plane of the facade.

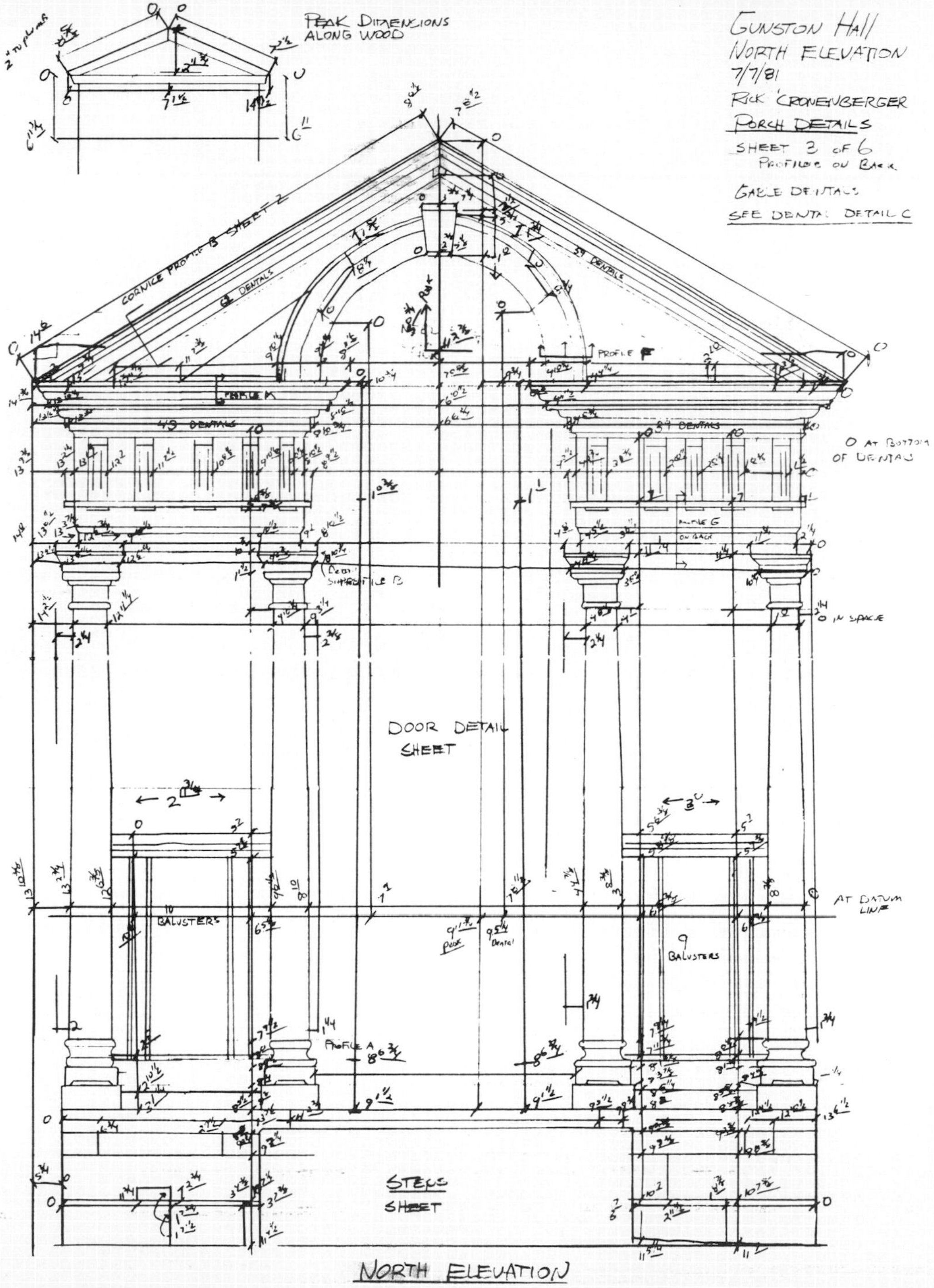

FIGURE 5.12

Field notes recording dimensions are the primary source material for a measured drawing. Note how many more dimensions and notes there are in the field notes in relation to the drawing. From the information in the field notes, the accuracy of the completed drawing can be judged.

else may be needed to produce a finished drawing. Sketches and measurements made in the field are recorded on graph paper and organized in what are called field notebooks to be filed as part of the field records. HABS/HAER considers field records informal documentation because they are not rigorously archival (although archival materials and processes are used) and are not easily reproducible. Field records are retained by HABS/HAER and transmitted to the Library of Congress along with other completed documentation.

Obtaining Measurements

Dimensions for measured drawings normally come from three sources: documents, hand measurements, and photographs. Documentary measurements come from original or alteration drawings, old views, published accounts, previous surveys, specifications, and so on. A more thorough discussion of documentary sources is included in chapter 3.

The tools and techniques used for taking measurements by hand vary in their sophistication. The measurements are produced by taping distances, by surveying (measuring angles and distances, often with the help of surveying instruments and electronic distance measuring equipment), or by measuring and then counting repetitive materials (see fig. 5.9).

Photography offers a wide variety of information-gathering capabilities that are discussed in great detail in chapter 4. Field photographs are used as an adjunct to field measurements and are invaluable for double-checking accuracy. They are very cost-effective. As a rule of thumb, the less accessible a site is for checking measurements, the more field photographs should be taken. Even a simple structure like a springhouse may require an entire roll of film to record all its details (see fig. 5.10). Large-format photographs are sharper and clearer than 35mm photographs. In large-format, great detail is discernible, even in contact prints,

A STEP-BY-STEP APPROACH TO HAND MEASURING

Planning

- ☐ Establish type and number of measured drawings to be produced.
- ☐ Develop methodology for taking measurements, including quality-control checks.
- ☐ Assess site constraints:
  - Floor level
  - Rooms square
  - Access and lighting
  - Safety

Measuring

- ☐ First sketch the areas to be measured and establish the locations for the principal reference points and overall dimensions. The sketches will become the basis for the field notes.
- ☐ Establish datum lines and planes as points of reference for taking measurements. Locate datum lines and planes in relation to each other and note on sketches.
- ☐ Begin by locating major points in relation to each other and any datum lines and planes. Take major dimensions. Record both in field notes.
- ☐ Double check accuracy of initial measurements, since all subsequent measurements will rely on them.
- ☐ Systematically take and record measurements to fill in the necessary dimensions for each drawing. Periodically tie your measurements back to the principal reference points or datum lines and planes to assure continued accuracy.

Checking

- ☐ An effective way to verify the accuracy of your measurements is to block out the major dimensions in a drawing while still in the field, then check how the component parts will fit into the overall drawing.
- ☐ The preliminary drawings should be produced in the field to ensure the accuracy and completeness of the field measurements.

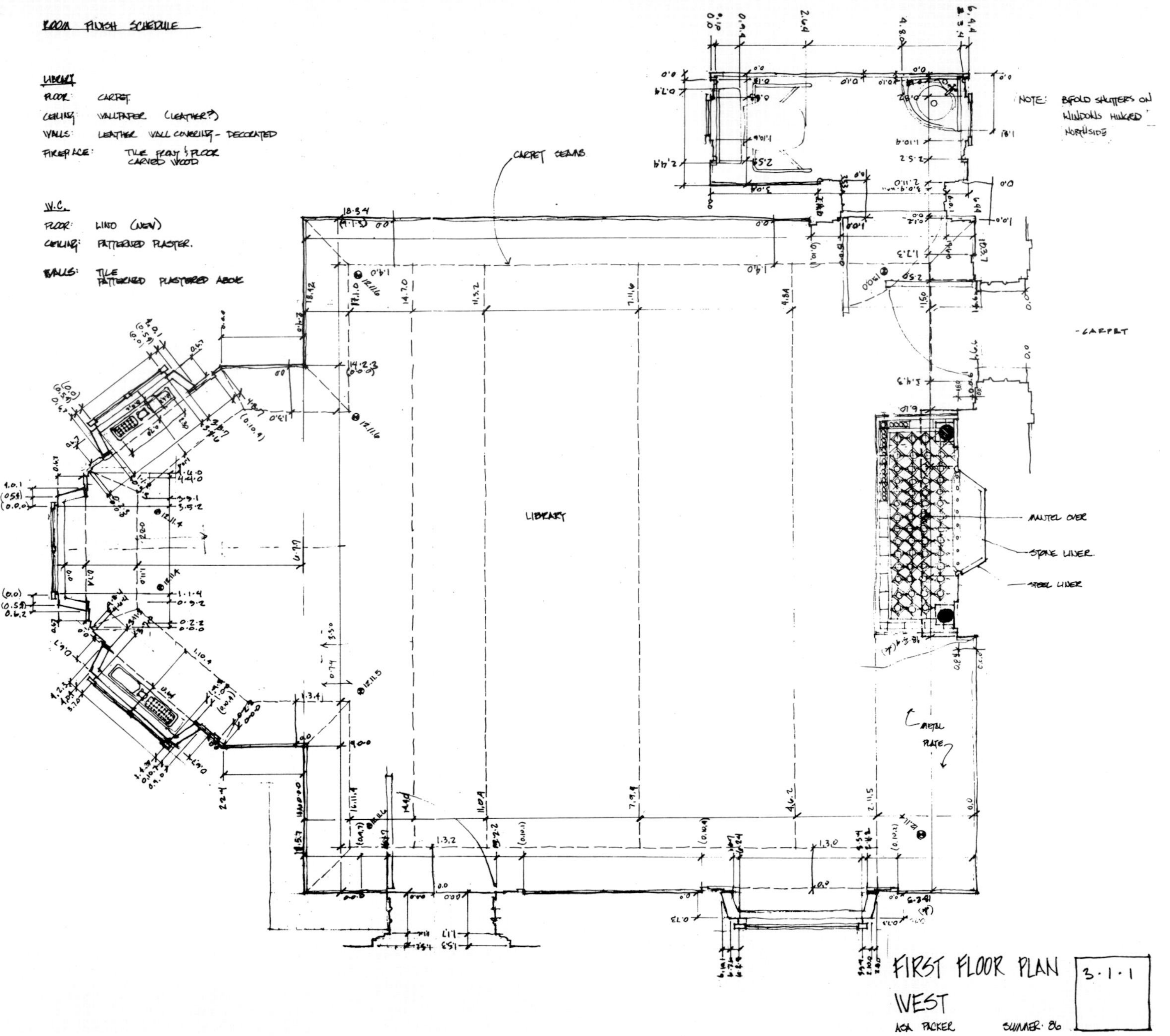

when viewed under a jeweler's loupe or magnifying glass. A measuring stick placed in the field of view of a photograph can be used to scale distances (see fig. 5.11). Photographs can be used in other, less common ways to produce measurements. The techniques of rectified photography, mono- and stereophotogrammetry, and analytical photogrammetry are discussed later in this chapter.

Obtaining Measurements from Documentary Sources

The easiest way to obtain measurements is to find a source that has already recorded them. Historical research should include a search for

FIGURE 5.13a

Field notes contain many more dimensions than are labeled on the final drawing. Note the use of cumulative measurements and targets indicating floor-to-ceiling heights and standardized notation for recording the dimensions. Compare these field notes with the completed drawing (fig. 5.29) to see the difference.

drawings, specifications, building permits, and other sources of dimensional information. If they are found, the reliability and accuracy of the dimensions must be assessed, as must their usefulness to the current project. Important questions include: who produced the measurements and for what purpose? Do the drawings reflect the structure as it was actually built and exists today? If not, how and why are the drawings different? Are some but not all of the drawings reliable?

The recorder must verify the accuracy of the information against the structure itself. If the drawings have few given dimensions, it may be possible to scale from the drawings. Scaled dimensions must be checked in both directions on a drawing to make sure there is no differential distortion. Paper will elongate or shrink differently along the grain than across the grain. Prints made by wrapping the drawing

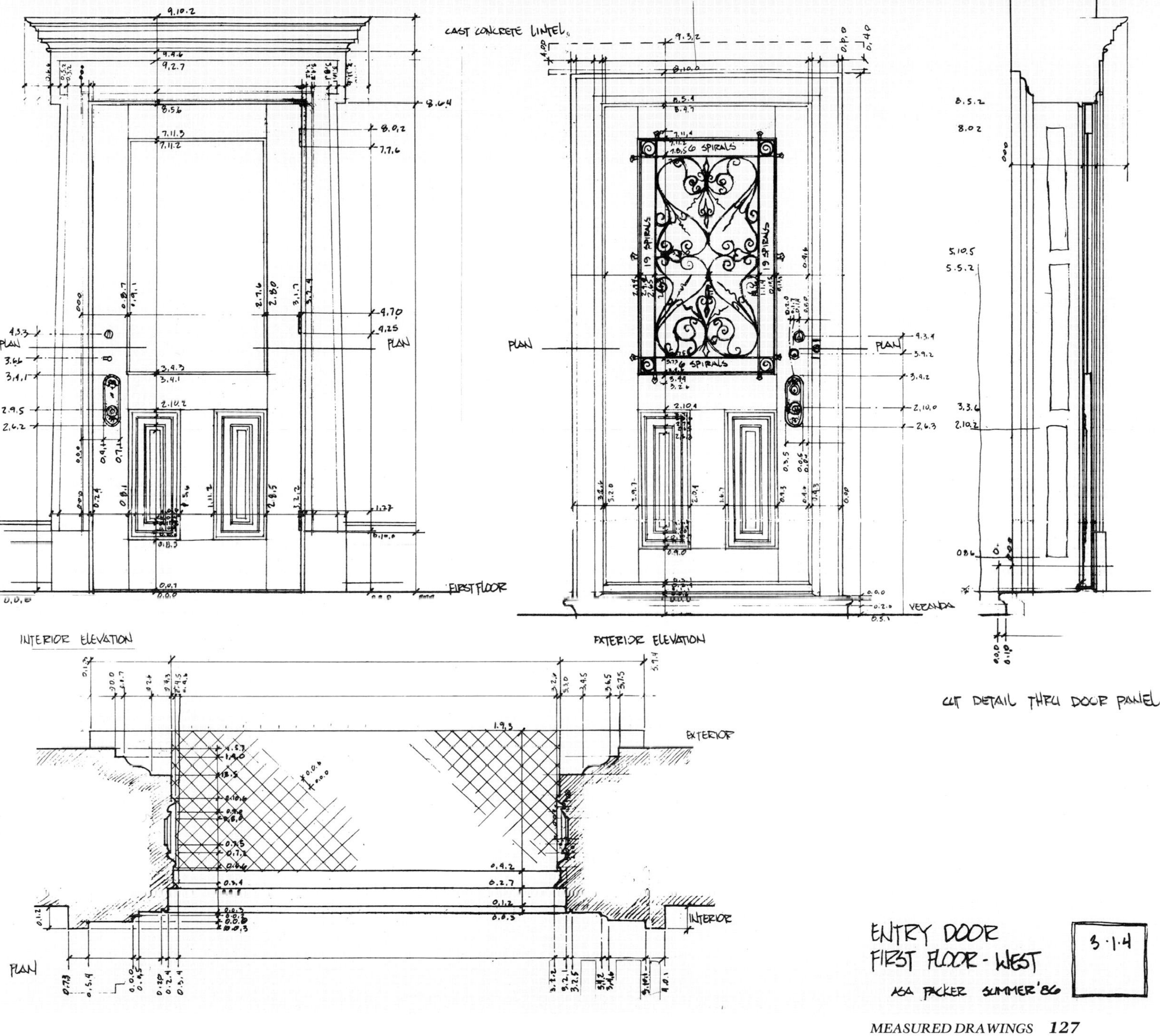

FIGURE 5.13b

The field notes for this door were made at a large scale because the final drawing will be at a large scale in order to show the necessary detail. Compare the level of detail with the same door in fig. 1.7.

and print paper around a tubular light source, the exposure method found in most blueprint machines, will be elongated in the direction of travel. For a four mil thick HABS/HAER drawing sheet and a two-inch diameter light source, the elongation would be approximately 5/32" in three feet, or the equivalent of eight scale inches at ¼"=1'-0". Thicker drawings will produce more elongation; thinner drawings will produce less.

Hand Measuring

Hand measuring is the most common way to obtain dimensions for measured drawings. Hand measuring can be highly accurate when done with careful planning and execution. The number of drawings, their accuracy, the scale used, and the sheet layout should be determined before planning the measuring, because those decisions help to determine the best way to measure a structure. Hand measuring only records that which is consciously measured and written down, making a methodical, systematic approach essential. Otherwise, errors of omission and commission will be difficult to avoid. Proceeding in a systematic manner not only gives organization to the measuring process, it also highlights errors when they do occur. You should plan more than one way to obtain each measurement—for example, by direct measurement, by calculations from other points, and by trigonometry—so that all dimensions will be verifiable (see fig. 5.12).

The number of people required for hand measuring a structure will vary. Three is an ideal number, two people to measure and one to record the dimensions. In teams of two, one person can measure while the other records the dimensions. It is difficult, however, and potentially dangerous for one person to measure anything other than small features or details. Large structures are documented more efficiently with several three- or two-person measuring teams rather than one large team.

Tools for Hand Measuring. The most common tools for hand measuring are a retractable steel tape stiff enough to extend across openings or up to ceilings (a one-inch-wide, twenty-five-foot tape is recommended), a one-hundred-foot tape, a six-foot folding carpenter's rule, a plumb bob or similar weight and string, a carpenter's spirit level, graph paper, a large clipboard, and a pencil (see fig. 5.14). Accurate measurements can be made and recorded with these simple tools and a knowledge of geometry. Additional equipment might include a profile gauge, magnetic compass, scale stick for field photographs, flashlight, and ladders or scaffolding. Safety equipment such as hard hats and safety ropes should be used as needed.

Establishing Datum Lines and Planes. The first step in hand measuring is to establish datum lines and planes from which to take measurements. In some structures it may be possible to use the floor as a datum plane, if it is found to be level. The first step in determining if a floor is level is to inspect it. Does it look level or feel level when you walk on it? If your observations indicate that the floor may be level, you should check it more carefully with a carpenter's level or by using the techniques described in the following paragraphs. An advantage to using the floor as a datum plane is that it requires only one vertical measurement (from the floor up instead of both up and down from a datum plane). Another consideration is whether the floor elevation changes from room to room or from wing to wing. Even if all the floors are level, changes in elevation may necessitate a common datum plane from which to measure.

If the floor is level, a convenient height for measuring is at waist level. It does not require you to stoop and is high enough to pass across most window openings. Remember to keep the tape level when measuring.

If the floor is not level, you must establish a datum plane independent of the structure. A horizontal datum line accurate enough to use for most small structures can be established by leveling a taut string with a carpenter's spirit level. The longer the level and the tighter the string, the more accurate the level line will be. The spirit level should be at least two feet long for optimum accuracy. The string should be tight enough to remove visible sags, which can be observed by sighting along the string. Also note if the string is hung up on anything. A small bubble level designed to hang on a string is significantly less accurate than this method. A chalk line can be used, but it may leave a permanent mark on some materials, so obtain permission before using one. By repeating the process, you can carry the datum line around a structure to establish a datum plane. To check accuracy, periodically tie back or relate subsequent datum lines to the first datum line.

A water level (consisting of a water-filled tube, like a hose, with transparent ends through which the water level can be viewed) can also be used to demarcate a horizontal datum plane that can be carried from room to room and even from the interior to the exterior of a structure. It works on the principle that water seeks its own level. Advantages of water levels are that they are accurate and flexible in that they can go around corners and through openings. They are also inexpensive and can be homemade. One problem with the technique is that if some water spills, you must both reset the level to compensate for the lost water and clean up the mess.

Vertical datum lines and planes can be established by running a plumb line up or down from known points. Horizontal relationships from floor to floor can be determined using this technique.

Aboard ships, the use of a transit to set datum planes may be essential (especially if the ship is afloat) for measuring the compound curves of the decks. Plumb bobs and levels are useless unless the vessel is in a dry dock or otherwise supported out of water on land. See the section on recording historic ships in chapter 6 for more detailed information.

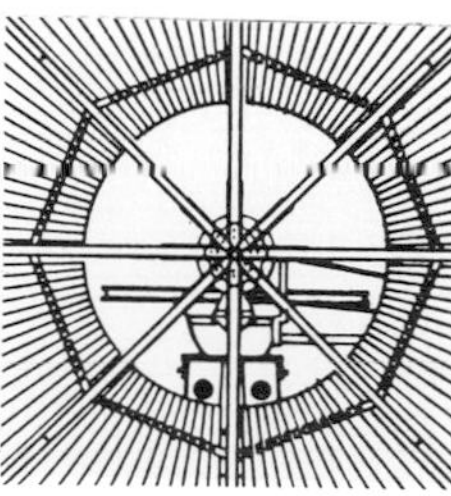

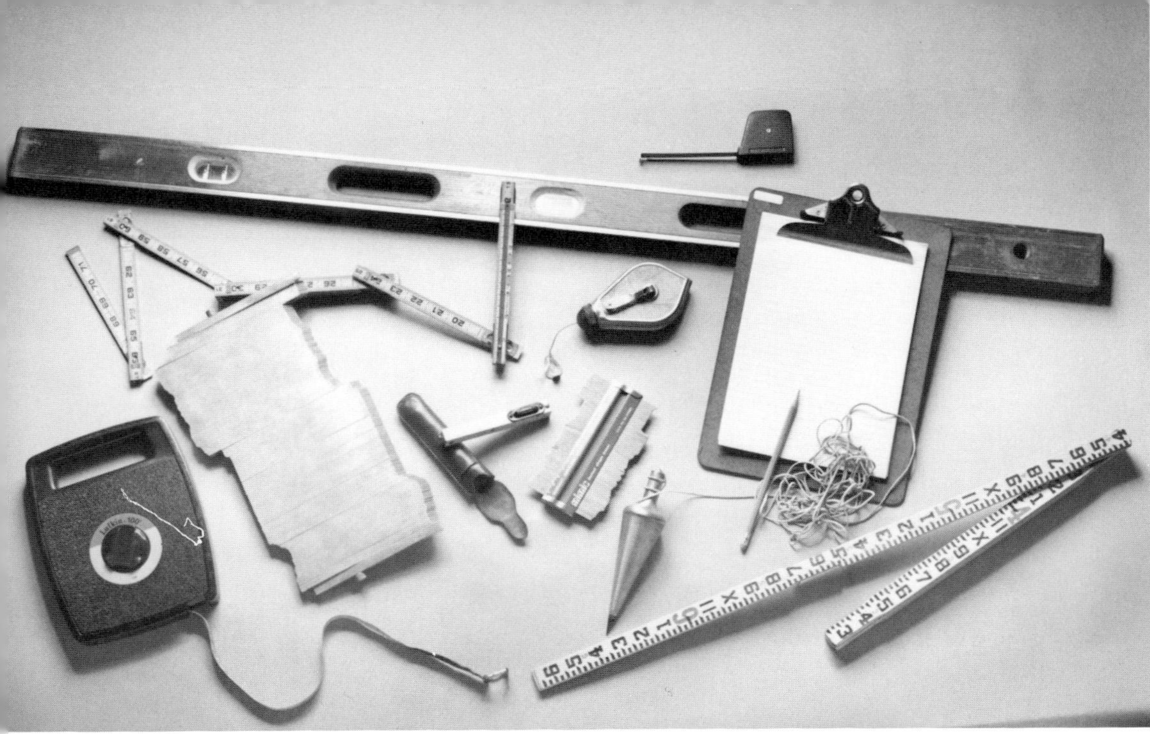

FIGURE 5.14

Hand measuring equipment.

FIGURE 5.15

Leitz SK telescoping digital measuring pole.

Hand Measuring Conventions. All measurements are assumed to be made in either horizontal or vertical planes. Vertical measurements can be made most accurately by using a plumb line to assure the verticality of the tape. When taking horizontal measurements, keep the tape taut to avoid sags. (Surveyors use a standard of twenty pounds of tension when taking measurements with steel tapes.) If you are using a transit to sight in a datum plane, the minimum dimension read in the scope, as you swing a tape from a point to the scope sightline, is in a direction perpendicular to the datum plane.

When direct horizontal measurements are not possible, inclined dimensions can be taken and converted to horizontal dimensions using trigonometry. Horizontal measurements made with one end of the tape higher than the other will actually be measuring a longer distance because of the inclination of the tape. It may be easier to measure inclined distances by breaking the slope into a series of stepped horizontal measurements. Vertical alignment of the tape at each step can be assured by using a plumb line.

Specialized Hand Measuring Tools. HABS/HAER uses several other types ofhand-measuring tools that are extremely useful. The Leitz/SK telescoping digital measuring pole allows one person to measure heights up to twenty-six feet with a direct readout of the dimension in feet, inches, and eighths of an inch (see fig. 5.15). The pole can also be used horizontally. The pole is just over four feet long when collapsed and weighs four pounds. It is made of nonconducting materials but nevertheless must be used with extreme caution around power lines. A second Leitz measuring tool is the builder's mini rod, similar to an oversized folding carpenter's rule. It comes in both six-and-one-half and nine-and-one-half foot lengths, with numbers that read vertically, and thus can be used as a scale stick in photographs. The shorter rod is just over fifteen inches long when folded and fits easily in a briefcase; the longer rod is twenty-two inches long when folded (see fig. 5.14). Marking one side of the rule in alternating black-and-white one-foot increments increases its usefulness as a scale stick when photographed from a distance.

Another measuring tool is a telescoping fiberglass rod with an oval cross section that is about five feet long but that extends to twenty-five feet. It has gradations marked every quarter inch on one side and alternating red and white one-foot increments on the other (see fig. 5.11).

Triangulation

The simplest form of surveying is triangulation, a technique suitable for hand measuring. Any point on a site can be located accurately by establishing its distance from two other points. An entire site can be measured by using a series of triangles and measuring the distances along their sides (see fig. 5.15). To ensure accuracy, you must periodically tie back to known points. This technique is particularly effective for flat sites, less so for sloping or hilly sites. The compensation for inclined measurements must be calculated using either the angle of inclination or the difference in height between the two points being measured. Both calculations are simple trigonometric functions. This technique is especially useful in irregular structures, for site plans, or on board ships.

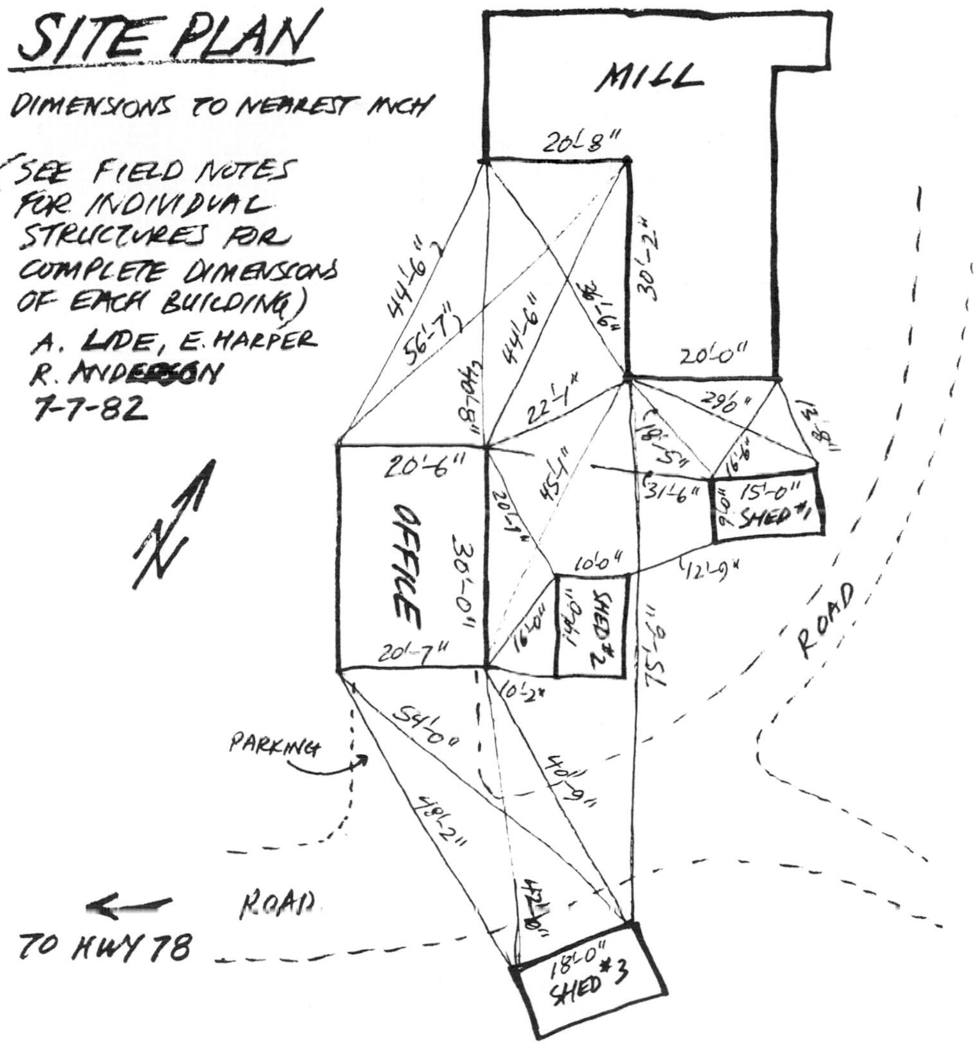

FIGURE 5.16

Measuring a series of triangles can locate structures in relation to one another without the use of surveying equipment. The technique is accurate when all the measurements are taken in a level plane. On a sloping site, the measurements must either be taken in vertically displaced level planes or inclined measurements converted mathematically to level measurements.

Basic Surveying

A rudimentary understanding of surveying techniques can make hand measuring faster, easier, and more accurate. Surveying is based on geometry and is an efficient method of establishing levels, measuring angles, and measuring distances. For more information on surveying, see the books listed in the bibliography.

Plane surveying should be used for documenting historic sites. Plane surveying does not compensate for the curvature of the earth, which is negligible even in large historic sites. All distance measurements are assumed to be either horizontal or vertical. Vertical measurements are taken in the direction of gravity, which can be determined by using a plumb line. Horizontal measurements are defined as being perpendicular to the direction of gravity. Inclined measurements up a hill, for instance, must be corrected to a horizontal measurement using trigonometry. A pocket calculator with trigonometric functions simplifies the mathematics.

Obtaining Measurements from Photographs

Measurements obtained from photographs can offer certain advantages over other methods of measurement. Photographs are generalized, that is, they record information without constraints. Everything seen by the camera is documented. Photographs also convey information on condition and texture.

Field photographs should include a scale stick or measuring tape to give approximate scale to elements in the view (see fig. 5.17). Another technique, especially useful for irregular features such as stonework or log walls, is to place a grid of known dimension over the subject being photographed. Such a grid can be made from a rigid frame of pipe, five feet square, with a string grid at one-foot intervals. Objects in or close to the plane of the tape or grid can be scaled relatively accurately. Objects in front of or beyond the plane of the tape or grid are either enlarged or diminished according to their displacement from the plane.

FIGURE 5.17

The measuring stick allows the viewer to understand the scale of the adobe bricks, which are much larger than regular brick. Without the scale stick as a reference, it is difficult to estimate the size of the masonry units.

Architectural Photogrammetry

Architectural photogrammetry combines principles of photography and geometry in a method in which scaled drawings can be obtained from photographs. The process makes use of photographs taken from known locations to create an optical model that can be scaled in all directions. There are several kinds of photogrammetry, which vary in technique, accuracy, and expense.

Rectified Photography

Rectified photography uses optical means to rectify or correct a photograph so that one plane of the subject is recorded without distortion. Because its accuracy is limited to one plane, rectified photography is best used for flat facades and room elevations (see fig. 5.18). The rectification can either be in exposure of the negative or in the printing process. If the photographer has access to a darkroom, the latter is easier.

Rectifying a negative requires the photographer to establish a grid on the object being photographed and to position the camera in relation to that grid so that the central axis of the lens is perpendicular to the center point of the grid and the film plane is parallel to the grid plane. This is a difficult and time-consuming task. However, the resulting negative can be enlarged conventionally to any desired scale.

The second technique rectifies the photograph in a darkroom by manipulating the negative as it is printed. This is usually accomplished by tilting the print easel in relation to the negative to remove the distortions. This is ideally accomplished with a rectifying enlarger designed for such work but can be accomplished with reasonable accuracy with an ordinary photographic enlarger (see figs. 5.18 and 5.19). Again, the negative can be enlarged to any desired scale. With either technique, any prints should be made on resin-coated (RC) paper because it is much less likely than fiber-based papers to change shape when immersed in developing chemicals, washed, and dried. Note, however, that resin-coated papers are not archivally stable.

Monophotogrammetry is a more accurate version of rectified photography. It makes use of metric cameras, the same type used in stereophotogrammetry, to make photographs without the optical distortions found in most camera systems. Metric cameras are heavy, rigid cameras with fixed, distortion-free, high resolution lenses that produce extremely high-quality photographs on glass plates. Glass plates are used because they are rigid, distortion-free, and dimensionally stable. The characteristics of the camera are precisely measured and recorded. Metric cameras have internal masks that place points called fiducial marks on each negative. The location of the fiducial marks is part of the known characteristics of the camera used in plotting the plates.

Perspective distortion is still present in monophotogrammetry, however, because metric cameras have fixed lenses. The perspective distortion is corrected in a special enlarger, called a rectifier, designed for that purpose. The resulting positive, made on another glass plate, is undistorted and may be scaled accurately in its principal image plane. Less expensive paper prints can be made, but they will be less accurate.

FIGURES 5.18, 5.19

The original of the field photograph was enlarged so that the image of the facade was to the same scale as the drawing of the facade. A perspective-corrected 35mm negative, normal photographic enlarger, and resin-coated (RC) enlarging paper were used to make the print. While not as accurate as rectified photography can be, this simple technique allowed the delineator to accurately position and rotate the window openings in the drawing. Notice the difference in the length of the gable ridge. In the photograph, it is diminished significantly in size because it is so far beyond the image plane of the facade.

Stereophotogrammetry

Stereogrammetry is the most accurate widely used type of photogrammetry (see fig. 5.20). Two or more overlapping photographs are taken at successive camera positions or stations, normally with the axes parallel. The locations of the camera stations are carefully measured in relation to the building, specifications of the camera are noted, and some points and dimensions are established on the structure or in the space before it. These data are known as survey control.

Paired photographs (stereopairs) are placed in a plotting instrument to produce an optical model that is scalable in three dimensions. The technique is highly specialized and requires the use of expensive cameras and plotting instruments operated by trained technicians. It is especially useful for structures that are too irregular, large, inaccessible, or dangerous to measure by hand (see fig. 5.21). The technique is limited by the fact that the cameras document only what is in their field of view. Objects hidden by foliage or projections are not measurable and must be recorded in some other manner.

One way in which photogrammetry can be used is in the preparation of stereopairs and survey control data that will be plotted and drawn only as necessary. Since plotting and drawing is the most expensive aspect of photogrammetry, this will allow more buildings to be documented for a given expenditure while still retaining the capability to produce measured drawings (see fig. 5.22). Two problems with this approach are that the informational content is not easily reproducible (glass plates are fragile and require special handling) and that it is not independently verifiable without putting the plates in a plotter.

Stereophotogrammetry may be either terrestrial or aerial. Terrestrial photogrammetry is used for showing individual buildings or groups of buildings in elevation. It is the best way to record small dimensions since the camera-to-subject distances are short.

Aerial photogrammetry is used for mapping and making plans for districts. Survey control in this case includes some targeting or knowledge of elevations, distances, and direction of points on the ground as well as the course, altitude, and speed of the plane and the time between successive exposures. Aerial photographs are generally taken with the axis within three degrees of perpendicular to the ground. A specialized aerial photogrammetry is low-level oblique, where the photographs are taken from low altitudes with the camera turned to the side to record elevations. The camera-to-subject distance is large, so the level of detail is not great. The technique is ideal, however, for recording large areas in a short time.

The products of both terrestrial and aerial processes are photographic stereopairs which, when placed in a plotting machine, present the illusion of a three-dimensional optical model. (The same principle is at work in a child's Viewmaster.) Using the survey control, this model can be accurately measured and points can be plotted on a drawing at any desired scale. A drafter then joins these points to produce a measured drawing in standard orthographic projection.

The number of stereopairs needed to document a site depends on the nature of the structure and its environment. Elevation drawings are best made from stereopairs taken perpendicular to the building, while oblique views are best for determining measurements of features in more than one plane, such as cornices or roofs. Repetitious views taken from several distances and angles may, therefore, be required. Series of pairs of photographs can be arranged in a mosaic by relating common points visible in adjacent pairs to cover large areas. Trees, adjacent structures, and other obstacles that obscure the view may also increase the number of stereopairs needed.

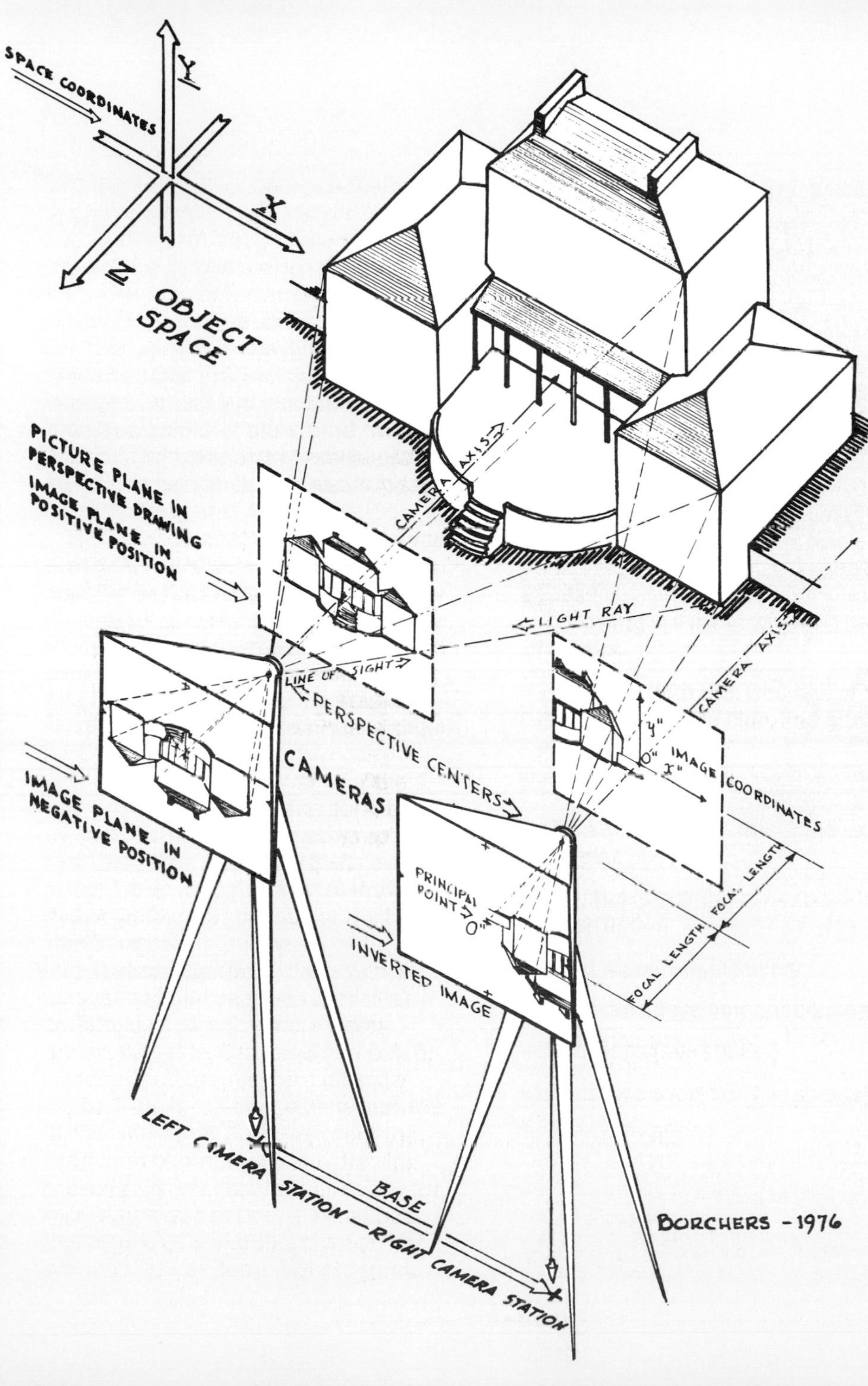

Analytical Photogrammetry

An analytical photogrammetry technique called reverse perspective analysis can be used to prepare drawings for structures that have been damaged or demolished but for which photographs remain and a few dimensions can be determined (see fig. 5.23).

The technique uses ordinary contemporary or historical photographs, sometimes in conjunction with contemporary photogrammetry. It combines the use of one or more photographs for which the camera position can be determined with geometric calculation of the major dimensions of the structure. Accuracy depends on the quantity and quality of photographs available and the number of known dimensions. The process is easier if the historic photographs can be combined with contemporary photogrammetry.

FIGURE 5.20

This diagram illustrates a typical setup for producing glass plate photogrammetric stereopairs using two camera stations. Note that it is the area of overlap of the two photographs, in this case the right half of the building, that can be measured from the plates.

HABS/HAER Measured Drawings

HABS/HAER measured drawings all have common elements of identification (see fig. 5.24). The title block includes the name of the project or sponsor; the name of the structure; the address, including city or vicinity; county and state; the HABS or HAER number; and the sheet number. Information in the drawing area includes the name of the delineator; date of the drawing; graphic scales, in both English and metric units; and north arrow on plans. Dimensions, materials indications, and annotations are also standard.

Drawing Scales and Drawing Accuracy

HABS/HAER uses common architectural and engineering scales in its drawings (see sidebar). Other scales can be used even though they are not common. An example would be a drawing done at 3⁄16"=1'-0" because it would not fit on a standard HAER Mylar at ¼"=1'-0".

ARCHITECTURAL SCALES

SCALE	RATIO	SMALLEST UNIT*	USE
1⁄16"=1'-0"	1:192	4"	*Drawings of large structures without details included. Materials shown in plan only.*
⅛"=1'-0"	1:96	2"	*Little detail possible. Materials shown in plan, only large units in elevation.*
¼"=1'-0"	1:48	1"	*The most common architectural scale. Reasonable amount of detail possible. HABS/HAER shows door and window frames, materials in both plan and elevation. At this scale, line weights can adversely affect accuracy. A 3 x 0 (0.25mm) line is approximately ½" thick.*
¾"=1'-0"	1:16	⅜"	*Most common scale for door/window elevations and other features of similar scale.*
1½"=1'-0"	1:8	3⁄16"	*Details of door/window jambs/frames, large tools, small machines, etc.*
3"=1'-0"	1:4	3⁄32"	*Details of objects such as hardware, tools, etc. and molding profiles.*
Full Size	1:1		*Small or intricate objects, elaborate moldings and ornamentation.*

** The smallest unit that can be drawn relates to the surveying practice of a drawing accuracy of 1⁄50" at map scale. This converts to approximately 1" at the scale of ¼"=1'-0" (a ratio scale of 1:48).*

ENGINEERING AND MAP SCALES

SCALE	RATIO	SMALLEST UNIT*	USE
1″=5,280′	1:62,500	104′	*USGS 15 minute maps.*
1″=2,000′	1:24,000	40′	*USGS 7.5 minute maps.*
1″=40′	1:480	0.8′	*Site maps.*
1″=20′	1:240	0.4′	*Very common scale for residential size site plans (at this scale a half-acre lot will fit comfortably on a legal size page in a deed book). Distances given in feet and hundredths.*
1″=16.66′	1:200	0.33′	*Site maps.*
1″=10′	1:120	0.2′	*Small site maps.*
1″=8.33′	1:100	0.166′	*Small site maps.*

* *The smallest unit that can be drawn relates to the surveying practice of a drawing accuracy of 1/50″ at map scale. This converts to approximately 5″ at the scale of 1″=20′ (a ratio scale of 1:240).*

Metric Scales

Metric scales are expressed in decimal ratios. Typical metric scales are very similar to English scales in the level of detail given. The metric scale commonly used for floor plans, 1:50, is only four percent smaller than the English scale of ¼″=1′-0″ (1:48). Since few historic structures in the United States were built using the metric system, HABS/HAER rarely uses metric measurements except as a convenience to users. The most common HABS/HAER use of the metric system is the inclusion of a metric graphic scale on measured drawings.

Before Drafting

All of the measured drawings in a set should be designed before the drafting begins. The composition of each measured drawing should be planned so that there is room for the drawing, the common information listed above, dimensions and annotations. While it is sometimes possible to place more than one drawing on an individual sheet, a

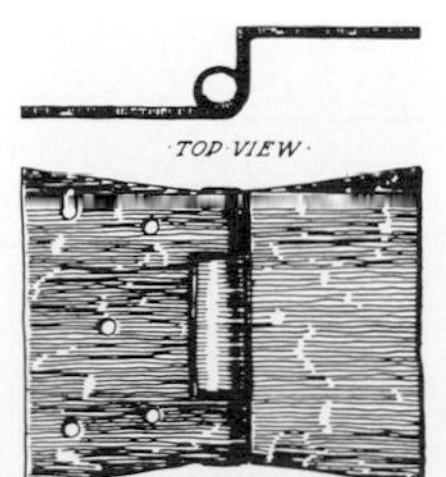

Figure 5.21

The documentation of Grant's Tomb presented problems of geometry (it is round), size (143' high), and access (scaffolding would have been prohibitively expensive). Stereophotogrammetry was an ideal choice. The open site, photographed after the leaves had fallen, allowed the necessary angles of view and the technique easily accommodated the size and shape of the monument. The perspective distortion apparent in the plate is corrected when the plates are plotted.

FIGURE 5.22

Because St. Mary's Seminary in Baltimore was threatened with imminent demolition, photogrammetry was the only practical means to record it, given the limited amount of time and money available. The circled and labeled targets are known and measured survey control points that allow other dimensions to be determined using a photogrammetric plotter. The survey control points also allow adjacent plates to be related precisely to each other by comparing points visible in both plates.

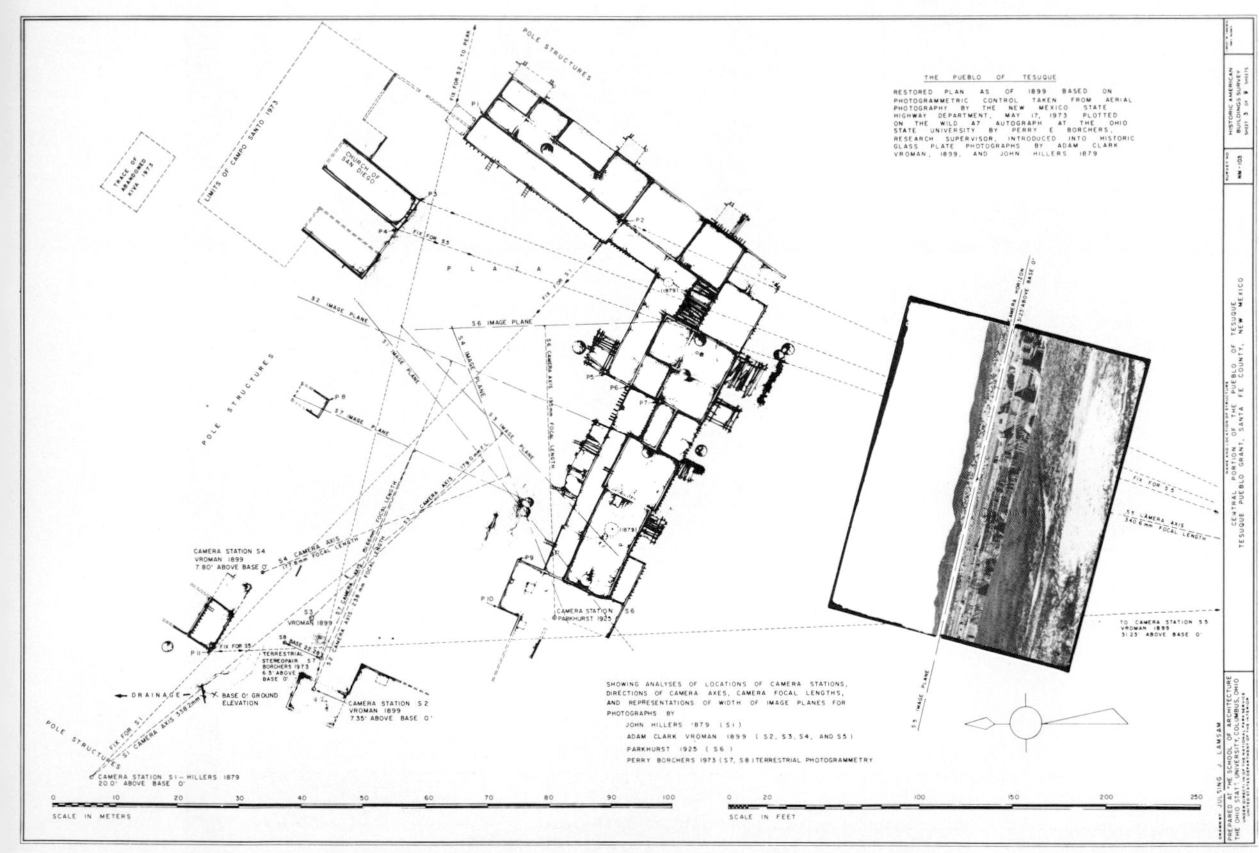

FIGURE 5.23

Using aerial photogrammetric glass plates from 1973, reverse perspective analysis was used to plot the camera stations, axes, and focal lengths for historic photographs of the Pueblo of Tesuque from 1879, 1899, and 1925. Using known dimensions from the 1973 photogrammetric studies, measured drawings could then be prepared for the three earlier views. This drawing shows the location of the earlier views superimposed on the 1973 plan of the site.

single drawing of a large structure or site may require several sheets. Do not mix sheet sizes in a single set of drawings. HABS/HAER achieves a unity of design throughout a set of measured drawings by establishing and following consistent drafting conventions regarding line weights, lettering, dimensions, annotations, materials indications, labels, north arrows, scales, and title blocks.

The final ink-on-Mylar HABS/HAER measured drawings are frequently tracings of preliminary drawings made from the field measurements. The consistency and accuracy of the set is worked out before the inking begins. The preliminary drawings are frequently done in pencil on Mylar. Pencil is used because it is easy to use and erase and is cheaper than ink. Mylar is preferred to tracing paper or vellum because of its dimensional stability. Paper and vellum change shape, particularly with changes in humidity, reducing the accuracy of a drawing and the final drawing that will be traced from it.

The preliminary measured drawings should be made on Mylar to ensure the highest level of accuracy. The drawings can be overlaid to reduce the amount of repetitive drafting and to check accuracy. The horizontal dimensions for an elevation or section drawing can be traced from a floor plan, for instance. The translucency of Mylar facilitates overlay drafting and checking.

HABS/HAER measured drawings should always be produced so that the drawing will remain legible when reproduced at a smaller size. At the Library of

Congress, the public sees page-size copies of HABS/HAER measured drawings, which fit in three-ring binders. The drawings reproduced in this book are significantly smaller than the original drawings. Extremely fine lines (smaller than 3x0 Rapidograph), small lettering (smaller than ⅛"), and closely spaced parallel lines are to be avoided if possible. Where necessary, they should be used with caution. When reproduced at a reduced scale, fine lines tend to fade out, small lettering becomes illegible, and closely spaced lines bleed together and read as a solid mass.

Title Sheet

The title sheet for the measured drawings component of the HABS/HAER documentation traditionally includes at least a site plan, statement of significance, and a project information statement (see fig. 5.25). In some cases, particularly when using the larger sheet size, there is enough room to include one of the measured drawings on the title sheet. The site plan includes enough of the surrounding area to establish the setting for the structure or object being recorded.

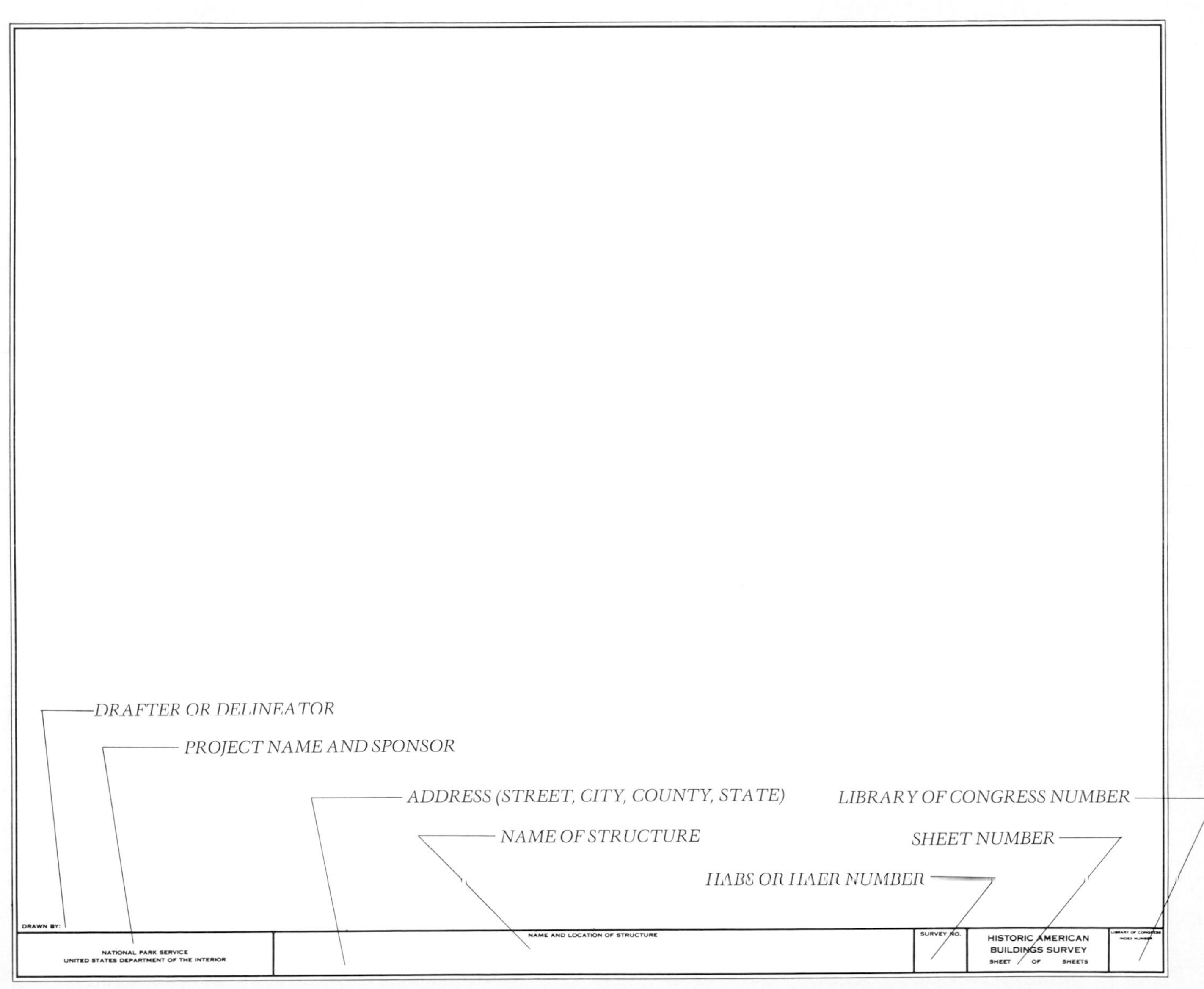

Figure 5.24

Common elements of identification in HABS/HAER measured drawings.

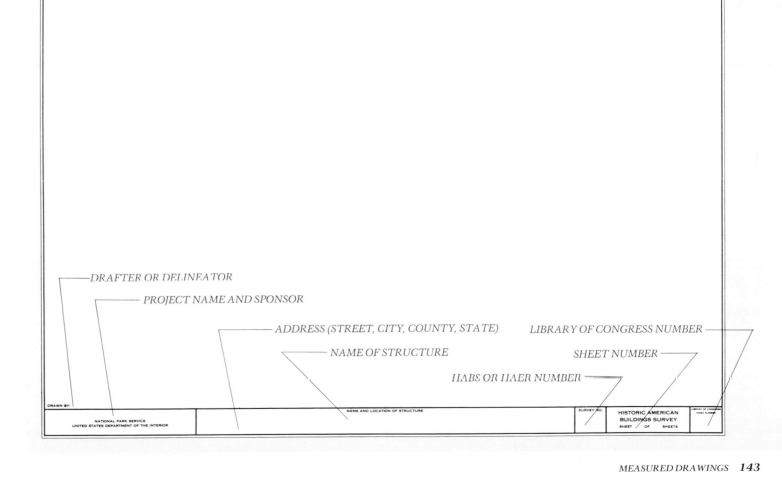

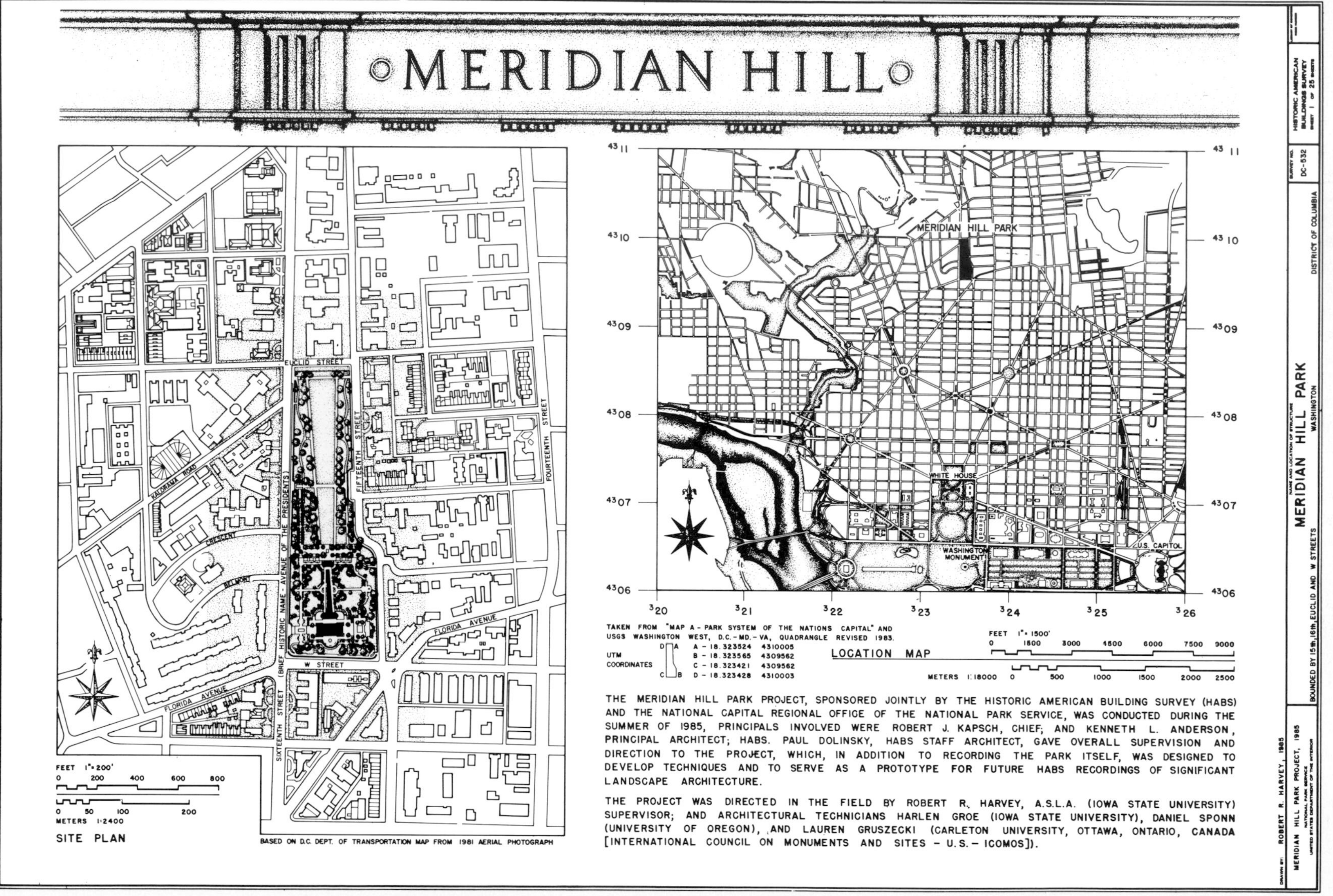

FIGURE 5.25

The title sheet for drawings of Meridian Hill Park in Washington, D.C., includes not only a United States Geological Survey location map but also a larger scale site plan for placing the park in a neighborhood context. The decorative detail across the top of the sheet is the frieze from the 16th Street fountain. All title sheets should include a brief statement of significance, as well as credits and acknowledgments.

There is no HABS/HAER requirement for specific site plan sources or scales because they are variable. Site maps frequently follow the civil engineering practice of measuring in feet and hundredths and drawing at engineering scales such as 1″=20′.

Site plans do not have to be measured by hand. The scale should be determined by the location, size, and significance of the site. Cities often have available detailed maps locating individual structures and lots. These can be copied, and the source, scale, and date cited (see fig. 5.23). HABS/HAER discourages photographically copying maps onto measured drawings because the resulting photographic image is not archivally stable.

For rural sites, maps should include enough of the surrounding area so that the structure can be reliably located. HABS/HAER typically copies United States Geological Survey (USGS) 7.5 minute maps as site maps. They are available for the entire country and are in a convenient scale (1″=2000′ or 1:24,000). If a USGS map is used, the Universal Transverse Mercator (UTM) coordinates for the site should be determined and the UTM grid marked with ticks along the neat lines (border) of the map (see fig. 5.27).

It may be possible to include the site immediately around a building as part of the first-floor plan. Sites with elaborate or significant grounds may warrant a site plan on a separate sheet or sheets, drawn at a scale large enough to illustrate the significant features of the site. Refer to the section on landscape documentation in chapter 6 for more detailed information.

The statement of significance, as in the written portion of the documentation, summarizes the significance of a site and often includes a brief interpretation. You should be able to determine from this statement, for instance, why a structure was judged significant enough to warrant measured drawings. The length of a statement of significance will vary. The significance of Mount Vernon, for example, can be simply and concisely stated. A coal mine, by contrast, may require several paragraphs to explain its features and operation.

The project information statement describes the history of a recording project. It includes the concept behind the documentation, the organizers and sponsors, persons and organizations completing the work, and the scope and limitations of the research. Academic as well as financial sponsors should be credited along with any cooperating agencies. Documentation is rarely a one-person effort and it is always appropriate to give credit where credit is due.

ATLANTIC BUILDING

CAST·IRON SIGN

3" = 1'·0" 1:4

FEET 3" = 1'·0" CENTIMETERS 1:4

920·930 F STREET NORTHWEST {COMMERCIAL BUILDINGS}

920, 922-24 AND 926 F STREET NORTHWEST ARE THREE SMALL-SCALE, BRICK COMMERCIAL STRUCTURES WHICH ILLUSTRATE THE TRADITIONAL BUILDING PATTERNS ASSOCIATED WITH THE LATE-19TH AND EARLY-20TH CENTURY COMMERCIAL DISTRICT. DESIGNED WITH RETAIL SPACES ON THE GROUND LEVEL AND OFFICES OR RESIDENTIAL SPACE ABOVE, THEY CONTINUE TO PRESENT THE MERCANTILE IMAGE OF A TURN-OF-THE-CENTURY DOWNTOWN. AS AN ENSEMBLE, THESE BUILDINGS HAVE BEEN RECOGNIZED AS INTEGRAL ELEMENTS OF THE HISTORIC F STREET STREETSCAPE AND ARE CITED BY THE D.C. HISTORIC PRESERVATION DIVISION AS CONTRIBUTING TO THE SIGNIFICANCE OF THE DOWNTOWN HISTORIC DISTRICT AND THE PENNSYLVANIA AVENUE NATIONAL HISTORIC SITE.

THE SCHWARTZ BUILDING, AT 920 F STREET NORTHWEST, WAS DESIGNED IN 1911 BY SAMUEL R. TURNER FOR BENJAMIN SCHWARTZ. FOUR STORIES TALL, THIS BRICK BUILDING FEATURES A THREE-STORY OCTAGONAL ORIEL AND A CAST-IRON DENTILLED CORNICE. THE BUILDING HOUSED SCHWARTZ'S TAILOR SHOP ON THE GROUND FLOOR AND VARIOUS INDEPENDENT OFFICES ON THE UPPER FLOORS UNTIL THE 1920S WHEN IT RECEIVED MAJOR ALTERATIONS TO ACCOMMODATE ITS CONVERSION TO HOTEL USE.

DATING TO THE 1870S, 922-24 F STREET NORTHWEST IS THE OLDEST OF THE THREE SMALL STRUCTURES. THIS BUILDING FEATURES A PRESSED BRICK FRONT AND CAST-IRON CORNICE BELOW THE MANSARD ROOF OF THE ATTIC STORY, CHARACTERISTIC OF THE SECOND EMPIRE STYLE POPULAR IN WASHINGTON AT THAT TIME. DESIGNED FOR COMMERCIAL USE ON THE GROUND FLOOR, THE BUILDING WAS OCCUPIED BY THE EVANS DINING ROOM FROM 1879 TO 1897, FOLLOWED BY THE EVANS DRUG STORE FROM 1901 TO 1910. IN 1912, THE SINGLE RETAIL SPACE AT STREET LEVEL WAS ALTERED TO ACCOMMODATE TWO SEPARATE STORES.

926 F STREET NORTHWEST WAS DESIGNED IN 1891 BY NOTED LOCAL ARCHITECT LEON DESSEZ AS OFFICES FOR THE PROMINENT LAW FIRM OF WOLF AND COHEN. THREE STORIES TALL, THIS BRICK BUILDING FEATURES DECORATIVE BRICK LINTELS AND A CORBELLED BRICK CORNICE. IN 1909, SALVATORE DESIO, A JEWELER, RELOCATED TO THE BUILDING AND CONTRACTED ARCHITECTS HUNTER AND BELL TO REMODEL THE STRUCTURE, INCLUDING LOWERING THE FIRST LEVEL AND ADDING AN ELABORATE STOREFRONT, SINCE REMOVED.

THE ATLANTIC BUILDING, AT 928-30 F STREET NORTHWEST, WAS DESIGNED IN 1887 BY PROMINENT WASHINGTON ARCHITECT JAMES GREEN HILL FOR THE ATLANTIC BUILDING COMPANY. HILL HAD SERVED AS SUPERVISORY ARCHITECT OF THE U.S. TREASURY AND WAS THE DESIGNER, AS WELL, OF NUMEROUS FINE PRIVATE BUILDINGS IN THE NATION'S CAPITAL. THE ATLANTIC BUILDING COMPANY WAS A SYNDICATE OF LOCAL INVESTORS, AND THE BUILDING IS NOTABLE AS ONE OF THE EARLIEST LARGE-SCALE COMMERCIAL DEVELOPMENTS IN WASHINGTON TO BE FINANCED BY LOCAL MONEY.

DESCRIBED IN THE CONTEMPORARY PRESS AS "ONE OF THE MOST MAGNIFICENT OFFICE STRUCTURES ON THE CONTINENT" AND AS "PRONOUNCED BY GOOD JUDGES AS IN MANY RESPECTS THE FINEST OFFICE BUILDING IN THE WORLD," THE ATLANTIC BUILDING REMAINS ONE OF THE FINEST EXAMPLES OF THE ROMANESQUE REVIVAL STYLE IN THE DISTRICT. ITS SKILLFULLY COMPOSED FACADE IS CONSTRUCTED OF BRICK AND BROWNSTONE WITH TERRA COTTA ORNAMENT, AND IRON AT THE FIRST FLOOR.

EIGHT STORIES TALL WITH AN ATTIC, THE ATLANTIC BUILDING WAS ONE OF THE LAST BUILDINGS OF ITS SIZE TO BE CONSTRUCTED OF LOAD-BEARING MASONRY WALLS IN WASHINGTON. THESE BRICK BEARING WALLS, WHICH INCLUDE ALL INTERIOR PARTITIONS, RANGE IN THICKNESS FROM 39" AT THE FOUNDATIONS TO 13" AT THE EIGHTH FLOOR. FLOOR STRUCTURE THROUGHOUT THE BUILDING CONSISTS OF WOOD FRAMING, EXCEPT FOR LIMITED AREAS OF THE FIRST AND SECOND FLOORS WHERE BRICK VAULTS RESTING ON IRON BEAMS WERE USED IN AN ATTEMPT TO PROVIDE FIREPROOFING AND SECURITY. ELSEWHERE, THE USE OF IRON FRAMING IS LIMITED TO SUPPORTING THE FACADE, THE ROOF, AND THE BRICK PARTITION WALLS ABOVE THE STORES AND THE REAR ROOM ON THE FIRST FLOOR.

ONE OF THE FIRST HIGH-RISE OFFICE BUILDINGS IN WASHINGTON, THIS SPECULATIVE STRUCTURE FEATURES TWO PASSENGER ELEVATORS PAIRED WITH A SUBSTANTIAL WOODEN STAIRCASE WRAPPED AROUND A SKYLIT STAIRWELL, AND COMMODIOUS OFFICE SPACES ON ALL EIGHT FLOORS. THE PLAN OF A TYPICAL FLOOR OF THE ATLANTIC BUILDING CONSISTS OF A DOUBLE-LOADED CORRIDOR, WITH ALL OFFICES CONNECTED INTERNALLY AS WELL AS TO THE CORRIDOR, TO FACILITATE SUITE ARRANGEMENTS. LIGHT WELLS, BOTH EXTERNAL AND INTERNAL, ARE USED TO PROVIDE LIGHT TO OFFICES ON THE LOWER FLOORS. THE PLAN WAS MODIFIED ON THE EIGHTH FLOOR TO PROVIDE TWO LARGE ASSEMBLY ROOMS. THESE ROOMS HAVE BEEN NOTED AS THE LOCATION OF NUMEROUS IMPORTANT PUBLIC MEETINGS, INCLUDING ONE AT WHICH THE NATIONAL ZOOLOGICAL PARK WAS FOUNDED. THE ATTIC CONSISTS OF AN APARTMENT FOR THE BUILDING'S CARETAKER.

THE ATLANTIC BUILDING IS LISTED INDIVIDUALLY ON THE NATIONAL REGISTER OF HISTORIC PLACES AND IS A PROMINENT MEMBER OF THE DOWNTOWN HISTORIC DISTRICT AND THE PENNSYLVANIA AVENUE NATIONAL HISTORIC SITE.

THIS DOCUMENTATION WAS PRODUCED UNDER A COOPERATIVE AGREEMENT BETWEEN THE HISTORIC AMERICAN BUILDINGS SURVEY / HISTORIC AMERICAN ENGINEERING RECORD OF THE NATIONAL PARK SERVICE, ROBERT J. KAPSCH, CHIEF, AND CLOVER F STREET ASSOCIATES, L.P., EDWARD L. DANIELS, PRESIDENT. THE MEASURED DRAWINGS WERE EXECUTED UNDER THE DIRECTION OF HABS/HAER ARCHITECT JOHN A. BURNS, A.I.A., BY SUPERVISORY ARCHITECT MARK SCHARA, GRADUATE OF THE UNIVERSITY OF VIRGINIA; DRAFTING FOREMAN CHRISTINE B. VINA, GRADUATE OF TEXAS TECH UNIVERSITY; AND ARCHITECTURE TECHNICIANS MARY ELLEN DIDION, GRADUATE OF THE CATHOLIC UNIVERSITY OF AMERICA, THOMAS P. FORDE, JR., VIRGINIA POLYTECHNIC INSTITUTE AND STATE UNIVERSITY, AND DORIS MICHAELA GROSSING, TECHNICAL UNIVERSITY OF VIENNA (ICOMOS/AUSTRIA). THE RECORDING WAS ASSISTED BY ARCHITECTURAL AND HISTORICAL DATA MADE AVAILABLE BY PATRICK BURKHART, A.I.A., OF SHALOM BARANES ASSOCIATES ARCHITECTS AND EMILY EIG OF TRACERIES. THE LARGE FORMAT PHOTOGRAPHS WERE TAKEN BY HABS PHOTOGRAPHER JACK E. BOUCHER.

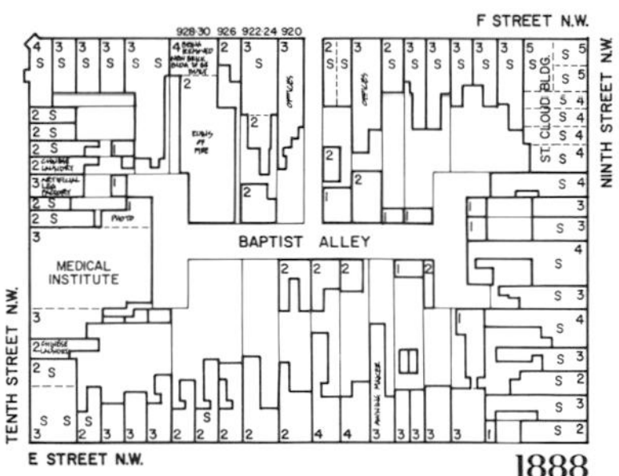

1888

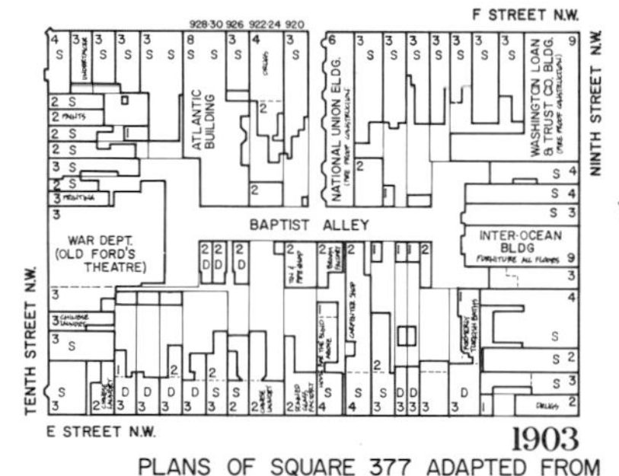

1903

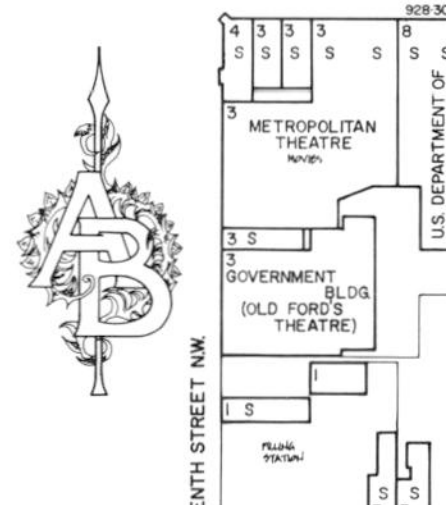

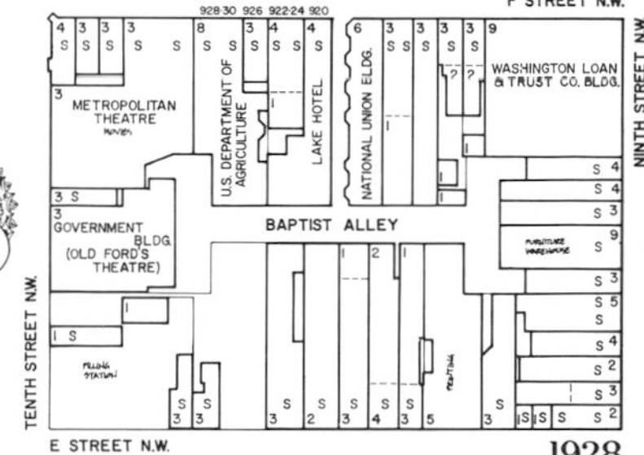

1928

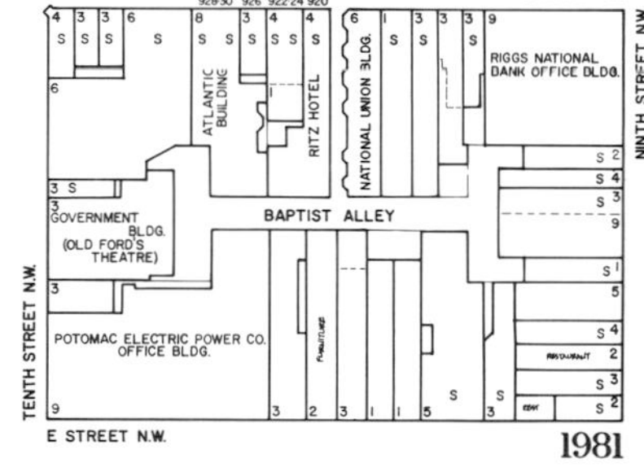

1981

PLANS OF SQUARE 377 ADAPTED FROM INSURANCE MAPS BY THE SANBORN MAP COMPANY

NUMBERS INDICATE NUMBER OF STORIES "S" DESIGNATES STORE "D" DESIGNATES DWELLING NO SCALE

DRAWN BY: MARY ELLEN DIDION / MARK SCHARA

920-930 F STREET NORTHWEST PROJECT, 1988

NATIONAL PARK SERVICE · UNITED STATES DEPARTMENT OF THE INTERIOR

920·930 F STREET NORTHWEST (COMMERCIAL BUILDINGS)

WASHINGTON · DISTRICT OF COLUMBIA

SURVEY NO. DC 569

HISTORIC AMERICAN BUILDINGS SURVEY SHEET 1 OF 26 SHEETS

Plans

Plans are an essential element of measured drawings. They cannot be documented adequately in photographs. Plan drawings are horizontal cuts through a structure that portray the arrangement and progression of spaces so that an observer can perceive what is being recorded. Plans are cut at a consistent height; the convention is to cut through openings such as doors, windows, and fireboxes. Plans should be projected views; that is, where "horizontal" surfaces are inclined or curve, as in the deck of a ship, they should be projected into a horizontal plane.

Plans are arranged in a logical progression. HABS/HAER orders them from the bottom up (the lowest level comes first, the highest level last) except with ships, where the order is reversed. Ideally, all plans should be drawn at the same scale so that the relationship between levels is constant. Where similar floor plans are repeated many times, as in tall buildings or row houses, typical floor plans can be drawn and annotated to note small differences among plans. Plans of attics and basements (often thought not worth recording or drawn at a smaller scale) can record valuable information about structural and mechanical systems. Moreover, attics and basements are traditionally unfinished spaces, allowing access to measure and record them.

Building plans are recorded from foundation to roof, although most sets of floor plans include only basement to top floor. Since foundations are rarely accessible, when information on footings and foundations is available, consideration should be given to recording that information (see fig. 6.12). It is the lack of information, not the lack of importance, that precludes the recording of most foundations. The foundations of engineering and industrial structures can be highly significant. Large machines may require special footings to isolate the surrounding structure from vibrations. Bearing points for bridges must accommodate the lateral movement of expansion and contraction in bridge structure (see fig. 5.28).

Basements are paradoxical. While they are usually the most abused and changed spaces in a structure, they often contain a great deal of information about the structural and mechanical systems of a building (see fig. 6.15). They are rarely finished as elaborately as the rest of a building and may be damp and dirty and difficult to measure. They are nevertheless worth documenting, especially if they reveal important information about a structure. There can be analogous spaces in industrial structures and aboard ships.

First-floor plans can fulfill several documentation needs. The first floor is frequently the most important floor in a structure (see fig. 5.29). It is sometimes the only floor plan documented with a measured drawing. Additionally, site plan information can be added to a first-floor plan to explain the relationship between interior and exterior spaces.

Upper floors are documented with measured drawings when they are significant enough to justify the effort. In houses, the second floor is where the private rooms are located. In commercial buildings, the upper floors are often given over to office space that may be completely different in character from first-floor commercial space. In both instances, the differences are significant enough to justify additional measured drawings. Repetitive plans may be recorded in a single drawing of

Figure 5.26

Urban sites with easily located street addresses have less need than others for a detailed map of the surrounding area. In this instance, four historic maps were used to illustrate the development of a block over time.

a typical floor, annotated to explain the differences between floors (see fig. 5.30).

Attic plans are similar to basement plans in that they can reveal a great deal of information about a structure (see fig. 5.31). Like basements, they can be uncomfortable to work in. Common drawbacks are low headroom, protruding nails, dirt, poor lighting, and the possibility of bird and insect infestations. Moreover, often they are also cold in the winter and hot in the summer. Discomforts notwithstanding, attics are worth documenting if they provide useful information.

Roof plans provide information about the arrangement and massing of a structure, particularly for large buildings and complexes. They can be included, albeit at a small scale, on the site plan. Roofs can, of course, be difficult and dangerous to measure.

Elevations

Elevation drawings show facades, room elevations, and other vertical elements of a structure projected into a vertical plane. Elevations show structures as we see them, upright and facing straight ahead (but without perspective). Buildings look like their elevation drawings more than any other measured drawing. The illusion of depth is provided by varying line weights, not by diminishing size as in a perspective drawing (see figs. 1.1, 1.14, 1.15, 5.7, and 6.20).

For buildings, the front facade is the most commonly drawn because it is usually the most important. Rear facades are usually secondary, as are side facades. Location is an important determinant. The land and river facades of a plantation house are both important, as would be the front and side facades of a commercial building on a corner. Secondary facades may be adequately recorded with large-format photography. In such instances, dimensional information could be obtained from plans and section drawings.

Industrial buildings that have facades of little significance in relation to their interiors can also have their facades adequately recorded with large-format photography. Technological objects are recorded with elevation drawings similar to building elevations. A machine may need four elevation drawings to reveal its complexities, while a ship may need only a starboard profile.

Sections

Section drawings are vertical cuts through a structure that show the vertical arrangement of spaces and objects (see fig. 5.32). What you see in a section drawing of a building is a series of room elevations in accurate relation to one another but separated by walls, floors, and ceilings. They are cut in one plane but may jog horizontally from floor to floor to reveal different information. The locations of section cuts are indicated on each floor plan so that they can be related. Section drawings are useful because they provide vertical information: floor-to-floor heights, ceiling heights, roof height, and the vertical progression of spaces. They are also valuable for structural details, interior decorative finishes, and the relation of functions.

Sections are similar to floor plans, except that they are cut perpendicular to the floor. Instead of the floor, the visible surface beyond the horizontal cut line of a plan, room elevations are the visible surfaces beyond the vertical cut line of a section.

Figure 5.27

Title sheets for rural structures often need several maps at different scales to locate the site in relation to adjacent properties, nearby towns, or major landscape features.

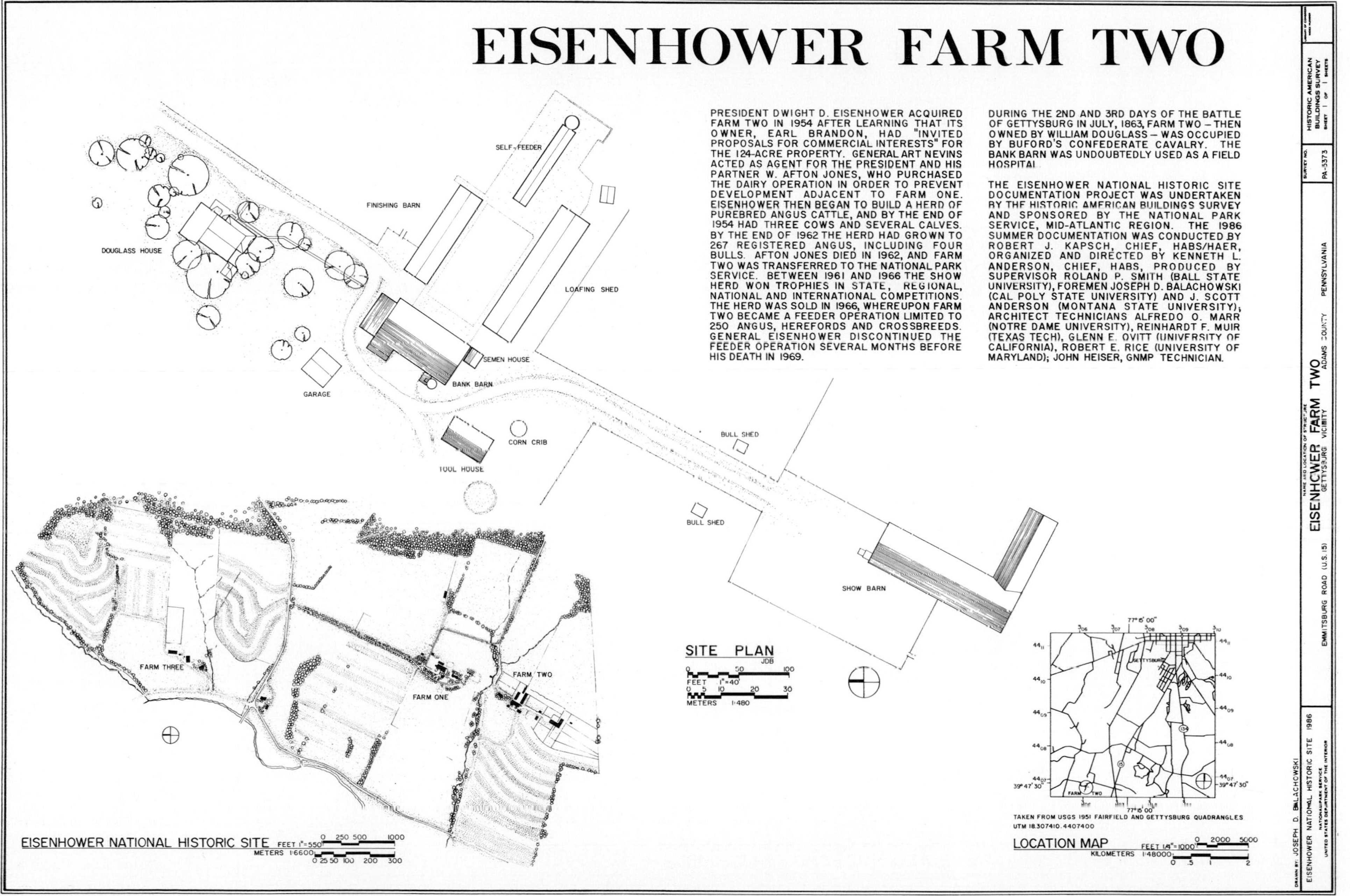

EISENHOWER FARM TWO
PRESIDENT DWIGHT D. EISENHOWER ACQUIRED FARM TWO IN 1954 AFTER LEARNING THAT ITS OWNER, EARL BRANDON, HAD "INVITED PROPOSALS FOR COMMERCIAL INTERESTS" FOR THE 124-ACRE PROPERTY. GENERAL ART NEVINS ACTED AS AGENT FOR THE PRESIDENT AND HIS PARTNER W. AFTON JONES, WHO PURCHASED THE DAIRY OPERATION IN ORDER TO PREVENT DEVELOPMENT ADJACENT TO FARM ONE. EISENHOWER THEN BEGAN TO BUILD A HERD OF PUREBRED ANGUS CATTLE, AND BY THE END OF 1954 HAD THREE COWS AND SEVERAL CALVES. BY THE END OF 1962 THE HERD HAD GROWN TO 267 REGISTERED ANGUS, INCLUDING FOUR BULLS. AFTON JONES DIED IN 1962, AND FARM TWO WAS TRANSFERRED TO THE NATIONAL PARK SERVICE. BETWEEN 1961 AND 1966 THE SHOW HERD WON TROPHIES IN STATE, REGIONAL, NATIONAL AND INTERNATIONAL COMPETITIONS. THE HERD WAS SOLD IN 1966, WHEREUPON FARM TWO BECAME A FEEDER OPERATION LIMITED TO 250 ANGUS, HEREFORDS AND CROSSBREEDS. GENERAL EISENHOWER DISCONTINUED THE FEEDER OPERATION SEVERAL MONTHS BEFORE HIS DEATH IN 1969.
DURING THE 2ND AND 3RD DAYS OF THE BATTLE OF GETTYSBURG IN JULY, 1863, FARM TWO – THEN OWNED BY WILLIAM DOUGLASS – WAS OCCUPIED BY BUFORD'S CONFEDERATE CAVALRY. THE BANK BARN WAS UNDOUBTEDLY USED AS A FIELD HOSPITAL.
THE EISENHOWER NATIONAL HISTORIC SITE DOCUMENTATION PROJECT WAS UNDERTAKEN BY THE HISTORIC AMERICAN BUILDINGS SURVEY AND SPONSORED BY THE NATIONAL PARK SERVICE, MID-ATLANTIC REGION. THE 1986 SUMMER DOCUMENTATION WAS CONDUCTED BY ROBERT J. KAPSCH, CHIEF, HABS/HAER, ORGANIZED AND DIRECTED BY KENNETH L. ANDERSON, CHIEF, HABS, PRODUCED BY SUPERVISOR ROLAND P. SMITH (BALL STATE UNIVERSITY), FOREMEN JOSEPH D. BALACHOWSKI (CAL POLY STATE UNIVERSITY) AND J. SCOTT ANDERSON (MONTANA STATE UNIVERSITY); ARCHITECT TECHNICIANS ALFREDO O. MARR (NOTRE DAME UNIVERSITY), REINHARDT F. MUIR (TEXAS TECH), GLENN E. OVITT (UNIVERSITY OF CALIFORNIA), ROBERT E. RICE (UNIVERSITY OF MARYLAND); JOHN HEISER, GNMP TECHNICIAN.
SELF-FEEDER
FINISHING BARN
DOUGLASS HOUSE
LOAFING SHED
SEMEN HOUSE
BANK BARN
GARAGE
CORN CRIB
TOOL HOUSE
BULL SHED
BULL SHED
SHOW BARN
SITE PLAN
JDB
FEET 1"=40'
METERS 1:480
FARM THREE
FARM ONE
FARM TWO
EISENHOWER NATIONAL HISTORIC SITE
FEET 1"=550'
METERS 1:6600
GETTYSBURG
TAKEN FROM USGS 1951 FAIRFIELD AND GETTYSBURG QUADRANGLES
UTM 18.307410.4407400
LOCATION MAP
FEET 1/4"=1000'
KILOMETERS 1:48000
DRAWN BY: JOSEPH D. BALACHOWSKI
EISENHOWER NATIONAL HISTORIC SITE 1986
NATIONAL PARK SERVICE
UNITED STATES DEPARTMENT OF THE INTERIOR
NAME AND LOCATION OF STRUCTURE
EISENHOWER FARM TWO
EMMITSBURG ROAD (U.S. 15)
GETTYSBURG VICINITY
ADAMS COUNTY
PENNSYLVANIA
SURVEY NO.
PA-5373
HISTORIC AMERICAN BUILDINGS SURVEY
SHEET 1 OF 1 SHEETS

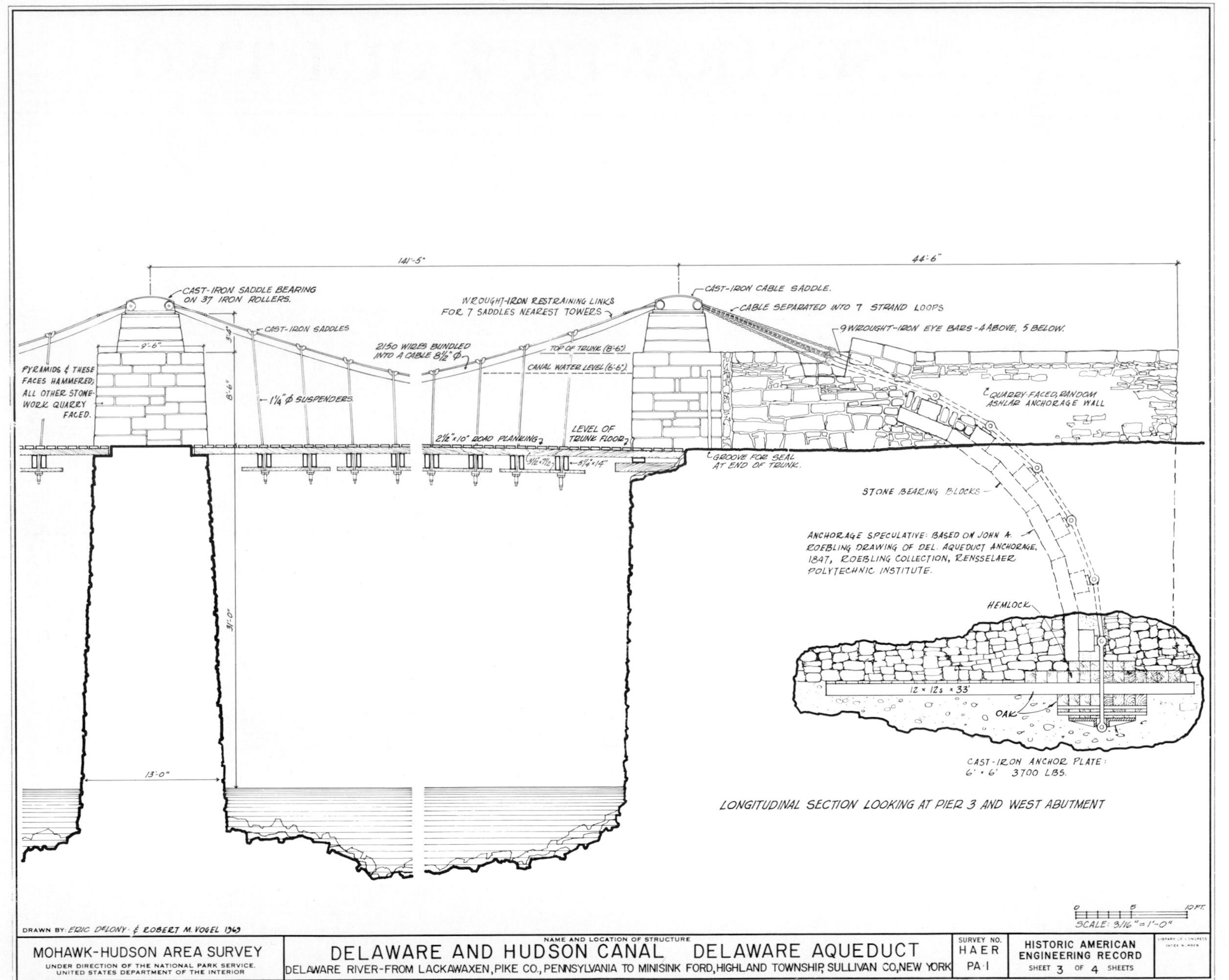

FIGURE 5.28

In this section of the Delaware and Hudson Canal Delaware Aqueduct, the site measurements were complemented with information taken from an 1847 drawing by John A. Roebling, designer of the aqueduct. Note the citation for the drawing of the anchorage with the comment that the information is speculative. The information contained on the drawing obviously cannot be confirmed. While it is likely that the anchorage was constructed as drawn, that conclusion can be assessed by the user of the documentation (see fig. 1.8).

Large-scale Details

Large-scale detail drawings explain how objects fit or work together. A door or window detail may include a plan; interior and exterior elevations; and jamb, lintel, and sill sections (see fig. 5.33). A detail of a power supply system in a mill will show how power is transferred through a series of shafts, pulleys, and belts to individual machines (see fig. 5.34). Exploded-view drawings allow a drafter to pull apart an object to

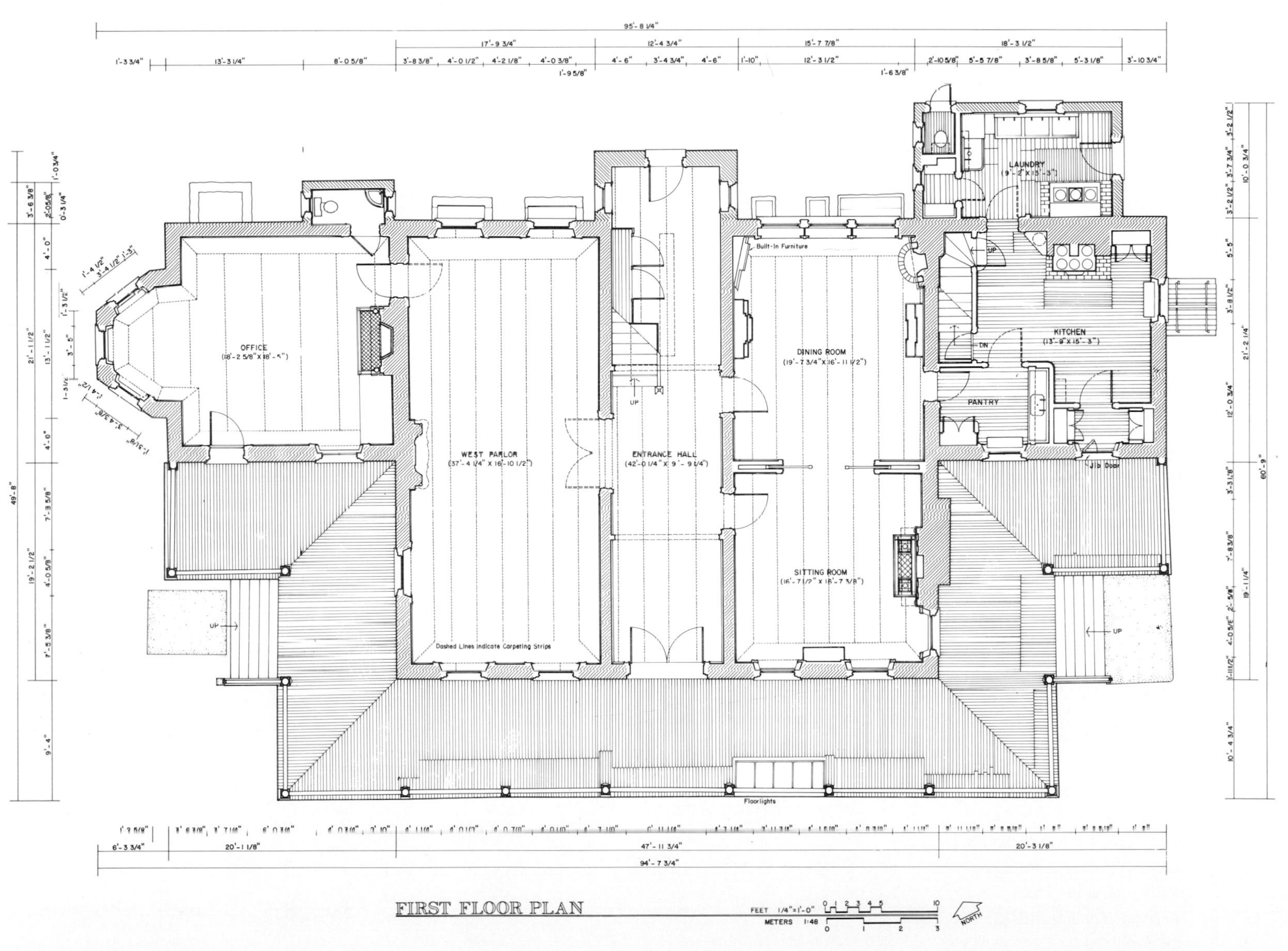

FIGURE 5.29

The plans of this elaborate late nineteenth-century house were recorded in detail, down to the porch floorboards and seams in the strip carpeting. A potential disadvantage of showing this much detail on a floor plan is that it can make the drawing harder to read. The graphic density of the closely spaced floorboards tends to draw the viewer's eye away from the carpeted major rooms. Also, the contrast between the flooring in the kitchen and the carpeting in the other rooms visually disguises the original symmetrical shape of the house.

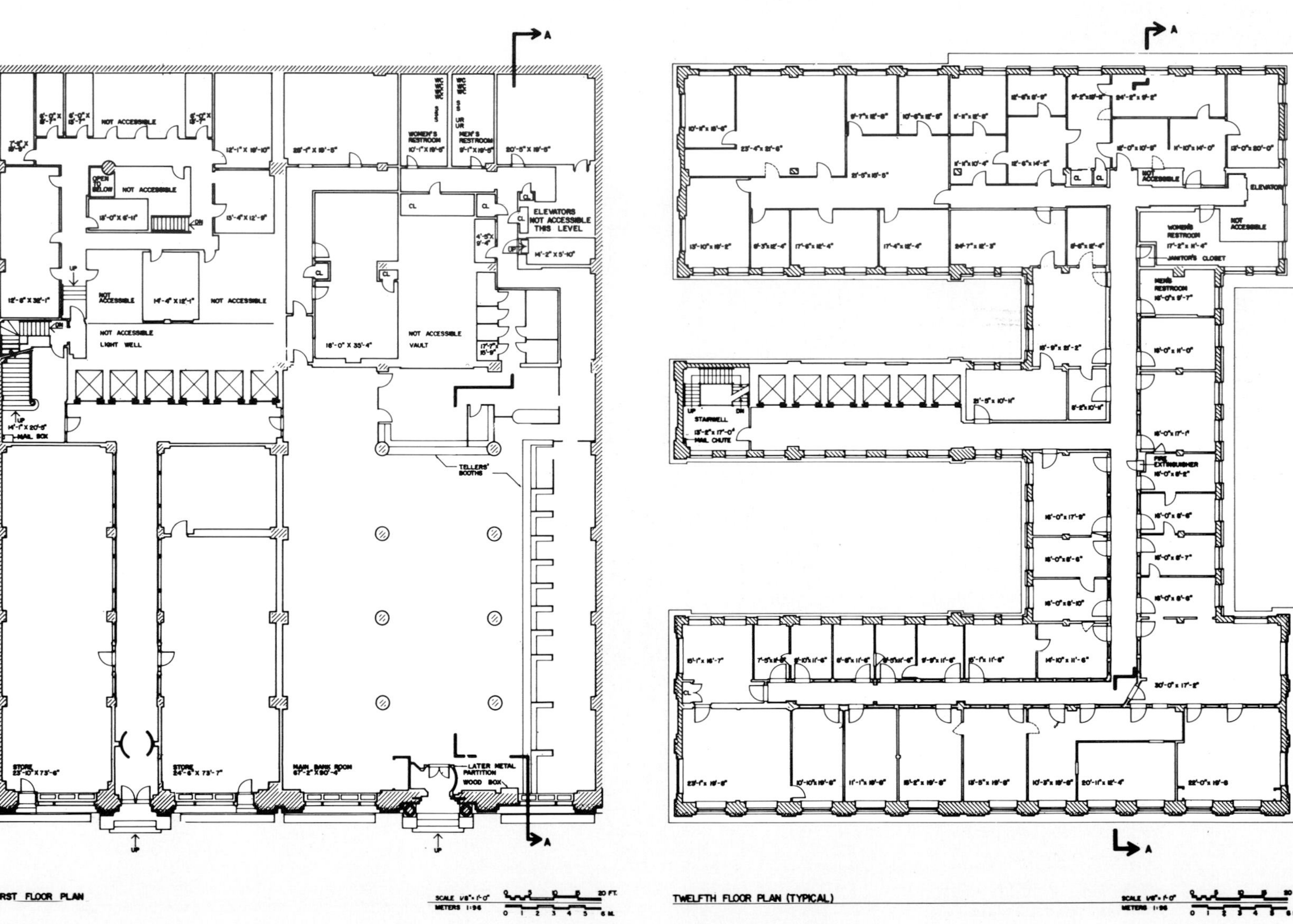

Figure 5.30

Tall buildings like the Munsey Building in Washington, D.C., commonly have a large number of identical or nearly identical floors. It is duplicative to record each floor individually; instead, a typical floor is recorded, then annotated to indicate the features that vary from floor to floor. Note how the upper floors differ from the first-floor plan, which covers the entire site. The upper floors, devoted to office space, were not hemmed in by adjacent buildings and needed lightwells to be marketable. The Munsey Building plan is typical of office buildings of its period, when offices depended on natural light and air circulation.

show how its component parts fit together. Often an exploded view is the only way to explain the intricacies of a heavy-timber framing joint or a pin connection in a bridge truss (see fig. 5.35). Large-scale drawings are appropriate for depicting complex objects, such as machines, that cannot be delineated adequately at a small scale (see fig. 5.36). The tools used in an industrial process are an important component of the work (see fig. 5.37). Remember, however, that it is difficult to portray the motion inherent in machinery operations in a two-dimensional drawing. Other objects such as mantels and newels can be recorded adequately with a large-format photograph using a scale stick in the field of view (see fig. 5.38).

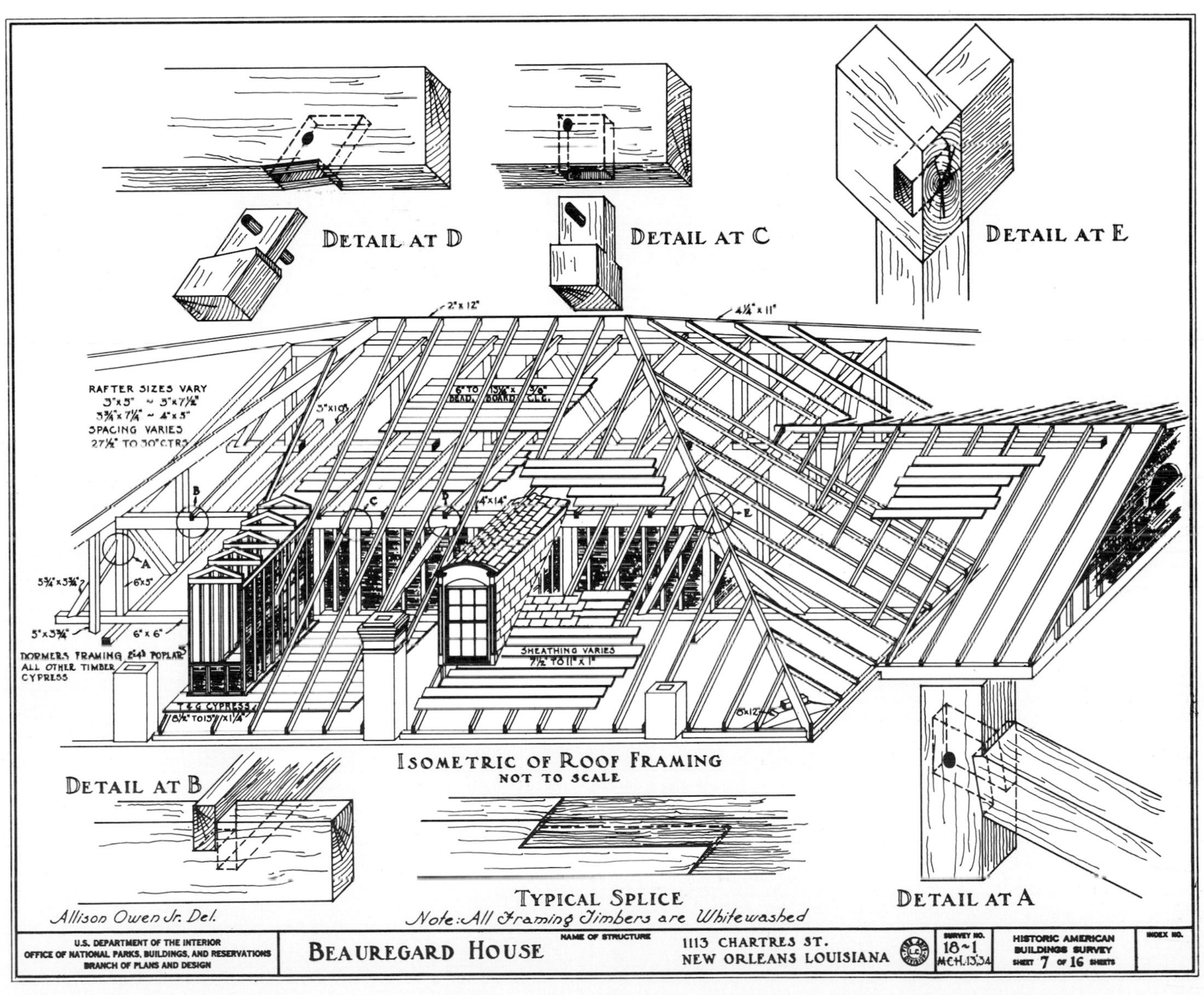

FIGURE 5.31

This drawing shows how the attic space of the Beauregard House in New Orleans was utilized and how the structure was arranged to carry the roof load. Joint and splice details show the representative construction technology of the period, and the roof and dormer cut-aways show typical construction practices.

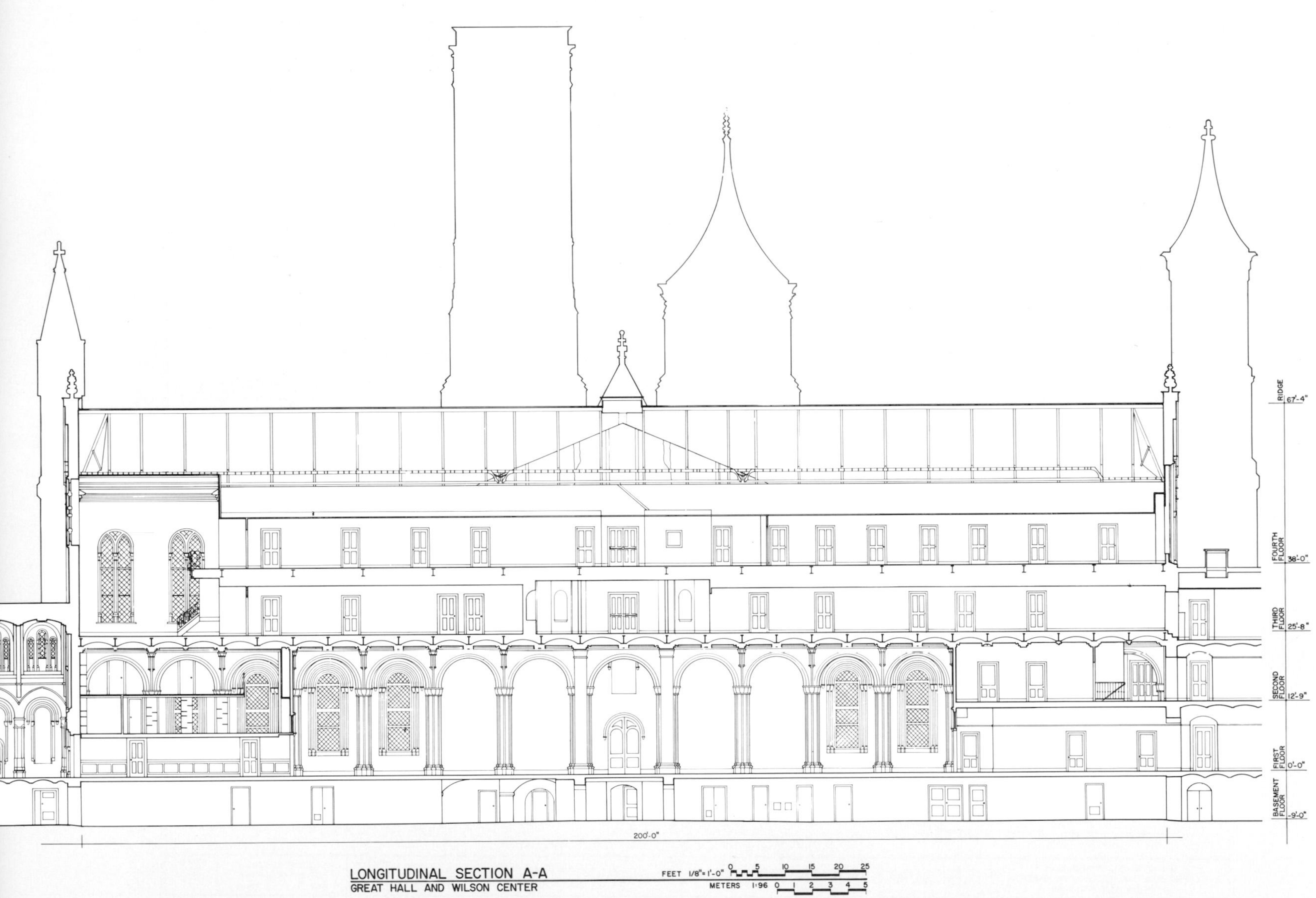

Figure 5.32

This drawing gives the 1984 appearance of the central portion of the original Smithsonian Institution Building. At the same time, it shows where additions have been made. The interior originally had two floors, with one large space, the Great Hall, on the first floor and three rooms on the second floor. The left three bays have had two intermediate floors added to house the papers of the first secretary of the Smithsonian, Joseph Henry. The right three bays had one floor added to provide office space. The original height of the second floor is visible in the left two bays. If you follow the cornice line across the drawing, you can see where the returns define the original room sizes. Masonry groin vaults support the first floor. The original second floor, now called the third floor, is supported on iron beams with brick barrel vaults.

Interpretive Drawings

Interpretive drawings can be produced in various ways. One way is to annotate a documentary drawing in order to explain information that may not be apparent from the delineation, as for the air circulation system of a theater superimposed on a section drawing. Research on a mill building uncovered few written records, so the most efficient way to explain the evolution of the site was through the use of Sanborn and other historical maps to produce a drawing that portrayed the chronological development of the mill (see fig. 5.39). In another example, the design evolution of an architecturally significant house was interpreted in a drawing that reproduced several historic drawings along with copies of the HABS measured drawings of the plan and elevation (see fig. 5.40).

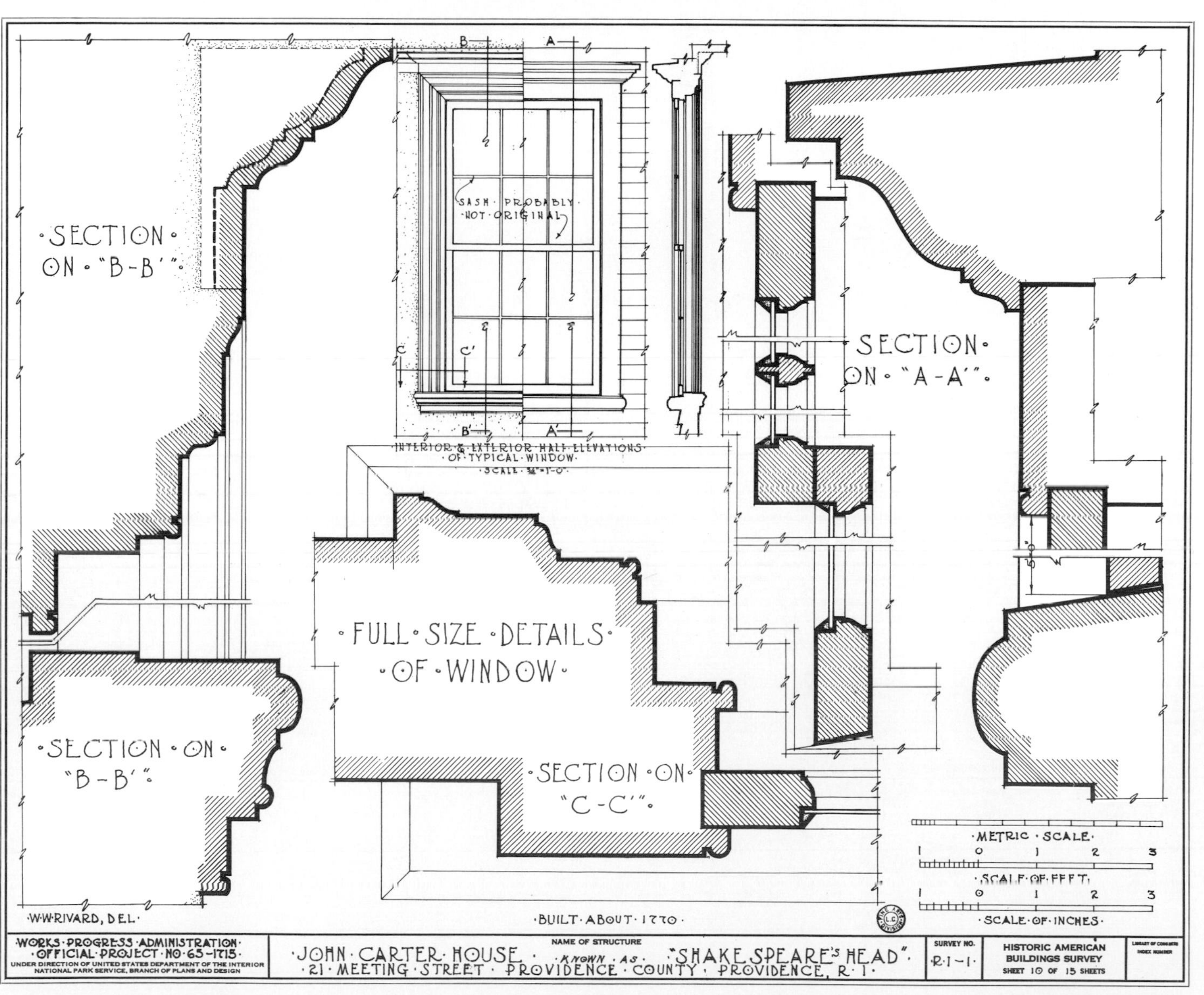

FIGURE 5.33

In these window details, exterior and interior sills and heads and jamb and sash details are drawn full size, with an exterior/interior elevation drawing of the window indicating the location of each detail.

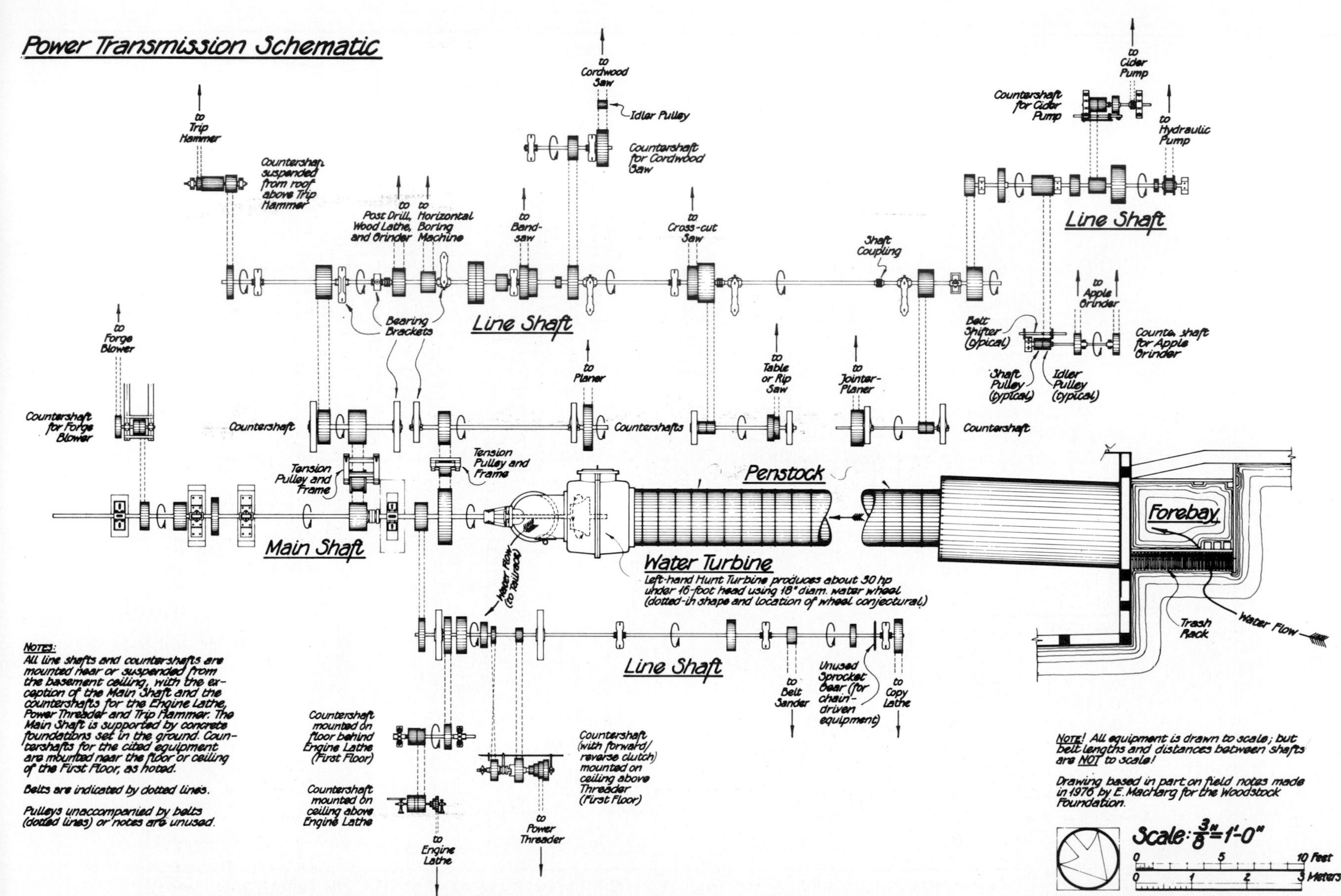

FIGURE 5.34

The transmission of power in mills used to be accomplished by a series of shafts and pulleys and belts. The main drive shaft was designed to operate at a constant speed. Individual line shaft speeds could be varied from the main shaft speed by using different sized pulleys. Machine speeds could be further controlled by changing their pulley sizes. The original power source was a water wheel. Some mills later converted to water turbines or steam engines to drive the shafts. Ultimately, the introduction of electric-motor-driven machinery eliminated the need for this type of power transmission.

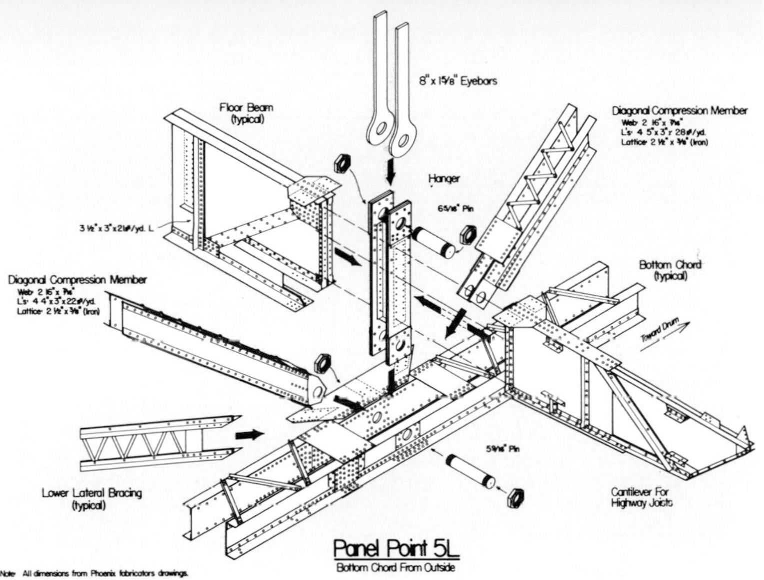

***Figure* 5.35**

The only way to adequately document a pin connection in a truss is to graphically explode the joint, pulling the members apart so that each component can be drawn and the fit of the assembly explained. This panel point actually has two pin connections, allowing the floor beams and deck some movement independent of the primary truss. Note that the dimensions were taken from fabrication drawings for the bridge.

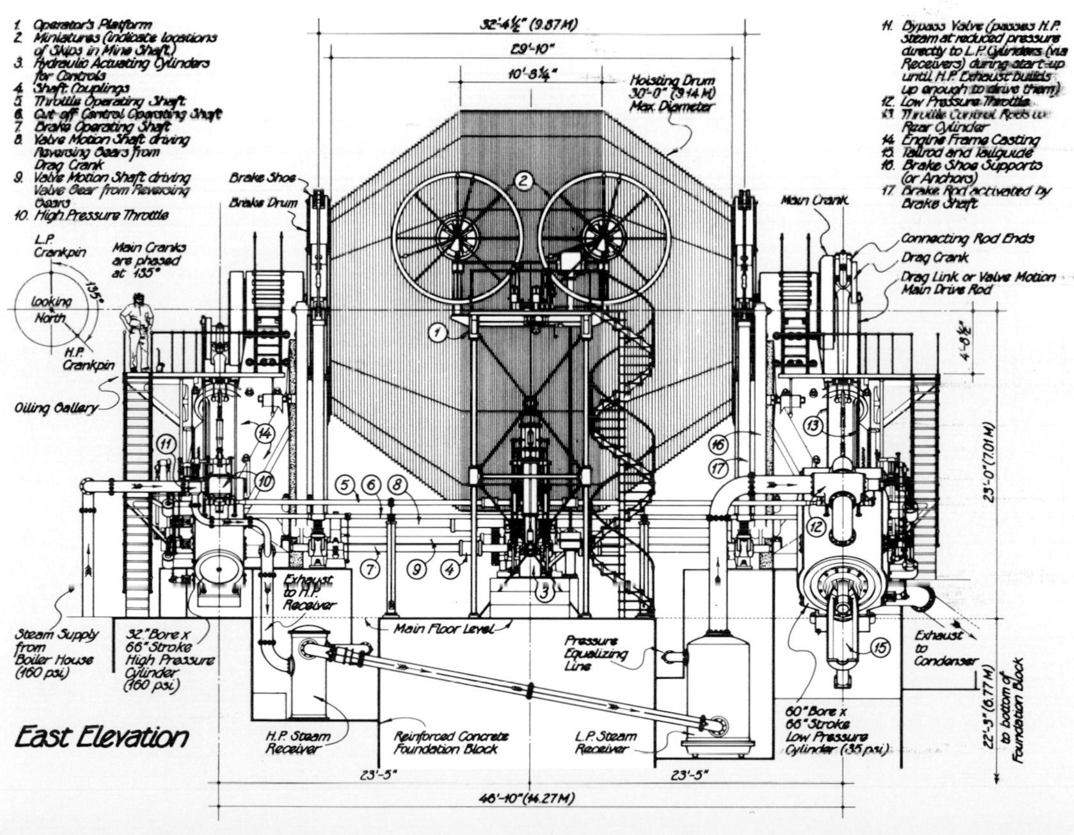

***Figure* 5.36**

The steam-powered cross-compound condensing hoist with a cylindro-conical drum for the no. 2 shaft of the Quincy copper mine in Hancock, Michigan, was manufactured by the Nordberg Manufacturing Company. It was placed in operation in 1920. The hoist was the largest in the world at the deepest mine in the Western Hemisphere. The drawing shows a longitudinal elevation with the individual parts labeled and major dimensions given. The drawing was based on original drawings, field checked by HAER, and shows the hoist in original condition.

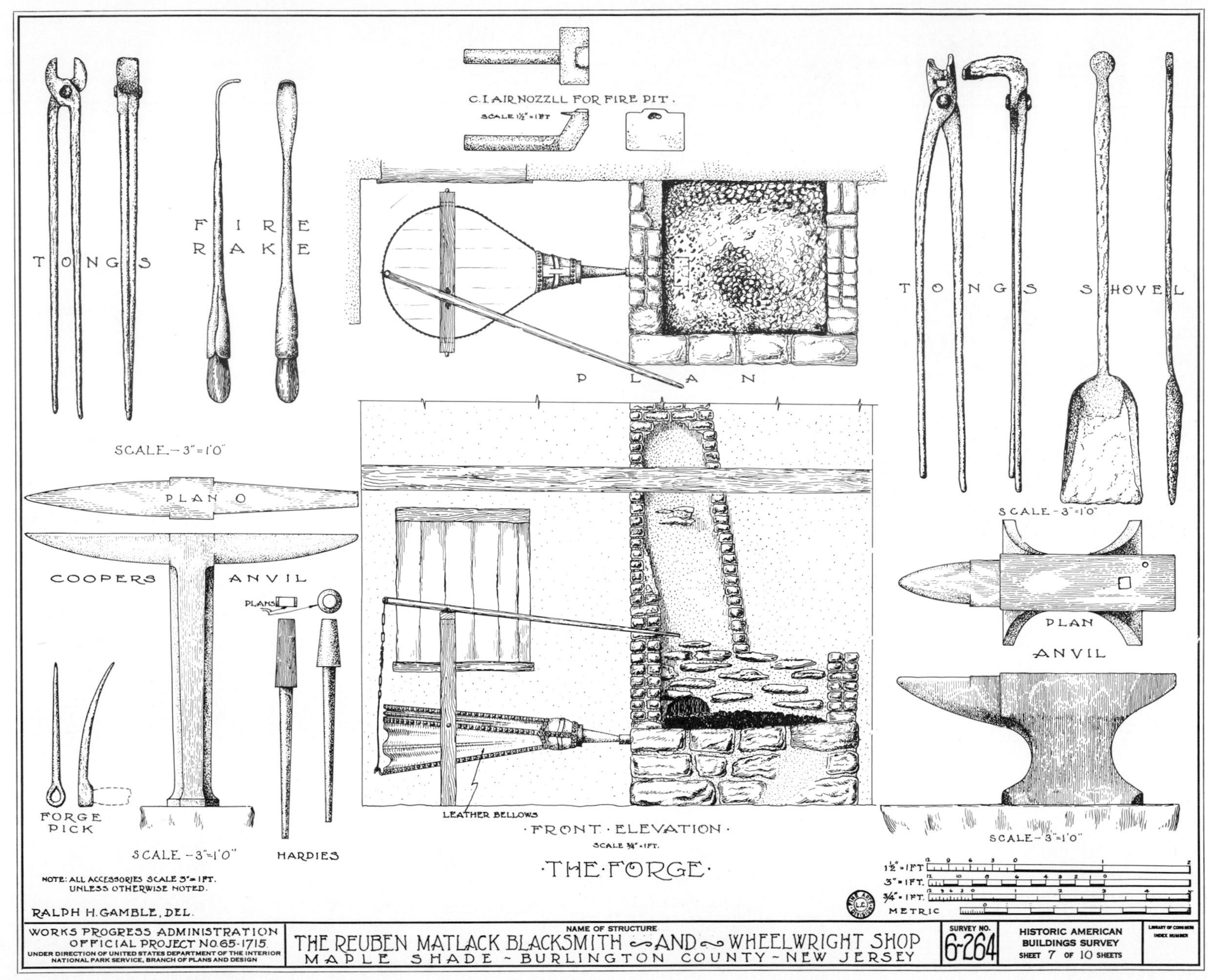
C.I. AIR NOZZLL FOR FIRE PIT.
SCALE 1½" = 1 FT
TONGS
FIRE RAKE
PLAN
TONGS
SHOVEL
SCALE - 3" = 1'0"
PLAN O
COOPERS ANVIL
PLANS
SCALE - 3" = 1'0"
PLAN
ANVIL
FORGE PICK
SCALE - 3" = 1'0"
HARDIES
LEATHER BELLOWS
· FRONT · ELEVATION ·
SCALE ¾" = 1 FT.
· THE · FORGE ·
SCALE - 3" = 1'0"
NOTE: ALL ACCESSORIES SCALE 3" = 1 FT.
UNLESS OTHERWISE NOTED.
RALPH H. GAMBLE, DEL.
1½" = 1 FT
3" = 1 FT.
¾" = 1 FT.
METRIC
FINE ARTS L.C. DIVISION
WORKS PROGRESS ADMINISTRATION
OFFICIAL PROJECT NO. 65-1715
UNDER DIRECTION OF UNITED STATES DEPARTMENT OF THE INTERIOR
NATIONAL PARK SERVICE, BRANCH OF PLANS AND DESIGN
NAME OF STRUCTURE
THE REUBEN MATLACK BLACKSMITH AND WHEELWRIGHT SHOP
MAPLE SHADE ~ BURLINGTON COUNTY ~ NEW JERSEY
SURVEY NO.
6-264
HISTORIC AMERICAN
BUILDINGS SURVEY
SHEET 7 OF 10 SHEETS
LIBRARY OF CONGRESS
INDEX NUMBER

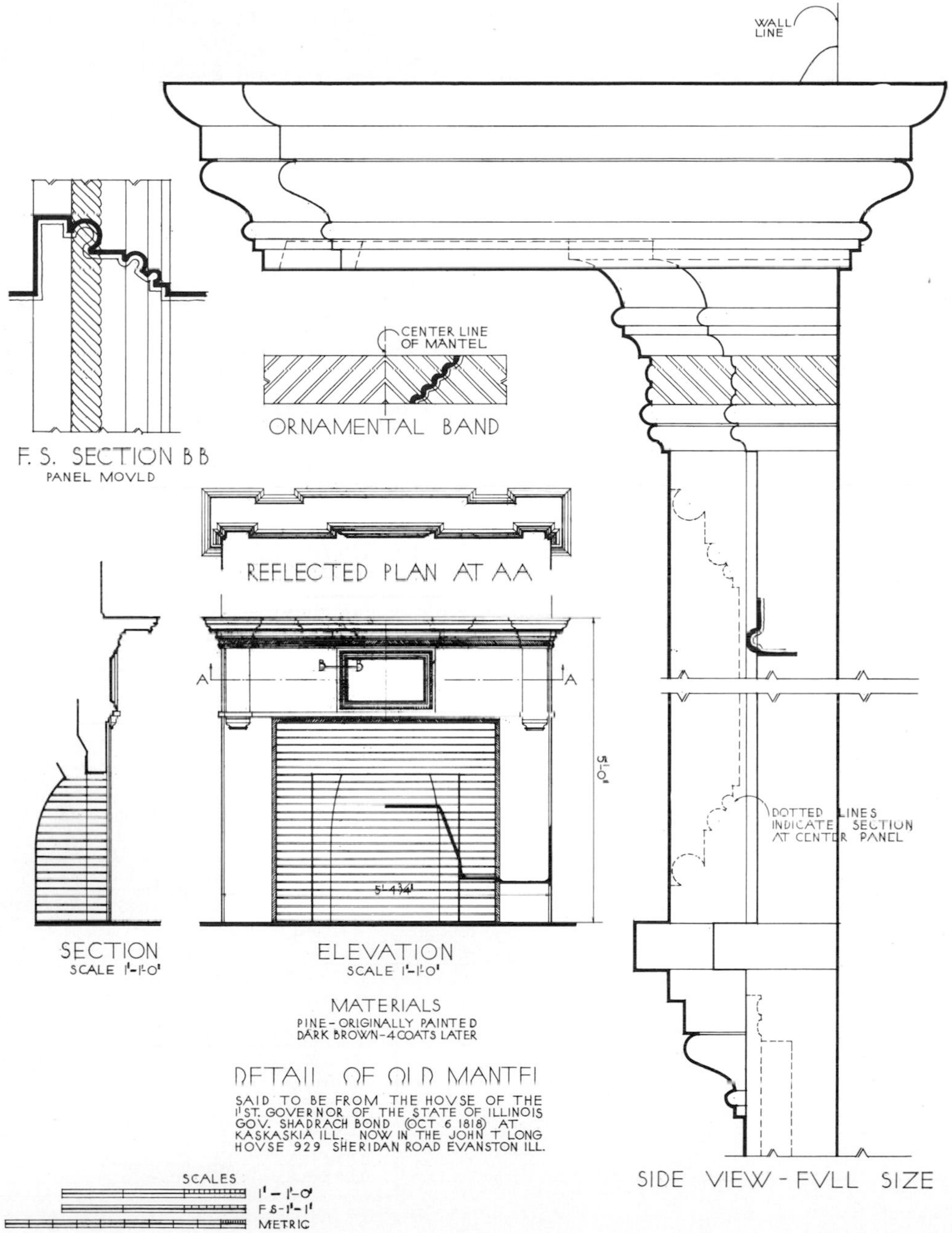

Figure 5.37

Measured drawings of a blacksmith's tools help to explain and interpret the work of a blacksmith more completely than would a measured drawing of the forge itself.

Figure 5.38

Two scale sticks were placed on this mantel. Basic dimensions can be determined from the resulting photograph with reasonable accuracy. The accuracy was enhanced by the photographer's positioning of the camera near the center point and perpendicular to the plane of the subject. Compare the photograph with the measured drawing to determine the types of information available from each recording technique.

WALL LINE

F. S. SECTION B B
PANEL MOVLD

CENTER LINE OF MANTEL

ORNAMENTAL BAND

REFLECTED PLAN AT AA

B B

A A

5'-0"

5'-4 3/4"

SECTION
SCALE 1"-1'-0"

ELEVATION
SCALE 1"-1'-0"

DOTTED LINES INDICATE SECTION AT CENTER PANEL

MATERIALS
PINE - ORIGINALLY PAINTED DARK BROWN - 4 COATS LATER

DETAIL OF OLD MANTEL

SAID TO BE FROM THE HOVSE OF THE 1ST. GOVERNOR OF THE STATE OF ILLINOIS GOV. SHADRACH BOND (OCT 6 1818) AT KASKASKIA ILL. NOW IN THE JOHN T LONG HOVSE 929 SHERIDAN ROAD EVANSTON ILL.

SCALES
1" - 1'-0"
F S - 1"- 1"
METRIC

SIDE VIEW - FVLL SIZE

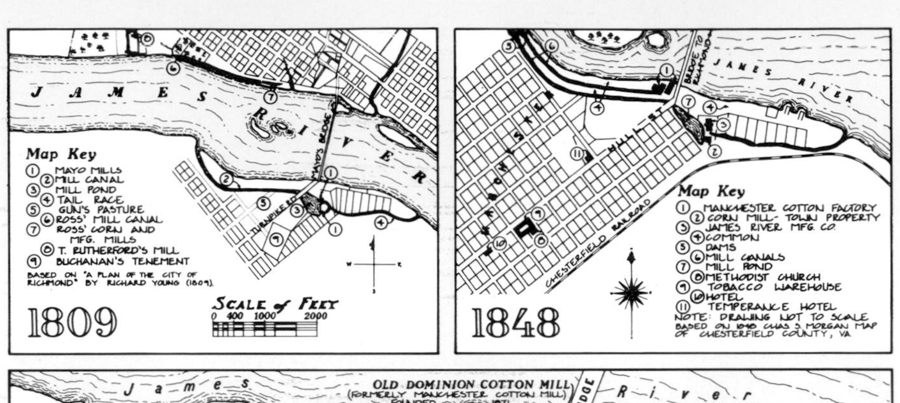

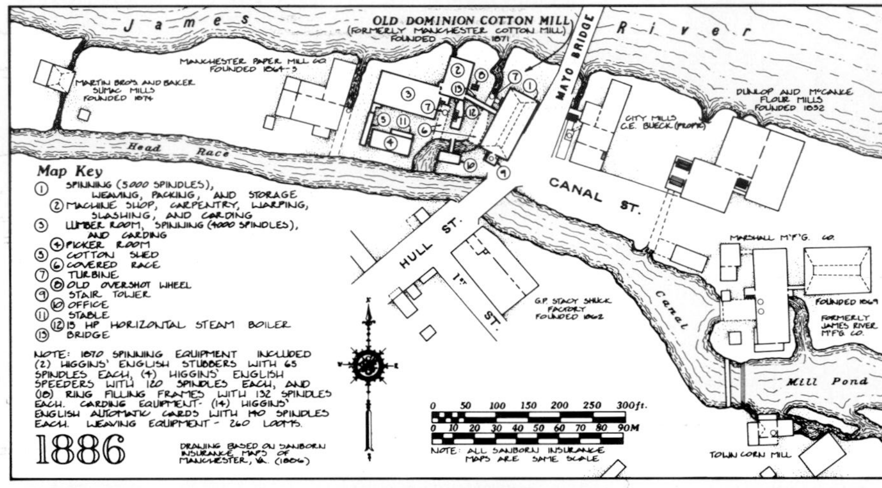

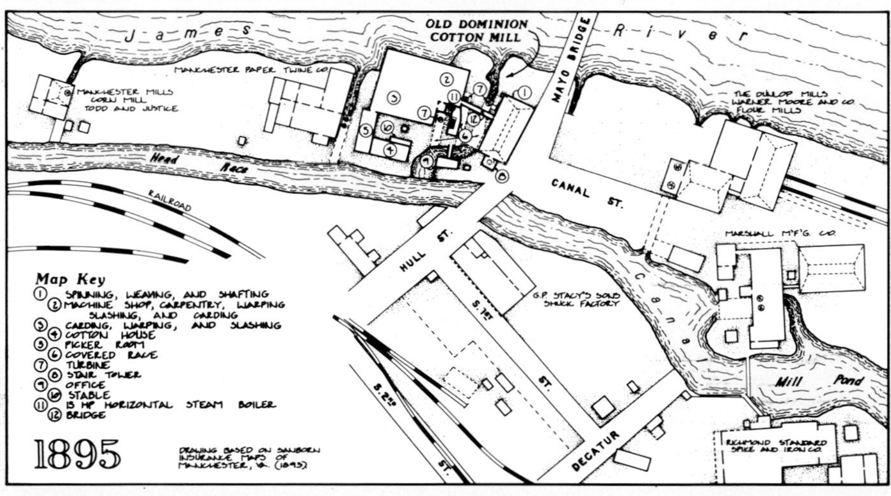

FIGURE 5.39

Manchester Mill was one of the few Richmond, Virginia, mills to survive the Civil War. Research turned up a substantial amount of graphic information, ranging from a Mathew Brady photograph in the National Archives to Sanborn insurance maps. Written records were found to be nearly nonexistent. The graphic records thus provided most of the clues, but not all of the answers, to the history of the mill. This drawing is one of two sheets adapted from historic maps that illustrate the evolution of the site.

Figure 5.40

Research completed shortly before the HABS drawings of the Wickham-Valentine House in Richmond were produced uncovered drawings showing the evolution of the design of the house. This sheet compares and contrasts the different designs by the architect, Alexander Parris, with the house as it existed in 1985.

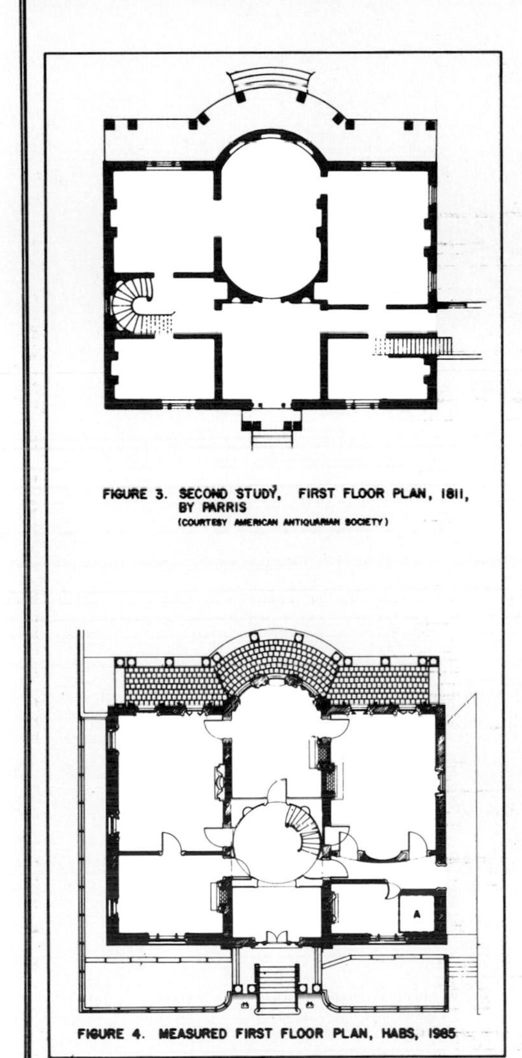

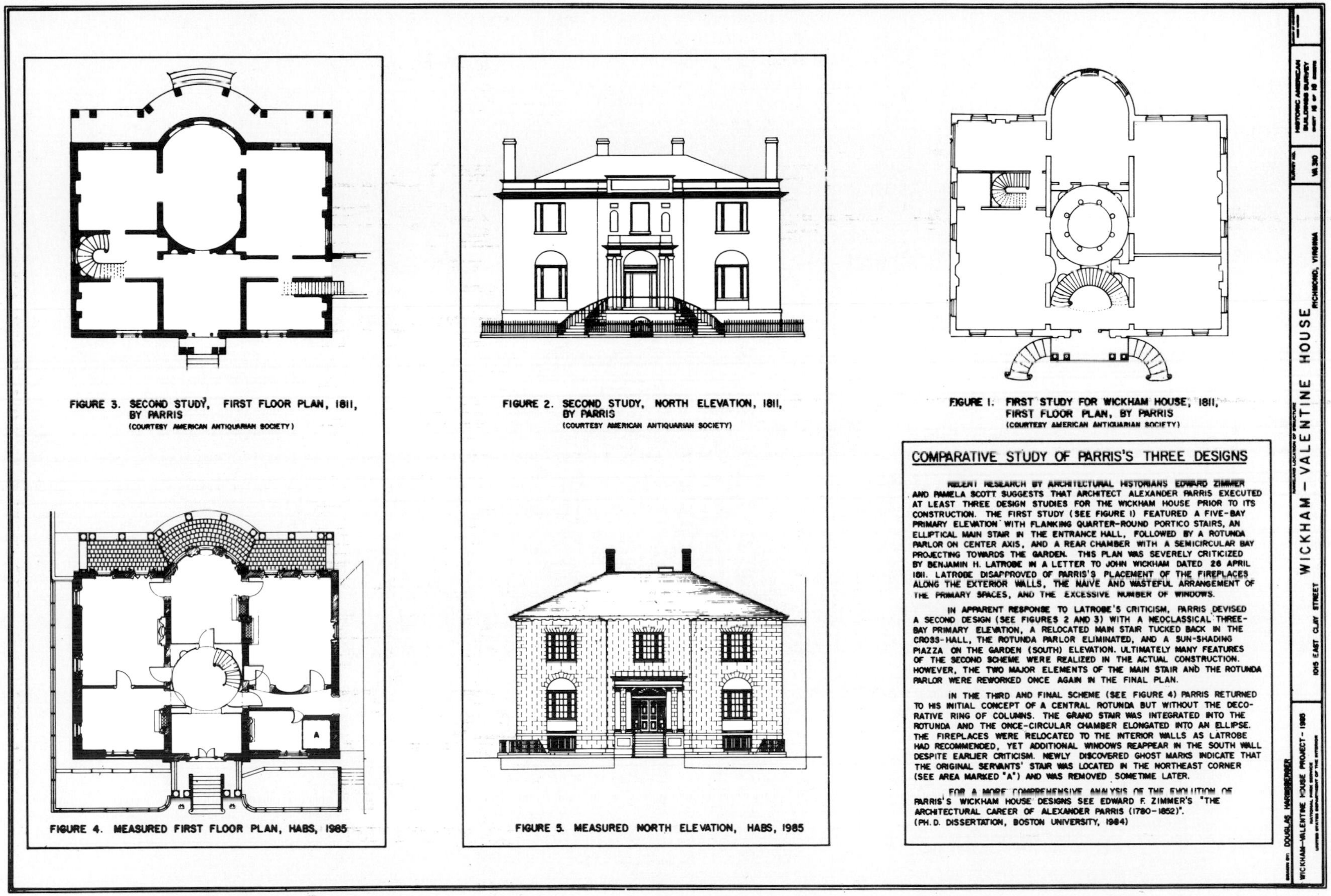

FIGURE 3. SECOND STUDY, FIRST FLOOR PLAN, 1811, BY PARRIS
(COURTESY AMERICAN ANTIQUARIAN SOCIETY)

FIGURE 4. MEASURED FIRST FLOOR PLAN, HABS, 1985

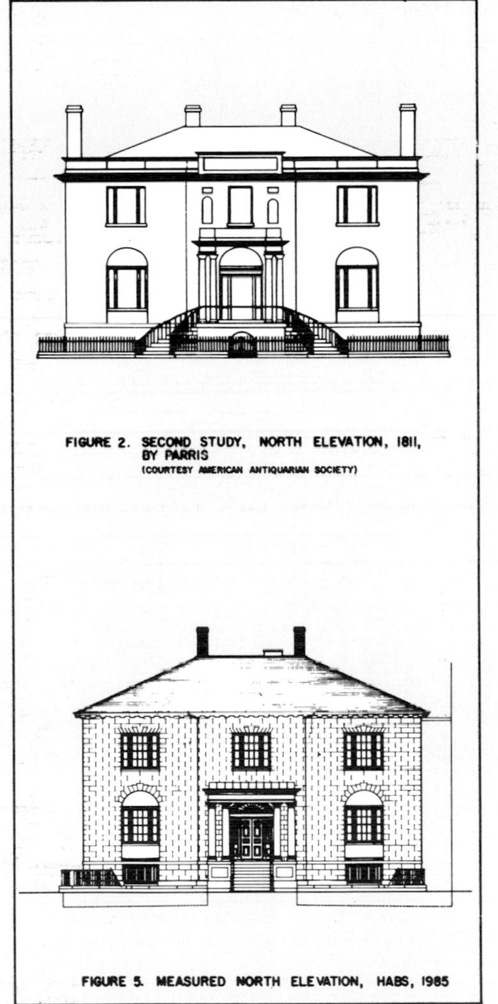

FIGURE 2. SECOND STUDY, NORTH ELEVATION, 1811, BY PARRIS
(COURTESY AMERICAN ANTIQUARIAN SOCIETY)

FIGURE 5. MEASURED NORTH ELEVATION, HABS, 1985

FIGURE 1. FIRST STUDY FOR WICKHAM HOUSE, 1811, FIRST FLOOR PLAN, BY PARRIS
(COURTESY AMERICAN ANTIQUARIAN SOCIETY)

COMPARATIVE STUDY OF PARRIS'S THREE DESIGNS

RECENT RESEARCH BY ARCHITECTURAL HISTORIANS EDWARD ZIMMER AND PAMELA SCOTT SUGGESTS THAT ARCHITECT ALEXANDER PARRIS EXECUTED AT LEAST THREE DESIGN STUDIES FOR THE WICKHAM HOUSE PRIOR TO ITS CONSTRUCTION. THE FIRST STUDY (SEE FIGURE I) FEATURED A FIVE-BAY PRIMARY ELEVATION WITH FLANKING QUARTER-ROUND PORTICO STAIRS, AN ELLIPTICAL MAIN STAIR IN THE ENTRANCE HALL, FOLLOWED BY A ROTUNDA PARLOR ON CENTER AXIS, AND A REAR CHAMBER WITH A SEMICIRCULAR BAY PROJECTING TOWARDS THE GARDEN. THIS PLAN WAS SEVERELY CRITICIZED BY BENJAMIN H. LATROBE IN A LETTER TO JOHN WICKHAM DATED 26 APRIL 1811. LATROBE DISAPPROVED OF PARRIS'S PLACEMENT OF THE FIREPLACES ALONG THE EXTERIOR WALLS, THE NAIVE AND WASTEFUL ARRANGEMENT OF THE PRIMARY SPACES, AND THE EXCESSIVE NUMBER OF WINDOWS.

IN APPARENT RESPONSE TO LATROBE'S CRITICISM, PARRIS DEVISED A SECOND DESIGN (SEE FIGURES 2 AND 3) WITH A NEOCLASSICAL THREE-BAY PRIMARY ELEVATION, A RELOCATED MAIN STAIR TUCKED BACK IN THE CROSS-HALL, THE ROTUNDA PARLOR ELIMINATED, AND A SUN-SHADING PIAZZA ON THE GARDEN (SOUTH) ELEVATION. ULTIMATELY MANY FEATURES OF THE SECOND SCHEME WERE REALIZED IN THE ACTUAL CONSTRUCTION. HOWEVER, THE TWO MAJOR ELEMENTS OF THE MAIN STAIR AND THE ROTUNDA PARLOR WERE REWORKED ONCE AGAIN IN THE FINAL PLAN.

IN THE THIRD AND FINAL SCHEME (SEE FIGURE 4) PARRIS RETURNED TO HIS INITIAL CONCEPT OF A CENTRAL ROTUNDA BUT WITHOUT THE DECORATIVE RING OF COLUMNS. THE GRAND STAIR WAS INTEGRATED INTO THE ROTUNDA AND THE ONCE-CIRCULAR CHAMBER ELONGATED INTO AN ELLIPSE. THE FIREPLACES WERE RELOCATED TO THE INTERIOR WALLS AS LATROBE HAD RECOMMENDED, YET ADDITIONAL WINDOWS REAPPEAR IN THE SOUTH WALL DESPITE EARLIER CRITICISM. NEWLY DISCOVERED GHOST MARKS INDICATE THAT THE ORIGINAL SERVANTS' STAIR WAS LOCATED IN THE NORTHEAST CORNER (SEE AREA MARKED "A") AND WAS REMOVED SOMETIME LATER.

FOR A MORE COMPREHENSIVE ANALYSIS OF THE EVOLUTION OF PARRIS'S WICKHAM HOUSE DESIGNS SEE EDWARD F. ZIMMER'S "THE ARCHITECTURAL CAREER OF ALEXANDER PARRIS (1780-1852)". (PH. D. DISSERTATION, BOSTON UNIVERSITY, 1984)

WICKHAM – VALENTINE HOUSE
1015 EAST CLAY STREET   RICHMOND, VIRGINIA

DRAWN BY: DOUGLAS HARNSBERGER

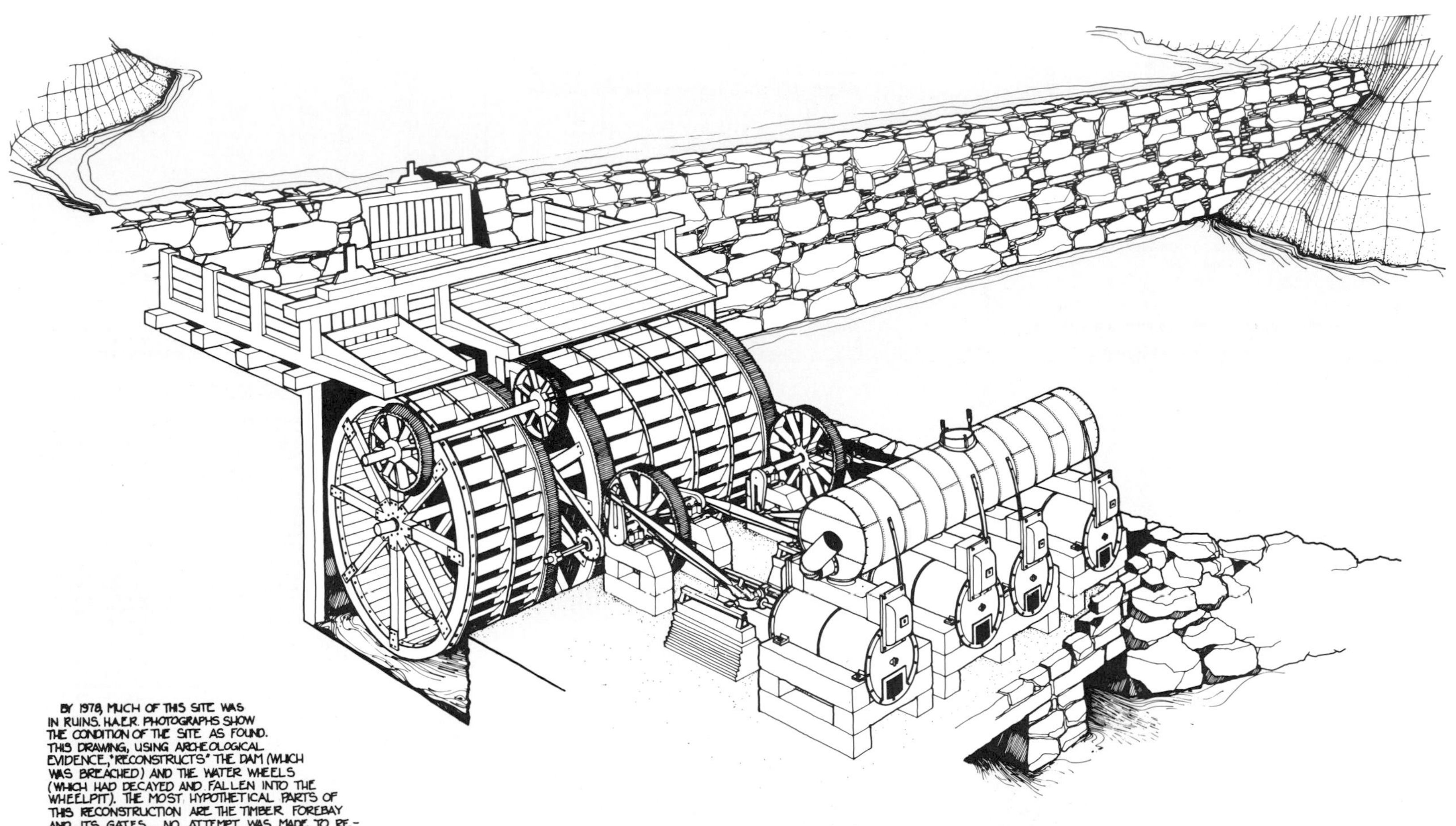

BY 1978, MUCH OF THIS SITE WAS
IN RUINS. H.A.E.R. PHOTOGRAPHS SHOW
THE CONDITION OF THE SITE AS FOUND.
THIS DRAWING, USING ARCHEOLOGICAL
EVIDENCE, "RECONSTRUCTS" THE DAM (WHICH
WAS BREACHED) AND THE WATER WHEELS
(WHICH HAD DECAYED AND FALLEN INTO THE
WHEELPIT). THE MOST HYPOTHETICAL PARTS OF
THIS RECONSTRUCTION ARE THE TIMBER FOREBAY
AND ITS GATES. NO ATTEMPT WAS MADE TO RE-
CONSTRUCT THE BUILDING THAT ONCE COVERED THE
MACHINERY.
PERSPECTIVE OF BLAST MACHINERY AND DAM

Figure 5.41

The blast machinery and dam of the Adirondack Iron and Steel Company in Tahawus, New York, were ruined when recorded by HAER in 1978. The physical remnants were studied and measured and graphically reassembled to produce this interpretive drawing of the original conditions. No attempt was made to draw the sheltering structure over the machinery. Conjectural portions of the drawing were identified in the note.

HABS makes extensive use of interpretive drawings to explain industrial processes and structural systems. At the site of an iron furnace, the blast machinery was found to be in ruinous condition. The pieces were measured and graphically assembled in a drawing to show how the machinery produced compressed air for the furnace (see fig. 5.41). In another example, the production of smokeless gunpowder at a military arsenal was explained in a series of drawings that followed the process step by step (see chapter 6). The structural subsystems of a bridge were depicted in a series of schematic drawings that identified each of the major components (see fig. 5.35).

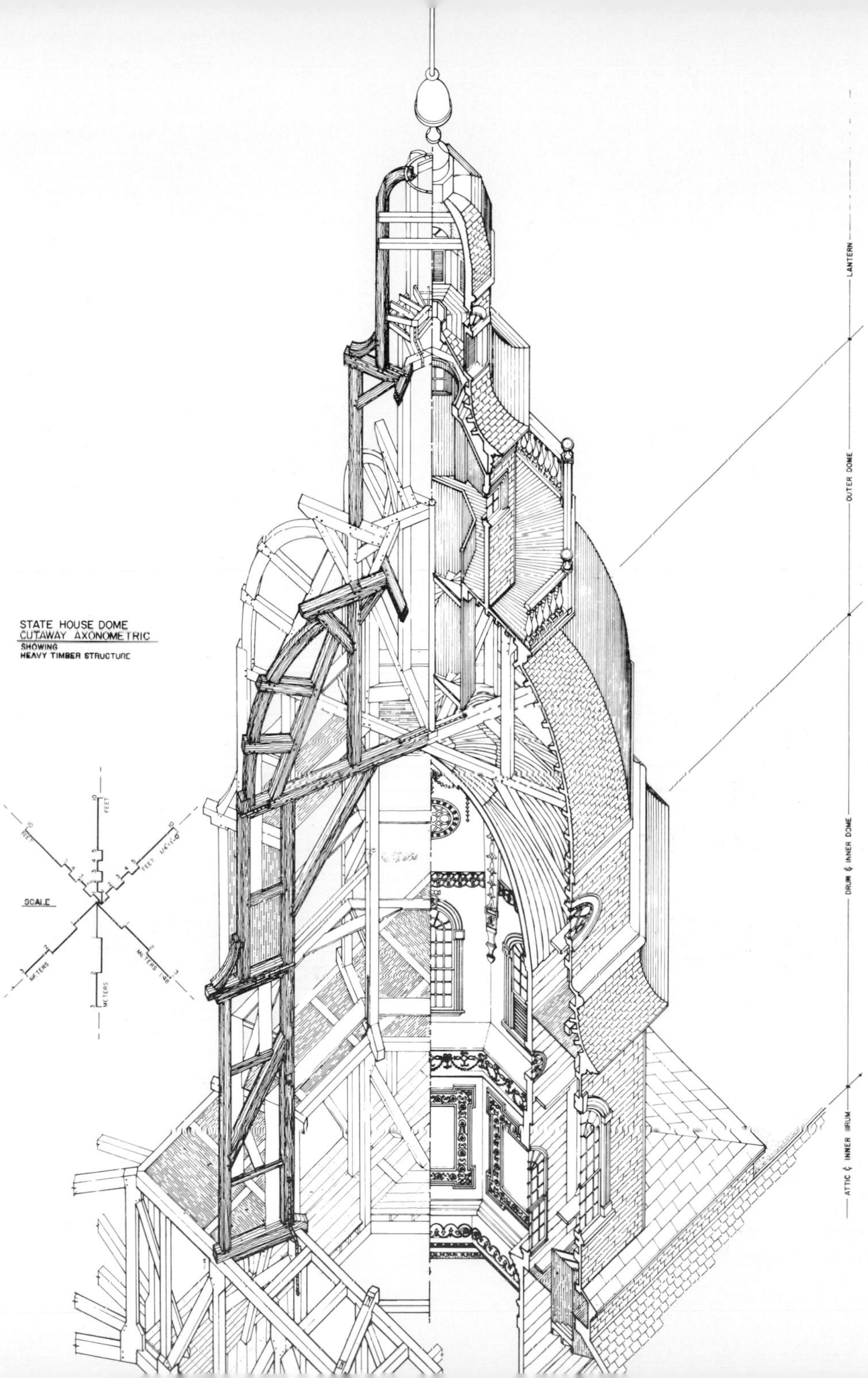

STATE HOUSE DOME
CUTAWAY AXONOMETRIC
SHOWING
HEAVY TIMBER STRUCTURE

SCALE

LANTERN

OUTER DOME

DRUM & INNER DOME

ATTIC & INNER DRUM

FIGURE 5.42

This axonometric drawing is cut away in two ways, to reveal information on the structural system on the left and the finish materials on the right.

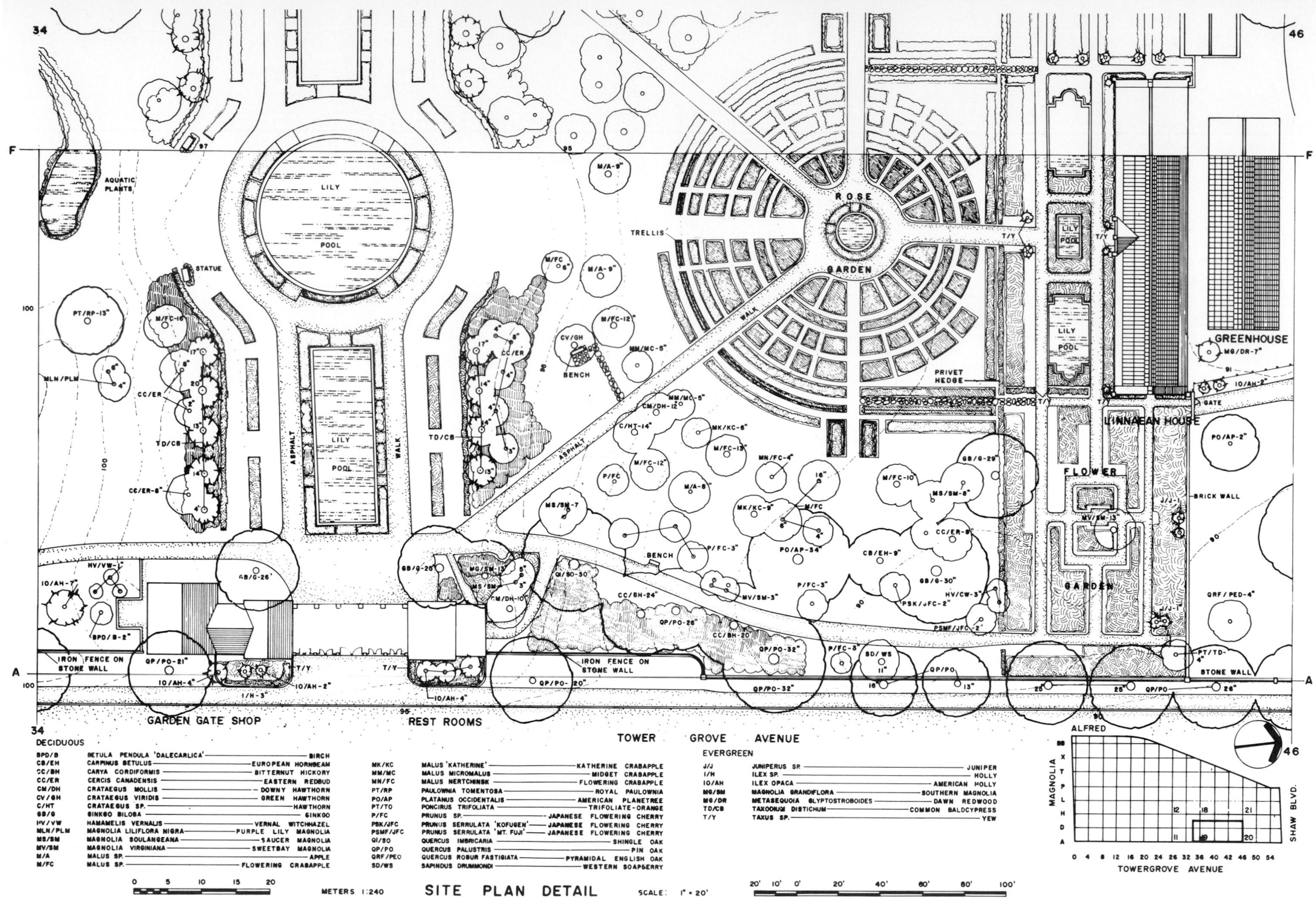
LILY POOL
ROSE GARDEN
TRELLIS
PRIVET HEDGE
GREENHOUSE
LINNAEAN HOUSE
FLOWER GARDEN
BRICK WALL
AQUATIC PLANTS
STATUE
BENCH
ASPHALT WALK
IRON FENCE ON STONE WALL
STONE WALL
GATE
GARDEN GATE SHOP
REST ROOMS
TOWER GROVE AVENUE
DECIDUOUS
BPD/B BETULA PENDULA 'DALECARLICA' — BIRCH
CB/EH CARPINUS BETULUS — EUROPEAN HORNBEAM
CC/BH CARYA CORDIFORMIS — BITTERNUT HICKORY
CC/ER CERCIS CANADENSIS — EASTERN REDBUD
CM/DH CRATAEGUS MOLLIS — DOWNY HAWTHORN
CV/GH CRATAEGUS VIRIDIS — GREEN HAWTHORN
C/HT CRATAEGUS SP. — HAWTHORN
GB/G GINKGO BILOBA — GINKGO
HV/VW HAMAMELIS VERNALIS — VERNAL WITCHHAZEL
MLN/PLM MAGNOLIA LILIFLORA NIGRA — PURPLE LILY MAGNOLIA
MS/SM MAGNOLIA SOULANGEANA — SAUCER MAGNOLIA
MV/SM MAGNOLIA VIRGINIANA — SWEETBAY MAGNOLIA
M/A MALUS SP. — APPLE
M/FC MALUS SP. — FLOWERING CRABAPPLE
MK/KC MALUS 'KATHERINE' — KATHERINE CRABAPPLE
MM/MC MALUS MICROMALUS — MIDGET CRABAPPLE
MN/FC MALUS NERTCHINSK — FLOWERING CRABAPPLE
PT/RP PAULOWNIA TOMENTOSA — ROYAL PAULOWNIA
PO/AP PLATANUS OCCIDENTALIS — AMERICAN PLANETREE
PT/TO PONCIRUS TRIFOLIATA — TRIFOLIATE-ORANGE
P/FC PRUNUS SP. — JAPANESE FLOWERING CHERRY
PSK/JFC PRUNUS SERRULATA 'KOFUGEN' — JAPANESE FLOWERING CHERRY
PSMF/JFC PRUNUS SERRULATA 'MT. FUJI' — JAPANESE FLOWERING CHERRY
QI/SO QUERCUS IMBRICARIA — SHINGLE OAK
QP/PO QUERCUS PALUSTRIS — PIN OAK
QRF/PEO QUERCUS ROBUR FASTIGIATA — PYRAMIDAL ENGLISH OAK
SD/WS SAPINDUS DRUMMONDI — WESTERN SOAPBERRY
EVERGREEN
J/J JUNIPERUS SP. — JUNIPER
I/H ILEX SP. — HOLLY
IO/AH ILEX OPACA — AMERICAN HOLLY
MG/SM MAGNOLIA GRANDIFLORA — SOUTHERN MAGNOLIA
MG/DR METASEQUOIA GLYPTOSTROBOIDES — DAWN REDWOOD
TD/CB TAXODIUM DISTICHUM — COMMON BALDCYPRESS
T/Y TAXUS SP. — YEW
ALFRED
MAGNOLIA
SHAW BLVD.
TOWERGROVE AVENUE
0 5 10 15 20
METERS 1:240
SITE PLAN DETAIL
SCALE: 1" = 20'
20' 10' 0' 20' 40' 60' 80' 100'

Figure 5.43

One problem in landscape recording is how to note all the plant material names and sizes without having the drawing dominated by the notes. The solution devised for this garden was to use abbreviations of the scientific and common names, separated by a slash, followed by the diameter of the trunk at breast height, a dimension that would be too small to draw accurately at this scale. Crown diameters were easier to draw and measure on the drawing, so they were left undimensioned. Adjacent plantings with the same name were tied to a single label by using fine lines. If the diameters varied, they were labeled individually. A key map located this section in relation to the overall garden.

Drawing techniques can help to interpret what is being recorded. Axonometric and isometric projections are two common forms of delineation that help to explain volume and mass (see fig. 6.10). Cut-away views graphically remove portions of a subject to reveal details underneath (see figs. 1.6 and 5.1). Often several techniques can be combined in one drawing (see fig. 5.42). See the section on interpretive drawings in chapter 6 for more information.

Landscape Documentation

Most landscapes are recorded as part of a project to document a historic structure. HABS does document historic landscapes and parks by themselves, however. Existing conditions in a botanical garden were documented in a project that located and identified all plant materials in a series of detailed drawings that provided a benchmark against which to measure future changes (see fig. 5.43). An urban park was documented with both existing condition drawings and interpretive drawings depicting the original design at maturity. See the section on landscape documentation in chapter 6 for more information.

Historic Ship Documentation

Historic vessels are recorded by many of the same techniques used for architectural and industrial structures. Specialized adaptations may be required, however, in field procedures to record decks and profiles or for lines lifting. Some measured drawing conventions specific to ships such as line drawings and construction plans may have to be produced. See the section on historic ship documentation in chapter 6 for more information.

In addition to the specialized measured drawings used to document historic ships, landscapes, and historic industrial processes, other specialized recording techniques and methods are used to document unusual sites. In the next chapter, case studies are used to explain the approaches used to produce HABS/HAER documentation for four disparate types of historic resources.

Case Studies

CHAPTER 6

Sally Kress Tompkins
Richard K. Anderson
John A. Burns
Paul D. Dolinsky

ertain historic resources possess special characteristics that call for adaptation of the precepts and guidelines described in earlier chapters of this book. These characteristics may be found in the evolution of a site over time, the distinctive features of a designed landscape, the structural details that are not apparent from a structure's exterior, an industrial process that requires interpretation, a historic ship whose hull is curved, or a complex building one of whose areas of significance lies in its mechanical systems.

In recording these resources, special attention must be paid to those characteristics that are different or distinctive. They add to the significance of the resource and challenge the would-be recorder. This chapter describes four different types of special resources and the approaches used by the Historic American Buildings Survey and Historic American Engineering Record (HABS/HAER) to document them. The case studies given are for a significant industrial process, a building whose multiple areas of significance included its mechanical systems, an important historic landscape, and two historic ships.

Interpretive Drawings

An interpretive drawing cross-references and integrates material by putting together details that may otherwise appear separately in accompanying written data, photographs, or standard measured drawings. Interpretive drawings help the user to see significant relationships and features impossible to present effectively with other documentary media. Characteristics that invite this treatment may be structural details, a manufacturing- or materials-handling process, the organization of machinery or other elements within a building or site, or the operative principles behind a particular engineering device or system. Interpretive drawings should be made when no other type of presentation is as efficient in terms of content conveyed, cost to produce, or time required for a user to study.

Several types of drawings are effective, depending on what kind of information is to be presented. They may range from the purely schematic, to the illustrative, to carefully scaled views. Some drawings may combine all these approaches. Examples include sequential maps or plans showing progressive development of a site or building. These may be diagrammatic or highly detailed, depending on the scales and types of changes being shown. Schematic flow charts are excellent for showing the movement of materials and energy between components. Interconnections, flow directions, temperatures, quantities, types of materials, time, power, and other factors often cannot be efficiently presented together in any other way. Isometric or perspective views showing the relationship between components in space can often clarify physical connections, relative sizes, functioning parts, or other factors when surrounding obstructions are graphically stripped away. Such drawings may also be used to carefully "restore" or re-create a site from surviving documentary or on-site information, especially when no other representation of the site in its intact condition is known to exist. Isometric "cutaways" or "exploded" views are ideal ways to show how something is made internally or assembled from various parts. All such drawings should be copiously annotated, but should not duplicate information more effectively left to a manuscript or to photography.

The question arises as to what distinguishes a good interpretive drawing from a bad one. Many of the technical rules governing typical measured drawings apply to interpretive drawings as well. The use of a variety of line weights, and the skillful application of illustrating techniques, such as stippling and shadowing, help to convey form and detail, add interest, and provide a visual framework. Drawings done in only one line weight with one or two lettering sizes can be both boring and confusing because they do not "read" well. Clarity is paramount, but this does not necessarily mean simplicity. Several levels of detail or types of information can be presented simultaneously without confusion if each addresses a different aspect of the subject. The rules of good scholarship also apply. Don't insert baseless information or speculation. If you represent something in a manner different from the way it exists or appears in other parts of the project package (in photos, for example), add a note stating what you changed and why. Things omitted for clarity should always be noted. Always cite any pre-existing sources on which you have based your work, such as other drawings, photographs, written or oral accounts, or published works. Cross-referencing features in a drawing to specific photographs, photocopied material, or parts of a written monograph about the site is strongly recommended. Labels, keys, descriptive and historical notes, and brief texts explaining your drawings are useful and informative. Scale may or may not be important, depending on its relevance to the information you are presenting. Finally, don't overlook the possibility of photocopying pre-existing interpretive drawings. Many industries may permit the reproduction of nonproprietary schematics and flow diagrams once used for managing their historical operations.

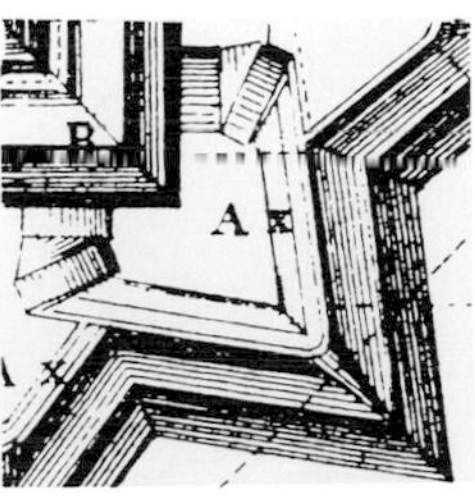

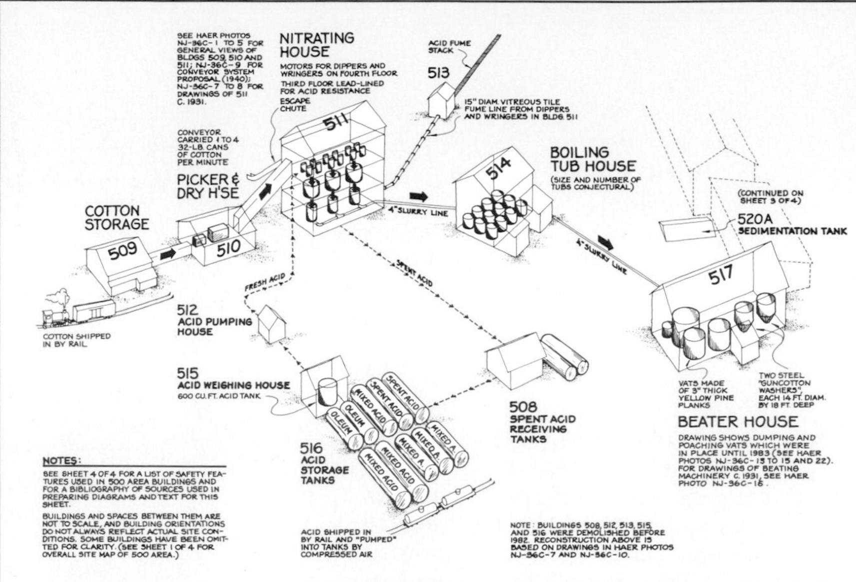

SMOKELESS POWDER PRODUCTION (1)

509 · COTTON STORAGE

COTTON WAS STORED HERE IN BALES AFTER SHIPMENT BY RAIL.

510 · PICKER & DRY HOUSE

COTTON WAS CLEANED OF DIRT AND OTHER IMPURITIES, WASHED, BLEACHED, AND DRIED. IT WAS THEN FLUFFED BY A PICKING MACHINE, CLEANED OF FINE DUST, AND DRIED TO 0.6% MOISTURE CONTENT. FINALLY IT WAS PACKED IN GALVANIZED CANS (32 LBS. PER CAN) TO SEAL OUT MOISTURE AND WAS CARRIED BY A CONVEYOR TO THE NITRATING HOUSE, BLDG. 511.

511 · NITRATING HOUSE

COTTON WAS NITRATED IN TWELVE DUPONT MECHANICAL NITRATORS BY MIXING IT WITH A SOLUTION THAT WAS ABOUT 35% NITRIC ACID [HNO_3], 33% SULFURIC ACID [H_2SO_4], AND 32% WATER BY MOLECULAR WEIGHT. (THE SULFURIC ACID ABSORBED EXCESS WATER PRODUCED BY NITRATING THE COTTON, THUS PREVENTING AN INHIBITORY DILUTION OF THE NITRIC ACID. THE RELATIVE PROPORTIONS OF THE ACIDS WERE EXTREMELY IMPORTANT, BECAUSE VARIATIONS OF ±10% WOULD PRODUCE A NITROCELLULOSE ("NC" FOR SHORT) INSOLUBLE IN ETHER-ALCOHOL AND THEREFORE UNPROCESSABLE IN THE POWDER FACTORY.) EACH NITRATOR, OR "DIPPER", WAS CHARGED BY SIMULTANEOUSLY ADDING COTTON AND ACID WHILE TWO SETS OF MOTOR-DRIVEN WOODEN PADDLES STIRRED THE MIXTURE. AGITATION CONTINUED FOR 20-30 MIN. AT ABOUT 86°F (30°C) AFTER CHARGING WAS COMPLETED. SINCE THE NITRATORS WERE GROUPED IN BATTERIES OF FOUR, THEY WERE CHARGED IN SEQUENCE SO THAT THE FOURTH ONE WAS BEING FILLED BY THE TIME THE FIRST WAS READY TO DISCHARGE ITS CONTENTS INTO THE CENTRIFUGE BENEATH THE BATTERY. AFTER THE SPENT ACID WAS WRUNG OUT, THE NC PASSED DOWN INTO A WATER-FILLED DROWNING TANK AND CONTINUED VIA PIPELINE AS A SLURRY TO BLDG. 514 (BOILING TUB HOUSE). SPENT ACID WAS RECOVERED IN BLDG. 508 AND REUSED AFTER FORTIFICATION WITH FRESH ACIDS FROM BLDG. 516 (ACID STORAGE HOUSE).

THE NITRATION OF COTTON RESULTED IN THREE CLASSES OF NC, GROUPED ACCORDING TO THEIR DEGREES OF NITRATION:

BELOW 12% --- PYROXYLIN (COMMERCIAL LAQUER BASE)

12% TO 12.75% -- PYROCOTTON OR PYROCELLULOSE (SMOKELESS POWDER BASE; 12.60 ± 0.10% USUALLY)

13.2% AND UP -- GUNCOTTON (HIGH EXPLOSIVES BASE)

(14.14% IS THEORETICALLY THE MAXIMUM POSSIBLE NITROGEN CONTENT IN NC.)

AFTER 1926, PICATINNY PURCHASED NC FROM COMMERCIAL MANUFACTURERS, AND BLDGS. 509-516 WERE USED PRIMARILY FOR THE PRODUCTION OF EXPERIMENTAL POWDERS. AT TIMES, WOOD PULP WAS SUBSTITUTED FOR COTTON AS A SOURCE OF CELLULOSE.

514 · BOILING TUB HOUSE

AFTER NITRATION, NC UNDERWENT LENGTHY PURIFICATION TO REMOVE UNDESIREABLE BY-PRODUCTS OF THE NITRATION PROCESS, NEUTRALIZE RESIDUAL ACIDS, AND REDUCE FIBER SIZE TO SPECIFICATION. NC FROM BLDG. 511 WAS SENT TO WOODEN TUBS EQUIPPED WITH STEAM LINES FOR HEATING AND CIRCULATING A SLIGHTLY ACID, OR "SOUR" WATER BATH (HENCE THE TERM "SOUR BOIL"). PYROCELLULOSE WAS BOILED FOR 16 HOURS IN AN 0.2% SULFURIC ACID SOLUTION, WHILE GUNCOTTON WAS BOILED FOR 30 HOURS IN AN 0.5% SOLUTION. THIS WAS FOLLOWED BY THREE 8-HOUR BOILINGS IN SUCCESSIVE FRESH WATER BATHS. THESE TREATMENTS REMOVED MUCH NITRATED OXY- AND HYDROCELLULOSE, CELLULOSE SULFATE, UNNITRATED CELLULOSE, AND SOME FREE ACIDS, BY-PRODUCTS WHICH WOULD CAUSE SMOKELESS POWDER TO DECOMPOSE SHORTLY IF THEY WERE NOT ELIMINATED.

517 · BEATER HOUSE

AFTER BOILING, NC FIBERS WERE BEATEN TO FINER LENGTHS BY PULPING MACHINES OF THE SORT USED BY CONTEMPORARY PAPER-MAKING INDUSTRIES. SODIUM CARBONATE [Na_2CO_3] WAS ADDED DURING BEATING TO NEUTRALIZE ACIDS FREED FROM THE FIBERS BY THE TREATMENT. FOLLOWING THIS, THE NC WAS PIPED TO BLDG. 520 FOR POACHING.

BY 1983, THIS BUILDING HAD BECOME A WING OF BLDG. 520 AND HAD BEEN RENUMBERED. EQUIPMENT IN IT HAD BEEN USED FOR DUMPING COMMERCIAL NC INTO WATER BATHS TO PREPARE IT FOR POACHING. NC WAS SHIPPED IN GALVANIZED CANS OF 220-236 LBS. NET WEIGHT, EACH CONTAINING ABOUT 150 LBS. OF NC AND 50 LBS. OF WATER (TO PREVENT FIRE). NC WAS DUMPED IN 60-CAN BATCHES AND MIXED WITH WATER IN ONE OF TWO STEEL "GUNCOTTON WASHERS," AFTER WHICH IT WAS PUMPED TO FOUR WOODEN TUBS OF VARIOUS SIZES IN BLDG. 517 (520) FOR AGITATION AND SETTLING. THESE FIRST STEPS IN THE POACHING OPERATION REMOVED SOME FREE ACIDS, PLUS WATER-SOLUBLE AND LIGHTER-THAN-WATER IMPURITIES. DECANTED WATER WAS PUMPED TO AN UNDERGROUND SEDIMENTATION TANK FOR REMOVAL OF RESIDUAL NC FIBERS WHILE THE NC SLURRY WAS PUMPED TO BLDG. 520 (POACHING HOUSE) FOR FURTHER PURIFICATION.

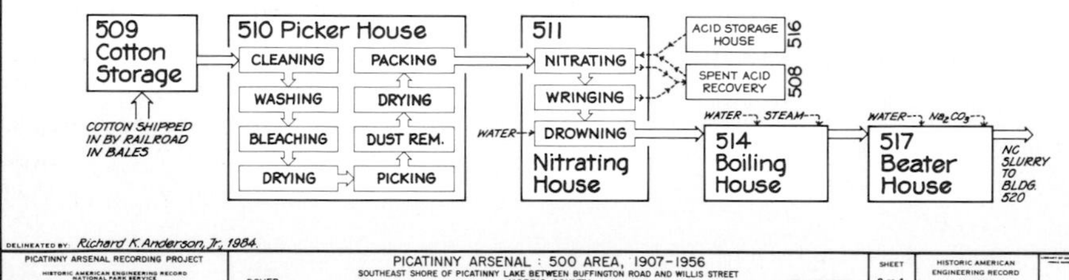

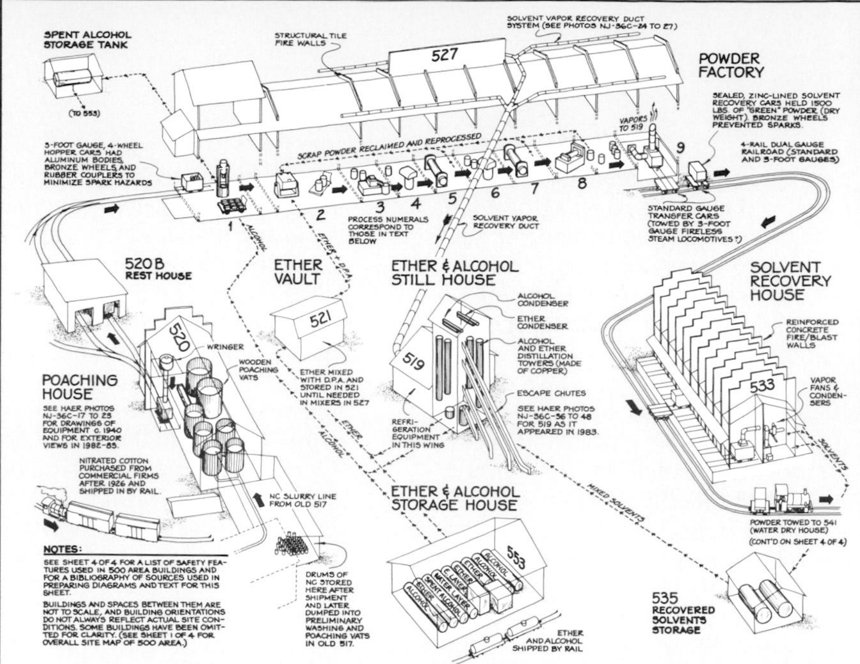

SMOKELESS POWDER PRODUCTION (2)

520 · POACHING HOUSE

HERE NITROCELLULOSE (OR "NC") RECEIVED A 6-HOUR BOILING IN AN 0.5% SODIUM CARBONATE [Na_2CO_3] BATH TO ELIMINATE ANY TRACES OF NITRATED OXY- AND HYDROCELLULOSE. THEN A 2-HOUR BOILING AND FOUR SUCCESSIVE 1-HOUR BOILINGS IN FRESH WATER BATHS, FOLLOWED BY TEN COLD WATER WASHINGS, REMOVED THE LAST TRACES OF FREE ACIDS. AFTER EACH BOILING OR WASHING, THE NC WAS ALLOWED TO SETTLE; THE WATER WAS THEN DECANTED AND FRESH WATER ADDED. IN ALL, ABOUT 50 GALS. OF WATER, 40-45 LBS OF STEAM, AND 150 HRS. WERE NEEDED TO PURIFY ONE POUND OF NC! (CONSIDERABLE RESEARCH WAS DONE IN THE 1930S AND 1940S TO FIND WAYS TO SHORTEN THIS TREATMENT WHILE PRESERVING THE LONG-TERM STABILITY OF THE NC.) AFTER THE LAST WASHING, THE NC WAS FORCED THROUGH A SCREEN WITH 0.012-0.025 INCH OPENINGS WHICH RETAINED ANY UNPULPED LUMPS. NC THAT PASSED THROUGH THE SCREEN WENT ON TO A 36 FT. BY 4 FT. WOODEN RIFFLE BOX WHICH REMOVED ANY SMALL, DENSE PARTICLES. TWO CENTRIFUGAL WRINGERS THEN REDUCED THE WATER CONTENT OF THE NC TO 30%. (170 LBS. OF NC WAS DRIED OUT IN EACH WRINGING.) IF THE NC PASSED ALL CHEMICAL AND STABILITY TESTS AT THIS POINT, IT WAS DUMPED INTO 3-FOOT GAUGE ALUMINUM HOPPER CARS, COVERED, AND PULLED INTO BLDG. 520-B (REST HOUSE) TO AWAIT MOISTURE TESTING.

527 · POWDER FACTORY

HERE A NINE-STEP PROCESS TURNED NC INTO SMOKELESS POWDER:

1) DEHYDRATION: THREE HYDRAULIC PRESSES FORCED ETHYL ALCOHOL [C_2H_5OH] AT 3,000 PSI THROUGH THE NC TO REMOVE WATER AND PRODUCE BLOCKS WEIGHING 27.77 LBS, DRY (1/9TH OF A 250 LB. MIXER LOAD).

2) MIXING: 8 MIXERS, EACH IN A SEPARATE ROOM, PRODUCED A COLLOIDED PASTE BY DISSOLVING THE NC IN A 2:1 MIXTURE OF ETHYL ETHER [$(C_2H_5)_2OH$] AND ETHYL ALCOHOL. OTHER COMPOUNDS WERE ALSO ADDED DURING THIS STAGE, SUCH AS D.N.T. [DINITROTOLUENE: $C_6H_3(NO_2)_2CH_3$], POTASSIUM SULFATE [K_2SO_4], AND EITHER D.P.A. [DIPHENYLAMINE, $(C_6H_5)_2NH$, A STABILIZER] OR D.B.P. [DIBUTYLPTHALATE: $C_6H_4(COO \cdot CH_2 \cdot CH_2 \cdot CH_2 \cdot CH_3)_2$, A GELATINIZING AND WATERPROOFING AGENT, AS WELL AS A STABILIZER]. MIXING TIME: 30 MINS. FOR 250 LBS. (DRY) OF NC AT 68°F (20°C).

3) MACERATING: 4 MACERATORS, EACH IN A SEPARATE ROOM, REDUCED THE SIZE OF THE COLLOID LUMPS TO DISTRIBUTE THE SOLVENTS AND COMPLETELY COLLOID THE MIXTURE. OPERATING TIME: 10 MINS.

4) PRELIMINARY BLOCKING: 2 PRESSES SHAPED PASTE INTO 12"x12"x24" BLOCKS AT 3,500 PSI, ONE MINUTE PER BLOCK.

5) SCREENING: 2 HORIZONTAL PRESSES REMOVED UNCOLLOIDED AND OVERSIZE LUMPS.

6) FINAL BLOCKING: 4 PRESSES REMOVED TRAPPED AIR AND UNCOLLOIDED COTTON AND SHAPED THE PASTE AT 3,500 PSI INTO CYLINDERS 12" DIAM. X 24" FOR FINAL PRESSING.

7) FINISH PRESSING: 4 PRESSES PRODUCED A FORMED, SPAGHETTI-LIKE GRAIN OF POWDER WITH PERFORATIONS AND DIMENSIONS ACCORDING TO SPECIFICATION.

8) CUTTING: THE EXTRUDED POWDER WAS CUT TO DESIRED LENGTHS BY 3 CUTTERS AND DUMPED INTO SOLVENT RECOVERY CARS.

9) PRELIMINARY SOLVENT RECOVERY: SUPPLY AND RETURN AIR LINES ATTACHED TO EACH CAR IN THE PRELIMINARY SOLVENT RECOVERY ROOM PICKED UP ETHER AND ALCOHOL FUMES FROM THE "GREEN" POWDER AND SENT THEM TO BLDG. 519 FOR RECTIFICATION. WHEN FILLED WITH POWDER, RECOVERY CARS WERE ROLLED ONTO TRANSFER CARS AND PULLED BY FIRELESS STEAM LOCOMOTIVES TO BLDG. 533 (SOLVENT RECOVERY HOUSE).

533 · SOLVENT RECOVERY

EACH CAR FROM BLDG. 527 WAS PLACED IN ITS OWN ROOM IN BLDG. 533 AND CONNECTED TO PIPELINES FOR STEAM, COOLING WATER, AND RECOVERED SOLVENTS. THE TEMPERATURE IN EACH CAR WAS RAISED TO 131°F (55°C) AND HELD THERE FOR 6-8 DAYS. SOLVENTS PASSED OFF AS VAPOR, CONDENSED ON COLD WATER LINES, AND FLOWED OFF TO BLDG. 519 FOR RECTIFICATION. WHEN THE POWDER'S SOLVENT CONTENT FELL TO 3-5% OF THE POWDER'S WEIGHT, THE POWDER WAS TRANSFERRED TO BLDG. 541 (WATER DRY HOUSE).

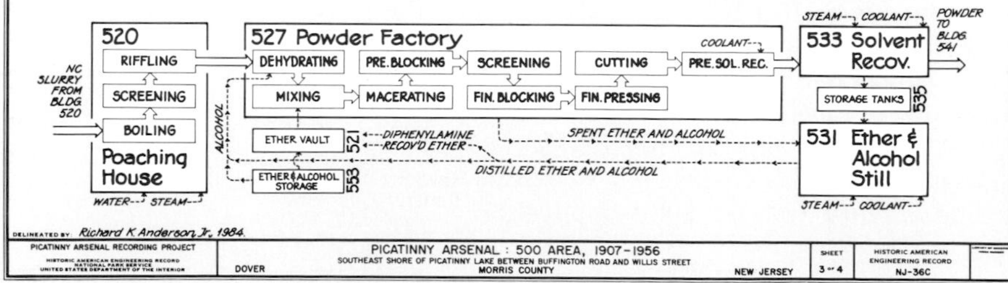

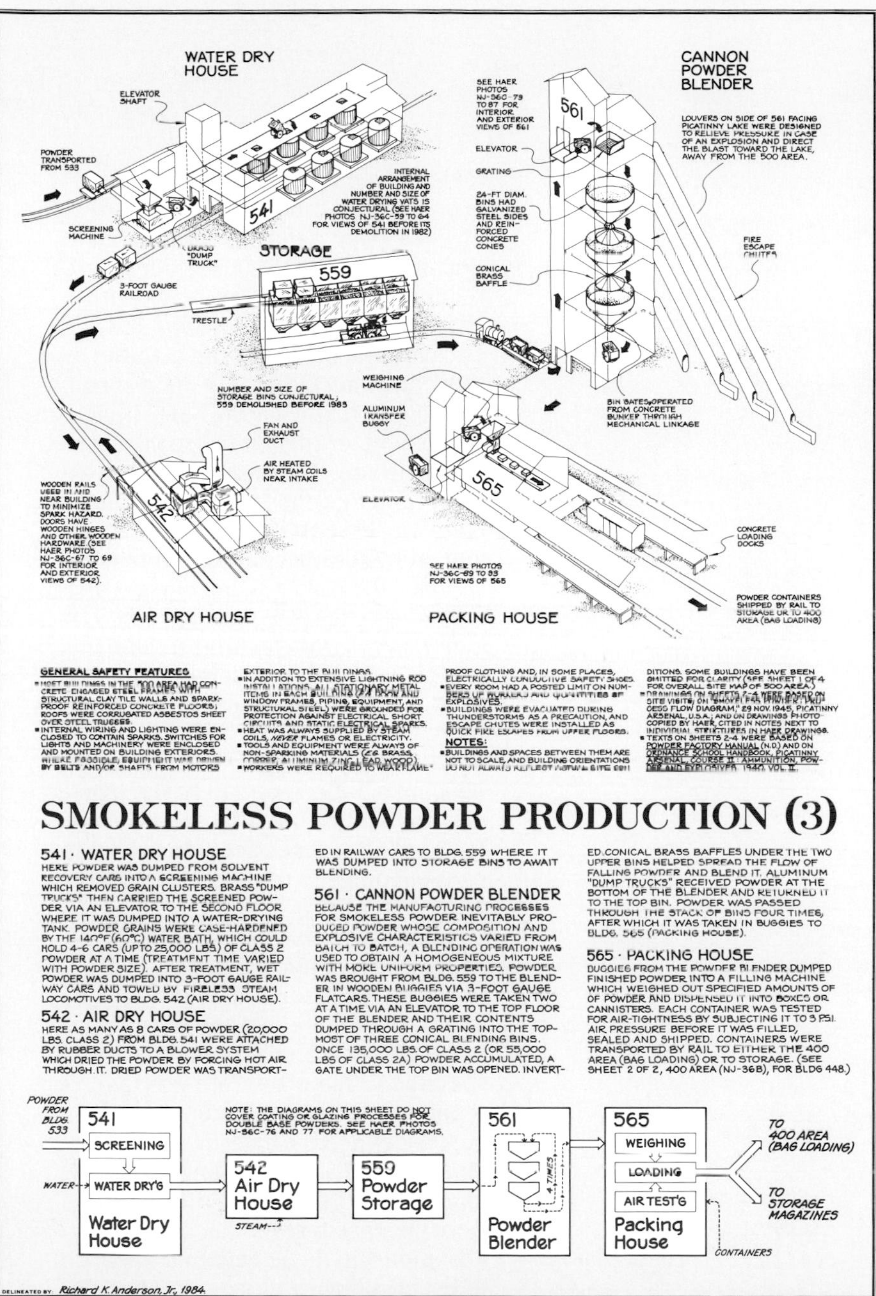

Figures 6.1, 6.2, 6.3

The "Smokeless Powder Production" presentation for the Picatinny Arsenal is not one diagram, but three parallel descriptions designed to supplement each other. Spread out over three sheets, the top level diagram "realistically" presents the forms of the buildings, examples of specific internal machinery, safety features, and major interconnections (pipes, ducts, railways). The verbal section provides detailed, step-by-step chemical data, while the bottom diagram presents the whole process schematically. This way, an observer can study the 500 Area of the Picatinny Arsenal at several different levels: where one function takes place relative to the others, how that function operates chemically, and how that function fits into the production concept.

Recording an Industrial Process

Built in 1926, the 500 Area at Picatinny Arsenal was documented in 1983 because the buildings, contaminated by explosives, were slated for demolition as obsolete and unsafe for adaptive reuse. The chemical processes and facilities—state-of-the-art designs for their time—played a major role in developing the powder production facilities that supplied U.S. forces during World War II.

The top diagram on each of the three drawing sheets (see figs. 6.1, 6.2, and 6.3) focuses on the chemical process used to produce smokeless powder at this particular plant—not powder production in general, not the building architecture, not even specific production machinery. Coverage of these secondary aspects was left to photography, photocopied original engineering drawings, or the project monograph (see figs. 6.4 and 6.5). A highly detailed written description of the process was included on the diagram because the general nature of the monograph did not easily accommodate such concentrated material. Items of secondary significance were treated in the diagram only to help a reader key in other parts of the documentation package.

The perspective diagram was laid out and inked freehand. Liberties were

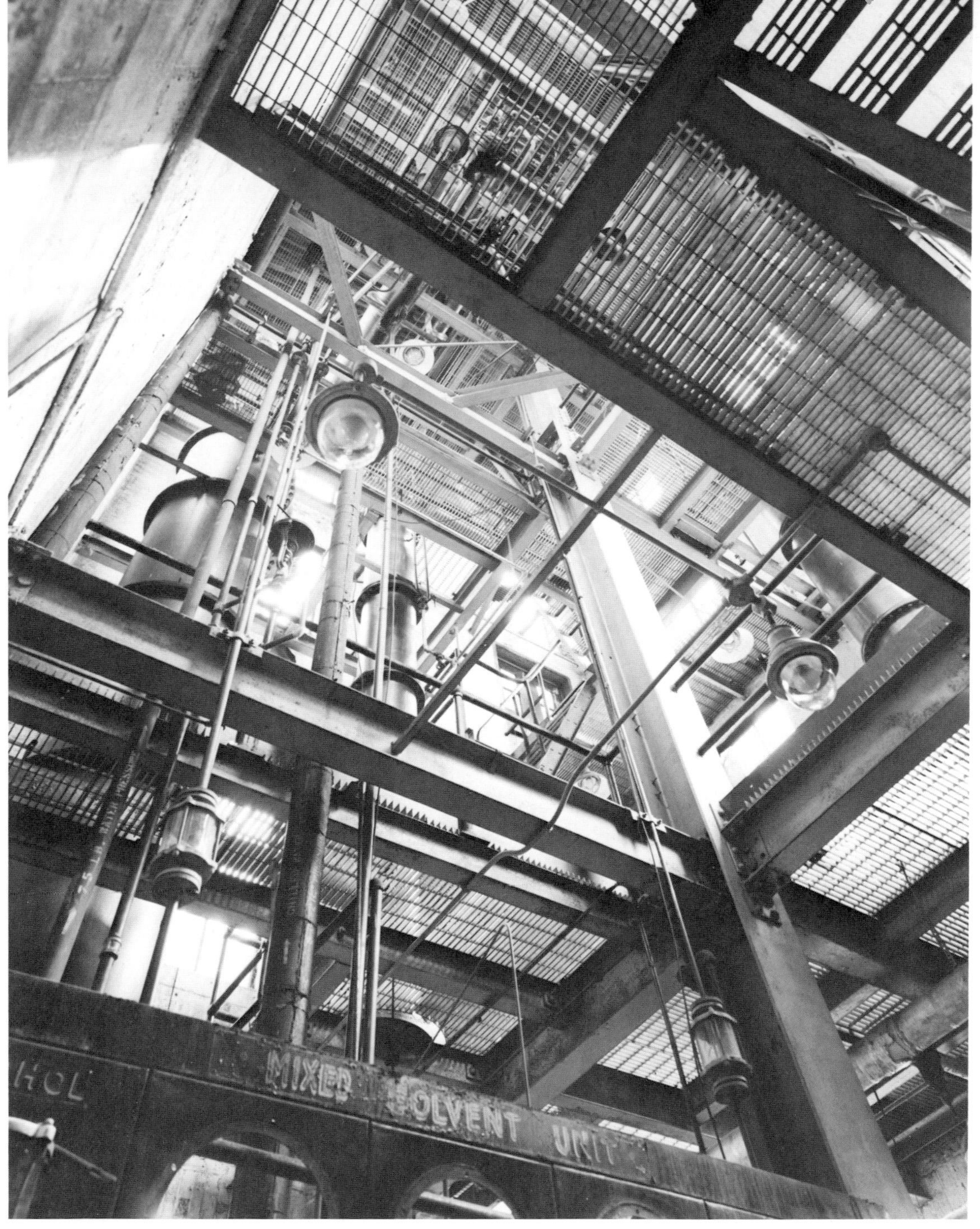

Figure 6.4

This photograph of the distillation towers inside Building 519 of the Picatinny Arsenal picks up in mechanical detail where the process drawing leaves off.

taken with the buildings' scale and orientation in order to clearly show the physical plant's functional interrelationships. Actual site conditions were recorded by the site plan and photographs (see figs. 6.6, 6.7, and 6.8). The pictorial quality of the diagram was enhanced by zeroing in on specific details, such as escape chutes, railway equipment, or the joints in a vitreous tile fume line. Buildings themselves were "ghosted" in, but with certain elements essential to their function and architectural character retained, such as fire walls, escape chutes, and roof overhangs (see figs. 6.2 and 6.9). Minor structures were omitted altogether. Functional elements (tanks, tubs, machines) were shaded to give them a firmer three-dimensional quality than the buildings. Flow arrows and building numbers were delineated boldly for prominence but often made to conform to the perspective planes of adjacent buildings to reinforce the pictorial quality of the drawing. Annotations were used profusely to refer readers to accompanying photographs, to identify buildings, to describe equipment, to indicate the materials and design of safety devices, and to point out speculative features. Care was taken to organize the notes in columns or blocks defined partially by the buildings in order to give the drawing an orderly appearance. Sources of information were clearly cited. As was done here, attention should be paid to the sizes of lettering, drawing details, and line

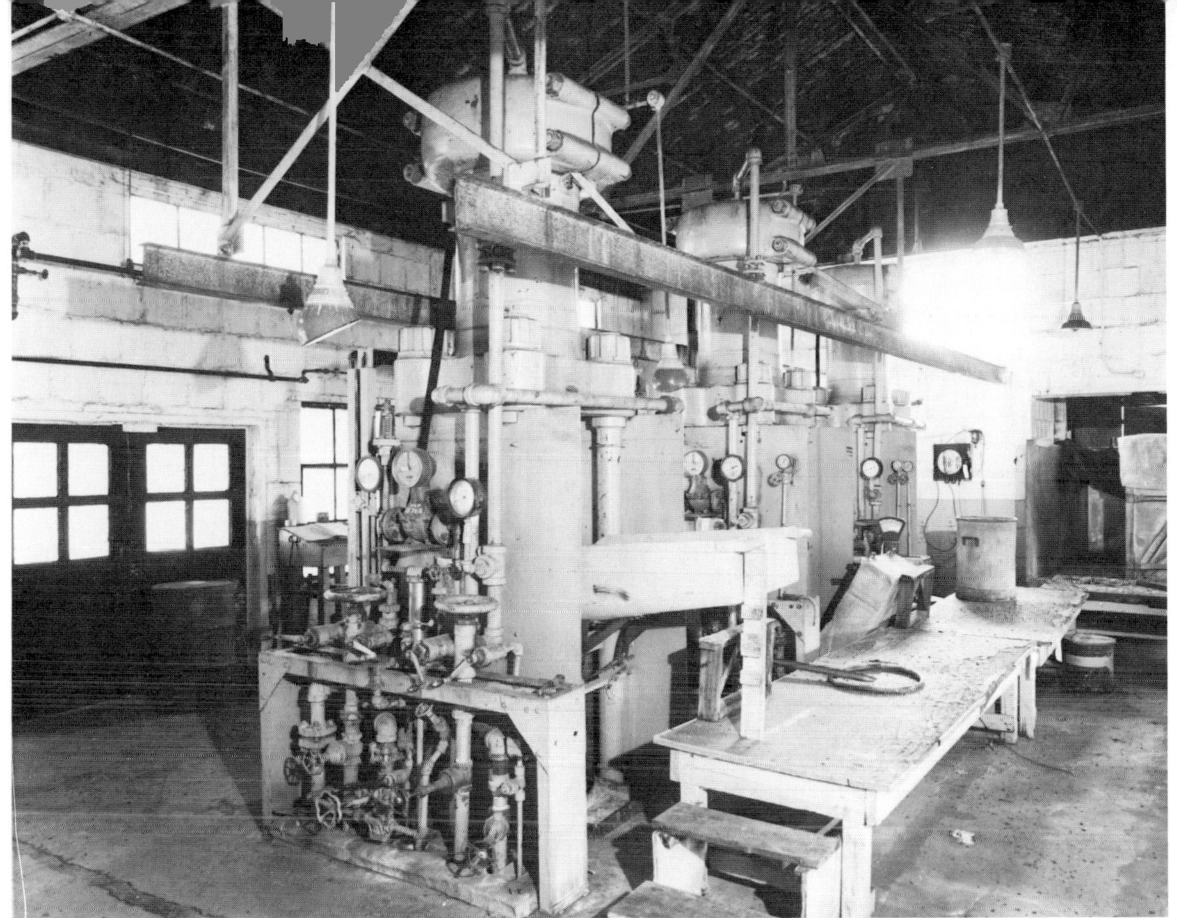

FIGURE 6.5

These presses in Building 527 of the Picatinny Arsenal, drawn schematically in fig. 6.2, removed water from pyrocotton slurry processed in Building 520.

FIGURE 6.6

This photograph of the cotton nitration line of the Picatinny Arsenal is one of many used instead of measured drawings to record the architectural appearance of Buildings 509, 510, and 511 of the arsenal. The measured drawings were reserved for the more significant chemical processes taking place inside the structures.

weights in interpretive drawings, since the drawings are often reduced in size, making legibility especially important.

The text for each sheet was composed with the intent to pack in as much relevant information as possible. With a chemical process, such factors as chemical formulas, weights, volumes, temperatures, pressures, times, reactants, products and by-products, purposes of procedures, and terminology are recorded in detail in order for the drawings to be of maximum benefit to future researchers. Relevant historical notes, numbers of machines, equipment design, and construction features are also included. The language is kept free of unexplained jargon and is organized in a building-by-building, step-by-step fashion. Descriptions of buildings are omitted since such information is covered elsewhere in the project record.

Figure 6.7

Building 519 of the Picatinny Arsenal, shown in Figure 6.2, recovered ether and alcohol vapors for reuse in the powder manufacturing process. Some of its exterior details, simplified in the process diagram, are made plain here.

The schematic portion of the presentation boils down the process to its simplest elements and steps, as described in the text, and organizes them by building. The flow of the schematic is from left to right, the same direction as the pictorial diagram and the text. To help interpret the hierarchy of elements more clearly, larger blocks and major labels for buildings are delineated more boldly than those for process steps or smaller buildings. The drawing sheets are laid out to parallel one another in their major divisions, so that all three sheets may be combined into one with little trouble, should any future user desire to do so.

Picatinny Arsenal is only one example of an interpretive presentation. The methods used in this case are not applicable in recording all industrial processes. In some cases, sequential views should be used to show principal motions (as in the case of an elliptical picture-frame lathe). Annotated sections of an object may suffice to present its operating features (as in the case of a blast furnace). Still others may benefit from a scaled isometric depiction of critical elements, with other features, such as a surrounding building, stripped away for clarity. The possibilities are numerous, but the idea is to balance relevant information, appropriate analytical presentation, clarity, and visual appeal.

FIGURE 6.8

This view of the cannon powder blender (Building 561 of the Picatinny Arsenal) from across Lake Picatinny shows a wall designed to relieve the forces of an explosion should any occur in the building. The isolation of the building further illustrates the potential danger of the operation.

FIGURE 6.9

Building 519 of the Picatinny Arsenal was equipped with slides for quick escape by workers in event of fire.

Recording Structural and Mechanical Systems

The Auditorium Building in Chicago (now Roosevelt University) was the largest structure of its kind in America at the time of its completion in 1890. The program included a hotel, an auditorium, and offices, with the hotel and office building wrapping around the theater in the center (see fig. 6.10). Economics had dictated the choice of the three different uses for the site. The developers planned to include income-producing functions to offset the large deficits expected in operating the theater. The Auditorium Building was thus an early example of mixed-use development. The arrangement of these functions was determined by real estate market conditions, light and ventilation requirements, and the site itself. The challenge to architects Dankmar Adler and Louis H. Sullivan was to integrate these three disparate functions, each with different needs, into a cohesive design (see fig. 6.11).

It is commonly thought that Dankmar Adler was the sole engineering genius behind the Auditorium, but responsibility for designing the foundations, the structural framing, and the heating and plumbing systems was spread over numerous consultants. The design of much of the various elevator, electrical, and service facilities was apparently the work of the manufacturers of the equipment. There was no general contractor on the Auditorium. Adler, who directed most of the construction work, acted much like a modern-day project manager, except that full-time supervision of the work was in the hands of an experienced builder.

Documenting the Auditorium Building in Chicago presented challenges that are becoming common as more structures built since the late nineteenth century are being recorded. The nineteenth century saw enormous changes in building technology. At the beginning of the century, building technologies were limited to masonry bearing-wall or heavy-frame construction, with fireplaces for heating, and outdoor privies. By the end of the century, technologies had evolved to include steel skeleton and light-frame construction; central heating; and other mechanical systems, such as plumbing and electricity. Architecture and engineering developed as professions during the century, along with many specialized building trades. The result was that buildings in general grew more complex in terms of materials, structure, and function. Large buildings became common.

The Auditorium Building exemplifies this trend in that it is a large building that has significance in many areas: design and construction, structural systems, mechanical systems, and aesthetics. It is also a building for which a great deal of documentary records exist, another increasingly common phenomenon. In fact, the volume of records available to review, cross-check, and verify presented a logistical problem. Nevertheless, this source material made possible the compilation of an extensive written history and description of the building. Historic photographs and drawings were also located and copied.

A major goal of the project was for Roosevelt University to be able to use the completed documentation in its stewardship of the building. This documentation would enable the university to consider historic significance and integrity when planning for the changing needs of the school. Moreover, Roosevelt University did not have a

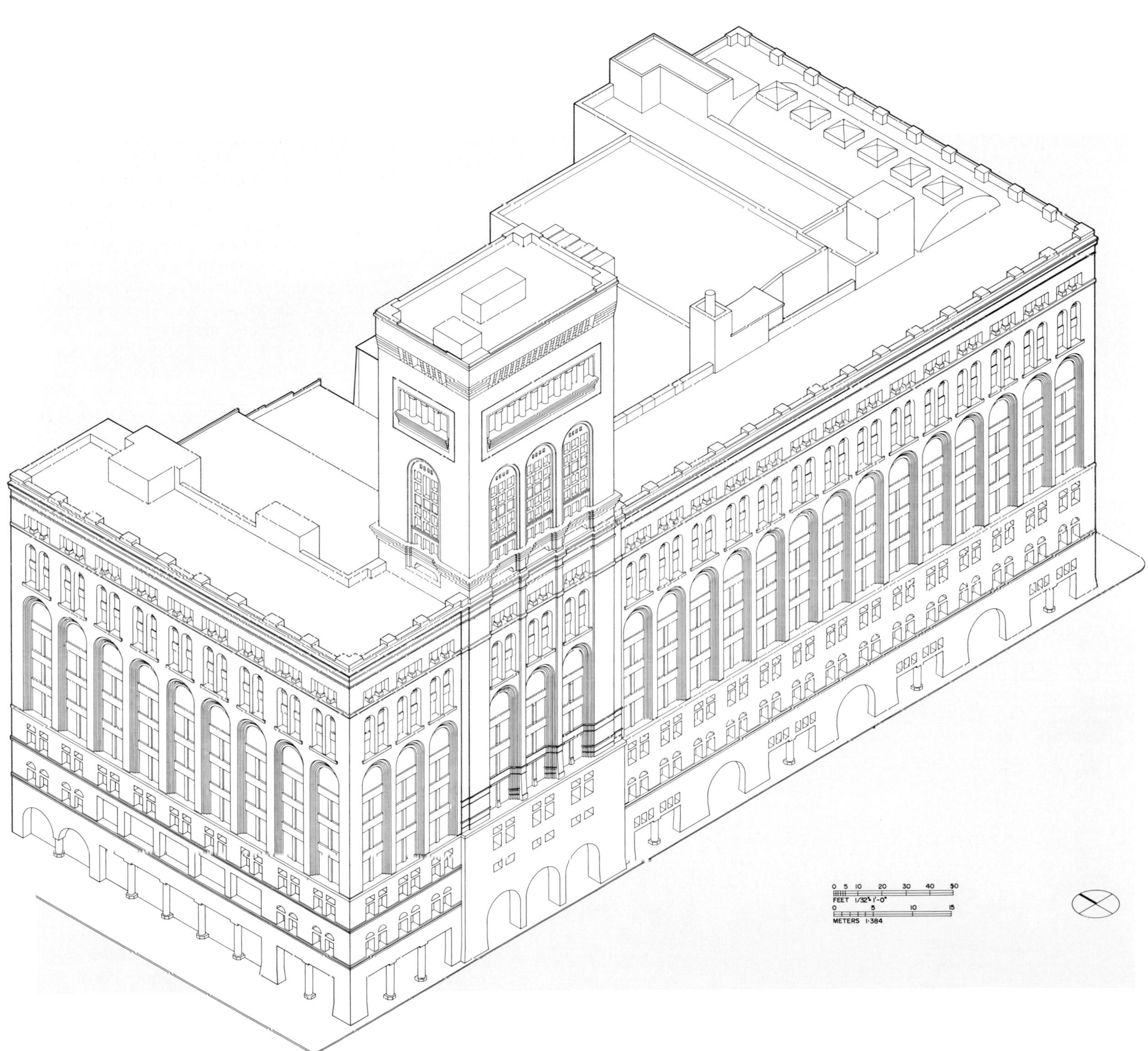

Figure 6.10

The program for the Auditorium Building in Chicago combined three unrelated functions—a theater, a hotel, and an office building. The design solution placed the theater in the interior, wrapped the hotel around two sides, and placed the office space along the third side, with one entrance on each street elevation. An aerial isometric drawing was used to portray the arrangement and massing of the three functions. The particular angle of view was chosen to delineate the west and south facades. The east facade was recorded in a separate elevation drawing (see fig. 6.20).

Figure 6.11

The imposing stone exterior of thc Auditorium Building In Chicago offers little hint of its interior complexities. This view, taken shortly after the building's completion in 1890, is not marred by the later fire escapes and shows the now removed weather station on top of the tower. Note that the ground level camera station does not reveal the functional massing of the building.

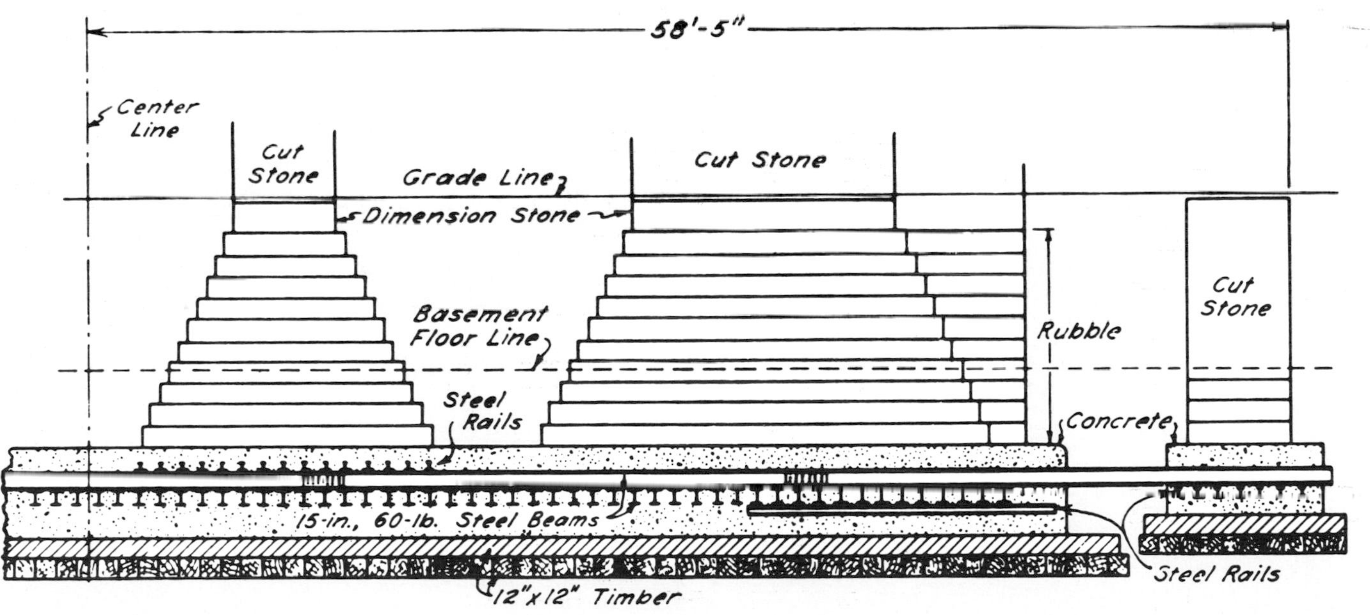

FIGURE 6.12

Other than original drawings and specifications, documentary records are rarely available for foundations because they are inaccessible. This illustration, from Observed and Computed Settlements of Structures In Chicago, *was probably based on a drawing published in the* Inland Architect *in July 1888. The widely varying point and linear loads of the Auditorium Building foundations and poor bearing capacity of the soil necessitated the use of spread footings. The center and left footings in this illustration, which are part of one large footing that carries the seventeen-story masonry tower, are considerably larger than the right footing, which carries the ten-story exterior wall.*

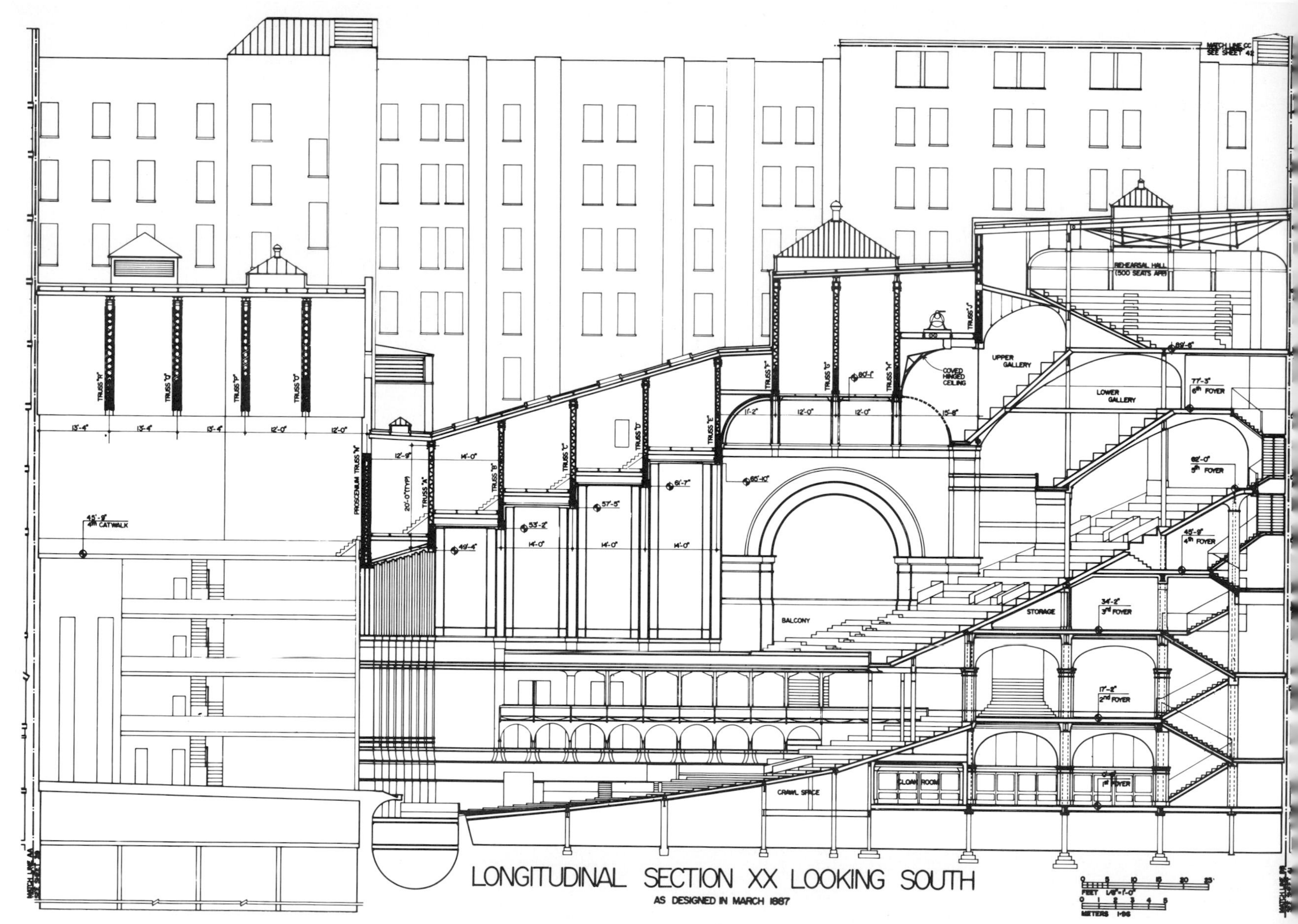
LONGITUDINAL SECTION XX LOOKING SOUTH
AS DESIGNED IN MARCH 1887
REHEARSAL HALL (500 SEATS APP.)
UPPER GALLERY
LOWER GALLERY
COVED HINGED CEILING
BALCONY
STORAGE
CRAWL SPACE
CLOAK ROOM
6th FOYER
5th FOYER
4th FOYER
3rd FOYER
2nd FOYER
1st FOYER
4th CATWALK
PROSCENIUM TRUSS "A"

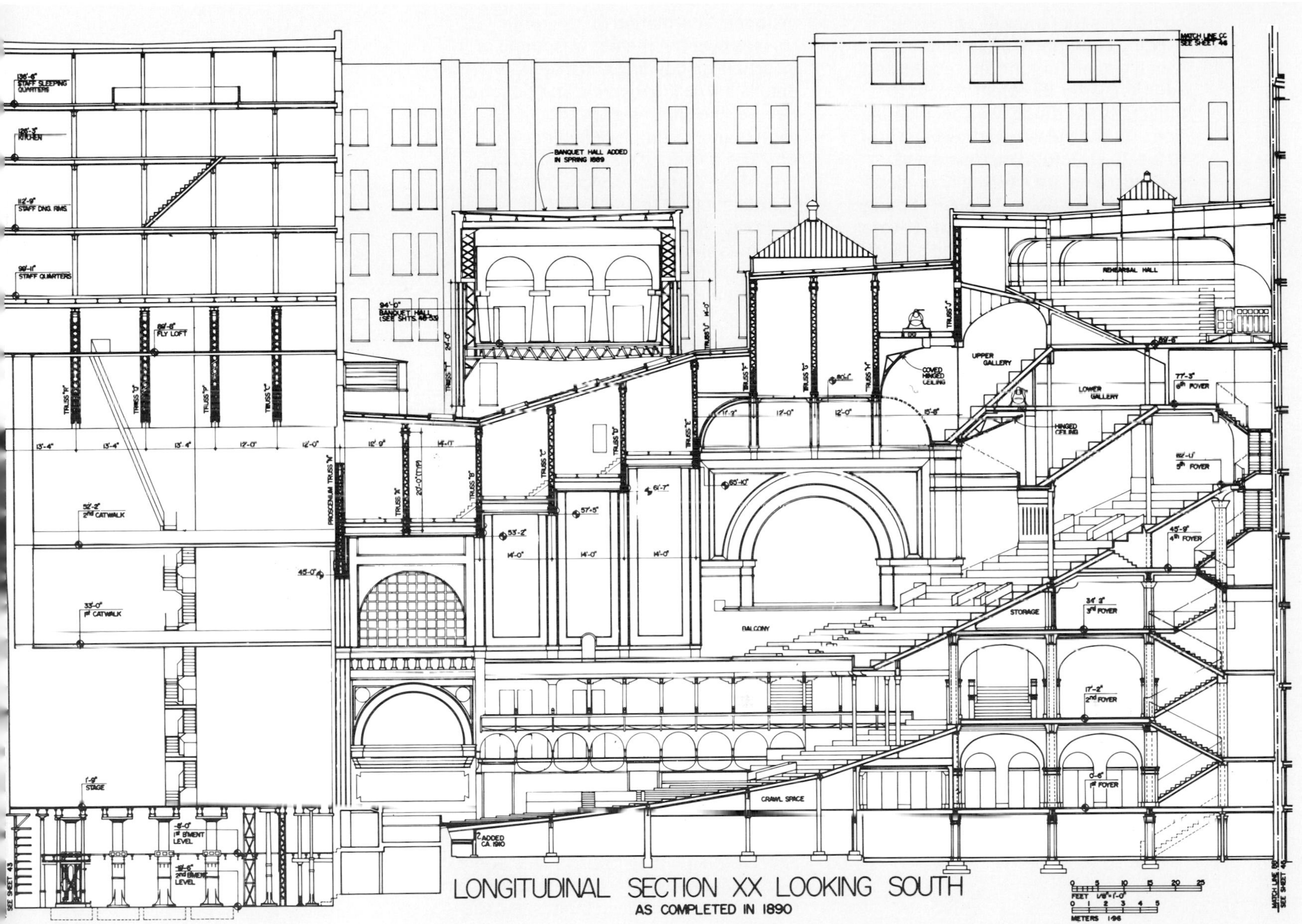

Figs. 6.13 and 6.14

Two section drawings were necessary to portray the major changes in the Auditorium Building's design made as construction progressed. These two sheets show only the theater portion as it was originally designed and as it was eventually completed four years later. Similar changes were made in the hotel and office portions of the building. In the stagehouse note the hydraulic equipment added under the stage and four floors of service space over the roof trusses. In the hall, the orchestra pit was modified, truss "A" was raised to accommodate the new organ, and a hinged ceiling was installed over the lower gallery. The roof trusses over the rehearsal hall were changed from Fink trusses to built-up plate girders. Above the roof of the theater the banquet hall was supported by two large trusses spanning the full width of the theater. These changes added more weight on the foundations, which had been designed to support the earlier design.

complete set of drawings showing existing conditions in the building, which had undergone alterations and additions after its construction. The university identified two specific functions for the measured drawings: first, to locate structural members and, second, to record existing floor plans and room functions. Because of budget constraints, floor plans for the theater were beyond the scope of the project, although the theater was recorded in the section drawings. For the same reasons, the project did not produce measured drawings of the decorative elements of the building.

Architectural research traditionally focuses on the architect as the principal person responsible for a building. Although the Auditorium Building research went beyond Adler and Sullivan, it was difficult to find detailed information on most of the other people associated with the building's design and construction. Time and budget constraints precluded an exhaustive search. Budgets notwithstanding, the point to remember is that structures with multiple areas of significance will probably require multiple areas of historical research if a complete history is to be compiled. For instance, information on the roof trusses over the theater was found in an article on building construction details in *The Engineering and Building Record*; the plumbing specifications were found in a book called *Industrial Chicago*, and drawings and a description of the foundation were found in a pamphlet on settlements of Chicago buildings (see fig. 6.12). A book with drawings and a description of the precedent for the hydraulic stage equipment (at the Budapest Opera House in Hungary) was serendipitously found in a used bookstore in Pennsylvania. Additional information was found in court records detailing the building's troubled financial history, including allegations of structural deficiencies.

Structural Systems

In modern terms, the Auditorium Building was built on a fast track, as its design was not complete when construction started. Moreover, the actual program for the building changed while it was under construction. The decision to add a banquet hall above the theater roof and four floors of service space above the stage house was made when the building was already at the fifth floor level. This was but one of many major changes made during construction.

Because of these modifications, historic drawings to which the recording team had access had to be verified against the building itself. In fact, some of what appeared in original drawings may not have ever been built, since the

Figure 6.15

The complexities of the structural system of the basement of the Auditorium Building are best revealed in a cutaway aerial isometric. An isometric drawing portrays the depth as well as the plan of the basement, illustrating the size and massing of the footings, and placement, size, and configuration of the bearing walls and columns. The annotations further explain features in the basement, such as the hydraulic stage equipment and the under-sidewalk vaults. Similar isometric drawings of each floor portray structural information in three dimensions. Non-bearing partitions were not shown, providing Roosevelt University, which now owns the building, with information on how to combine the small hotel rooms into larger spaces.

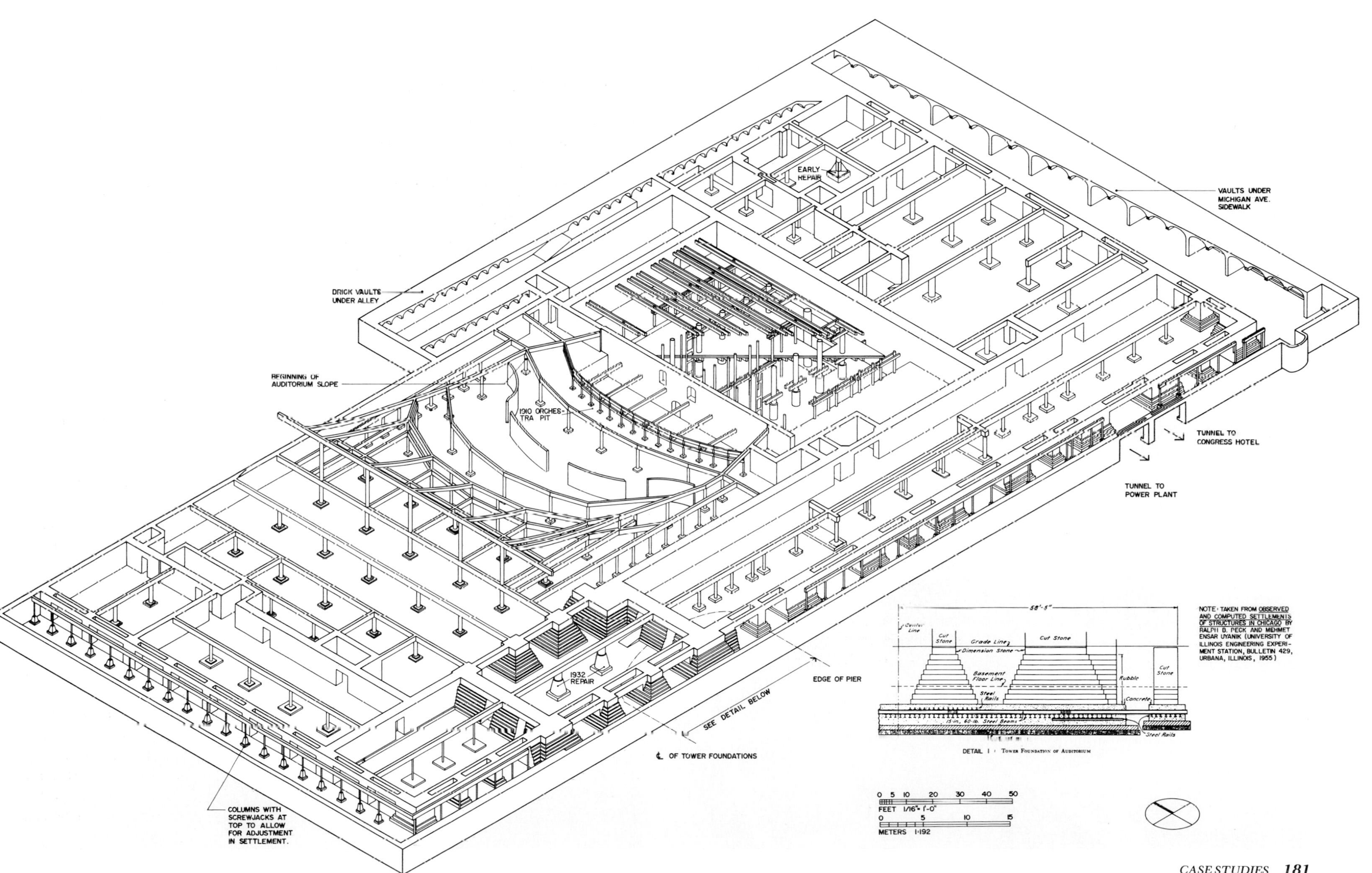

VAULTS UNDER MICHIGAN AVE. SIDEWALK
EARLY REPAIR
BRICK VAULTS UNDER ALLEY
BEGINNING OF AUDITORIUM SLOPE
1910 ORCHESTRA PIT
TUNNEL TO CONGRESS HOTEL
TUNNEL TO POWER PLANT
1932 REPAIR
EDGE OF PIER
SEE DETAIL BELOW
℄ OF TOWER FOUNDATIONS
COLUMNS WITH SCREWJACKS AT TOP TO ALLOW FOR ADJUSTMENT IN SETTLEMENT.
58'-5"
Center Line
Cut Stone
Grade Line
Cut Stone
Dimension Stone
Basement Floor Line
Rubble
Cut Stone
Steel Rails
Concrete
15 in. 60 lb. Steel Beams
Steel Rails
NOTE: TAKEN FROM OBSERVED AND COMPUTED SETTLEMENTS OF STRUCTURES IN CHICAGO BY RALPH B. PECK AND MEHMET ENSAR UYANIK (UNIVERSITY OF ILLINOIS ENGINEERING EXPERIMENT STATION, BULLETIN 429, URBANA, ILLINOIS, 1955)
0 5 10 20 30 40 50
FEET 1/16"=1'-0"
0 5 10 15
METERS 1:192

DETAIL 1 : TOWER FOUNDATION OF AUDITORIUM

design changed as construction progressed. Two versions of the longitudinal section were made to compare the structure as designed in 1886 to the structure as completed in 1890 (see figs. 6.13 and 6.14).

A further complication in documenting structural and mechanical systems is that HABS/HAER is nondestructive in its investigations. HABS/HAER does not open up walls or remove fireproofing from steel beams to determine their construction details. The Auditorium documentation relied on earlier documentary sources for information on hidden features. Where possible, the information was visually

Figure 6.16

Fire protection for the trusses in the theater attic of the Auditorium Building is provided by the heavy plaster ceiling of the theater and the terra-cotta deck over the trusses, which support the roof surface. While not ideal from a fire safety standpoint, the trusses were easy to record in large-format photographs.

***Figure* 6.17**

Among the only remaining original plumbing equipment in the Auditorium Building are these two sewage ejector pumps that still pump sewage up to the level of the street sewer from the stage basement.

***Figure* 6.18**

The hydraulic rams in the Auditorium Building have been fixed in position at stage level, making the rams inoperable. A new floor was built at the level the stage would have been when lowered.

verified. Structural information was delineated by isometric drawings of each floor so that the columns and beams and bearing walls could be located (see fig. 6.15). Structural details were recorded through reference to documentary sources supplemented by construction photographs where possible. Exposed structural members, chiefly the major roof trusses, were photographed (see fig. 6.16).

Mechanical Systems

Several of the original mechanical systems have nearly vanished. Heat has been supplied to the building from off-site boilers since 1893. The foundations for the direct-current dynamos are all that remain of the power plant under the Wabash Avenue sidewalk. Information on the plumbing comes primarily from the published specifications, with two still-operating sewage ejector pumps among the only remaining original equipment (see fig. 6.17). The hydraulic stage equipment is substantially intact, although the stage has been immobilized and the water tanks that supplied the necessary head were removed from the tower (see fig. 6.18). The hydraulic elevator equipment, which operated off the same water supply as the stage equipment, has been replaced. In spite of these limitations, a reasonably complete history and description of the systems was compiled from the remaining physical evidence and documentary sources. Significant remaining equipment was photographed. Only the ventilation systems of the theater and banquet hall were recorded in measured drawings (see fig. 6.19).

Aesthetics

The basic scheme of a theater wrapped by a hotel and office building is recognizable throughout the evolution of the design for the building. There are records for seven different designs for the facades. In the measured drawings the Michigan Avenue facade was recorded using photogrammetry (see fig. 6.20). The massing of the building was recorded in an aerial axonometric drawing that shows the Congress Street and Wabash Avenue facades and the roof configuration (see fig. 6.11). The north elevations of the tower and the Congress Street wing of the hotel were recorded in the longitudinal section of the theater.

The designs of the interior spaces were recorded with both historic and contemporary large-format photographs and written documentation, but not with measured drawings, as they were outside the scope of this project. The overall design for the interior of the theater was recorded in section drawings of the building, but with little detail. The majority of the graphic records for the decorative elements of the interior consist of copies of historic photographs (see fig. 6.21).

The banquet hall was the one interior space recorded in some detail, as it was undergoing restoration and easily accessible for measuring. Hand-measured drawings of the plans and structural and mechanical systems were complemented by a photogrammetric drawing of both extant and missing decorative features produced from contemporary and historic photographs (see fig. 6.22).

The documentation for the Auditorium Building includes 61 measured drawings, 111 large-format photographs, 86 pages of written data, eight photogrammetric glass plates, and several folders of field records, making it one of the most thoroughly documented structures in the collection. Within HABS/HAER, it was a pioneering effort at recording the multiple areas of significance typically found in a large commercial building.

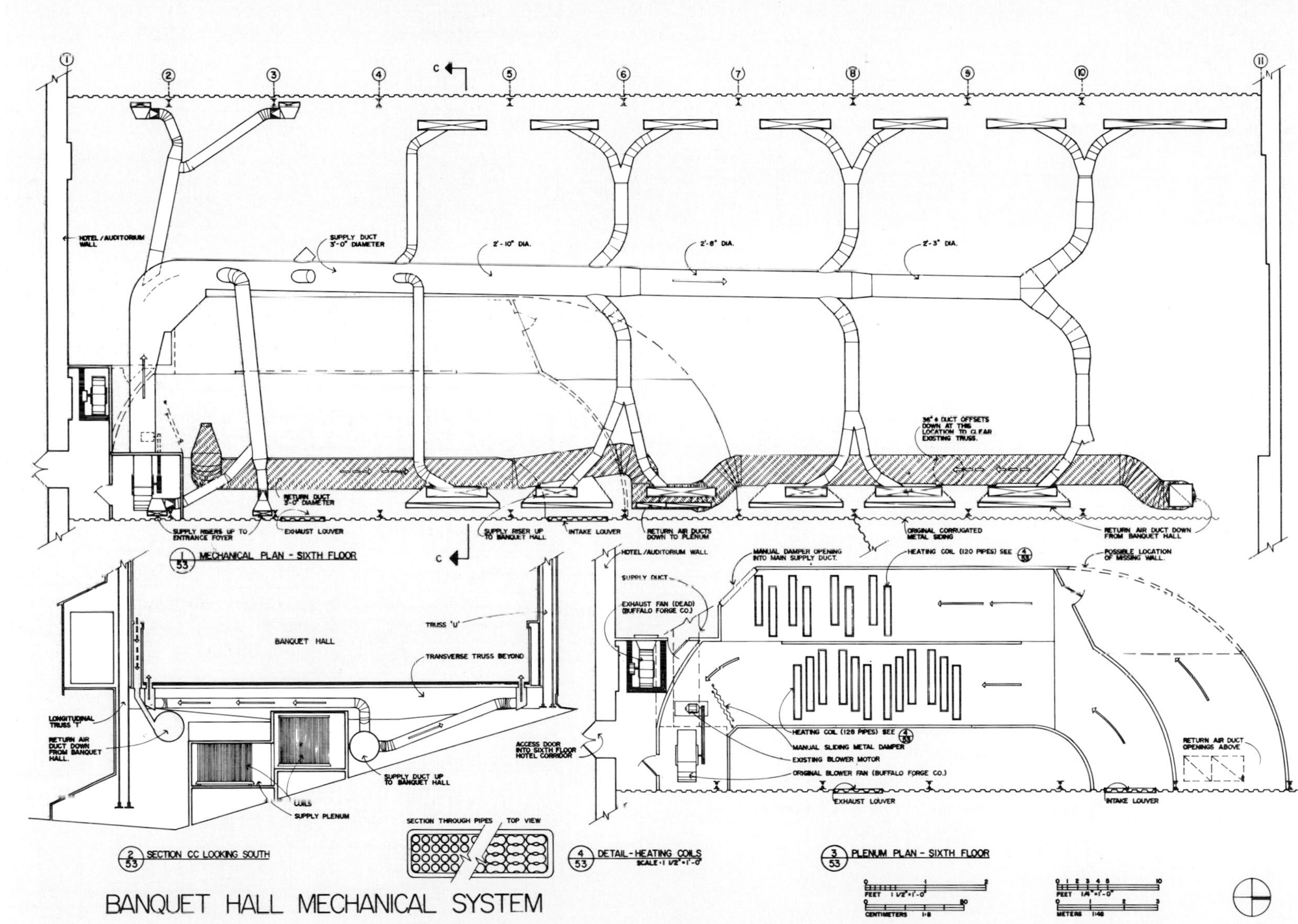

FIGURE 6.19

The restoration of the banquet hall in the Auditorium Building allowed access to the self-contained heating and ventilating system of the room. The system is independent of the main building since it sits above the theater roof.

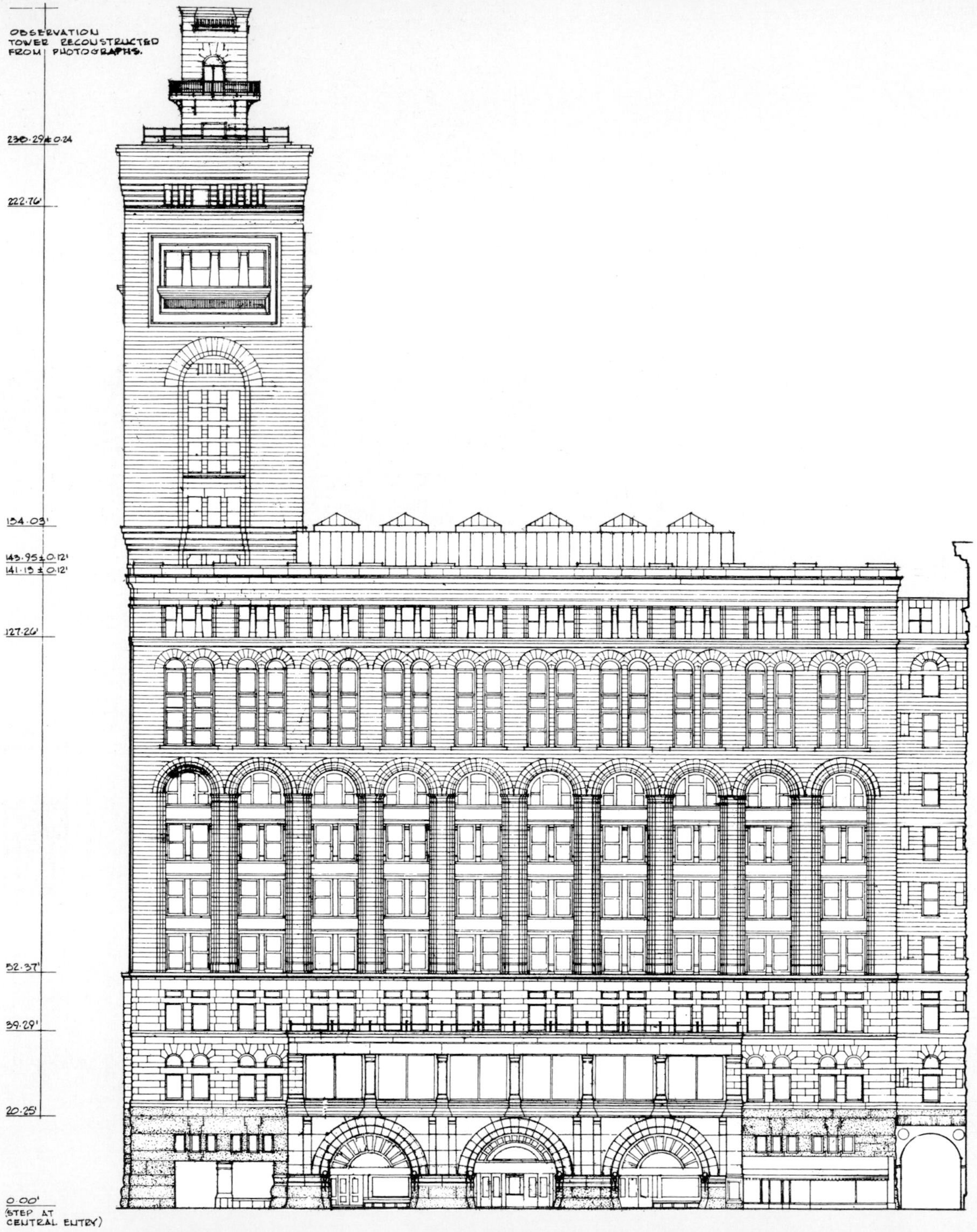

OBSERVATION TOWER RECONSTRUCTED FROM PHOTOGRAPHS.

230.29±0.24
222.76'
154.03'
143.95±0.12'
141.15±0.12'
127.26'
52.37'
39.29'
20.25'
0.00' (STEP AT CENTRAL ENTRY)

Figure 6.20

The Michigan Avenue facade of the Auditorium Building was recorded in 1963 using photogrammetric plates. Historic photographs of the observation tower together with information from the contemporary photogrammetric plates enabled the drawing to include the now removed structure.

FIGURE 6.21

Photocopies of promotional photographs made of the Auditorium Building shortly after completion form the basis for the HABS photographs of decorative features of the building, saving a great deal of on-site time for the contemporary photographer. Copying historic photographs may not always be possible if their owners are not willing to let them pass into the public domain.

CROSS SECTION LOOKING NORTH TO ORIGINAL MUSICIANS' GALLERY

FIGURE 6.22

Contemporary photogrammetric plotting combined with photogrammetric analysis of historic photographs of the Auditorium Building allowed the delineation of the original musicians' gallery in the banquet hall and re-creation of the removed lighting fixtures. Dimensions for the missing elements were determined photogrammetrically from the dimensions of objects in the historic photographs that had survived. This technique is called reverse perspective analysis.

FIGURE 6.23

Condition of the pilot schooner Alabama *at the time of the HABS recording project is documented with large-format photography. The original sailing rig had been removed sometime in the 1950s.*

FIGURE 6.24

This is a print of a circa 1926 photograph copied by HAER with the vessel owner's permission. The photograph can be dated by the name Alabama *on the starboard bow (research of the ship registry showed this to have been the ship's name from 1926 to 1928). This photograph was one of many historical photographs used to reconstruct the* Alabama*'s original sailing rig on the first sheet of the measured drawings (see fig. 6.25).*

Recording Historic Ships

The documentation of historic ships is a specialized case of documenting historic engineering and architectural structures. In concept, the three most common media used to document land-based structures—written reports, photography, and measured drawings—are easily adapted to the documentation of vessels. The preparation of reports and photographs for a ship will usually require the same research methods, skills, and equipment as for a stationary structure. Creating measured drawings of ships, on the other hand, introduces some unique challenges. In contrast to land-based structures, most vessels contain very few

FIGURE 6.25

The original profile of the Alabama *shown here was derived from several historic photographs as well as HAER field data; notes below the graphic scale record the sources and give limitations of the effort. This title sheet also gives the official description of the ship, a brief history, and the details of the recording project.*

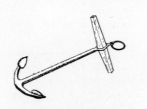

PILOT SCHOONER

ALABAMA

1926

Designed by noted fishing vessel designer Thomas F. McManus of Boston, Massachusetts, the schooner ALABAMA was built of the "finest materials" in 1926 by the Pensacola Shipbuilding Co. in Pensacola, Florida for the Mobile Bay Bar Pilots Association of Mobile, Alabama. She was meant to replace an earlier vessel of the same name launched in 1908 by the Tarr & James Co. of Essex, Massachusetts. Until the first vessel was sold to a Carribean shipping company by the Pilots Association, ALABAMA bore the name ALABAMIAN.

ALABAMA was originally outfitted with two engines and twin screws in addition to her two masted rig, which had been designed mainly for steadying purposes and for back-up propulsion in the event of engine failure. The Pilots Association also specified a short overhang aft to prevent the stern from pounding when at anchor off Fort Morgan in Mobile Bay. Three feet were added to the stern when a wheelhouse was built (sometime before 1945), and after World War Two, her masts were removed and replaced with short steel masts designed to carry only lights and radio antenna. During the war, she served in the Coast Guard Reserve as CGR 9031.

ALABAMA was built to accomodate pilots who guided incoming vessels through the Bay. Belowdecks are a galley up forward, an engine room amidships, and the pilots' cabin aft. Pilots were transferred to and from incoming vessels by small boats, which when idle were hauled out on the boat davits. In earlier days these boats were oar-powered yawlboats; toward the end of ALABAMA's service, 25 foot powerboats were used.

In 1966, ALABAMA was purchased by Robert S. Douglas of Vineyard Haven, Massachusetts, after which she underwent several modifications. The wheelhouse and steel masts were removed and her engines, auxiliaries, and deck replaced. Her stockless, self-stowing anchors were also removed. Her sailing rig has not yet been returned however. The profile which appears nearby is based on photographs taken shortly after she was launched, while the remaining drawings depict her in her present condition.

The ALABAMA Recording Project is part of the Historic American Engineering Record (HAER), a long-range program which includes the documentation of historically significant vessels in the United States. As a part of the National Park Service, U.S. Department of the Interior, the HAER program is administered by the Historic American Buildings Survey/Historic American Engineering Record Division (HABS/HAER), Robert J. Kapsch, Chief. The ALABAMA Recording Project was cosponsored during the summer of 1986 by HAER under the general direction of Sally Kress Tompkins, Deputy Chief, HABS/HAER; by the National Trust for Historic Preservation, Washington, D.C.–Marcia Myers, Vice President, Maritime Division; and by Mystic Seaport Museum, Mystic, Connecticut–J. Revell Carr, Director. Mr. Robert S. Douglas, owner of ALABAMA, granted access to the vessel and generously provided data and historic photographs essential to the ALABAMA's documentation. This project was part of a multi-year effort by the National Trust and HABS/HAER to develop national standards for documenting historic vessels.

The field work, measured drawings, historical report, and photographs were prepared under the project management of Richard K. Anderson, Jr., Staff Architect, HAER. The recording team consisted of Richard K. Anderson, Jr.; Deborah M. Rehn, Field Supervisor; Elizabeth M. Kunin, and Christopher A. Cyzewski, Architectural Technicians. The team received invaluable assistance from numerous members of the Mystic Seaport Museum shipyard staff under Dana Hewson, Shipyard Director. Paul Lipke of Plymouth, Massachusetts, aided the team in the field. Final drawings were inked by Robbyn L. Jackson, Architect, HAER. The formal photography was done by Jet Lowe, HAER Staff Photographer, in 1986.

OFFICIAL DESCRIPTION

Official №: 226177

Built of Wood

Length (original): 81.4' overall
Length (1986): 88.63' overall
Beam: 21.6'
Depth: 9.7'

Masts: 2 (originally)
Decks: 2

Gross Tonnage: 70
Net Tonnage: 35

Rig: Schooner

Sail Area: 1510 ± 20 sq. ft.

Mechanical Propulsion: Twin screw, two engine installations.

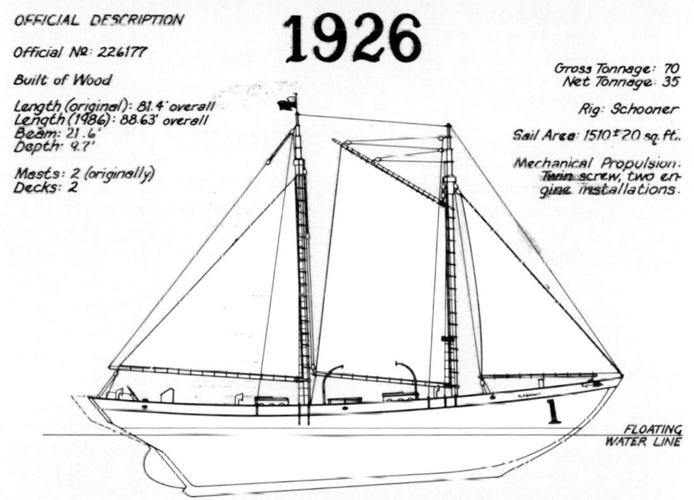

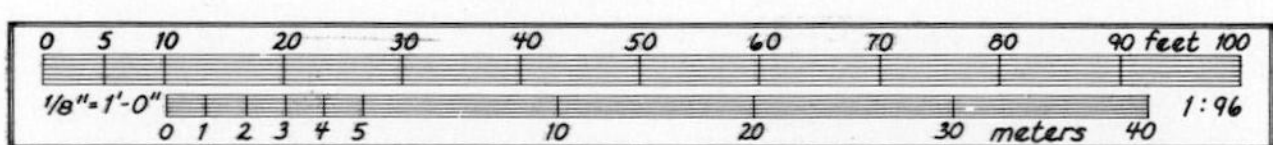

A. The hull and rail are based on field measurements taken by Robert S. Douglas in 1967 and by HAER in 1986. All other features are based on historical information and photographs supplied by Mr. Douglas.

B. Reverse perspective analysis was used to arrive at dimensions for the masts and booms. Some rigging details were derived from historic photographs, others from typical schooner rig details. Some features appearing in the historical photographs (see HAER photos MA-64-23 to MA-64-30) were not drawn above for lack of further dimensional data. Accuracy of the drawing above the rail is estimated to be ±6". A sail plan for re-rigging ALABAMA was drawn by Robert S. Douglas in 1971; a copy is enclosed with the field records.

Robbyn L. Jackson 1987

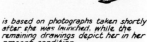

PILOT SCHOONER "ALABAMA" (1926)

VINEYARD HAVEN MARTHA'S VINEYARD DUKES COUNTY MASSACHUSETTS

SHEET 1 – 12

HISTORIC AMERICAN ENGINEERING RECORD MA-64

NOTES

A. No determination was made of the wood species used in construction of the vessel except for the deck (pine).

B. ALABAMA had no masts or rigging in 1986.

C. The position of the rail stanchions on the starboard side differ slightly from those on the port side (±1½").

D. Approximately 3 feet was added to the transom (date unknown) while the vessel served in Mobile, Alabama. This area was inaccessible for measurement.

E. No observations or measurements were made by HAER below the waterline. Data for the lines, keel and rudder were based on work done by Robert C. Douglas in 1967.

F. The bilges were filled with ballast and were inaccessible for measurement.

G. ALABAMA's two engines are Gray Marine Diesel, Model Number 64 HNS, manufactured by the Detroit Diesel Engine Division, General Motors Corp., Detroit, Michigan.

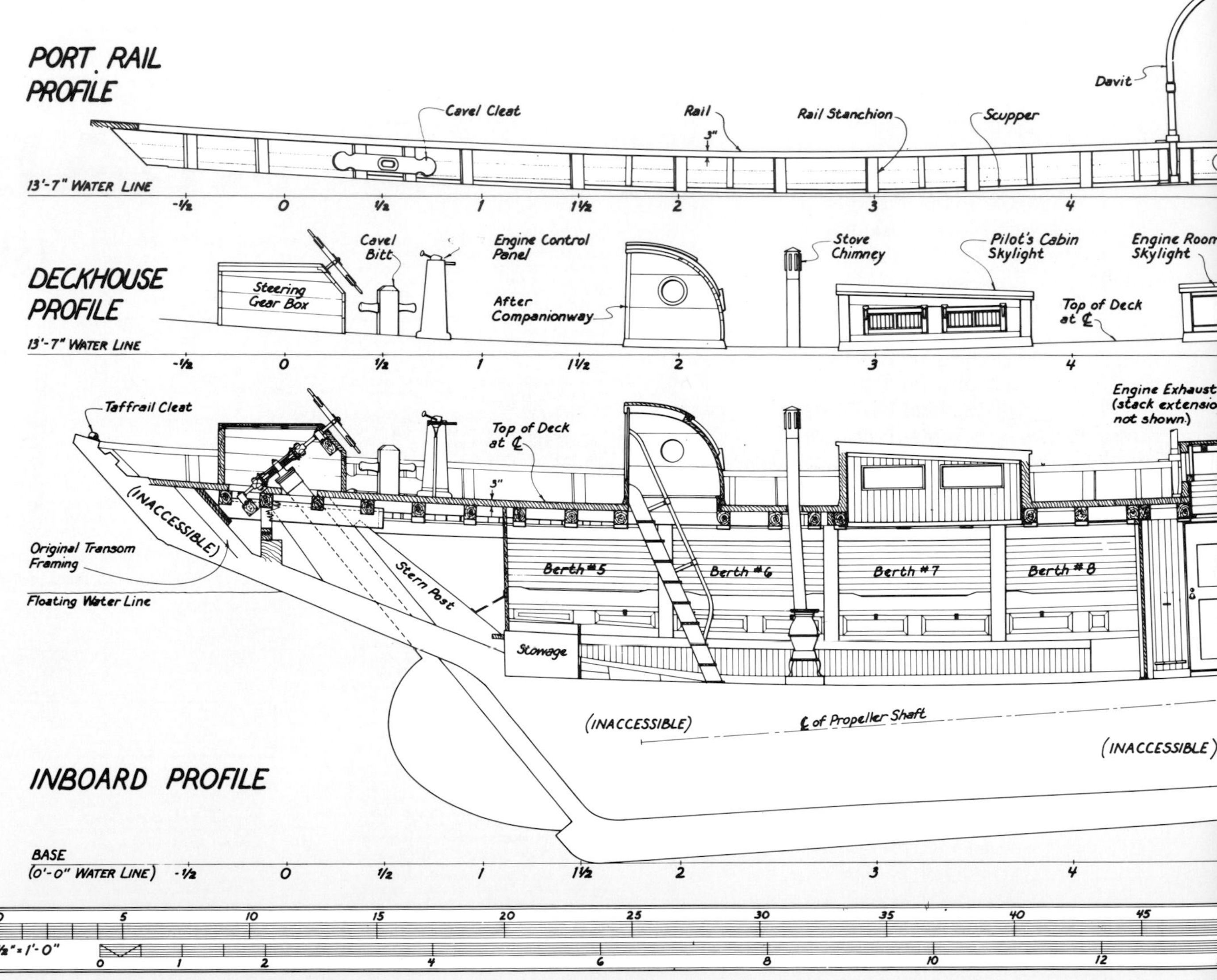

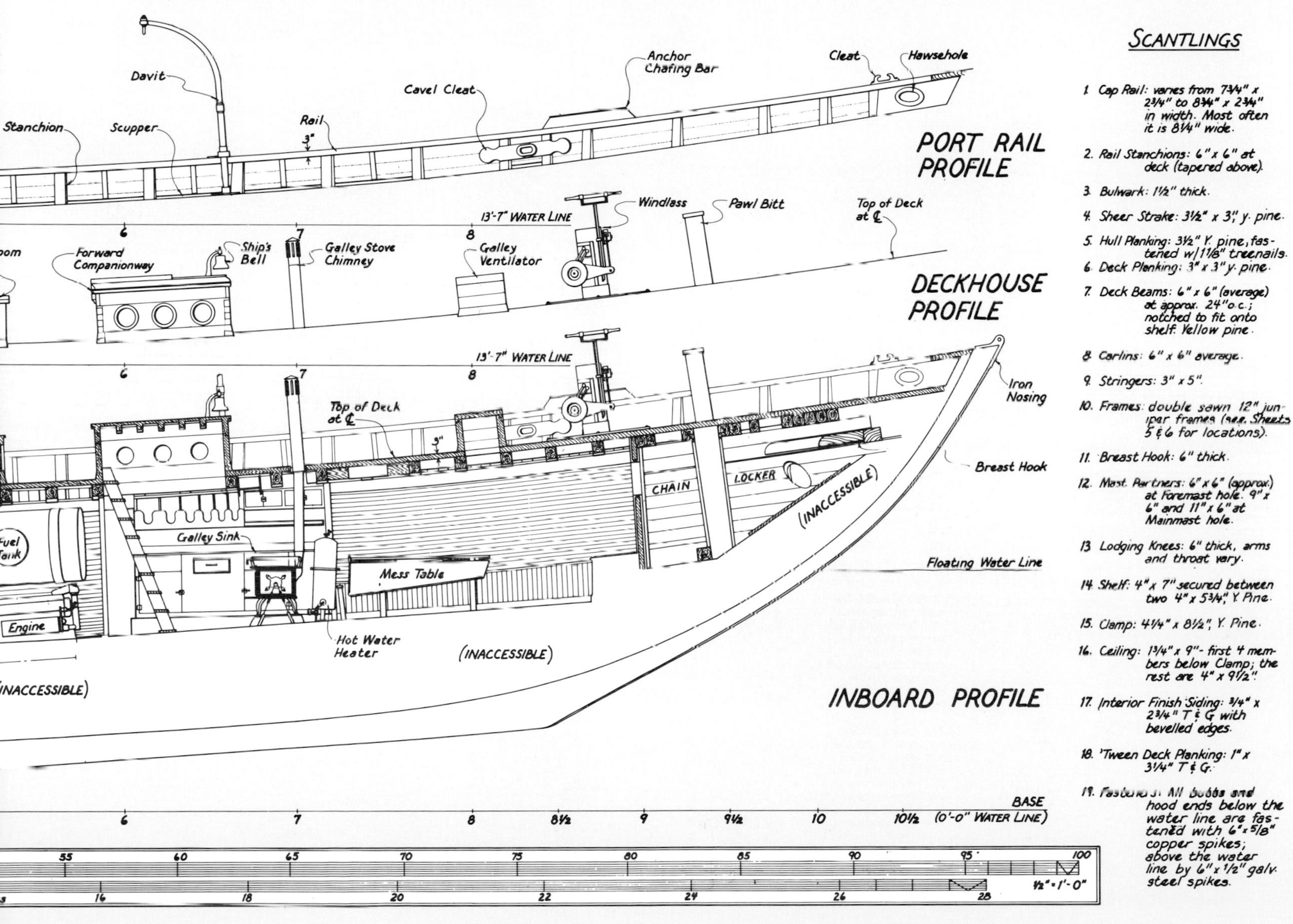

Davit
Anchor Chafing Bar
Cleat
Hawsehole
Cavel Cleat
Stanchion
Scupper
Rail
3"
PORT RAIL PROFILE
13'-7" WATER LINE
Windlass
Pawl Bitt
Top of Deck at ℄
Room
Forward Companionway
Ship's Bell
Galley Stove Chimney
Galley Ventilator
DECKHOUSE PROFILE
13'-7" WATER LINE
Iron Nosing
Top of Deck at ℄
3"
Breast Hook
CHAIN LOCKER
(INACCESSIBLE)
Fuel Tank
Galley Sink
Mess Table
Floating Water Line
Engine
Hot Water Heater
(INACCESSIBLE)
(INACCESSIBLE)
INBOARD PROFILE
BASE (0'-0" WATER LINE)
SCANTLINGS
1. Cap Rail: varies from 7¾" x 2¾" to 8¾" x 2¾" in width. Most often it is 8¼" wide.
2. Rail Stanchions: 6" x 6" at deck (tapered above).
3. Bulwark: 1½" thick.
4. Sheer Strake: 3½" x 3"; y. pine.
5. Hull Planking: 3½" Y. pine, fastened w/1⅛" treenails.
6. Deck Planking: 3" x 3" y. pine.
7. Deck Beams: 6" x 6" (average) at approx. 24" o.c.; notched to fit onto shelf. Yellow pine.
8. Carlins: 6" x 6" average.
9. Stringers: 3" x 5".
10. Frames: double sawn 12" junipar frames (see Sheets 5 & 6 for locations).
11. Breast Hook: 6" thick.
12. Mast Partners: 6" x 6" (approx.) at Foremast hole. 9" x 6" and 11" x 6" at Mainmast hole.
13. Lodging Knees: 6" thick, arms and throat vary.
14. Shelf: 4" x 7" secured between two 4" x 5¾" Y. Pine.
15. Clamp: 4¼" x 8½", Y. Pine.
16. Ceiling: 1¾" x 9" - first 4 members below Clamp; the rest are 4" x 9½".
17. Interior Finish Siding: ¾" x 2¾" T & G with bevelled edges.
18. 'Tween Deck Planking: 1" x 3¼" T & G.
19. hood ends below the water line are fastened with 6" x ⅝" copper spikes; above the water line by 6" x ½" galv. steel spikes.

FIGURES 6.26 and 6.27

This section through the Alabama was carefully drawn at ½" scale from field data. Inaccessible areas are noted, as are other observations pertinent to the vessel's structure and the team's recording procedures. A long graphic scale is included to enable users to scale from enlargements, reductions, or the drawing itself.

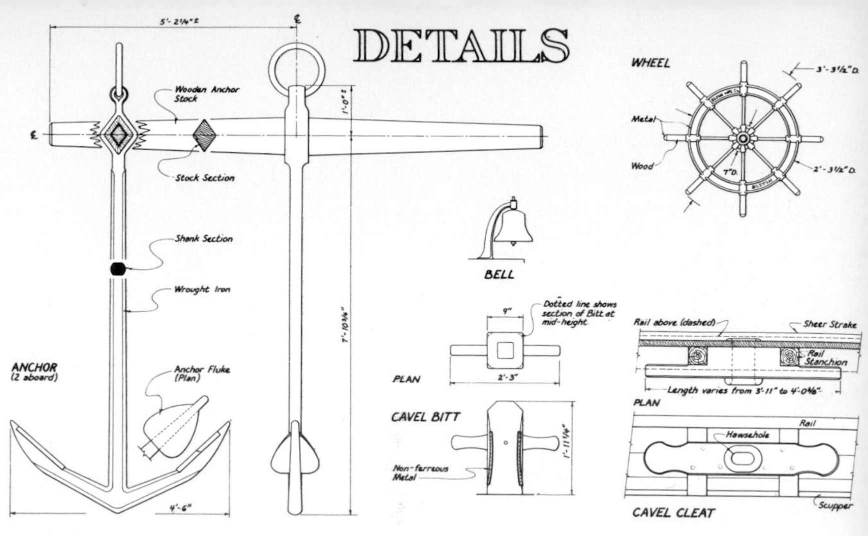

Notes

A. The locations of the frames were estimated by eye from their positions between the deck beams. (Accuracy ±½")

B. The positions of the rail stanchions on the starboard side differ from those on the port side by ±1½" (fore and aft).

C. ALABAMA's structure was inaccessible aft of the sternpost. The locations of the ends of the clamps and shelves were not determined, but the drawings reflect the assumption that they are just forward of the original transom.

D. Approximately 3 feet was added to the transom (date unknown) while the vessel served in Mobile, Alabama. The interior construction of this addition was inaccessible for measurement.

E. The location of frames aft of Station ½ were not determined in the field.

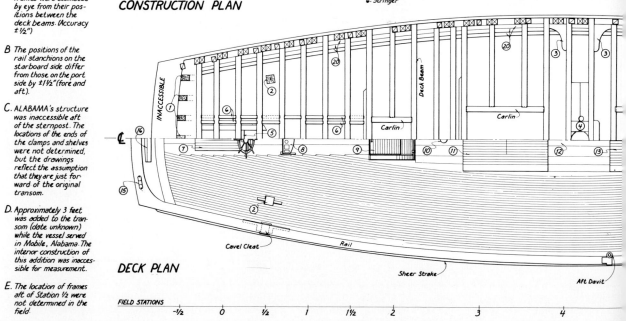

⊠ FRAME (SEE NOTE A)

▨ RAIL STANCHION (SEE NOTE B)

1. Original Transom Framing (See note C)
2. Cavel Bitt
3. Lodging Knee
4. Mast Partners
5. Stern Post
6. Stringer
7. Steering Gear Box
8. Engine Control Panel
9. Aft Companionway
10. Stove Chimney
11. Pilot's Cabin Skylight
12. King Plank
13. Engine Roo
14. Engine Exha
15. Taffrail Clea
16. Transom Ver

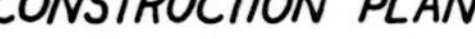

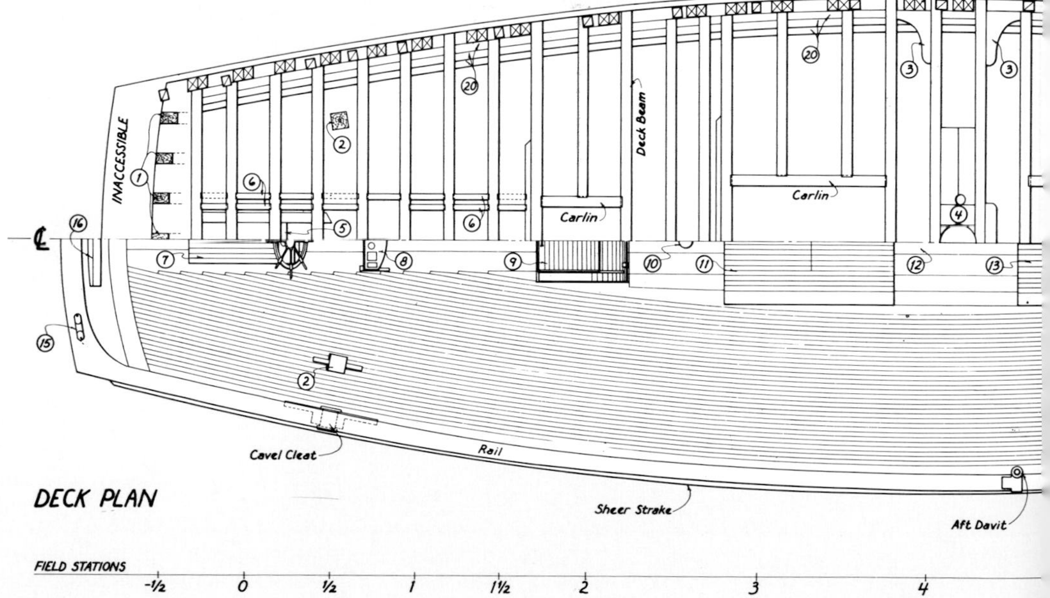

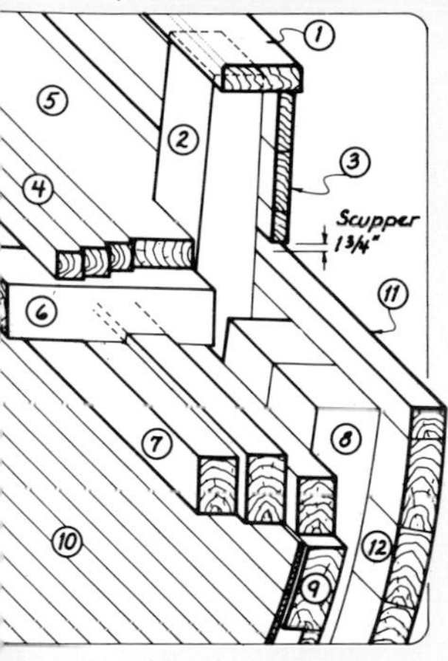

TYPICAL CONSTRUCTION DETAIL

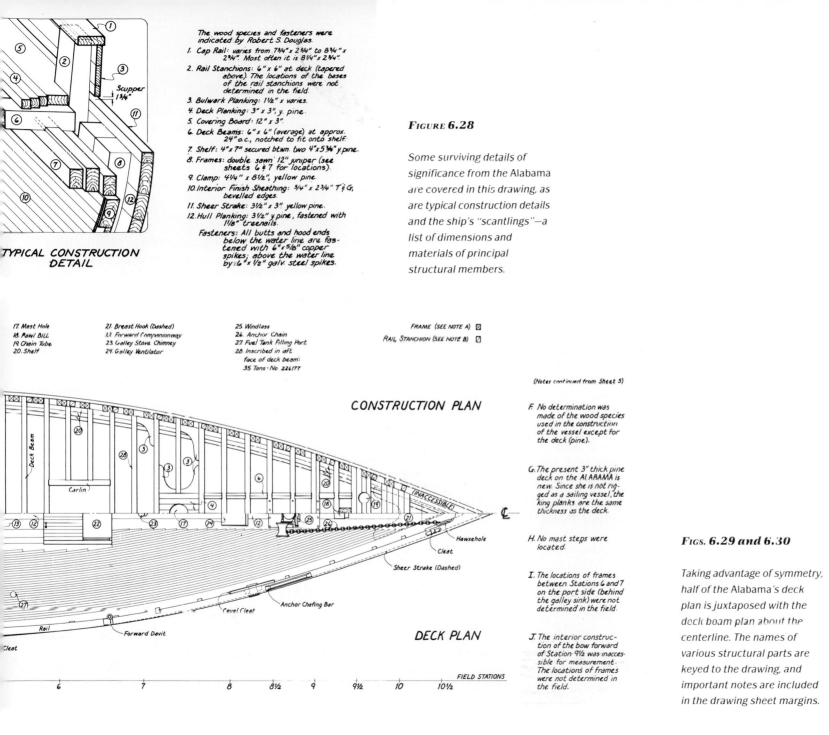

The wood species and fasteners were indicated by Robert S. Douglas.

1. Cap Rail: varies from 7¾" x 2¾" to 8¾" x 2¾". Most often it is 8¼" x 2¾".
2. Rail Stanchions: 6" x 6" at deck (tapered above). The locations of the bases of the rail stanchions were not determined in the field.
3. Bulwark Planking: 1½" x varies.
4. Deck Planking: 3" x 3", y. pine.
5. Covering Board: 12" x 3".
6. Deck Beams: 6" x 6" (average) at approx. 24" o.c., notched to fit onto shelf.
7. Shelf: 4" x 7" secured btwn. two 4" x 5¾" y. pine.
8. Frames: double sawn 12" juniper (see sheets 6 & 7 for locations).
9. Clamp: 4¼" x 8½", yellow pine.
10. Interior Finish Sheathing: ¾" x 2¾" T & G, bevelled edges.
11. Sheer Strake: 3½" x 3" yellow pine.
12. Hull Planking: 3½" y. pine, fastened with 1⅛" treenails.

Fasteners: All butts and hood ends below the water line are fastened with 6" x ⅝" copper spikes; above the water line by 6" x ½" galv. steel spikes.

Figure 6.28

Some surviving details of significance from the Alabama are covered in this drawing, as are typical construction details and the ship's "scantlings"—a list of dimensions and materials of principal structural members.

17. Mast Hole
18. Pawl Bill
19. Chain Tube
20. Shelf
21. Breast Hook (Dashed)
22. Forward Companionway
23. Galley Stove Chimney
24. Galley Ventilator
25. Windlass
26. Anchor Chain
27. Fuel Tank Filling Port
28. Inscribed in aft face of deck beam: 35 Tons · No 226177

FRAME (SEE NOTE A) ☒
RAIL STANCHION (SEE NOTE B) ▱

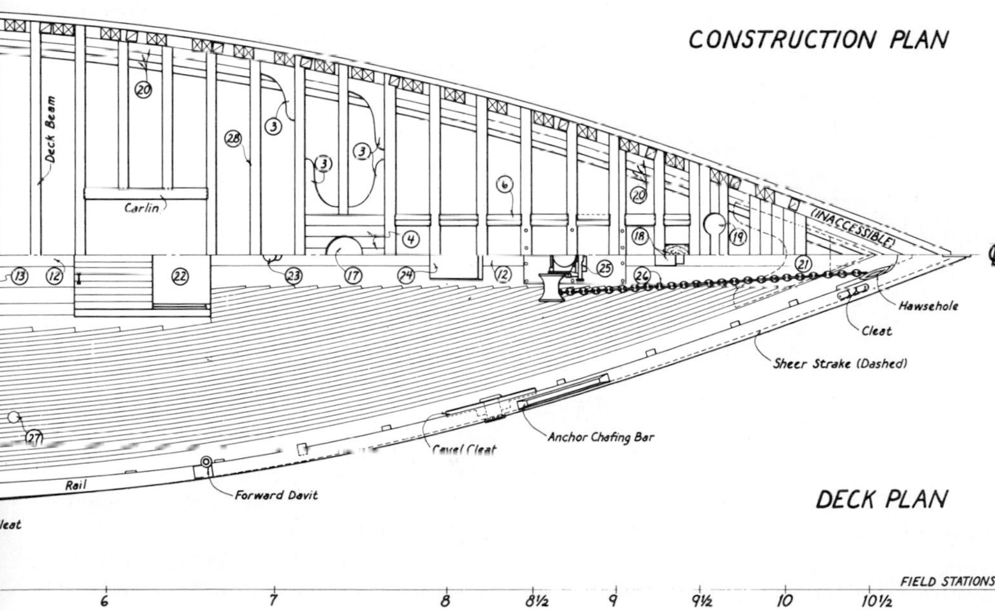

(Notes continued from Sheet 5)

F. No determination was made of the wood species used in the construction of the vessel except for the deck (pine).

G. The present 3" thick pine deck on the ALABAMA is new. Since she is not rigged as a sailing vessel, the king planks are the same thickness as the deck.

H. No mast steps were located.

I. The locations of frames between Stations 6 and 7 on the port side (behind the galley sink) were not determined in the field.

J. The interior construction of the bow forward of Station 9½ was inaccessible for measurement. The locations of frames were not determined in the field.

Figs. 6.29 and 6.30

Taking advantage of symmetry, half of the Alabama's deck plan is juxtaposed with the deck beam plan about the centerline. The names of various structural parts are keyed to the drawing, and important notes are included in the drawing sheet margins.

straight lines or flat surfaces. A firm grasp of geometry and measurement techniques will be necessary to properly handle the measurement complications introduced by a vessel's orientation and the compound curves of the hull, decks, and other features. Methods of obtaining the lines and recording structural features of a vessel may depend on her size, location (floating or in a dry dock), condition (intact or deteriorated), and attitude (upright, listing, or upside down).

A full set of measured drawings of a ship will commonly contain at least a starboard profile (right side elevation), deck plans, an inboard profile (longitudinal section) and sections (cross sections). Further sheets may show a port profile (left side elevation); sail and rigging plans, or engine room and propulsion machinery; significant hull structure, interior features, and details of fittings and hardware. Conceptually, these views are analogous to the types of drawings produced for buildings. Principal information about the shape of a vessel's hull, however, is recorded in the "lines" drawings. These are essentially a series of topographic maps of the hull viewed from the three cartesian coordinate axes: water lines (seen from above), buttock lines (seen from the side), and sections (seen from the ends). One to three diagonal sections may also be taken in addition. Ordinarily, only the port or starboard half of the hull is diagrammed this way, since symmetry is assumed. Documentation of both sides of a hull, however, may be warranted if information is sought on nonsymmetrical changes of shape.

The two case studies that follow focus on some of the field techniques used to measure and draw ships, since approaches for written and photographic coverage do not require specialized changes analogous to those needed for measured drawings.

Recording the Schooner Alabama

The scope of the *Alabama* Recording Project included both lines drawings and construction drawings, as well as a written history and large-format photographs. The *Alabama* is a wooden-hulled, sail-assisted pilot schooner built in 1926 for the Mobile Bay Pilots Association of Mobile, Alabama. It was built in Pensacola, Florida, to the designs of Thomas F. McManus, a noted designer of fishing schooners from the northeastern United States. The lines of several of his vessels were recorded for the Historic American Merchant Marine Survey (HAMMS) in the 1930s, but no construction drawings were included.

The *Alabama* was recorded afloat, since there were no funds or opportunities to haul the ship and perform field work out of the water. Since the lines had already been lifted by the owner, HAER replotted them from the owner's notes, and focused most field work on construction drawings. In addition to lines, the drawing schedule called for plans of the main and 'tween (the first full length deck between the main deck and the hold) decks, inboard and outboard profiles, sections, and details. Since the ship lacked masts and rigging at the time of recording, the team searched for historical photographs that could be relied upon in "restoring" these features in a drawing (see figs 6.23, 6.24, and 6.25).

Because the *Alabama*'s decks and features were a combination of compound curves and inclined surfaces, horizontal measurements alone were not enough to produce accurate drawings. Vertical measurements had to be made to some datum plane—in this case, an arbitrary plane locked to and moving with the ship, since the ship was afloat. This datum was created by setting up a transit midships (halfway between sides and ends) on top of a deckhouse, "leveling" it first athwartships (side to side) with respect to the ship, and then fore and aft with respect to the earth's horizon.

Leveling athwartships was performed by setting the telescope to 0° vertical inclination and then adjusting the

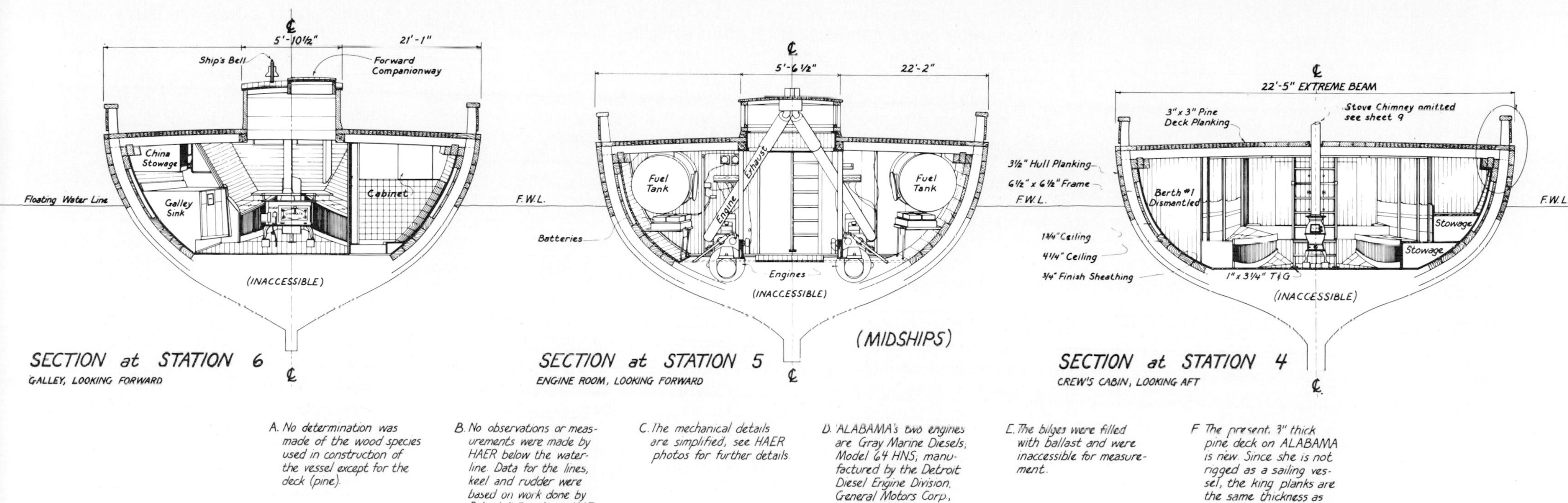

5'-10½"
21'-1"
Ship's Bell
Forward Companionway
China Stowage
Galley Sink
Cabinet
Floating Water Line
F.W.L.
(INACCESSIBLE)
SECTION at STATION 6
GALLEY, LOOKING FORWARD
5'-6½"
22'-2"
Fuel Tank
Engine Exhaust
Fuel Tank
Batteries
Engines
(INACCESSIBLE)
(MIDSHIPS)
SECTION at STATION 5
ENGINE ROOM, LOOKING FORWARD
22'-5" EXTREME BEAM
3"x 3" Pine Deck Planking
Stove Chimney omitted see sheet 9
3½" Hull Planking
6½" x 6½" Frame
F.W.L.
Berth #1 Dismantled
Stowage
Stowage
1¾" Ceiling
4¼" Ceiling
¾" Finish Sheathing
1" x 3¼" T&G
(INACCESSIBLE)
F.W.L.
SECTION at STATION 4
CREW'S CABIN, LOOKING AFT
A. No determination was made of the wood species used in construction of the vessel except for the deck (pine).
B. No observations or measurements were made by HAER below the waterline. Data for the lines, keel and rudder were based on work done by Robert C. Douglas in 1967.
C. The mechanical details are simplified, see HAER photos for further details.
D. ALABAMA's two engines are Gray Marine Diesels, Model 64 HNS, manufactured by the Detroit Diesel Engine Division, General Motors Corp., Detroit, Michigan.
E. The bilges were filled with ballast and were inaccessible for measurement.
F. The present, 3" thick pine deck on ALABAMA is new. Since she is not rigged as a sailing vessel, the king planks are the same thickness as the deck.

FIGURE 6.31

Cross-sections of the Alabama *further document the interior arrangements of structure and spaces.*

instrument's leveling screws until the scope sighted equal measurements above the extreme edges of the deck at points directly to port and starboard of the transit station. Leveling fore and aft was achieved by adjusting the leveling screws (not the scope) until the scope approximately sighted the horizon (water) over the stern, taking into account the up-and-down motion caused by waves. (Unlike leveling athwartships, leveling of the transit fore-and-aft is not particularly critical.) The distance to the tip of the bow beneath this plane was then recorded as one means to recover the plane in case the scope should be accidentally upset. From this stage, all vertical measurements were taken by setting the zero end of a tape to the point whose height was needed, then following readings through the scope until a minimum reading was found as the tape was inclined in various directions. These readings were then recorded in the field notes. (Geometrically, the minimum distance from a point to a plane is the "true" distance between them—it also lies on a line normal or "square" to the plane.)

The plan of the main deck was recorded by a combination of horizontal and vertical measurements. To begin, a copper nail (to prevent rust marks) was set in the rail at the ship's bow at what appeared to be the ship's centerline, and the location recorded. The end of a hundred-foot tape was then secured to the nail, and a series of other copper nails was set in the centerlines of the port and starboard rails, going aft to the stern of the ship. Each pair of nails (one port, one starboard) was set equidistant from the bow nail. The distances of each pair of nails from the bow nail and from each other were recorded, as were their distances beneath the datum plane. An error estimate of plus or minus ¼ inch for vertical measurements was allowed for any movement of the transit caused by the deckhouse roof's deflection under the transit operator's shifting weight. Less was allowed for the horizontal dimensions. Later on, these dimensions made it possible for the team to draw a plan of the rail projected into a horizontal plane with the aid of trigonometry.

Though the ship was assumed to be symmetrical, a centerline check was performed by setting the transit scope approximately parallel to the ship's centerline and sighting measurements on a tape drawn athwartships between each pair of rail tacks. These points were plotted after the rail plan was drawn to see if they lay in a straight line. Similar check measurements were made to the deck edges.

Measurements of deckhouses, planking, anchor winch, steering box, and other features were made along the deck. Error introduced by the deck camber (upward curve or crown of deck) was judged to be negligible in this instance when projecting dimensions taken athwartships into a plan view. Profiles (elevations) were made of deckhouses and other features in which diagonal measurements (in planes parallel to the ship's vertical centerline plane) were carefully recorded as well as the distances of corners and peaks of roofs beneath the transit datum plane. Materials were noted as well.

Once the main deck was completed, vertical measurements were made through the fore-and-aft ventilators to spots carefully marked on the 'tween deck centerline below. The transit was then moved below deck for use on the 'tween deck. A datum plane was set parallel to the one above by procedures similar to those used on the main deck—sightings were made up to the underside of the main deck when leveling the instrument athwartships, and fore-and-aft alignment was made using the spots marked earlier on the 'tween deck. Measurements above these spots were subtracted from the ones made from the first datum plane and the leveling screws adjusted until the same result was obtained at both spots. Then the distance between these two planes was recorded. Vertical measurements of 'tween deck features were then taken in the same way as on the main deck.

Below decks, the team was careful to record all structures, such as deck beams, clamps, frames, deck stanchions, carlins, mast partners, knees, ceiling planking, and so forth (see figs. 6.26, 6.27, and 6.28). Expert ship carpenters from a museum inspected the vessel with the team to help identify materials and point out matters of significance or interest. Features on deck were recorded by offsets from a centerline (marked on deck with a chalkline) and by triangulations among features. Bunks, galley and cabin stoves, appliances, engines, and auxiliaries were recorded, as were certain pieces of hardware. As much information as possible regarding equipment was collected from builders' plates. Even so, much of the *Alabama*'s structure was inaccessible, principally frames behind the ceiling planking and keelsons in the bottom. Field photographs were taken liberally to supplement field notes.

After the ship's lines were plotted and faired, a profile and plan of the main deck and rails were made. (The team was gratified to see that the sheer line they had measured agreed almost exactly with the owner's twenty-year-old lines information!) All drawings were executed at a scale of ½″=1′-0″ to preserve detail (see figs. 6.26, 6.27, 6.29, 6.30, and 6.31). Since the drawings are projected views of a nonrectilinear object, considerable use of trigonometry, triangulation, and cross-references between plan and profile views was necessary to construct accurate views. Frequently, fore-and-aft measurements had to be plotted on the profile before they could be projected onto the deck plan, and vice versa. The *Alabama*'s owner possessed a valuable collection of photographs that had been made shortly after the ship was built. Reverse perspective analysis of these was used to arrive at approximate measurements of the rig for inclusion in an outboard profile on the title sheet of the drawing set. All drawings were accompanied by scales and liberal notes relating to field procedures, materials, names of parts, and sources of information. The historical photographs were photocopied with the owner's permission and included with the large-format photographs taken by the project photographer. (In addition to their historical value, the older photographs were used to verify the drawings of the *Alabama*'s rig.) Using primary and secondary sources, a history was written to preserve information about the *Alabama*'s design and construction, designer, builder, owners, service provided, and significance in United States maritime history and engineering.

In recording ships, a full set of drawings should be annotated and highly detailed, covering every significant aspect of the project's field work and of the ship's appearance, design, construction, propulsion, interior features, and auxiliary equipment. The amount of effort required will depend on the size of the vessel and what significant features require the most concentrated attention, as well as available funds, personnel, and expertise.

FIGURE 6.32

Before the schooner Wawona *was dry-docked, a rectangular coordinate system for lining up measuring frames was laid out in the dry dock using a surveying transit. Here a centerline has been set on the keel blocks, and lines-lifting stations are being set beneath it on the dry dock deck.*

Lifting the Lines of the Wawona

The *Wawona* lines-lifting project was a recording effort of limited scope aimed primarily at recording the contours of this 1897 sailing ship's wooden hull. No attempt was made to gather data sufficient to produce a full set of construction drawings covering the ship's profiles, plans, sections, and details. The taking of lines, however, is a task of high priority when recording a historic vessel if the designed hull shape is an important factor in the ship's historic significance or if the data are needed for repairs or other preservation measures. If extensive drawing of a ship's hull structure includes numerous cross-sections, the lifting of lines will be essential, even if the hull's *shape* as such is not particularly significant. Usually the lines are taken on only one side, since the hull is assumed to be symmetrical. In the case of the *Wawona*, however, both sides were measured in order to detect any distortions caused by age or deterioration.

Lifting the lines of a ship can be accomplished in many ways. The choice of method depends on the size of the vessel, its location, its condition, and its historically significant features. Ultimately, some sort of convenient reference system must be devised that suits the field conditions of a vessel and permits measurements of its hull to be made accurately and efficiently.

In order to measure the *Wawona*, the ship was first lined up in a floating dry-dock within a predetermined reference system set up with a surveying transit (see figs. 6.32 and 6.33). A very large horizontal wooden straightedge with two large vertical scales (or squares) was then set up repeatedly around the hull at thirteen different predetermined points along the ship's length. Measurements were made to both sides of the ship's hull from the squares and straightedge after these instruments were aligned with the dry dock reference system (see fig. 6.34). The field data were then reduced at each station to plots on a drawing board for verification (see fig. 6.35). Each of these plots constituted a section of the hull, and since these sections were located at known points along the

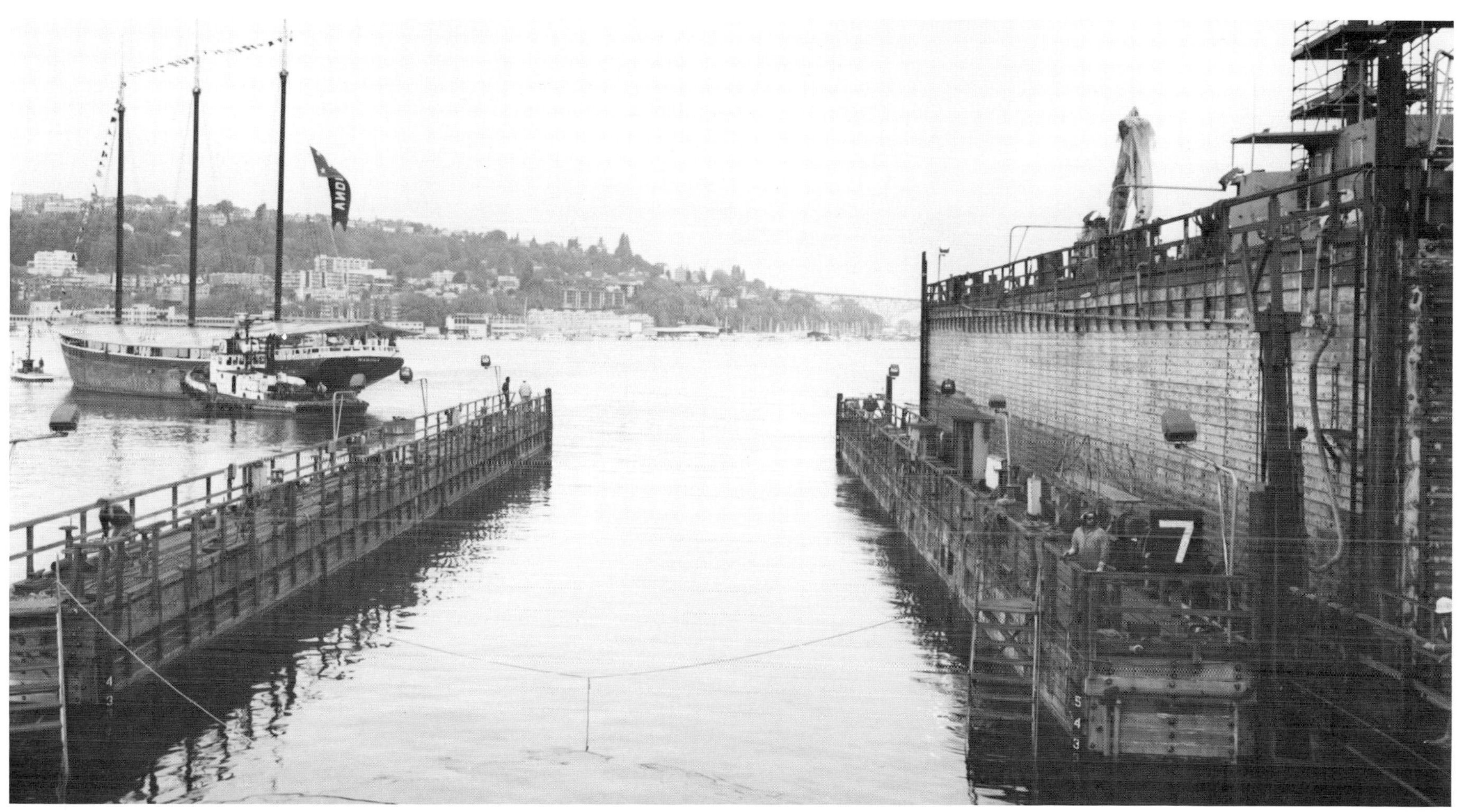

FIGURE 6.33

Tugs slowly move the Wawona *into temporarily submerged dry dock, later raised for a lines-lifting project.*

Figure 6.34

Using two measuring tapes and a pole, the recording team measures points on the Wawona*'s hull from points on the horizontal and vertical scales of the lines-lifting frames. Dimensions are written down by another team member. Points on the hull are taken only in the plane set by the frames (easily found by eye). Where the curves in the hull are quicker, more points are taken to ensure good documentation of the curve.*

Figure 6.35

The shape of Wawona*'s hull at each station is carefully plotted and faired on site from field data before any measuring equipment is moved to the next station. Any serious errors in measurement or recording can be easily found and checked at this stage of operations.*

ship's length, sufficient information was available to plot the ship's lines in plan and profile. The entire lines-lifting process took six days and consumed about five hundred work-hours, not including actual dry-docking or re-floating of the ship, or the drafting time for finished lines drawings.

Numerous problems in setting up the dry dock reference system and measuring instruments had to be overcome in this project, and many potential sources of error had to be monitored during the field work. Many of these problems were peculiar to the use of a floating dry dock and are not factors in all lines-lifting efforts. Constant changes of attitude inherent in a floating dry dock made it impractical to use ordinary levels and surveying techniques except over small distances or in special cases where error was judged to be within acceptable limits. These problems could have been controlled far more consistently and to finer limits (plus or minus ¼ inch maximum error in all directions) if more time-consuming procedures had been used, or if the ship had been placed in a land-based facility where no shifts in attitude could occur. During this project, whenever a surveying transit was used, it was set up in the dry dock and adjusted to the dry dock reference system, not to the leveling devices in the instrument. Any influences from the shifting attitude of the dry dock were thus avoided. Plumb bobs and spirit levels were used only over distances not exceeding five feet, except for plumbing the large squares in the fore-and aft direction. In this latter case, a possible error of plus or minus 1½ inches at the tops of the squares was accepted, due to the excessive time and effort that would have been required to ensure that the tops were "square" to the base plane of the reference system within an accuracy of plus or minus ¼ inch. A maximum error of plus or minus ⅛ inch for dimensions up to twenty feet, and plus or minus ¼ inch for those up to a hundred feet would have been preferred.

Back in the office, the data were redrawn at a scale of ¼" to the foot. Two sets of lines were then drawn for the *Wawona*: one showing the ship's actual condition, where the keel was hogged about 9½" amidships, and the second showing the probable condition of the ship when it was new (see figs. 6.36, 6.37, and 6.38). Extensive notes documenting field and drafting room procedures were added to the drawings, including error estimates, so that future users might follow the project's methodological development and have an adequate basis for judging its accuracy. Because of the project's limitations, no further drawings were made to show the ship's structural details except for a small-scale profile on the title sheet of the drawing set. Masts and rigging were drawn using existing drawings in the owners' possession, and these sources were noted in the title sheet profile (see fig. 6.39).

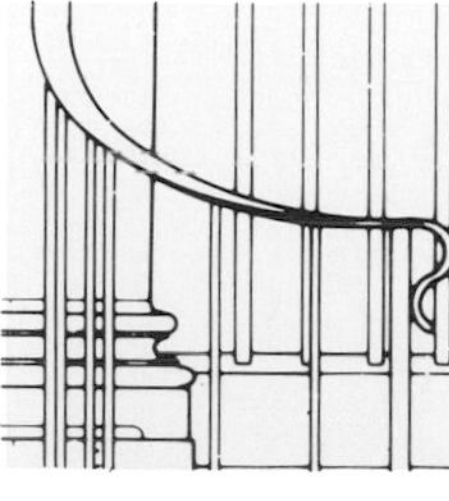

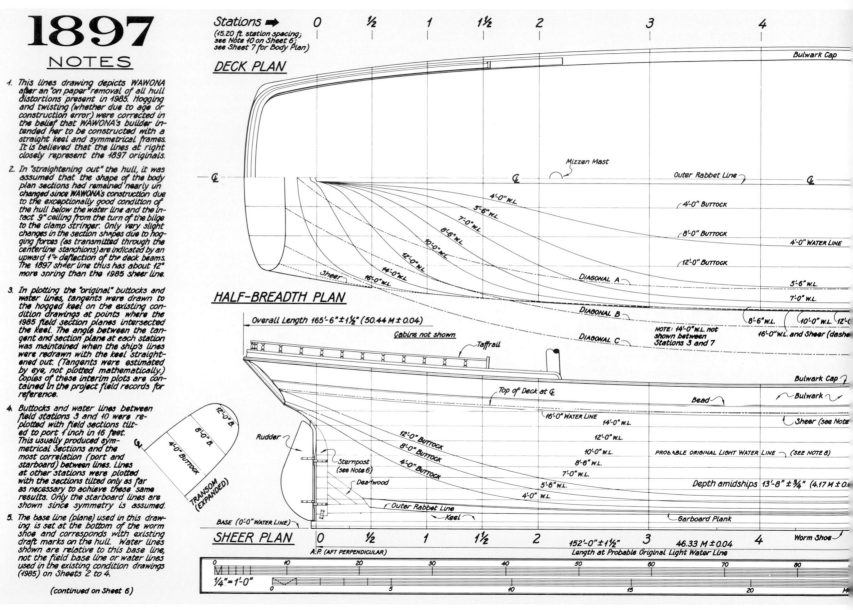

1897

NOTES

1. This lines drawing depicts WAWONA after an "on paper" removal of all hull distortions present in 1985. Hogging and twisting (whether due to age or construction error) were corrected in the belief that WAWONA's builder intended her to be constructed with a straight keel and symmetrical frames. It is believed that the lines at right closely represent the 1897 originals.

2. In "straightening out" the hull, it was assumed that the shape of the body plan sections had remained nearly unchanged since WAWONA's construction due to the exceptionally good condition of the hull below the water line and the intact 9" ceiling from the turn of the bilge to the clamp stringer. Only very slight changes in the section shapes due to hogging forces (as transmitted through the centerline stanchions) are indicated by an upward 1"+ deflection of the deck beams. The 1897 sheer line thus has about 12" more spring than the 1985 sheer line.

3. In plotting the "original" buttocks and water lines, tangents were drawn to the hogged keel on the existing condition drawings at points where the 1985 field section planes intersected the keel. The angle between the tangent and section plane at each station was maintained when the ship's lines were redrawn with the keel straightened out. (Tangents were estimated by eye, not plotted mathematically.) Copies of these interim plots are contained in the project field records for reference.

4. Buttocks and water lines between field stations 3 and 10 were replotted with field sections tilted to port 1 inch in 16 feet. This usually produced symmetrical sections and the most correlation (port and starboard) between lines. Lines at other stations were plotted with the sections tilted only as far as necessary to achieve these same results. Only the starboard lines are shown since symmetry is assumed.

5. The base line (plane) used in this drawing is set at the bottom of the worm shoe and corresponds with existing draft marks on the hull. Water lines shown are relative to this base line, not the field base line or water lines used in the existing condition drawings (1985) on Sheets 2 to 4.

(continued on Sheet 6)

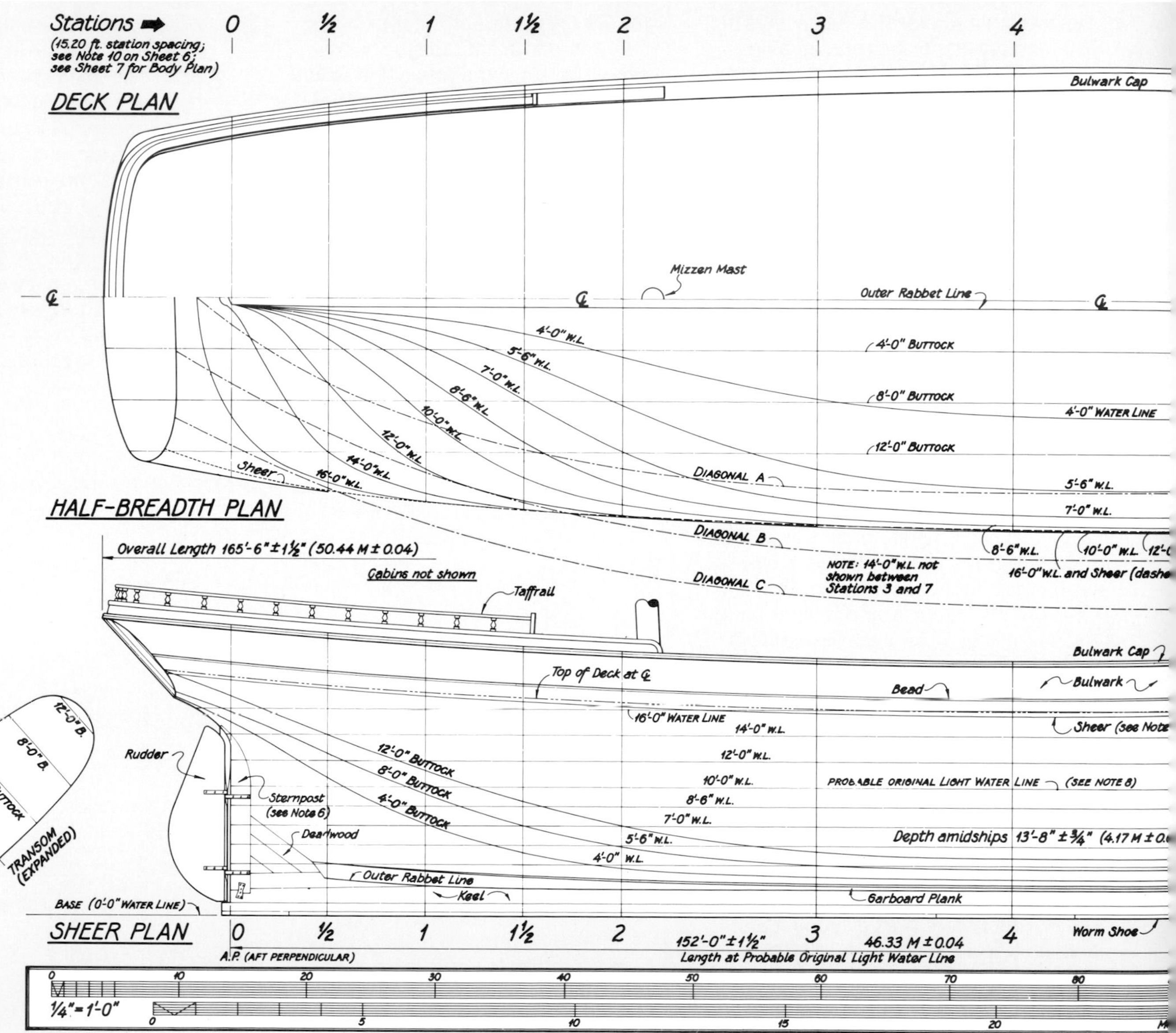

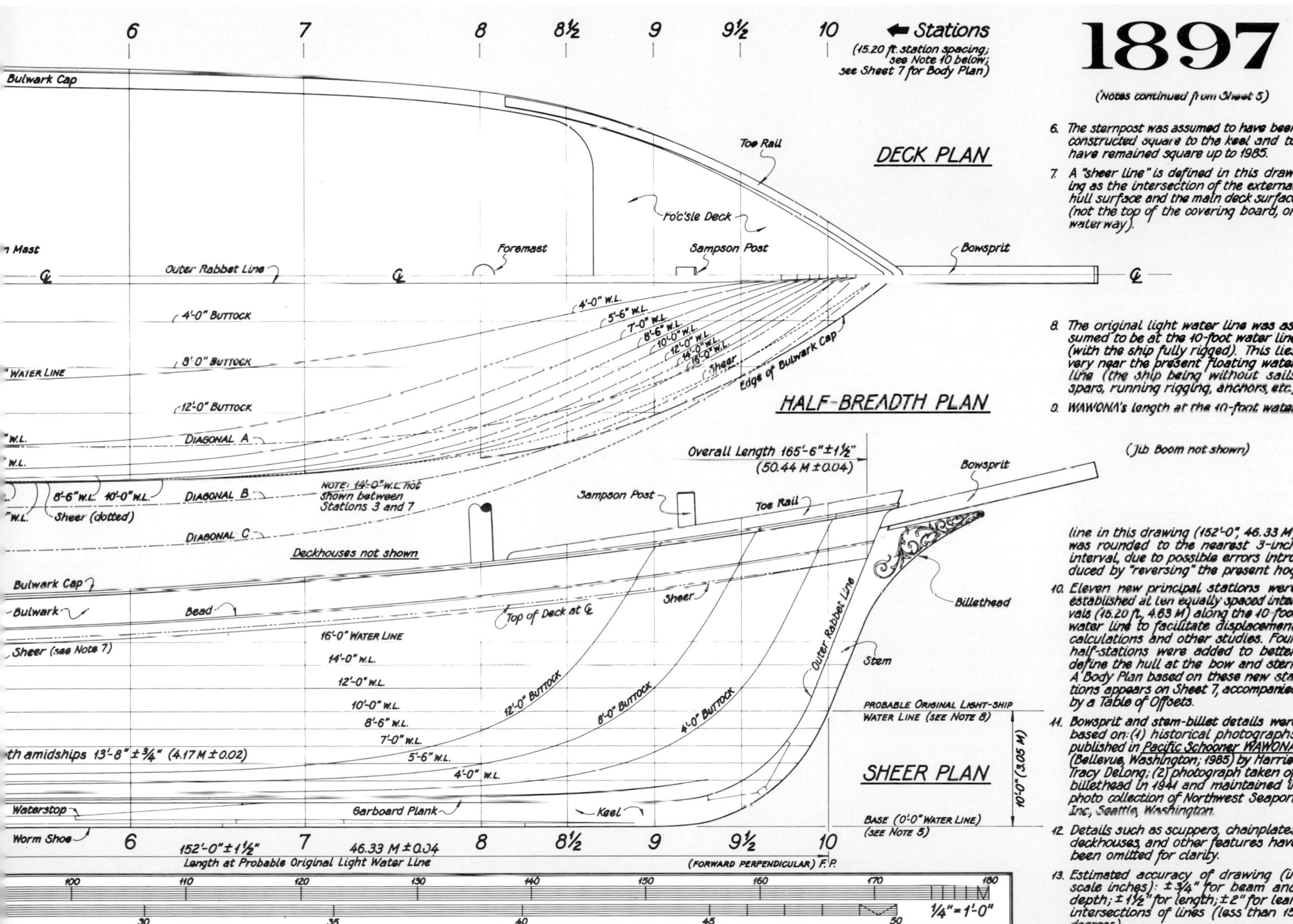

6
7
8
8½
9
9½
10
← Stations
(15.20 ft. station spacing; see Note 10 below; see Sheet 7 for Body Plan)
1897
(Notes continued from Sheet 5)
6. The sternpost was assumed to have been constructed square to the keel and to have remained square up to 1985.
7. A "sheer line" is defined in this drawing as the intersection of the external hull surface and the main deck surface (not the top of the covering board, or waterway).
8. The original light water line was assumed to be at the 10-foot water line (with the ship fully rigged). This lies very near the present floating water line (the ship being without sails, spars, running rigging, anchors, etc.).
9. WAWONA's length at the 10-foot water line in this drawing (152'-0", 46.33 M) was rounded to the nearest 3-inch interval, due to possible errors introduced by "reversing" the present hog.
10. Eleven new principal stations were established at ten equally spaced intervals (15.20 ft., 4.63 M) along the 10-foot water line to facilitate displacement calculations and other studies. Four half-stations were added to better define the hull at the bow and stern. A Body Plan based on these new stations appears on Sheet 7, accompanied by a Table of Offsets.
11. Bowsprit and stem-billet details were based on: (1) historical photographs published in Pacific Schooner WAWONA (Bellevue, Washington; 1985) by Harriet Tracy DeLong; (2) photograph taken of billethead in 1941 and maintained in photo collection of Northwest Seaport, Inc., Seattle, Washington.
12. Details such as scuppers, chainplates, deckhouses, and other features have been omitted for clarity.
13. Estimated accuracy of drawing (in scale inches): ±¾" for beam and depth; ±1½" for length; ±2" for lean intersections of lines (less than 15 degrees).
DECK PLAN
HALF-BREADTH PLAN
SHEER PLAN
Bulwark Cap
Toe Rail
Fo'c'sle Deck
Foremast
Sampson Post
Bowsprit
Outer Rabbet Line
4'-0" Buttock
8'-0" Buttock
12'-0" Buttock
Diagonal A
Diagonal B
Diagonal C
Edge of Bulwark Cap
Sheer
8'-6" W.L.
10'-0" W.L.
Sheer (dotted)
NOTE: 14'-0" W.L. not shown between Stations 3 and 7
Overall Length 165'-6" ± 1½" (50.44 M ± 0.04)
(Jib Boom not shown)
Deckhouses not shown
Bulwark
Bead
Top of Deck at ℄
Billethead
Stem
16'-0" Water Line
14'-0" W.L.
12'-0" W.L.
10'-0" W.L.
8'-6" W.L.
7'-0" W.L.
5'-6" W.L.
4'-0" W.L.
Sheer (see Note 7)
Waterstop
Worm Shoe
Garboard Plank
Keel
Probable Original Light-Ship Water Line (see Note 8)
Base (0'-0" Water Line) (see Note 5)
10'-0" (3.05 M)
152'-0" ± 1½"
46.33 M ± 0.04
Length at Probable Original Light Water Line
(Forward Perpendicular) F.P.
¼" = 1'-0"

Figs. 6.36, 6.37

The probable original (1897) contours of the Wawona's hull were carefully derived from the 1985 field work. Field and drawing-room procedures are outlined in notes on the drawings along with error estimations for these two phases of the documentation.

TABLE OF OFFSETS

ALL DIMENSIONS BELOW ARE GIVEN IN FEET, INCHES, AND EIGHTHS OF AN INCH
(See Notes 1 and 2)

		STATIONS														
		0	½	1	1½	2	3	4	5	6	7	8	8½	9	9½	10
HEIGHTS ABOVE BASE	UNDERSIDE BUL. CAP	22-0-4	21-4-6	20-10-6	20-5-6	20-1-0	19-7-0	19-5-0	19-7-2	20-2-4	21-2-6	22-5-6	23-3-4	24-2-6	25-4-2	26-6-6
	SHEER	18-2-4	17-6-2	16-11-4	16-6-6	16-2-2	15-8-2	15-6-4	15-8-4	16-5-2	17-3-6	18-7-4	19-5-2	20-4-0	21-5-4	22-8-0
	16' BUTT.				12-5-0	9-10-6	7-2-4	6-3-2	6-1-0	6-6-0	8-4-2					
	12' BUTT.	17-0-0	14-0-0	11-3-2	8-10-0	7-0-2	5-0-4	4-6-6	4-6-4	4-8-4	5-3-6	8-3-2	13-2-6	24-1-6		
	8' BUTT.	15-9-0	12-6-0	9-5-4	7-0-4	5-4-4	4-0-2	3-9-0	3-9-0	3-10-2	4-1-0	5-4-4	7-4-4	12-0-4	23-4-0	
	4' BUTT.	14-11-2	10-8-0	7-1-6	4-10-0	3-9-6	3-1-2	2-11-0	2-11-0	2-11-4	3-1-0	3-6-2	4-4-6	6-5-0	11-11-0	25-9-0
	RABBET		2-11-0	2-4-4	2-2-0	2-1-6	←				→	2-1-6	2-2-0	2-2-2	3-11-6	14-9-4
HALF-BREADTHS	BUL. CAP	13-6-4	14-7-4	15-4-2	15-11-0	16-5-2	17-1-0	17-5-4	17-7-4	17-5-2	17-0-0	15-9-2	14-4-6	12-0-4	8-7-6	4-3-4
	SHEER	13-5-4	14-11-4	15-10-0	16-5-0	16-10-6	17-6-4	17-10-4	18-0-4	17-6-6	17-3-0	15-6-0	13-8-2	11-0-6	7-5-2	3-0-4
	26' W.L.															4-1-2
	24' W.L.													11-11-4	8-2-4	3-5-2
	22' W.L.	13-7-2										15-8-2	14-1-4	11-4-6	7-7-4	2-9-6
	20' W.L.	13-11-0	14-9-0	15-5-6	15-11-6	16-5-4				17-5-4	17-0-4	15-7-2	13-9-4	10-11-4	6-11-4	2-2-0
	18' W.L.	13-3-6	15-0-0	15-9-6	16-3-4	16-7-4	17-2-6	17-7-2	17-9-2	17-7-4	17-2-6	15-5-0	13-4-6	10-4-6	6-4-0	1-6-6
	16' W.L.	9-1-0	14-4-4	15-9-2	16-5-4	16-10-6	17-6-0	17-9-6	18-0-0	17-10-2	17-3-4	15-2-4	12-11-2	9-8-6	5-7-6	1-0-4
	14' W.L.	1-0-2	12-0-2	15-2-4	16-5-0	17-0-2	17-8-0	17-11-4	18-1-0	17-11-0	17-3-0	14-9-6	12-3-4	8-11-0	14-0-4	
	12' W.L.	0-6-4	6-7-0	13-2-4	15-9-2	16-10-4	17-8-4	18-0-0	18-1-6	17-11-0	17-1-0	14-2-4	11-5-4	7-11-4	4-0-2	
	10' W.L.	0-6-4	3-2-0	9-1-6	13-11-6	16-0-4	17-6-0	17-10-6	18-0-0	17-9-0	16-8-0	13-3-0	10-3-6	6-9-4	3-0-6	
	8'-6" W.L.	0-6-4	2-0-2	6-0-4	11-3-0	14-7-4	16-11-0	17-6-4	17-8-0	17-4-4	16-0-6	12-2-2	9-1-4	5-8-4	2-4-4	
	7' W.L.	0-6-4	1-5-0	3-9-4	7-11-0	12-0-0	15-9-0	16-8-4	16-10-6	16-6-0	14-10-2	10-7-0	7-6-4	4-6-0	1-8-2	
	5'-6" W.L.	0-6-4	1-0-4	2-5-4	5-0-2	8-3-0	13-3-4	14-8-6	14-10-6	14-4-2	12-5-0	8-2-0	5-7-0	3-2-4	1-1-6	
	4' W.L.	0-6-4	0-9-4	1-6-4	2-9-0	4-5-0	7-10-2	9-3-4	9-3-4	9-2-6	8-8-4	7-8-2	5-1-4	3-5-0	1-11-2	
	HALF-SIDING	0-6-4	0-8-0	←											→	0-8-0
DIAGONALS	A	2-2-2	6-8-0	9-7-0	11-9-0	13-3-0	14-8-6	15-0-4	15-0-4	14-11-2	14-7-4	13-3-2	11-9-0	9-5-4	6-0-6	1-3-0
	B	6-8-2	10-6-6	13-6-4	15-10-4	17-7-6	19-7-4	20-2-4	20-3-0	20-0-6	19-3-2	16-9-6	14-6-4	11-5-6	7-6-4	2-5-4
	C	11-6-4	14-11-4	17-7-0	19-9-0	21-4-2	23-1-6	23-10-0	23-11-6	23-8-2	22-5-4	19-2-0	16-6-2	13-1-4	8-10-4	3-8-6

1897

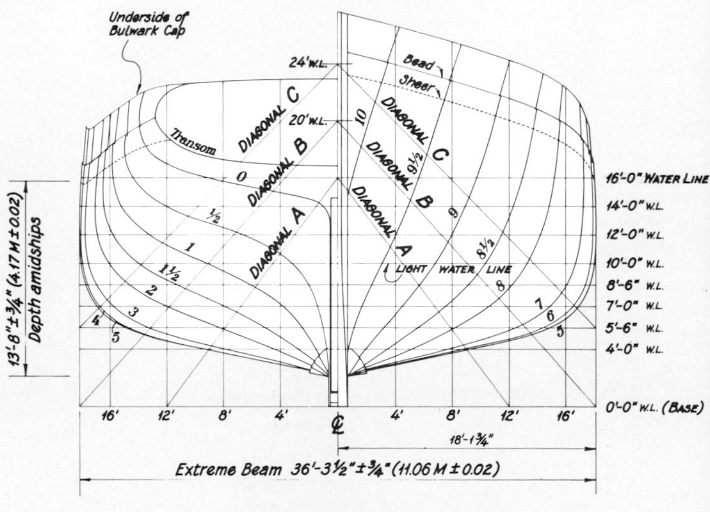

BODY PLAN

1/4" = 1'-0"

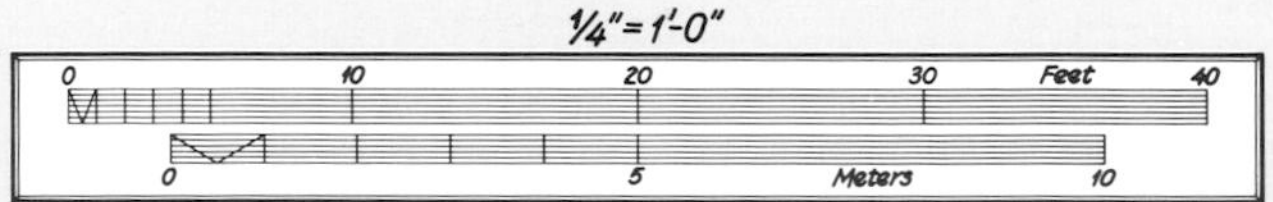

FIGURE 6.38

The table of offsets for the Wawona records numerically what is shown in the body plan. The body plan is analogous to "slices" of the hull's shape and shows only half the hull from midships forward and the other half from midships aft, since the hull is symmetrical.

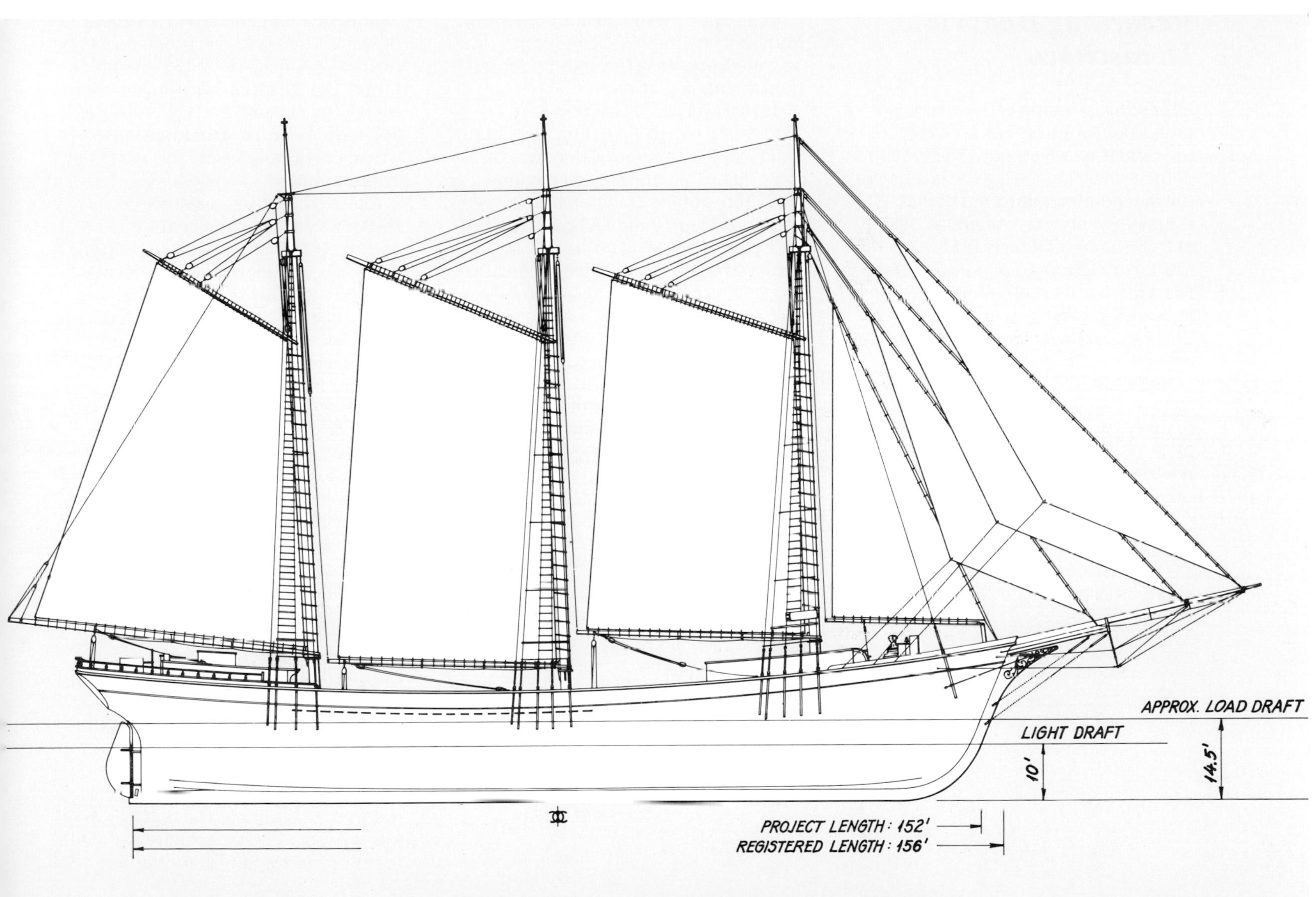
APPROX. LOAD DRAFT
LIGHT DRAFT
10'
14.5'
PROJECT LENGTH: 152'
REGISTERED LENGTH: 156'
Hull based on project field measurements; all other features based on HAER photos, historical photos, and profile by E. Harry Anderson of Seattle, Washington.

Figure 6.39

The title sheet for the lines drawings of the Wawona *includes an outboard profile whose hull is based on field measurement and whose rigging is based on pre-existing documentation. Sources are footnoted below the drawing.*

Recording Historic Landscapes

Although landscape architecture is a profession as ancient as architecture, the term is relatively new. The growth of the profession during the last half of the nineteenth century led to the establishment of the American Society of Landscape Architects (ASLA) in 1899. The statement of purpose of the ASLA defines its profession as "the art of design, planning or management of the land and the arrangement of natural and man-made elements upon it."

HABS focuses on the designed environment; land management is not its primary concern. The designed environment is more than individual buildings, however. The landscape architect's mission—the arrangement of land and spaces upon it—significantly modifies our built environment. Landscape architecture, therefore, merits serious documentation efforts.

In many respects, there is little difference between architectural and landscape architectural documentation. Measured drawings of garden structures utilize traditional measured drawing documentation techniques. A site plan, depending on complexity, usually requires only standard measuring techniques. Challenges occur when one attempts to graphically record the intangible qualities peculiar to a landscape. Unlike architecture, in which the structure and its changes are tangible, a landscape is intended to mature and develop. Capturing this ephemeral quality in a two-dimensional measured drawing can be very limiting, and the value of photography to landscape documentation becomes apparent. The three-dimensional nature of a photograph explains spatial transitions which cannot be fully captured in a measured drawing. These graphic products can be further enhanced by written documentation. Design intent and implementation of the plan are not necessarily as apparent as with a structure, and written data can provide this essential information.

Charles E. Peterson, founder of HABS, was trained as a landscape architect, and has always stressed the importance of methodical landscape documentation. Predictably, this took the form of site plans and site details of great American homes. The natural progression in landscape documentation was from specific historic sites and estates to large-scale historic districts.

The documentation of landscapes, however, remained subordinate to the architectural focus of HABS. The documentation of Meridian Hill Park, undertaken in 1985, represents a response to a national interest in historic landscapes and the growing sophistication of HABS/HAER documentation techniques. With increased awareness of the importance and vulnerability of these landscapes, HABS has begun to develop standards for landscape documentation.

Meridian Hill Park, part of the Rock Creek National Park in Washington, D.C., was selected as a pilot project for landscape documentation. Since HABS routinely documented landscapes, this was viewed as an opportunity not only to refine our traditional measuring techniques but also to experiment with some rapidly developing technology.

Meridian Hill Park is located a mile and a-half north of the White House in Washington, D.C. (see fig. 5.25). It is one of the first public gardens in the United States designed in the Classical tradition. Built over a period of twenty-five years beginning in 1912, the park represents an alliance of landscape architecture, architecture, and advanced concrete technology (see fig. 6.40).

Meridian Hill Park is designed in the Italian Renaissance tradition of landscape architecture. Similar to many of

Figure 6.40

The frieze of the Sixteenth Street Fountain bears the name of Meridian Hill Park. Like all other architectural features, it was constructed of exposed aggregate concrete. The massive rustication pattern replicates Italian Renaissance masonry.

FIGURE 6.41

The premier feature of Meridian Hill Park is the great cascade, a device found in numerous Italian Renaissance gardens. Beginning with a jet in the triumphal arch, water cascades over thirteen basins, finally coming to rest in a large reflecting pond.

***Figure* 6.42**

Large-format photographs of Meridian Hill Park, enlarged onto drafting film, were used to construct a drawing showing earlier conditions and appearance (see fig. 6.49).

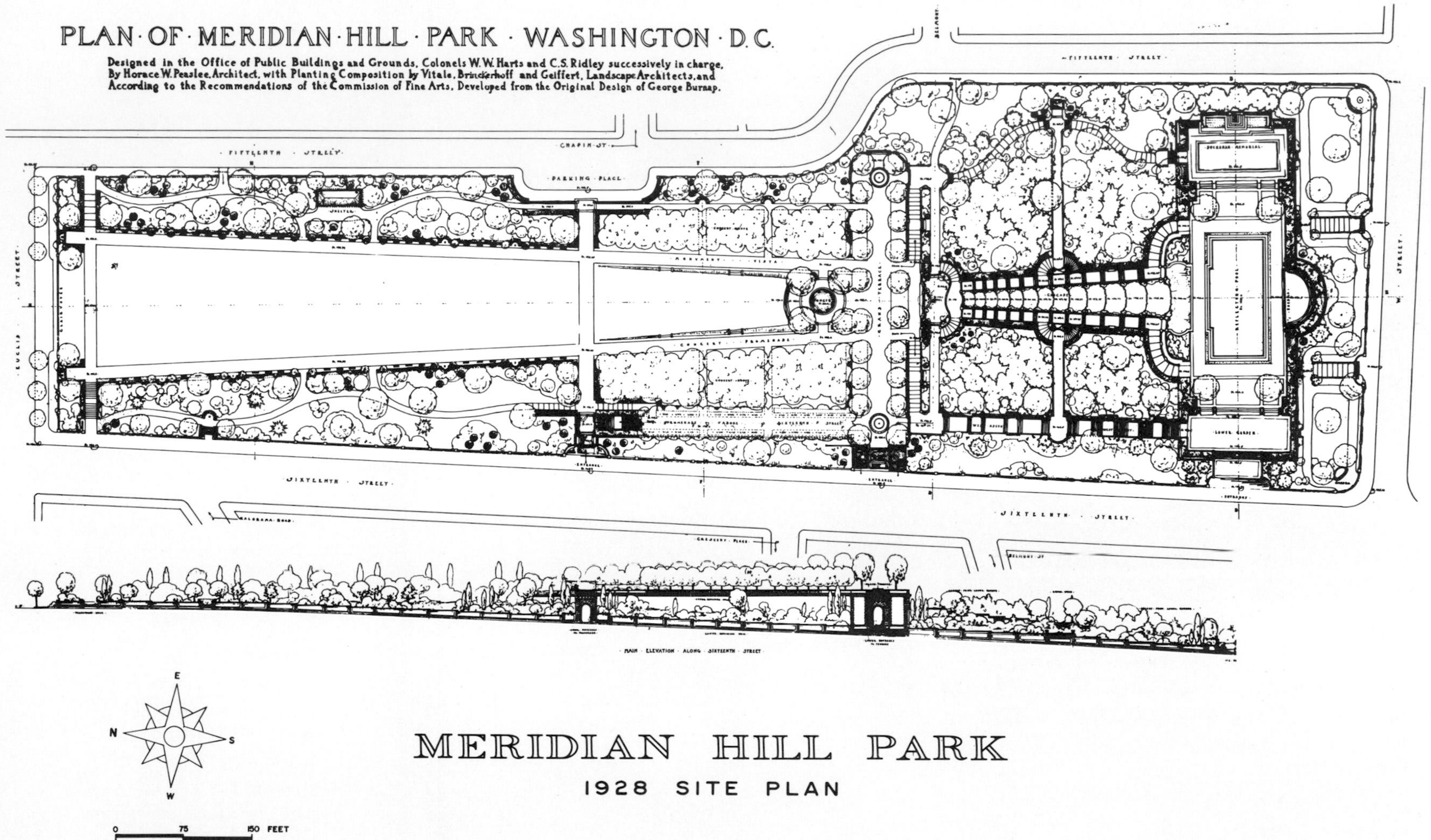
PLAN · OF · MERIDIAN · HILL · PARK · WASHINGTON · D.C.
Designed in the Office of Public Buildings and Grounds, Colonels W. W. Harts and C.S. Ridley successively in charge, By Horace W. Peaslee, Architect, with Planting Composition by Vitale, Brinckerhoff and Geiffert, Landscape Architects, and According to the Recommendations of the Commission of Fine Arts, Developed from the Original Design of George Burnap.
CHAPIN ST
PARKING PLACE
MAIN · ELEVATION · ALONG · SIXTEENTH · STREET
E
N
S
W
MERIDIAN HILL PARK
1928 SITE PLAN
0
75
150 FEET

Figure 6.43

The 1928 illustrative plan of Meridian Hill Park in Washington, D.C. shows the design as approved by the District of Columbia Commission of Fine Arts. This plan illustrates the projected design at completion. Although minor details are not discernible at this scale, this serves as an overall site plan. Certain elements which appear on the 1928 plan were never fully realized, such as the circular concert pavilion at the crest of the retaining wall and the Sixteenth Street entrance in the retaining wall (see fig. 6.48).

the hill gardens of Italy, it was developed on two levels along a major axis with numerous cross axes. The upper garden is a nine-hundred-foot level mall that culminates in a great terrace overlooking the Washington, D.C., skyline. The lower garden is an Italian water garden. Located within a triumphal arch in the great terrace retaining wall is a fountain from which water cascades over thirteen basins. At the base of the cascade is a large reflecting pool where the water finally comes to rest. On axis at the base of the cascade is an exedra from which the spectacle can be viewed (see figs. 6.41 and 6.42).

George Burnap, landscape architect with the Office of Public Buildings and Grounds, Washington, D.C., designed the first plan for Meridian Hill Park. The project came to fruition, however, under Horace W. Peaslee, who succeeded Burnap in the same position. As a public project, the design of the park received the finest professional criticism with final approval given by the U.S. Commission of Fine Arts (see fig. 6.43).

Although its precedents are found in the Italian Renaissance, the technology employed in the construction of Meridian Hill Park is clearly twentieth century. The innovative use of concrete made possible its grand scale development which would have been financially prohibitive in cut stone. John J. Early, an architectural sculptor, developed a technique of cast-in-place concrete. This method utilized selected washed aggregate, which was exposed by wire brushing and acid washes to replicate the subtleties of sixteenth-century Italian garden mosaics. This technique was employed in all retaining walls, cascade basins, walkways, balustrades, and decorative architectural elements (see figs. 6.44 and 6.45).

The planting design was mastered by Feruccio Vitale, an Italian-born and educated landscape architect. Steeped in the great Italian landscape tradition, he was particularly qualified to design the planting for this "American Renaissance Garden." The upper mall is a formal grass allée surrounded by hemlock hedges and American elms. The water garden is surrounded by an Italian bosco, or thickly planted grove.

As with any other documentation project undertaken by HABS/HAER, the first step in recording a historic landscape is to determine the salient features to be analyzed and documented. In the case of a landscape, it is important to determine the designer's intent regarding the seasonal variations, the ever-changing nature of the subject, and the progression of spaces within the landscape. Such a task necessitates comprehensive documentation. Individually, measured drawings, photography, or written data will not satisfactorily document this comprehensively. By combining these three approaches, however, the importance of a landscape can be captured.

When a project is as complicated as Meridian Hill Park, planning is paramount. This is not to say, however, that plans cannot be modified.

Any model for documentation must be flexible enough to allow for the needs of an individual sponsor. In this case, the sponsor, the National Capital Region of the National Park Service, needed an accurate record of existing conditions for maintenance and rehabilitation. This general purpose, together with the goal of HABS to fully develop a landscape model, resulted in a comprehensive documentation proposal for Meridian Hill Park.

A number of alternate design proposals and construction drawings exist for Meridian Hill Park. This material resulted

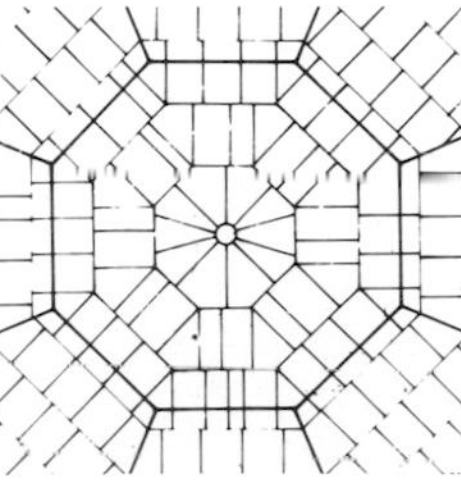

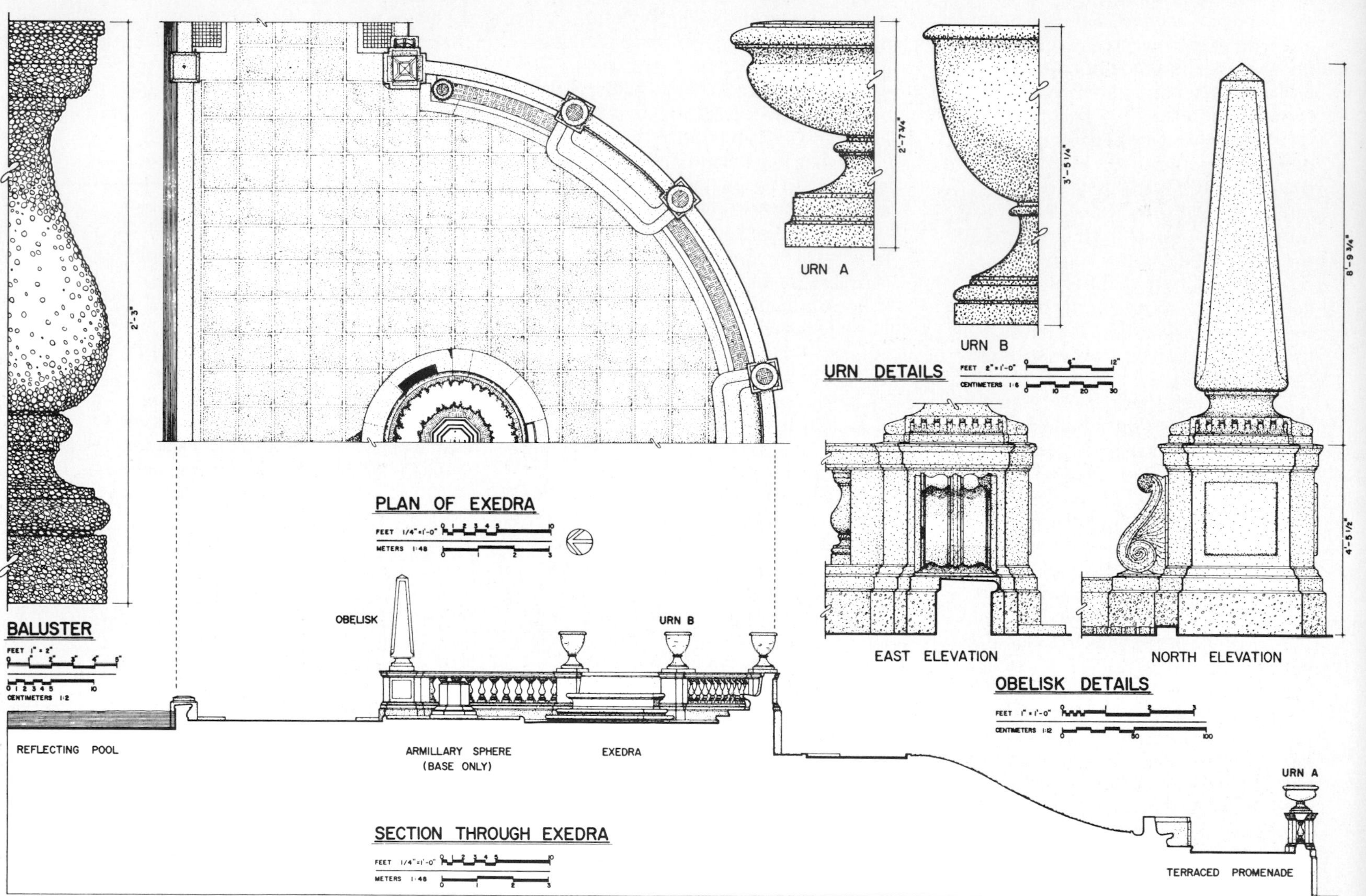

Figure 6.44

Drawings were completed of areas of Meridian Hill Park which received intensive design focus. An exedra terminating the major axis of the park was the subject of great design refinement. Plan, section, and details were completed. The exposed aggregate concrete textures were delineated at various scales.

Figure 6.45

John J. Earley, engineer for the decorative concrete finishes in Meridian Hill Park, was a pioneer in concrete technology. Meridian Hill Park provided an opportunity to replicate Renaissance masonry inexpensively. Through the use of poured-in-place, exposed aggregate concrete, classical elements could be easily replicated. Such technology allowed a high level of artistry, as illustrated in the photograph of the balustrade. The use of strong sidelighting highlights the texture of the pebble aggregate.

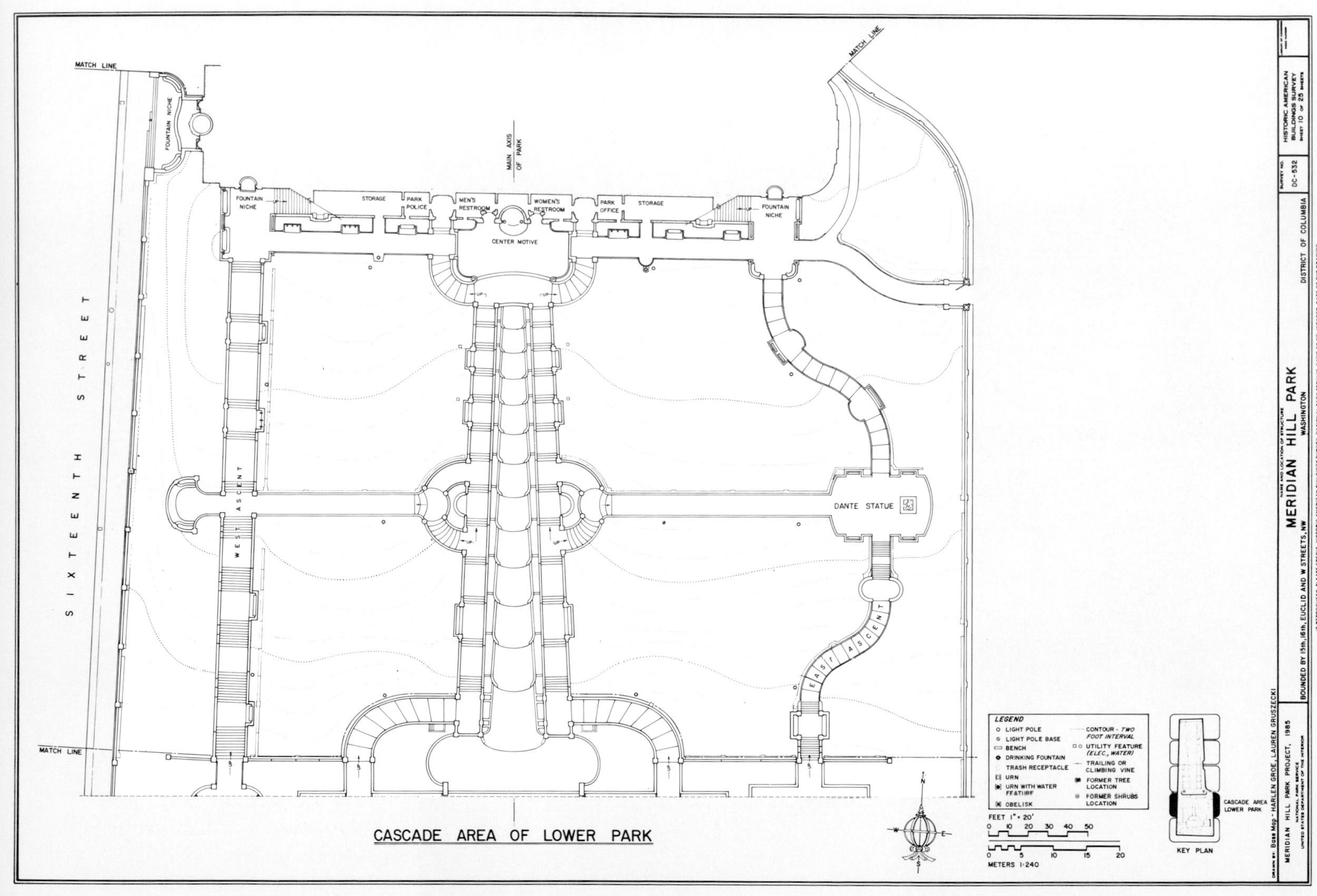

from the reviews given to every public project in Washington, D.C., and the long construction period. HABS research revealed an early design proposal for the park, which was reproduced in the written data. Similarly, a 1928 plan approved by the Commission of Fine Arts was reproduced onto drafting film and included in the measured drawings. Historic photographs were reshot with current views to further support the 1985 existing conditions survey. Numerous tasks had to be undertaken simultaneously because of time constraints.

Figure 6.46

In order to capture landscape details graphically, Meridian Hill Park was divided into five contiguous areas. This required linking five 24" x 36" HABS format drafting film sheets. In the lower right-hand corner of each sheet is a key map showing the location of the section within the park. Delineated on these sheets are "hard features" such as sidewalks, steps, light poles, and benches.

Utilizing historic plans, a transit, and measuring tapes, the overall plan of Meridian Hill Park was developed. Because of the approximate twelve-acre size and the need to develop plans at a 1″=20′ usable scale, the site was divided into five sections from north to south. Each section fits on a large HABS drawing sheet with a sufficient border for annotations. On these five sheets are delineated the hard base features: walkways, concrete features, fountains, benches, light poles, and so on (see fig. 6.46).

In order to save time, drafters used a pin bar, a flat metal bar with tabs upon which a sheet of drafting film is hooked. Base maps were inked on these sheets. Consecutive sheets were overlaid, inked

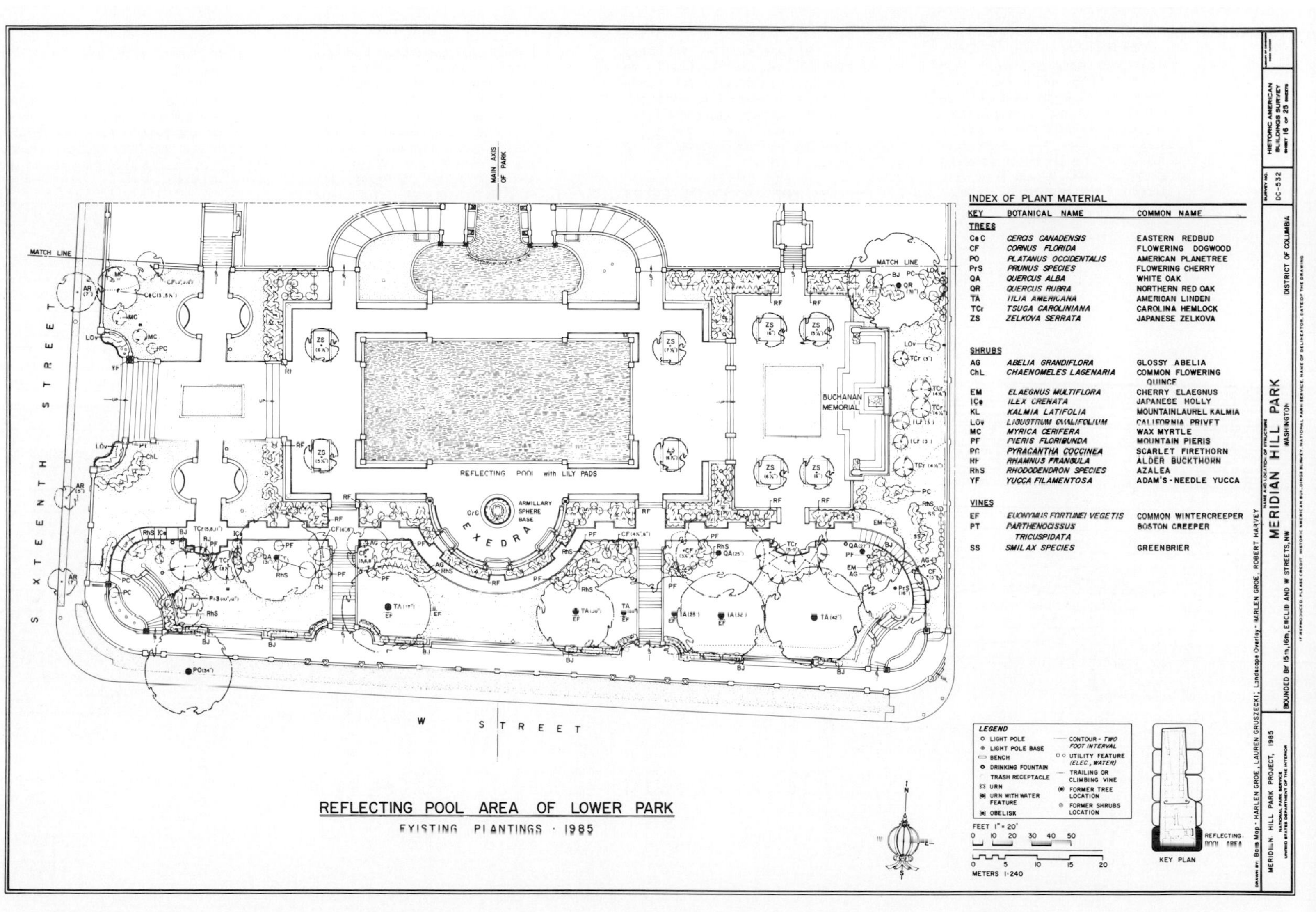

MAIN AXIS OF PARK
MATCH LINE
SIXTEENTH STREET
W STREET
REFLECTING POOL with LILY PADS
ARMILLARY SPHERE BASE
EXEDRA
BUCHANAN MEMORIAL
INDEX OF PLANT MATERIAL
KEY BOTANICAL NAME COMMON NAME
TREES
CeC CERCIS CANADENSIS EASTERN REDBUD
CF CORNUS FLORIDA FLOWERING DOGWOOD
PO PLATANUS OCCIDENTALIS AMERICAN PLANETREE
PrS PRUNUS SPECIES FLOWERING CHERRY
QA QUERCUS ALBA WHITE OAK
QR QUERCUS RUBRA NORTHERN RED OAK
TA TILIA AMERICANA AMERICAN LINDEN
TCr TSUGA CAROLINIANA CAROLINA HEMLOCK
ZS ZELKOVA SERRATA JAPANESE ZELKOVA
SHRUBS
AG ABELIA GRANDIFLORA GLOSSY ABELIA
ChL CHAENOMELES LAGENARIA COMMON FLOWERING QUINCE
EM ELAEGNUS MULTIFLORA CHERRY ELAEGNUS
ICe ILEX CRENATA JAPANESE HOLLY
KL KALMIA LATIFOLIA MOUNTAINLAUREL KALMIA
LOv LIGUSTRUM OVALIFOLIUM CALIFORNIA PRIVET
MC MYRICA CERIFERA WAX MYRTLE
PF PIERIS FLORIBUNDA MOUNTAIN PIERIS
PC PYRACANTHA COCCINEA SCARLET FIRETHORN
RF RHAMNUS FRANGULA ALDER BUCKTHORN
RhS RHODODENDRON SPECIES AZALEA
YF YUCCA FILAMENTOSA ADAM'S-NEEDLE YUCCA
VINES
EF EUONYMUS FORTUNEI VEGETIS COMMON WINTERCREEPER
PT PARTHENOCISSUS TRICUSPIDATA BOSTON CREEPER
SS SMILAX SPECIES GREENBRIER
REFLECTING POOL AREA OF LOWER PARK
EXISTING PLANTINGS · 1985
KEY PLAN
MERIDIAN HILL PARK
WASHINGTON
DISTRICT OF COLUMBIA
DC-532

FIGURE 6.47

The complex planting plan for Meridian Hill Park required a separate overlay sheet. Onto a "pin bar" registered overlay of the hardline base map were delineated the landscape plantings. These included trees, shrubs, and vines, as well as their canopy size and caliper. The water features were highlighted.

MERIDIAN HILL PARK, LOCATED BETWEEN 15th, 16th, W, AND EUCLID STREETS, NW, IS ONE OF THE MOST DISTINGUISHED EXAMPLES OF LANDSCAPE DESIGN IN WASHINGTON. THE HILLY TERRAIN OF THE TWELVE ACRE SITE AND THE BEAUX-ARTS TRAINING OF THE DESIGNERS PRODUCED A DESIGN THAT IS AN ELABORATE ARCHITECTURAL COMPOSITION AS WELL AS A LANDSCAPED PARK. AMONG THE MAJOR FEATURES ARE THE MALL, THE ITALIANATE CASCADE, THE GREAT TERRACE, AND THE MONUMENT TO PRESIDENT BUCHANAN. THE ARCHITECTURAL ELEMENTS ARE CONSTRUCTED WITH EXPOSED PEBBLE CONCRETE, AND REPRESENT SOME OF THE EARLIEST USES OF THIS MATERIAL IN THE UNITED STATES.

THE PARK OWES ITS EXISTENCE TO EFFORTS OF MARY FOOTE HENDERSON, WHO LOBBIED IN CONGRESS FOR ITS PURCHASE FOR DEVELOPMENT AS FORMAL GARDENS. AFTER 1910, MERIDIAN HILL PARK PROPERTY WAS TRANSFERRED TO THE OFFICE OF PUBLIC BUILDINGS AND GROUNDS. ON MARCH 20, 1914, THE FINE ARTS COMMISSION GAVE APPROVAL TO A PRELIMINARY SCHEME FOR THE PARK'S DEVELOPMENT THAT WAS PREPARED BY LANDSCAPE ARCHITECT GEORGE BURNAP. THE ARCHITECTURAL ELEMENTS WERE DEVELOPED AND THE BURNAP PLAN WAS REFINED BY HORACE W. PEASLEE UNDER THE SUPERVISION OF THE FINE ARTS COMMISSION. PLANTING PLANS WERE PREPARED BY VITALE, BRINCKERHOFF, AND GEIFFERT, LANDSCAPE ARCHITECTS OF NEW YORK. FULL DEVELOPMENT OF THE PARK TOOK SEVERAL DECADES, FINALLY BEING COMPLETED IN OCTOBER OF 1936.

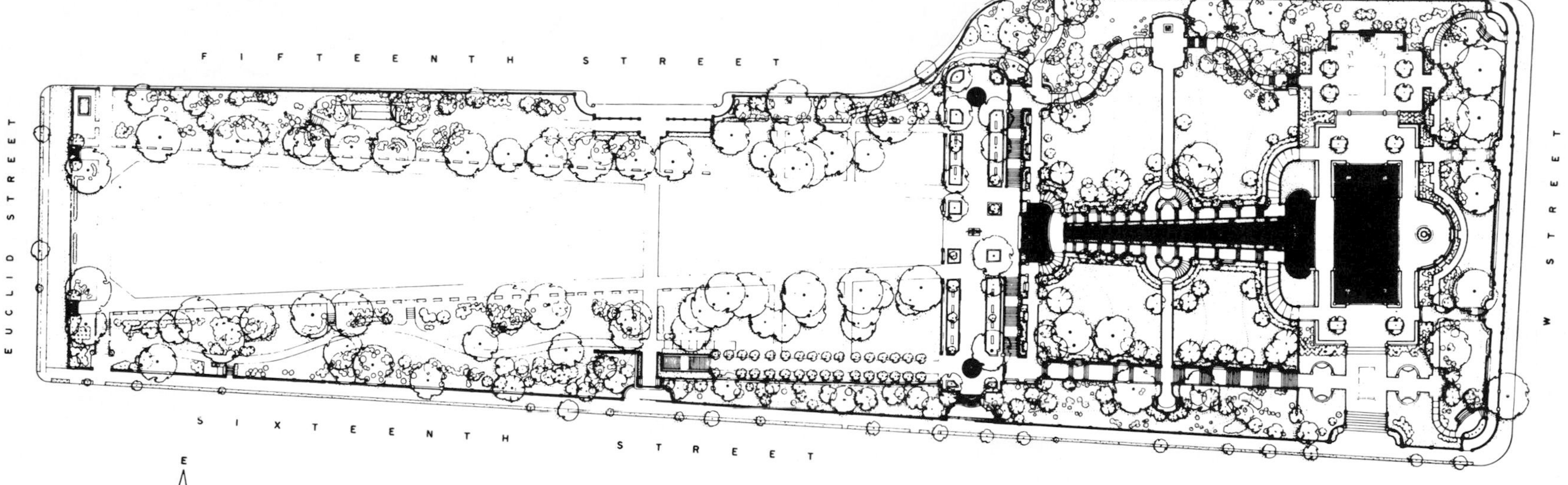

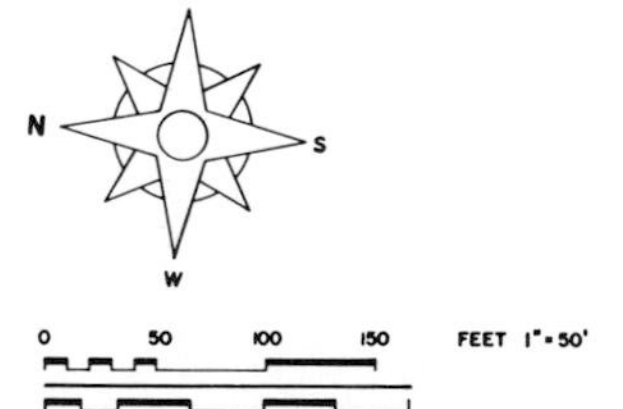

MERIDIAN HILL PARK

1985 SITE PLAN

Figure 6.48

The 1985 site plan of Meridian Hill Park is a document of existing conditions. It was developed by linking the five detailed plans together and photographically reducing them to the same scale as the 1928 plan. In spite of the 1"-50' scale, the deviations from the 1928 plan (see fig. 6.43) are very clear. A brief historical overview is also included on this sheet.

with the new information, and reproduced photographically to create a new sheet. This allowed multiple usage of a base sheet on which are delineated the hard features. On these overlay sheets were delineated the soft features, such as trees, shrubs, and vines. Also included on these sheets are tree caliper, canopy size, and the common and botanical names of plants and trees. These sheets also feature some graphic enhancement for illustrative purposes (see fig. 6.47).

Unlike traditional architectural documentation, in which the base sheet is usually the final record, a landscape base sheet serves a separate purpose. It depicts any land configuration or surface without plant material. This record serves as an excellent management tool for the maintenance of the hard surfaces.

To further add to the value of the 1928 approved plan of the park, the five HABS sheets were photographically reduced to the same 1928 scale and printed onto a single sheet of drafting film. A simple comparison of the two sheets reveals a great wealth of information regarding "as designed" versus "as built" features as well as certain elements that were never undertaken (see figs. 6.43 and 6.48).

Many photographs were taken to capture the three-dimensional nature of the landscape. An experiment that used both photography and drawing proved to be very useful, especially for recording areas of the park that had undergone considerable change. For example, a large-format photograph was made of the reflecting pool and exedra (see fig. 6.42). This was enlarged and half-toned into a sheet of drafting film and a registered graphic overlay was produced. This overlay recreates via documentary sources and historic photographs the appearance of the park at its peak (see fig. 6.49).

To avoid confusion over the numerous construction campaigns, one sheet, the landscape development concept map, gave information regarding construction dates, responsible organization, and designers as they relate to various sections of the park (see fig. 6.50).

Following is a list of the final drawings:

- Title sheet with U.S. Geological Survey location map, site plan, and statement of significance.
- 1928 site plan
- 1985 site plan at same scale as 1928 site plan
- Structures existing prior to park construction
- 1916 topographic survey
- Landscape development concept map
- Base maps (five sheets)
- Landscape overlays (five sheets)
- Exedra details
- Sixteenth Street fountain details
- Retaining wall/triumphal arch detail
- Halftone photographs with graphic overlays (five sheets)

In addition to these twenty-five measured drawings, the Meridian Hill Park project produced sixty-seven pages of historical information and fifty-one large-format photographs. The Meridian Hill Park documentation serves as a model for future landscape recording projects (see figs. 6.48, 6.49, and 6.50).

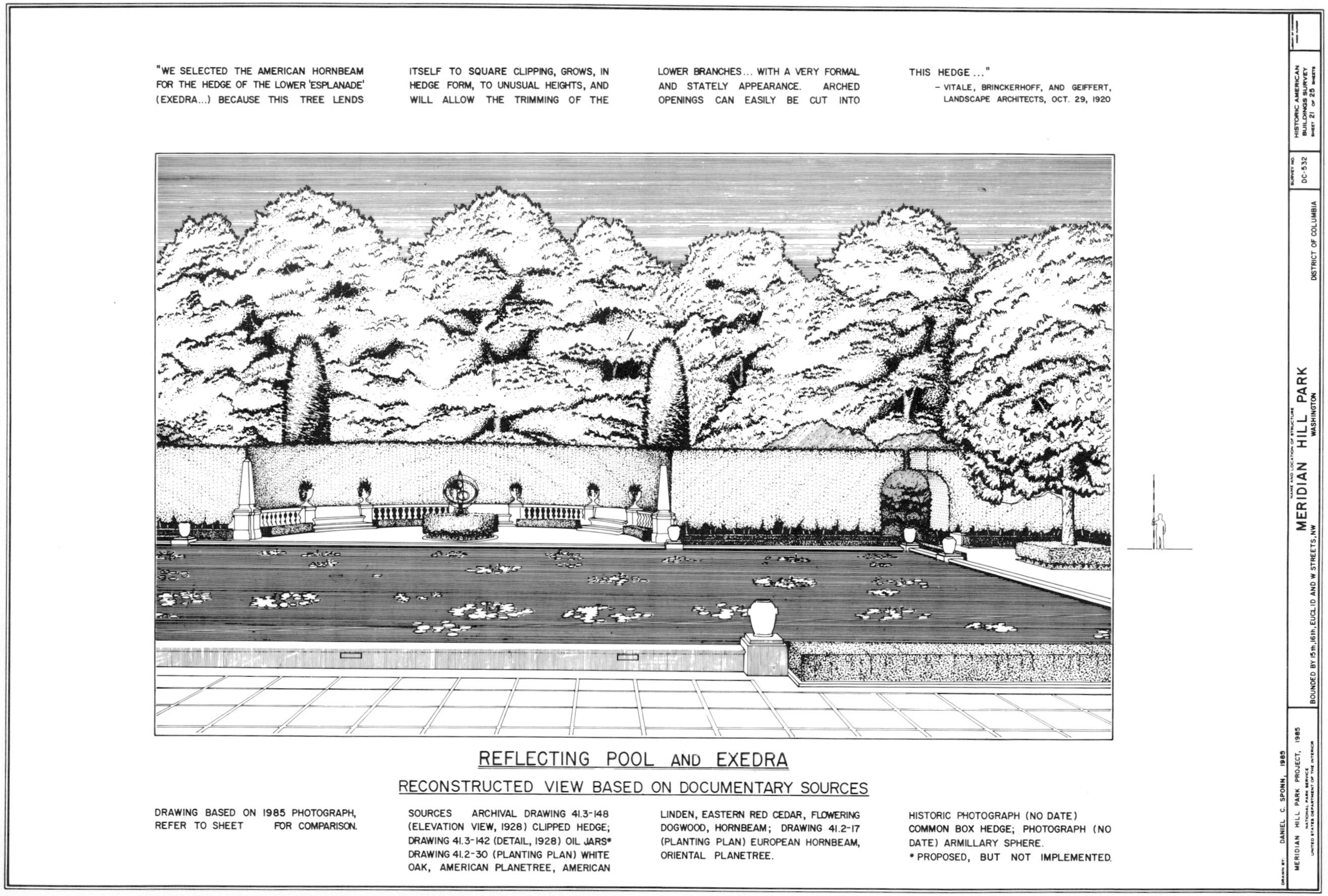

"WE SELECTED THE AMERICAN HORNBEAM FOR THE HEDGE OF THE LOWER 'ESPLANADE' (EXEDRA...) BECAUSE THIS TREE LENDS ITSELF TO SQUARE CLIPPING, GROWS, IN HEDGE FORM, TO UNUSUAL HEIGHTS, AND WILL ALLOW THE TRIMMING OF THE LOWER BRANCHES... WITH A VERY FORMAL AND STATELY APPEARANCE. ARCHED OPENINGS CAN EASILY BE CUT INTO THIS HEDGE..."

– VITALE, BRINCKERHOFF, AND GEIFFERT, LANDSCAPE ARCHITECTS, OCT. 29, 1920

REFLECTING POOL AND EXEDRA

RECONSTRUCTED VIEW BASED ON DOCUMENTARY SOURCES

DRAWING BASED ON 1985 PHOTOGRAPH, REFER TO SHEET FOR COMPARISON.

SOURCES ARCHIVAL DRAWING 41.3-148 (ELEVATION VIEW, 1928) CLIPPED HEDGE; DRAWING 41.3-142 (DETAIL, 1928) OIL JARS* DRAWING 41.2-30 (PLANTING PLAN) WHITE OAK, AMERICAN PLANETREE, AMERICAN LINDEN, EASTERN RED CEDAR, FLOWERING DOGWOOD, HORNBEAM; DRAWING 41.2-17 (PLANTING PLAN) EUROPEAN HORNBEAM, ORIENTAL PLANETREE. HISTORIC PHOTOGRAPH (NO DATE) COMMON BOX HEDGE; PHOTOGRAPH (NO DATE) ARMILLARY SPHERE.

* PROPOSED, BUT NOT IMPLEMENTED.

DRAWN BY: DANIEL C. SPONN, 1985

MERIDIAN HILL PARK PROJECT, 1985
NATIONAL PARK SERVICE
UNITED STATES DEPARTMENT OF THE INTERIOR

NAME AND LOCATION OF STRUCTURE
MERIDIAN HILL PARK
BOUNDED BY 15th, 16th, EUCLID AND W STREETS, NW
WASHINGTON
DISTRICT OF COLUMBIA

SURVEY NO. DC-532

HISTORIC AMERICAN BUILDINGS SURVEY
SHEET 21 OF 25 SHEETS

FIGURE 6.49

A pin bar registered overlay of an enlarged photograph was developed to recreate historic conditions in Meridian Hill Park. The reflecting pool and exedra had been heavily landscaped with hornbeam hedges and extensive plantings which are no longer extant. These conditions were graphically recreated, and notes were added which indicate the documentary sources for the overlay (see fig. 6.42).

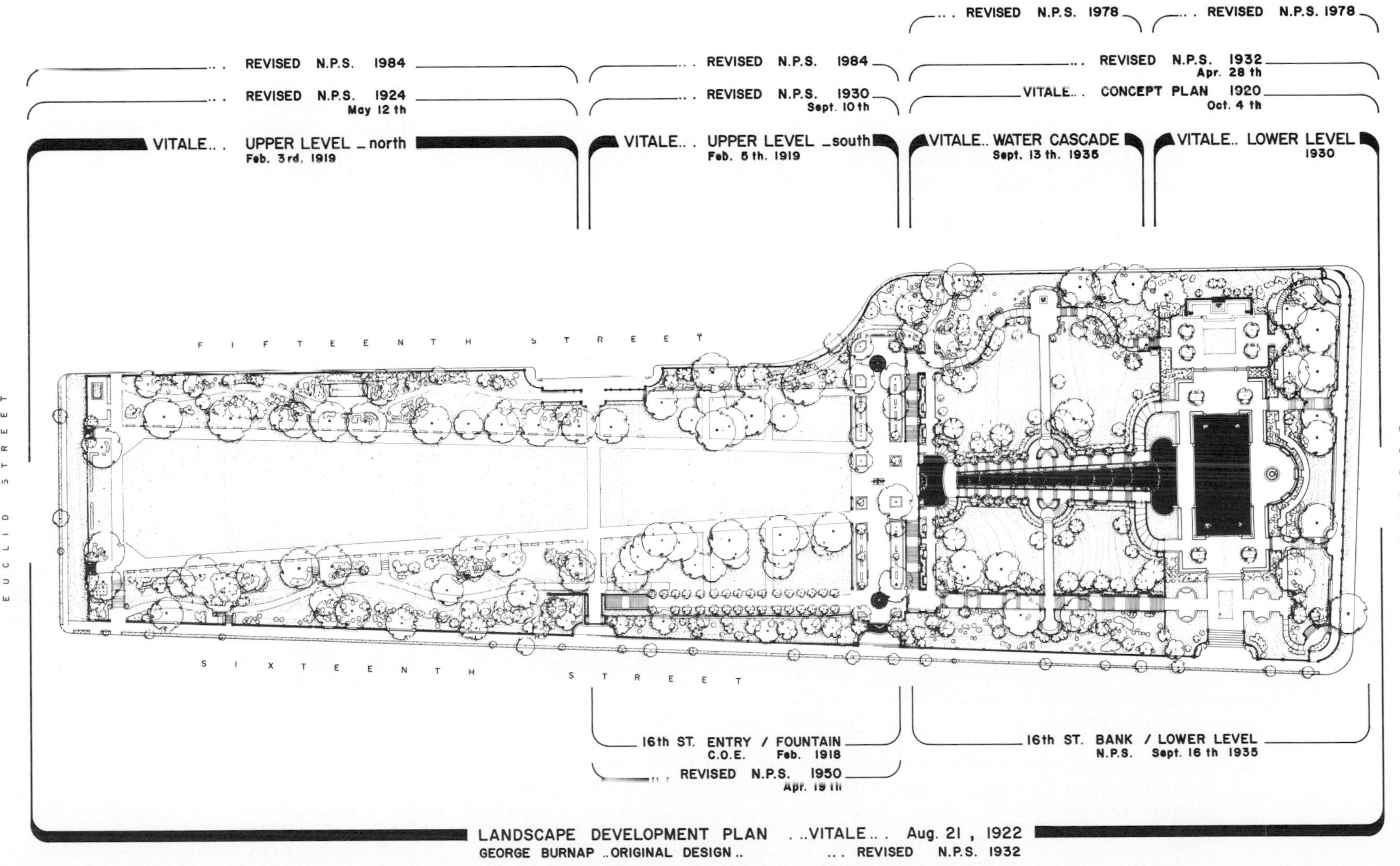

FIGURE 6.50

The landscape development concept sheet for Meridian Hill Park traces changes to the park since 1919. Because of the numerous construction campaigns, a key map was needed to delineate these modifications graphically.

LIST OF ILLUSTRATIONS

Figure 2.5
United States Naval Academy, Superintendent's Quarters (HABS No. MD-329-5). Annapolis, Anne Arundel County, Maryland. HABS/HAER Inventory card. Inventoried by Sally K. Tompkins, 1980.

Figure 2.6
United States Naval Academy, Superintendent's Quarters (HABS No. MD-329-5). Annapolis, Anne Arundel County, Maryland. HABS/HAER Inventory card. Inventoried by Sally K. Tompkins, 1980.

Figure 2.7
Utica Cement Company, Laboratory Building. Utica, LaSalle County, Illinois. HABS/HAER Inventory card. Inventoried by Gray Fitzsimons and Doug Kupel, 1980.

Figure 2.8
Utica Cement Company, Laboratory Building. Utica, LaSalle County, Illinois. HABS/HAER Inventory card. Inventoried by Gray Fitzsimons and Doug Kupel, 1980.

Figure 2.9
HABS Survey. Ottawa, LaSalle County, Illinois. Typical survey page. Inventoried by Jeanne C. Lawrence and Mary K. Shipe, 1987. From: *An Inventory of Historic Structures Within the Illinois and Michigan Canal National Heritage Corridor, Volume III: Ottawa* (Washington D.C.: HABS/HAER, 1987).

Figure 2.10
Hacienda Azucarera La Esperanza, Steam Engine (HAER No. PR-1-A). Manati, Tierras Nuevas, Puerto Rico. ¾ view of 6 column beam engine and flywheel, looking southeast. Photograph by Fred Gjessing, National Park Service, 1976.

Figure 2.11
Photo identification sheet. National Park Service.

Figure 2.12
Fort Jay (HABS No. NY-4-6). Governors Island, New York, New York County, New York. Aerial view, looking north. Photograph by Jet Lowe, 1983.

Figure 2.13
United States Military Academy (HABS No. NY-5708). West Point, Orange County, New York. The plain and camptown as seen from the northwest, circa 1830. Courtesy USMA Archives.

Figure 2.14
United States Military Academy (HABS No. NY-5708). West Point, Orange County, New York. Engineering training on the plain, circa 1881. Courtesy USMA Archives.

Figure 2.15
United States Military Academy (HABS No. NY-5708). West Point, Orange County, New York. Aerial view of the academy looking north, circa 1933. Courtesy USMA Archives.

Figure 3.1
McLachlen Building. Washington, District of Columbia. Architectural catalog, 1923. *J. H. de Sibour, Architect, Washington D.C.* Source: Reproduced courtesy Collection, of the Columbia Historical Society, Washington, D.C.

Figure 3.2
Homer Building. Washington, District of Columbia. Specifications. Source: National Archives and Records Service, Washington, D.C., Building Permits.

Figure 3.3
Ottawa Republican-Times. Source: Reddick Library, Ottawa, Illinois.

Figure 3.4
Summit city directory. Source: Village Clerk's Office, Summit, Illinois.

Figure 3.5
Scotty's Castle (HABS No. CA-2257). Death Valley, Inyo County, California. Letter from Aztec Forged Hardware Co., 21 March 1929.

Figure 3.6
Washington Public Library (HABS No. DC-457). Washington, District of Columbia. *Programme of Competition for the Washington Public Library Building.* Source: Martin Luther King Memorial Library, Washingtonia Room.

Figure 3.7
Sanborn map of Passaic, New Jersey, Sheet 3, September 1886. Courtesy Geography and Map Division, Library of Congress.

Figure 3.8
Spring Valley House (HABS No. IL-1150). Utica vicinity, LaSalle County, Illinois. First floor plan, Sheet 3 of 8. Drawing by Ellen Stoner, 1987.

Figure 3.9
Leland Stanford House (HABS No. CA-1709). Sacramento, Sacramento County, California. Historic views. Photocopies of 1862 Wood Engraving (CA-1709-1), Pre-1870 Photograph (CA-1709-2), and 1902 Photograph (CA-1709-7).

Figure 3.10
Cambria Iron Company. Johnstown, Cambria County, Pennsylvania. Photograph of a bird's-eye view. Field photograph by Gray Fitzsimons.

Figure 3.11
Milo S. Ketchum, *The Design of Highway Bridges*, Figure 162 (New York: McGraw-Hill Book Company, 1908).

Figure 3.12
Oliver Evans, *The Young Mill-Wright and Miller's Guide*, Plate XIX and Plate XXI (Philadelphia: Blanchard and Lea, 1853).

Figure 4.1
Maurice Bathhouse (HABS No. AR-28-C). Hot Springs National Park, Hot Springs, Garland County, Arkansas. West elevation, Sheet 1 of 3. Drawing by Gregory C. McCall, 1985.

Figure 4.2
Maurice Bathhouse (HABS No. AR-28-C). Hot Springs National Park, Hot Springs, Garland County, Arkansas. General view of west front. Photograph by Jack E. Boucher, 1983.

Figure 4.3
Maurice Bathhouse (HABS No. AR-28-C). Hot Springs National Park, Hot Springs, Garland County, Arkansas. West front, from southwest. Photograph by Jack E. Boucher, 1984.

Figure 4.4
East Boston Pumping Station (HAER No. MA-65). Boston, Suffolk County, Massachusetts. Engine room, horizontal Corliss (Engine #3), taken from east. Photograph by Jet Lowe, 1986.

Figure 4.5
Statue of Liberty (HAER No. NY-138). Liberty Island, New York City, New York County, New York. Detail, profile view of right side of face. Photograph by Jet Lowe, 1984.

Figure 4.6
Central Furnace (HAER No. OH-12). Cleveland, Cuyahoga County, Ohio. Detail, corroded stairs on stoves to central furnaces. Photograph by Jet Lowe, 1979.

Figure 4.7
Gunston Hall (HABS No. VA-141). Lorton vicinity, Fairfax County, Virginia. General view of house and grounds from north. Photograph by Jack E. Boucher, 1981.

Figure 4.8
Jack E. Boucher by Manuel A. Ovalles, *Chattanooga Times*.

Figure 4.9
Field photograph by Robert Vogel.

Figure 4.10
Hanchett Residence Park (HABS No. CA-2010). San Jose, Santa Clara County, California. 1241 Martin Avenue, southeast front. Photograph by Jane Lidz, 1980.

Figure 4.11
203 East York Street (House, Iron Balustrade) (HABS No. GA-287). Savannah, Chatham County, Georgia. Ironwork on front steps. Photograph by L. D. Andrew, 1936.

Figure 4.12
Lowther Hall (HABS No. GA-14-59). Clinton, Jones County, Georgia. Interior stairs. Photograph by Branan Sanders, 1934.

Figure 4.13
Taking photographs to aid hand measurement. From a diagram by Melvin Rotsch. Source: Harley J. McKee, *Recording Historic Buildings* (Washington, D.C.: GPO, 1970), p. 41.

Figure 4.14
Winthrop College, Tillman Building (HABS No. SC-619-B). Rock Hill, York County, South Carolina. First floor, stairway, looking southwest. Photograph by Jack E. Boucher, 1986.

Figure 4.15
Chesapeake Bugeye *Louise Travers* (HAER No. MD-55). Solomons Island, Calvert County, Maryland. View of stern. Photograph by Jet Lowe, 1986.

Figure 4.16
Bethlehem Steel Company's Lackawanna Plant (HAER No. NY-198). Buffalo, Erie County, New York. Incline skip. Photograph by Jet Lowe, 1985.

Figure 4.17
Chicago Stock Exchange Building (HABS No. IL-1034). Chicago, Cook County, Illinois. Elevated view from northeast and spandrel detail. Photographs by Cervin Robinson, 1963.

Figure 4.18
Borough House (HABS No. SC-362). Stateburg, Sumter County, South Carolina. South elevation, conservatory, wide-angle lens. Photograph by Jack E. Boucher, 1984.

Figure 4.19
Borough House (HABS No. SC-362). Stateburg, Sumter County, South Carolina. South elevation, conservatory, distant view showing roof of main house, normal lens. Photograph by Jack E. Boucher, 1984.

Figure 4.20
Borough House (HABS No. SC-362). Stateburg, Sumter County, South Carolina. South elevation, conservatory, distant view showing roof of main house, wide angle lens. Photograph by Jack E. Boucher, 1984.

Figure 4.21
Corrigan, McKinney Steel Company (Republic Steel Company) (HAER No. OH-13). Cleveland, Cuyahoga County, Ohio. Roughing stands, 84-inch strip mill. Photograph by Jet Lowe, 1979.

Figure 4.22
Healy Building (HABS No. DC-248). Georgetown University, Washington, District of Columbia. Detail of east elevation near north end pavilion. Photograph by Jack E. Boucher, 1969.

Figure 4.23
Pantigo Windmill (HAER No. NY-143). East Hampton, Suffolk County, New York. Stairway, looking from floor 2 to floor 1. Photograph by Jet Lowe, 1978.

Figure 4.24
Lake Lynn Hydroelectric Power House and Dam (HAER No. WV-30). Cheat River, Morgantown vicinity, Monongalia County, West Virginia. General view of power house interior, looking southwest. Photograph by Jet Lowe, 1980.

Figure 4.25
Large-format camera and accessories. Photograph by Jack E. Boucher, 1987.

Figure 4.26
Copper River and Northwestern Railway, Million Dollar Bridge (HAER No. AK-10). Cordova, Alaska. Looking east from Childs Glacier to Miles Glacier. Photograph by Jet Lowe, 1984.

Figure 4.27
Diagram comparing sizes of negatives.

Figure 4.28
Octagon House. Washington, District of Columbia. Oblique view shot with 35mm Nikon camera with 28mm PC lens. Oblique view shot with 4" x 5" HORSEMAN camera with 90mm Schneider lens. Photographs by William L. Lebovich, 1988.

Figure 4.29
Battle Creek Hydroelectric Project (HAER No. CA-2). Manton vicinity, Tehama County, California. Detail of gate values and needle valve controls. Photograph by Jet Lowe, 1979.

Figure 4.30
East Broad Top Railroad (HAER No. PA-127). Wrays Hill Tunnel, Orbisonia vicinity, Huntingdon County, Pennsylvania. Tunnel interior. Photograph by Jack E. Boucher, 1986.

Figure 4.31
Watkins Woolen Mill (HAER No. MO-1). Lawson, Clay County, Missouri. Third floor, north side, four jacks. Photograph by Jet Lowe, 1978.

Figure 4.32
HABS/HAER Photographic Services Request Form.

Figure 4.33
Reading-Halls Station Bridge (HAER No. PA-55). Muncy vicinity, Lycoming County, Pennsylvania. Oblique view, two panels of truss. Photograph by Jet Lowe, 1984.

Figure 4.34
Joseph Banks House (HABS No. SC-593). St. Matthews, Calhoun County, South Carolina. Interior, first floor central stairway. Photograph by Jack E. Boucher, 1987.

Figure 4.35
White House (HABS No. DC-37). Washington, District of Columbia. North front. Photograph by Jack E. Boucher, 1976.

Figure 4.36
Higgins Armory. Worcester, Worcester County, Massachusetts. Historic structure field photo record.

Figure 4.37
Higgins Armory. Worcester, Worcester County, Massachusetts. Great Hall, third floor. Photograph by Jack E. Boucher, 1988.

Figure 4.38
James J. Hill Mansion. St. Paul, Ramsey County, Minnesota. Sample HABS negative, negative sleeve, and mount card. Photograph by Jet Lowe, 1987.

FIGURE 4.39
Stan Hywet Hall (HABS No. OH-50). Akron, Summit County, Ohio. Rectified photograph. Chambers and Chambers, Architects.

FIGURE 4.40
Stan Hywet Hall (HABS No. OH-50). Akron, Summit County, Ohio. Floor plan annotated with locations of rectified photographs. Drawing by Chambers and Chambers, Architects.

FIGURE 4.41
Stan Hywet Hall (HABS No. OH-50). Akron, Summit County, Ohio. Detail showing bay window of solarium, east front. Photography by Jack E. Boucher, 1982.

FIGURE 4.42
Dorchester Heights Monument (HABS No. MA-1171). Boston, Suffolk County, Massachusetts. North elevation, level 5 (photogrammetric plate LC-HABS-GS11-D, 1981-N6R). Photograph by Dennett, Muessig and Associates, Ltd., 1981.

FIGURE 4.43
Diagram showing location of x-ray generator, subject and film cassette. Reproduced courtesy David M. Hart, AIA.

FIGURE 4.44
Typical locations for radiographs of the structure of a braced frame building. Reproduced courtesy David M. Hart, AIA.

FIGURE 4.45
Radiograph of stair rail and newel post. Reproduced courtesy David M. Hart, AIA.

FIGURE 4.46
Corrigan, McKinney Steel Co. (HAER No. OH-13). Cleveland, Cuyahoga County, Ohio. Furnace No. 3 (no longer in use), looking northwest. Photograph by Jet Lowe, 1979.

FIGURE 5.1
Shutt House (HABS No. IL-1123-F). Springfield, Sangamon County, Illinois. Structural framing axonometric, Sheet 5 of 5. Drawing by Lesley M. Gilmore, 1986.

FIGURE 5.2
Gunston Hall (HABS No. VA-141). Lorton vicinity, Fairfax County, Virginia. Palladian Room, Sheet 14 of 30. Drawing by Richard J. Cronenberger, 1981.

FIGURE 5.3
Gunston Hall (HABS No. VA-141). Lorton vicinity, Fairfax County, Virginia. View from northwest. Photograph by Jack E. Boucher, 1981.

FIGURE 5.4
Ben Thresher's Mill (HAER No. VT-10). Barnet Center, Caledonia County, Vermont. First floor, Sheet 6 of 11. Drawing by Anastasios Kokoris, 1979.

FIGURE 5.5
Woodrow Wilson House (HABS No. DC-133). Washington, District of Columbia. Section A-A, Sheet 11 of 13. Drawing by Kenneth S. Williams, Jr., 1977.

FIGURE 5.6
Fort McCoy, Building 7042. Sparta vicinity, Monroe County, Wisconsin. General view. U.S. Army photograph, 1941. Reproduced courtesy U.S. Army.

FIGURE 5.7
Independence Hall (HABS No. PA-1430). Philadelphia, Philadelphia County, Pennsylvania. North elevation. Photogrammetry and drawing by Dennett, Muessig, Ryan and Associates.

FIGURE 5.8
Valery Nichols House (Casa Flinard) (HABS No. LA-33). New Orleans, Orleans County, Louisiana. Sketch plan and elevation. Sketch by G.B. Drennan, 1938.

FIGURE 5.9
City Hall (HABS No. NY-5444). Utica, Oneida County, New York. East elevation of tower, field notes. Field notes by Harley J. McKee, 1966.

FIGURE 5.10
Lundale Farm, Springhouse (HABS No. PA-1308-A). Pughtown vicinity, Chester County, Pennsylvania. Contact print of field photographs. Photographs by John A. Burns, 1975.

FIGURE 5.11
Hopkinton Supply Company (HABS No. MA-1227). Hopkinton, Middlesex County, Massachusetts. South front with scale. Photograph by Jack E. Boucher, 1988.

FIGURE 5.12
Gunston Hall (HABS No. VA-141). Lorton vicinity, Fairfax County, Virginia. North elevation porch details, Sheet 3 of 6. Field notes by Richard J. Cronenberger, 1981. Land Front Porch, Sheet of 11 of 30. Drawing by Richard J. Cronenberger, 1981.

FIGURE 5.13A and 5.13B
Asa Packer Mansion (HABS No. PA-5330). Jim Thorpe, Carbon County, Pennsylvania. First floor plan west, Sheets 3.1.1 and 3.1.4, Field notes by Timothy A. Buehner, Patrick P. Koby, Sandra Moore, and Eric A. Zehrung, 1986.

FIGURE 5.14
Hand measuring equipment.

Figure 5.15
Leitz/SK telescoping digital measuring pole.

Figure 5.16
Triangulated field notes. Illustration by Richard K. Anderson, 1988.

Figure 5.17
Cameron Valley Housing, Alexandria, Virginia. Detail of adobe brick and window. Photograph by Jet Lowe, 1988.

Figure 5.18
Lundale Farm, House (HABS No. PA-1308). Pughtown vicinity, Chester County, Pennsylvania. North (rear) elevation. Photograph by John A. Burns, 1975.

Figure 5.19
Lundale Farm, House (HABS No. PA-1308). Pughtown vicinity, Chester County, Pennsylvania. North elevation, Sheet 6 of 6. Drawing by Susan M. Dornbusch, 1978.

Figure 5.20
Typical camera positions for stereophotogrammetry. Diagram by Perry E. Borchers, 1976.

Figure 5.21
Grant Monument (Grant's Tomb) (HABS No. NY-5429). New York, New York County, New York. Photogrammetric negative LC-HABS-GS05-T-2564-102L. Photograph by Perry E. Borchers, 1963.

Figure 5.22
St. Mary's Seminary. Baltimore, Maryland. Photogrammetric image LC-HABS-GS05-B1974-801R. Photograph by Perry E. Borchers, 1974.

Figure 5.23
Central Portion of the Pueblo of Tesuque (HABS No. NM-103). Santa Fe County, New Mexico. Restored plan as of 1899, Sheet 3 of 9. Photogrammetric plotting by Perry E. Borchers. Drawing by Julsing J. Lamsam, 1973.

Figure 5.24
Common elements of identification in HABS/HAER measured drawings.

Figure 5.25
Meridian Hill Park (HABS No. DC-532). Washington, District of Columbia. Title sheet, Sheet 1 of 25. Drawing by Robert R. Harvey, 1985.

Figure 5.26
920-930 F Street NW (Commercial Buildings) (HABS No. DC-569). Washington, District of Columbia. Title sheet, Sheet 1 of 26. Drawing by Mary Ellen Didion and Mark Schara, 1988.

Figure 5.27
Eisenhower Farm Two (HABS No. PA-1967). Gettysburg vicinity, Adams County, Pennsylvania. Title sheet, Sheet 1 of 1. Drawing by Joseph D. Balachowski, 1988.

Figure 5.28
Delaware and Hudson Canal Delaware Aqueduct (HAER No. PA-1). Spanning Delaware River from Lackawaxen, Pike County, Pennsylvania, to Minisink Ford, Sullivan County, New York. Longitudinal section looking at Pier 3 and west abutment, Sheet 3 of 4. Drawing by Eric N. DeLony and Robert M. Vogel, 1969.

Figure 5.29
Asa Packer Mansion (HABS No. PA-5330). Jim Thorpe, Carbon County, Pennsylvania. Section A-A, Sheet 11 of 15. Drawing by Timothy Buehner, Paul Dolinsky, Patrick Koby, Sandra Moore, and Eric Zehrung, 1987.

Figure 5.30A and 5.30B
Munsey Building (HABS No. DC-358). Washington, District of Columbia. First floor and twelfth floor plans, Sheets 2 and 3 of 6. Drawings by Joan B. Duncan and Michael J. Kopchik, 1979.

Figure 5.31
Beauregard House (HABS No. LA-1). New Orleans, Orleans Parish, Louisiana. Isometric of roof framing, Sheet 7 of 16. Drawing by Allison Owen, Jr., 1934.

Figure 5.32
Smithsonian Institution Building (HABS No. DC-141). Washington, District of Columbia. Longitudinal section A-A, Sheet 19 of 22. Drawing by Mark R. Freudenwald, 1984.

Figure 5.33
John Carter House (HABS No. RI-1). Providence, Providence County, Rhode Island. Full size details of window, Sheet 10 of 15. Drawing by W.W. Rivard, 1936.

Figure 5.34
Ben Thresher's Mill (HAER No. VT-10). Barnet Center, Caledonia County, Vermont. Power transmission schematic, Sheet 7 of 11. Drawing by Richard K. Anderson, Jr., 1981.

Figure 5.35
Pacific Short Line Bridge (HAER No. IA-1). Sioux City, Woodbury County, Iowa. Panel point 5L, Sheet 4 of 5. Drawing by Hans Muessig and Marie Neubauer, 1981.

Figure 5.36
Quincy Mining Company, No. 2 Hoist Engine (HAER No. MI-2). Hancock, Houghton County, Michigan. East elevation, Sheet 16 of 34. Drawing by Richard K. Anderson, Jr., 1979.

Figure 5.37
Reuben Matlack Blacksmith and Wheelwright Shop (HABS No. NJ-264). Maple Shade, Burlington County, New Jersey. Forge, Sheet 7 of 10. Drawing by Ralph H. Gamble, 1936.

Figure 5.38
John T. Long House (Shadrach Bond Mantel) (HABS No. IL-26-31). Evanston, Cook County, Illinois. Elevation, mantel. Photograph by Albert J. DeLong, 1934.

Figure 5.39
Manchester Cotton and Woolen Manufacturing Company (HAER No. VA-44). Richmond, Virginia. Historic site plans, Sheet 2 of 8. Drawing by Deborah Joy Cooper, based on historic maps.

Figure 5.40
Wickham-Valentine House (HABS No. VA-310). Richmond, Virginia. Comparative study of Parris's three designs, Sheet 16 of 18. Drawing by Douglas Harnsberger, 1985.

Figure 5.41
Adirondack Iron and Steel Company "New Furnace" (HAER No. NY-123). Tahawus, Essex County, New York. Perspective of blast machinery and dam, Sheet 12 of 13. Drawing by Barry A. Richards, 1978.

Figure 5.42
Maryland State House (HABS No. MD-245). Annapolis, Anne Arundel County, Maryland. Dome, Sheet 45 of 45. Drawing by Andrew Wenchel, 1986.

Figure 5.43
Missouri Botanical Garden (HABS No. MO-1135). St. Louis, Missouri. Site plan detail, Sheet 21 of 24. Drawing by Theodore S. Torpy and Stuart M. Mertz, 1975.

Figure 6.1
Picatinny Arsenal: 500 Area (HAER No. NJ-36C). Dover, Morris County, New Jersey. Process diagram of the 500 Area Smokeless Powder Production Plant, Sheet 2 of 4. Drawing by Richard K. Anderson, Jr., 1984.

Figure 6.2
Picatinny Arsenal: 500 Area (HAER No. NJ-36C). Dover, Morris County, New Jersey. Process diagram of the 500 Area Smokeless Powder Production Plant, Sheet 3 of 4. Drawing by Richard K. Anderson, Jr., 1984.

Figure 6.3
Picatinny Arsenal: 500 Area (HAER No. NJ-36C). Dover, Morris County, New Jersey. Process diagram of the 500 Area Smokeless Powder Production Plant, Sheet 4 of 4. Drawing by Richard K. Anderson, Jr., 1984.

Figure 6.4
Picatinny Arsenal: 500 Area (HAER No. NJ-36C-44). Dover, Morris County, New Jersey. Distillation towers, Building 519. Photograph by Jet Lowe, 1983.

Figure 6.5
Picatinny Arsenal: 500 Area (HAER No. NJ-36C-29). Dover, Morris County, New Jersey. Presses, Building 527. Photograph by Jet Lowe, 1983.

Figure 6.6
Picatinny Arsenal: 500 Area (HAER No. NJ-36C-2). Dover, Morris County, New Jersey. Cotton nitration line. Photograph by Jet Lowe, 1983.

Figure 6.7
Picatinny Arsenal: 500 Area (HAER No. NJ-36C-37). Dover, Morris County, New Jersey. Exterior details, Building 519. Photograph by Jet Lowe, 1983.

Figure 6.8
Picatinny Arsenal: 500 Area (HAER No. NJ-36C-84). Dover, Morris County, New Jersey. Cannon powder blender, Building 561. Photograph by Jet Lowe, 1983.

Figure 6.9
Picatinny Arsenal: 500 Area (HAER No. NJ-36C-39). Dover, Morris County, New Jersey. Slides, Building 519. Photograph by Jet Lowe, 1983.

Figure 6.10
Auditorium Building (HABS No. IL-1007). Chicago, Cook County, Illinois. Aerial isometric drawing of the west and south facades, Sheet 1 of 53. Drawing by Willie Graham and David T. Marsh, Jr., 1981.

Figure 6.11
Auditorium Building (HABS No. IL-1007). Chicago, Cook County, Illinois. Auditorium from Michigan Avenue, Photograph No. IL-1007-75. Photocopy of photograph by J.W. Taylor, 1890.

Figure 6.12
Auditorium Building (HABS No. IL-1007). Chicago, Cook County, Illinois. Tower foundations of auditorium, from Sheet 13 of 53. From *Observed and Computed Settlements of Structures in Chicago* by Ralph B. Peck and Ensar Uyanik (University of Illinois Engineering Experiment Station, Bulletin 429, Urbana, Illinois, 1955).

Figure 6.13 and 6.14
Auditorium Building (HABS No. IL-1007). Chicago, Cook County, Illinois. Longitudinal section X-X looking south as designed in 1887, Sheet 40 of 53. Longitudinal section X-X looking south as completed in 1890, Sheet 44 of 53. Drawings by August Ventura, 1980.

Figure 6.15
Auditorium Building (HABS No. IL-1007). Chicago, Cook County, Illinois. Basement, structure, Sheet 13 of 53. Drawing by Laura L. Hochuli, 1980.

Figure 6.16
Auditorium Building (HABS No. IL-1007). Chicago, Cook County, Illinois. View looking northwest from between trusses B and C of theater attic, Photograph No. IL-1007-52. Photograph by Jet Lowe, 1979.

Figure 6.17
Auditorium Building (HABS No. IL-1007). Chicago, Cook County, Illinois. Original Shone's hydro-pneumatic sewage ejectors in stage basement. Photograph No. IL-1007-15. Photograph by Jet Lowe, 1979.

Figure 6.18
Auditorium Building (HABS No. IL-1007). Chicago, Cook County, Illinois. North side of south bank of hydraulic rams, Photograph No. IL-1007-29. Photograph by Jet Lowe, 1979.

Figure 6.19
Auditorium Building (HABS No. IL-1007). Chicago, Cook County, Illinois. Banquet hall mechanical system, Sheet 53 of 53. Drawing by Tobin Kendrick and Cathy Berlow, 1979-1980.

Figure 6.20
Auditorium Building (HABS No. IL-1007). Chicago, Cook County, Illinois. East (front) elevation, Sheet 3 of 7. Drawing by Harry H. Lau, 1963.

Figure 6.21
Auditorium Building (HABS No. IL-1007). Chicago, Cook County, Illinois. Auditorium interior from balcony, Photograph IL-1007-89. Photocopy of photograph by J.W. Taylor, 1890.

Figure 6.22
Auditorium Building (HABS No. IL-1007). Chicago, Cook County, Illinois. Musicians' gallery of banquet hall, Sheet 1 of 1. Drawing by Varathor Bookaman and Joseph A. Tripicone, Jr., 1979.

Figure 6.23
Pilot Schooner *Alabama* (HAER No. MA-64). Vineyard Haven, Dukes County, Massachusetts. Starboard profile or *Alabama* In 1986. Photograph MA-64-1. Photograph by Jet Lowe, 1986.

Figure 6.24
Pilot Schooner *Alabama* (HAER No. MA-64). Vineyard Haven, Dukes County, Massachusetts. View of *Alabama* from the starboard bow, circa 1926. Photograph MA-64-24. Photographer unknown, courtesy of Robert S. Douglas.

Figure 6.25
Pilot Schooner *Alabama* (HAER No. MA-64). Vineyard Haven, Dukes County, Massachusetts. Reconstructed profile of the *Alabama* as the vessel appeared in 1926, Sheet 1 of 12. Drawing by Robbyn L. Jackson, 1987.

Figure 6.26
Pilot Schooner *Alabama* (HAER No. MA-64). Vineyard Haven, Dukes County, Massachusetts. Inboard profile of afterbody, Sheet 9 of 12. Drawing by Robbyn L. Jackson, 1987.

Figure 6.27
Pilot Schooner *Alabama* (HAER No. MA-64). Vineyard Haven, Dukes County, Massachusetts. Inboard profile of forebody, Sheet 10 of 12. Drawing by Robbyn L. Jackson, 1987.

Figure 6.28
Pilot Schooner *Alabama* (HAER No. MA-64). Vineyard Haven, Dukes County, Massachusetts. Details of vessel, Sheet 12 of 12. Drawing by Robbyn L. Jackson, 1987.

Figure 6.29
Pilot Schooner *Alabama* (HAER No. MA-64). Vineyard Haven, Dukes County, Massachusetts. Main deck plan of vessel, Sheet 5 of 12. Drawing by Robbyn L. Jackson, 1987.

Figure 6.30
Pilot Schooner *Alabama* (HAER No. MA-64). Vineyard Haven, Dukes County, Massachusetts. Main deck plan of vessel, Sheet 6 of 12. Drawing by Robbyn L. Jackson, 1987.

Figure 6.31
Pilot Schooner *Alabama* (HAER No. MA-64). Vineyard Haven, Dukes County, Massachusetts. Cross-sections of vessel, Sheet 11 of 12. Drawing by Robbyn L. Jackson, 1987.

***Figure* 6.32**
Schooner *Wawona* (HAER No. WA-64). Seattle, King County, Washington. Field photograph by Richard K. Anderson, Jr., 1985.

***Figure* 6.33**
Schooner *Wawona* (HAER No. WA-64). Seattle, King County, Washington. Tugs move *Wawona* into dry dock, Photograph WA-14-55. Photograph by Jet Lowe, 1985.

***Figure* 6.34**
Schooner *Wawona* (HAER No. WA-64). Seattle, King County, Washington. Field photograph by Richard K. Anderson, Jr., 1985.

***Figure* 6.35**
Schooner *Wawona* (HAER No. WA-64). Seattle, King County, Washington. Photograph by Tom E. Sandry, 1985.

***Figure* 6.36**
Schooner *Wawona* (HAER No. WA-14). Seattle, King County, Washington. Half-breadth plan and sheer plan of *Wawona*, Sheet 5 of 7. Drawing by Richard K. Anderson, Jr., 1986.

***Figure* 6.37**
Schooner *Wawona* (HAER No. WA-14). Seattle, King County, Washington. Half-breadth plan and sheer plan of *Wawona*, Sheet 6 of 7. Drawing by Richard K. Anderson, Jr., 1986.

***Figure* 6.38**
Schooner *Wawona* (HAER No. WA-14). Seattle, King County, Washington. Body plan and table of offsets of *Wawona*, Sheet 7 of 7. Drawing by Richard K. Anderson, Jr., 1986.

***Figure* 6.39**
Schooner *Wawona* (HAER No. WA-14). Seattle, King County, Washington. Outboard profile of *Wawona*, Sheet 1 of 7. Drawing by Richard K. Anderson, Jr., 1986.

***Figure* 6.40**
Meridian Hill Park (HABS No. DC-532). Washington, District of Columbia. Sixteenth Street fountain, 1985, Photograph No. DC-532-2. Photograph by Jack E. Boucher, 1985.

***Figure* 6.41**
Meridian Hill Park (HABS No. DC-532). Washington, District of Columbia. Cascade and reflecting pool, Photograph No. DC-532-16. Photograph by Jack E. Boucher, 1985.

***Figure* 6.42**
Meridian Hill Park (HABS No. DC-532). Washington, District of Columbia. Reflecting pool and exedra. Photograph by Jack E. Boucher, 1985.

***Figure* 6.43**
Meridian Hill Park (HABS No. DC-532). Washington, District of Columbia. 1928 Site plan, Sheet 2 of 25. Drawing by Robert R. Harvey, 1985.

***Figure* 6.44**
Meridian Hill Park (HABS No. DC-532). Washington, District of Columbia. Exedra plan, section, and details, Sheet 17 of 25. Drawing by Lauren Gruszecki and Daniel Sponn, 1985.

***Figure* 6.45**
Meridian Hill Park (HABS No. DC-532). Washington, District of Columbia. Balustrade detail, Photograph No. DC-532-30. Photograph by Jack E. Boucher, 1985.

***Figure* 6.46**
Meridian Hill Park (HABS No. DC-532). Washington, District of Columbia. Cascade area of lower park, Sheet 10 of 25. Drawing by Harlen Groe and Lauren Gruszecki, 1985.

***Figure* 6.47**
Meridian Hill Park (HABS No. DC-532). Washington, District of Columbia. Cascade area of lower park with pin bar overlay, Sheet 16 of 25. Drawing by Harlen Groe, Lauren Gruszecki, and Robert Harvey, 1985.

***Figure* 6.48**
Meridian Hill Park (HABS No. DC-532). Washington, District of Columbia. 1985 Site plan, Sheet 3 of 25. Drawing by Daniel Sponn, 1985.

***Figure* 6.49**
Meridian Hill Park (HABS No. DC-532). Washington, District of Columbia. Reflecting pool and exedra, reconstructed view, 1985, Sheet 21 of 25. Drawing by Daniel Sponn, 1985.

***Figure* 6.50**
Meridian Hill Park (HABS No. DC-532). Washington, District of Columbia. Landscape development concept, Sheet 6 of 25. Drawing by Harlen Groe, 1985.

BIBLIOGRAPHY

CHAPTER 1

The National Park Service has issued dozens of instructive publications on the techniques of recording, starting with the HABS "Bulletins" and "Circulars" of the 1930s and ending with the HABS and HAER "Field Instructions" and "Procedures Manuals" of the 1980s. For that reason they are not all listed here. The most current versions of this supplementary material are available from the HABS/HAER office in Washington, D.C. (see Appendix B).

In addition to the book *Historic America*, cited below, there were several earlier national catalogs of both the HABS and HAER collections. Many state, local, and topical catalogs of the HABS and HAER collections have also been published. An up-to-date list of these catalogs is available from HABS/HAER in Washington, DC (see Appendix B).

McKee, Harley J. *Recording Historic Buildings*. Washington, DC: Government Printing Office, 1970.

Peterson, Charles E. "The Historic American Buildings Survey Continued," *Journal of the Society of Architectural Historians*. Vol. XVI, No. 3 (October 1957), pp. 29-31.
Contains the text of Peterson's 1933 memorandum proposing the establishment of HABS.

Smith, Carol C. *Fifty Years of the Historic American Buildings Survey, 1933-1983*. Alexandria, VA: The HABS Foundation, 1983.

Stamm, Alicia, and C. Ford Peatross, eds. *Historic America: Buildings, Structures, and Sites*. Washington, DC: Library of Congress, 1983.
Published for the fiftieth anniversary of HABS, the book includes sixteen essays and a checklist of the HABS and HAER collections as of January 1, 1982.

U.S. Department of the Interior, National Park Service. "Secretary of the Interior's Standards and Guidelines for Architectural and Engineering Documentation." *Federal Register*. Vol. 48, No. 190 (Thursday, 29 September 1983), Notices, pp. 44730-44734 (see Appendix A).

CHAPTER 2

Standards

U.S. Department of the Interior, National Park Service. "Secretary of the Interior's Standards and Guidelines, Archeology and Historic Preservation. *Federal Register*. Vol. 48, No. 190 (Thursday, 29 September 1983), Notices, pp. 44716-44740.

Styles

Blumenson, John J. G. *Identifying American Architecture: A Pictorial Guide to Styles and Terms, 1600-1945*. Nashville: AASLH, 1986. 2nd ed.

Gottfried, Herbert, and Jan Jennings. *American Vernacular Design 1870-1940: An Illustrated Glossary*. New York: Van Nostrand Reinhold, 1985.

McAlester, Virginia and Lee. *A Field Guide to American Houses*. New York: Alfred A. Knopf, 1986.

Poppeliers, John C., S. Allen Chambers, and Nancy B. Schwartz. *What Style Is It?* Washington, DC: Preservation Press, 1983.

Rifkind, Carole. *A Field Guide to American Architecture*. New York: New American Library, 1980.

Whiffen, Marcus. *American Architecture Since 1780: A Guide to the Styles*. Cambridge, MA: MIT Press, 1969.

Surveys

Interagency Resources Division, National Park Service, U.S. Department of the Interior. *Guidelines for Local Surveys: A Basis for Preservation Planning*, National Register Bulletin 24. Washington, DC: National Park Service, 1977, revised 1985.

CHAPTER 3

This bibliography includes reference works cited in the chapter, such as where to find architectural drawings or information on specific architects. It does not include basic texts in architectural history or American history. The scholarship in these fields is extensive and ongoing. Rather, this list includes bibliographies on American architecture, which will point the reader in the direction of some basic works.

Bibliographies

These bibliographies each have a different area of interest, and most begin with a list of general sources. In addition, both the Society of Architectural Historians and the Vernacular Architecture Forum publish current bibliographies in their newsletters.

American Association of Architectural Bibliographers. *Papers*, Volumes I-XXII. The first eleven volumes were published by The University Press of Virginia between 1965 and 1975, Volume XI being the cumulative index. Volume XII was published by Garland Publishing, Inc., 1977.

Cuthbert, John A., Barry Ward, and Maggie Keeler. *Vernacular Architecture in America: A Selected Bibliography*. Boston: G. K. Hall & Co., 1985.

Hitchcock, Henry-Russell. *American Architectural Books: A List of Books, Portfolios, and Pamphlets on Architecture and Related Subjects Published in America Before 1895*. Minneapolis: University of Minnesota Press, 1946, 1962.

Roos, Frank J., Jr. *Bibliography of Early American Architecture: Writings on Architecture Constructed Before 1860 in Eastern and Central United States*. Urbana: University of Illinois Press, 1968.

Schlereth, Thomas J., ed. *Material Culture: A Research Guide*. Lawrence, Kansas: University Press of Kansas, 1985.

Wodehouse, Lawrence. *American Architects from the Civil War to the First World War: A Guide to Information Sources*. Detroit: Gale Research Co., 1976.

———. *American Architects from the First World War to the Present: A Guide to Information Sources*. Detroit: Gale Research Co., 1977.

Architects

For biographical information on specific architects, these three sources are indispensable. Note also the Wodehouse bibliographies, cited above.

Columbia University. *Avery Obituary Index of Architects and Artists*. Boston: G. K. Hall & Co., 1963.

Placzek, Adolf K., ed. *Macmillan Encyclopedia of Architects*. New York: The Free Press, 1982.

Withey, Henry F., and Elise Rathburn Withey. *Biographical Dictionary of American Architects, Deceased*. Los Angeles: New Age Publishing Co., 1956.

Architectural Drawings

Columbia University. *Avery Index to Architectural Periodicals*. Boston: G. K. Hall & Co., 1973 .

National Union Index to Architectural Records, at Prints and Photographs Division, Library of Congress, Washington, DC

Original architectural drawings are difficult to locate, and are most likely found in the building itself or in the architect's office. For drawings that have been published, the *Avery Index* is a good source. The *National Union Index*, begun as the *Cooperative Preservation of Architectural Records (COPAR)*, is a guide to architects' drawings in various repositories.

Architectural Terms

These four works contain the standard definitions and uses of architectural terms.

Harris, Cyril M. *Dictionary of Architecture and Construction*. New York: McGraw-Hill, 1975.

Harris, Cyril M. *Historic Architecture Sourcebook*. New York: McGraw-Hill, 1977.

Saylor, Henry H. *Dictionary of Architecture*. New York: Wiley, 1952.

Sturgis, Russell. *A Dictionary of Architecture and Building*, 3 volumes. New York: The Macmillan Company, 1902; republished by the Gale Research Company, 1966.

Grammar

The Chicago Manual of Style. Chicago: University of Chicago Press, 1982. 13th ed.

Turabian, Kate L. *A Manual for Writers*. Chicago: University of Chicago Press, 1987. 5th ed.

HABS/HAER and many other institutions follow the grammar rules set forth by the University of Chicago Press. Turabian's book is a condensation of the *Manual of Style*, geared toward unpublished works.

Technological History

Armstrong, Ellis L., ed. American Public Works Association. *History of Public Works in the United States, 1776-1976*. Chicago: American Public Works Association, 1976.

Furgueson, Eugene S. *Bibliography of the History of Technology*. Cambridge, MA, 1968.

Kemp, Emory, and Theodore Sande, eds. *Historic Preservation of Engineering Works: Proceedings of the Engineering Foundation Conference, Franklin Pierce College, Rindge, New Hampshire, June 1978*. New York: American Society of Civil Engineers, 1981.

Koch, Jean. *Industrial Archeology: An Introductory Bibliography*. Vance Bibliographies, Monticello, Illinois, 1979.

Kranzberg, Melvin, and Carroll W. Pursell, Jr., eds. *Technology in Western Civilization*. 2 vols. New York: Oxford University Press, 1967.

Rothenberg, Marc. *The History of Science and Technology in the United States: A Critical and Selective Bibliography.* New York: Garland Publishing, Inc., 1982.

Starbuck, David, ed. *An Introductory Bibliography in Industrial Archeology*. Society for Industrial Archeology, 1983.

CHAPTER 4

The American National Standards Institute, New York City, publishes industry standards for the photography and conservation industries. Its list of publications should be consulted for specific discussions on various aspects of permanence of films. The Society of American Archivists, Chicago, has publications on conservation. They should be consulted for specific discussion on this issue.

Ansel Adams was the author of numerous how-to photographic books and television shows. In the early 1980s (he died in 1984), he revised his series on photography and it has been republished as *The New Ansel Adams Photography Series* (4 volumes) by New York Graphic Society, New York. Another excellent volume by Adams is *Examples: The Making of 40 Photographs*, also published by the New York Graphic Society.

Borchers, Perry E. "Photogrammetric Recording of Cultural Resources." Washington, DC: National Park Service, 1977.

Boucher, Jack E. "Suggestions for Producing Publishable Photographs." Washington, DC: National Trust for Historic Preservation, no date.

______. *A Record In Detail: The Architectural Photographs of Jack E. Boucher.* Columbia, MO: University of Missouri Press, 1988.

Buchanan, Terry. *Photographing Historic Buildings*. London: Royal Commission on Historic Monuments, Her Majesty's Stationery Office, 1983.

Chambers, Henry, AIA. "Rectified Photography and Photo Drawing for Historic Preservation." Washington, DC: National Park Service, 1973.

Dean, Jeff. *Architectural Photography, Techniques for Architects, Preservationists, Historians, Photographers, and Urban Planners.* Nashville, TN: American Association of State and Local History, 1981.

Hart, David M., AIA. *X-Ray Examination of Historic Structures* ("Draft"). Washington, DC: National Park Service, 1975.

HABS/HAER. "Specifications for the Production of Photographs (for the use and guidance of contract Photographers)." Washington, DC: HABS/HAER, 1984.

Hockey, William B. "Scaled-Rectified Photography on Site." *APT Bulletin*, Vol. VII, No. 3, 1975, pp. 36-77.

Jones, Harvie P. "Enhancement of Historic Photographs." *APT Bulletin*, Vol. XI, No. 1, 1979, pp. 4-15.

Langford, M. J. *Basic Photography: A Primer for Professionals*. New York, 1965.

Lowe, Jet. *Industrial Eye*. Washington, DC: Preservation Press, 1986.

Lyons, Thomas R., and Thomas Eugene Avery. *Remote Sensing. A Handbook for Archeologists and Cultural Resource Managers*. Washington, DC: National Park Service, 1977.

McGrath, Norman. *Photographing Buildings Inside and Out*. New York, 1987

Pare, Richard. *Photography and Architecture: 1839-1939*. Montreal: Canadian Centre for Architecture, 1982.

Preservation Assistance Division, National Park Service, U.S. Department of the Interior. "Using Photogrammetry to Monitor Materials Deterioration and Structural Problems on Historic Buildings: The Dorchester Heights Monument; Case Study." Washington, DC: National Park Service, 1985.

Robinson, Cervin, and Herschman, Joel. *Architecture Transformed: A History of the Photography of Buildings from 1839 to Present*. Cambridge, MA: MIT Press, 1987.

Shulman, Julius. *The Photography of Architecture and Design: Photographing Buildings, Interiors, and the Visual Arts*. New York, 1977.

CHAPTER 5

American Institute of Architects. *Architectural Graphic Standards*, eighth edition. New York: John Wiley & Sons, Inc., 1988.
The standard reference for architectural information, this edition is the first to have a chapter on historic preservation, including four pages on HABS. Earlier editions have some material now considered historic, such as glass block details.

Bodey, Hugh, and Michael Hallas. *Elementary Surveying for Industrial Archeologists*. Aylesbury, England: Shire Publications Ltd., 1978.
Excellent for surveying all types of historic structures, not just industrial sites. Bibliography.

Brunskill, R. W. *Illustrated Handbook of Vernacular Architecture*. Boston: Faber and Faber, 1978.
A standard work. Bibliography.

Bullick, Orin M. *The Restoration Manual*. Norwalk, CT: Silvermine Publishers Incorporated, 1966.
A standard reference. Glossary and bibliography.

Chitham, Robert. *Measured Drawing for Architects*. London: The Architectural Press Ltd., 1980.
Good reference, but mostly English subject matter.

Cramer, Johannes. *Handbuch der Bauaufnahme*. Stuttgart: Deutsche Verlags-Anstalt, 1984.
Excellent, if you read German.

Kissim, Philip. *Surveying for Civil Engineers*. New York: McGraw-Hill Book Company, Inc., 1981.
Good reference on surveying.

Pannel, John Percival Masterman, and J. Kenneth Major. *The Techniques of Industrial Archeology*. Newton Abbot, England: David & Charles, 1974.
Excellent for documenting all types of historic structures, not merely industrial sites. Bibliography.

Patterson, Robert M. *Manual for the Preparation of "As Found" Drawings*. Victoria, Canada: British Columbia Heritage Trust, 1982.
Short booklet on recording historic buildings. Bibliography.

van der Putten, H. M. *Interim Guide for Measuring, Recording & Drawing of Historic Structures*. Ottawa: National Parks Canada, 1968.
Canadian equivalent of *Recording Historic Buildings*.

CHAPTER 6

Interpretive Drawings

Historic American Engineering Record, National Park Service, U.S. Department of the Interior. "HAER Field Instructions." Washington, DC: National Park Service, 1981.

Tufte, Edward R. *The Visual Display of Quantitative Information*. Cheshire, CT: Graphics Press, 1983.

Multiple Areas of Significance

The books listed below concentrate on historic construction technologies. For information on architectural history, consult the bibliography for Chapter 3.

Condit, Carl. *American Building Art: The Nineteenth Century*. New York: Oxford University Press, 1960.

______. *American Building Art: The Twentieth Century*. New York: Oxford University Press, 1961.

Cowan, Henry J. *An Historical Outline of Architectural Science*. New York: Elsevier Publishing Company, 1966.
Bibliography on the history of building science.

Cowan, Henry J. *The Master Builders*. New York: John Wiley & Sons, Inc., 1977.

Cowan, Henry J. *Science and Building*. New York: John Wiley & Sons, Inc., 1977.

Guedes, Pedro, ed. *Encyclopedia of Architectural Technology*. New York: McGraw-Hill Book Company, 1979.

Jandl, H. Ward, ed. *The Technology of Historic American Buildings*. Washington, DC: Foundation for Preservation Technology, 1983.

Peterson, Charles E., ed. *Building Early America*. Radnor, PA: Chilton Book Company, 1976.

Maritime Documentation

Albion, Robert G. *Naval and Maritime History: An Annotated Bibliography*. Mystic, CT: The Marine Historical Association, Inc., 1972.

Brouwer, Norman J. *International Register of Historic Ships*. Annapolis, MD: United States Naval Institute Press, 1985.

Historic American Engineering Record, National Park Service, U.S. Department of the Interior. *Guidelines for Recording Historic Ships*. Washington, DC: National Park Service, 1988.
Includes bibliography.

Jackson, Melvin H., ed. *The Historic American Merchant Marine Survey: Works Progress Administration, Federal Project No. 6*. Salem, NH: Ayer Company, Inc., 1983.
Available from the Ayer Company, Inc., P.O. Box 958, Salem, NH 03079. Copies of individual drawings may be obtained by writing the Division of Transportation—Room 5010, National Museum of American History, Smithsonian Institution, Washington, DC 20560.

Kinnell, Susan K., and Suzanne R. Ontiveros, eds. *American Maritime History: A Bibliography*. Santa Barbara, CA: ABC-Clio, Inc.

Labaree, Benjamin W. *A Supplement (1971-1986) to Robert G. Albion's Naval and Maritime History: An Annotated Bibliography*. Mystic, CT: Mystic Seaport Museum, Inc., 1988.

National Museum of American History. *Ship Plan List: Maritime Collection*. Washington, DC: Smithsonian Institution, 1984.
This catalog contains ordering information and a complete list of all available merchant ship plans from a dozen collections maintained by the Smithsonian. There is a separate catalog covering warships, *The Smithsonian Collection of Warship Plans*. Write to Ship Plans, Division of Transportation—Room 5010, National Museum of American History, Smithsonian Institution, Washington, DC 20560.

National Trust for Historic Preservation. *Guidelines for Maritime Documentation*. Washington, DC: National Trust, 1988.
This publication contains guidelines for the documentation of artifacts, folklore, and other maritime-related subjects in addition to ships and buildings. Contact the Maritime Department, National Trust for Historic Preservation, 1785 Massachusetts Avenue, N.W., Washington, DC 20036.

Landscape Documentation

Burnap, George. *Parks: Their Design, Equipment and Use*. Philadelphia: J.B. Lippincott Company, 1916.
An excellent source book.

Landscape Architecture. Vol. 77, No. 4 (July/August 1987), and Vol. 77, No. 5 (September/October 1987).
Both issues contain articles on the documentation and preservation of historic landscapes.

Liberty Hyde Bailey Hortorium. *Hortus Third, A Concise Dictionary of Plants Cultivated in the United States and Canada*. New York: Macmillan Publishing Co., Inc., 1976.
A standard reference on plant materials.

Newton, Norman T. *Design on the Land. The Development of Landscape Architecture*. Cambridge, MA: The Belknap Press of Harvard University Press, 1971.
A history of landscape architecture.

APPENDIX A

SECRETARY OF THE INTERIOR'S STANDARDS FOR ARCHITECTURAL AND ENGINEERING DOCUMENTATION

These standards concern the development of documentation for historic buildings, sites, structures and objects. This documentation, which usually consists of measured drawings, photographs and written data, provides important information on a property's significance for use by scholars, researchers, preservationists, architects, engineers, and others interested in preserving and understanding historic properties. Documentation permits accurate repair or reconstruction of parts of a property that is to be demolished.

These Standards are intended for use in developing documentation to be included in the Historic American Building Survey (HABS) and the Historic American Engineering Record (HAER) Collections in the Library of Congress. HABS/HAER, in the National Park Service, have defined specific requirements for meeting these Standards for their collections. The HABS/HAER requirements include information important to development of documentation for other purposes such as State or local archives.

Standard I. Documentation Shall Adequately Explicate and Illustrate What Is Significant or Valuable About the Historic Building, Site, Structure or Object Being Documented.

The historic significance of the building, site, structure or object identified in the evaluation process should be conveyed by the drawings, photographs and other materials that comprise documentation. The historical, architectural, engineering or cultural values of the property together with the purpose of the documentation activity determine the level and methods of documentation. Documentation prepared for submission to the Library of Congress must meet the HABS/HAER Guidelines.

Standard II. Documentation Shall Be Prepared Accurately from Reliable Sources with Limitations Clearly Stated to Permit Independent Verification of the Information.

The purpose of documentation is to preserve an accurate record of historic properties that can be used in research and other preservation activities. To serve these purposes, the documentation must include information that permits assessment of its reliability.

Standard III. Documentation Shall Be Prepared on Materials That Are Readily Reproducible, Durable and in Standard Sizes.

The size and quality of documentation materials are important factors in the preservation of information for future use. Selection of materials should be based on the length of time expected for storage, the anticipated frequency of use and size convenient for storage.

Standard IV. Documentation Shall Be Clearly and Concisely Produced.

In order for documentation to be useful for future research, written materials must be legible and graphic materials must contain scale information and location references.

SECRETARY OF THE INTERIOR'S GUIDELINES FOR ARCHITECTURAL AND ENGINEERING DOCUMENTATION

Introduction

These Guidelines link the Standards for Architectural and Engineering Documentation with more specific guidance and technical information. They describe one approach to meeting the Standards for Architectural Engineering Documentation. Agencies, organizations or individuals proposing to approach documentation differently may wish to review their approaches with the National Park Service.

The Guidelines are organized as follows:

- Definitions
- Goal of Documentation
- The HABS/HAER Collections
- Standard I: Content
- Standard II: Quality
- Standard III: Materials
- Standard IV: Presentation
- Architectural and Engineering Documentation Prepared for Other Purposes

Definitions

These definitions are used in conjunction with these Guidelines:

Architectural Data Form—a one page HABS form intended to provide identifying information for accompanying HABS documentation.

Documentation—measured drawings, photographs, histories, inventory cards or other media that depict historic buildings, sites, structures or objects.

Field Photography—photography other than large-format photography, intended for the purposes of producing documentation, usually 35mm.

Field Records—notes of measurements taken, field photographs and other recorded information intended for the purpose of producing documentation.

Inventory Card—a one page form which includes written data, a sketched site plan and a 35mm contact print drymounted on the form. The negative with a separate contact sheet and index should be included with the inventory card.

Large-Format Photographs—photographs taken of historic buildings, sites, structures or objects where the negative is a 4" x 5", 5" x 7" or 8" x 10" size and where the photograph is taken with appropriate means to correct perspective distortion.

Measured Drawings—drawings produced on HABS or HAER formats depicting existing conditions or other relevant features of historic buildings, sites, structures or objects. Measured drawings are usually produced in ink on archivally stable material, such as Mylar.

Photocopy—a photograph, with large-format negative, of a photograph or drawings.

Select Existing Drawings—drawings of historic buildings, sites, structures or objects, whether original construction or later alteration drawings that portray or depict the historic value or significance.

Sketch Plan—a floor plan, generally not to exact scale although often drawn from measurements, where the features are shown in proper relation and proportion to one another.

Goal of Documentation

The Historic American Buildings Survey (HABS) and Historic American Engineering Record (HAER) are the national historical architectural and engineering documentation programs of the National Park Service that promote documentation incorporated into the HABS/HAER collections in the Library of Congress. The goal of the collections is to provide architects, engineers, scholars, and interested members of the public with comprehensive documentation of buildings, sites, structures and objects significant in American history and the growth and development of the built environment.

The HABS/HAER Collections: HABS/HAER documentation usually consists of measured drawings, photographs and written data that provide a detailed record which reflects a property's significance. Measured drawings and properly executed photographs act as a form of insurance against fires and natural disasters by permitting the repair and, if necessary, reconstruction of historic structures damaged by such disasters. Documentation is used to provide the basis for enforcing preservation easement. In addition, documentation is often the last means of preservation of a property; when a property is to be demolished, its documentation provides future researchers access to valuable information that otherwise would be lost.

HABS/HAER documentation is developed in a number of ways. First and most usually, the National Park Service employs summer teams of student architects, engineers, and historians to develop HABS/HAER documentation, under the supervision of National Park Service professionals. Second, the National Park Service produces HABS/HAER documentation in conjunction with restoration or other preservation treatment of historic buildings managed by the National Park Service. Third, Federal agencies, pursuant to Section 110(b) of the National Historic Preservation Act, as amended, record those historic properties to be demolished or substantially altered as a result of agency action or assisted action (referred to as mitigation projects). Fourth, individuals and organizations prepare documentation to HABS/HAER standards and donate the documentation to the HABS/HAER collections. For each of these programs, different Documentation Levels will be set.

The Standard describe the fundamental principals of HABS/HAER documentation. They are supplemented by other material describing more specific guidelines, preferred techniques for architectural photography, and formats for written data. This technical information is found in the HABS/HAER Procedures Manual.

These Guidelines include important information about developing documentation for State or local archives.The State Historic Preservation Officer or the State library should be consulted regarding archival requirements if the documentation will become part of their collection. In establishing archives, the important questions of durability and reproducibility should be considered in relation to the purposes of the collection.

Documentation prepared for the purpose of inclusion in the HABS/HAER collections must meet the requirements below. The HABS/HAER office of the National Park Service retains the right to refuse to accept documentation for inclusion in the HABS/HAER collections when that documentation does not meet HABS/HAER requirements, as specified below.

Standard I: Content

1. Requirement: Documentation shall adequately explicate and illustrate what is significant or valuable about the historic building, site, structure or object being documented.

2. Criteria: Documentation shall meet one of the following documentation levels to be considered adequate for inclusion in the HABS/HAER collections.

a. Documentation Level I:

1. Drawings: a full set of measured drawings depicting existing or historic conditions.

2. Photographs: photographs with large-format negatives of exterior and interior views; photocopies with large-format negatives of select existing drawings or historic views where available.

3. Written data: history and description.

b. Documentation Level II:

1. Drawings: select existing drawings, where available, should be photographed with large-format negatives or photographically reproduced on Mylar.

2. Photographs: photographs with large-format negatives of exterior and interior views, or historic views, where available.

3. Written data: history and description.

c. Documentation Level III:

1. Drawings: sketch plan.

2. Photographs: photographs with large-format negatives of exterior and interior views.

3. Written data: architectural data form.

d. Documentation Level IV: HABS/HAER inventory cards.

3. Test: Inspection of the documentation by HABS/HAER staff.

4. Commentary: The HABS/HAER office retains the right to refuse to accept any documentation on buildings, sites, structures or objects lacking historical significance. Generally, buildings, sites, structures or objects must be listed in, or eligible for listing in, the National Register of Historic Places to be considered for inclusion in the HABS/HAER collections.

The kind and amount of documentation should be appropriate to the nature and significance of the buildings, site, structure or object being documented. For example, Documentation Level I would be inappropriate for a building that is a minor element of a historic district, notable only for streetscape context and scale. A full set of measured drawings for such a minor building would be expensive and would add little, if any, information to the HABS/HAER collections. Large-format photography (Documentation Level III) would usually be adequate to record the significance of this type of building.

Similarly, the aspect of the property that is being documented should reflect the nature and significance of the building, site, structure or object being documented. For example, measured drawings of Dankmar Adler and Louis Sullivans' Auditorium Building in Chicago should indicate not only facades, floor plans and sections, but also the innovative structural and mechanical systems that were incorporated in that building. Large-format photography of Gunston Hall in Fairfax County, Virginia, to take another example, should clearly show William Buckland's hand-carved moldings in the Palladian Room, as well as other views.

HABS/HAER documentation is usually in the form of measured drawings, photographs, and written data. While the criteria in the section have addressed only these media, documentation need not be limited to them. Other media, such as films of industrial processes, can be and have been used to document historic buildings, sites, structures or objects. If other media are to be used, the HABS/HAER office should be contacted before recording.

The actual selection of the appropriate documentation level will vary, as discussed above. For mitigation documentation projects, this level will be selected by the National Park Service Regional Office and communicated to the agency responsible for completing the documentation. Generally, Level I documentation is required for nationally significant buildings and structures, defined as National Historic Landmarks and the primary historic units of the National Park Service.

On occasion, factors other than significance will dictate the selection of another level of documentation. For example, if a rehabilitation of a property is planned, the owner may wish to have a full set of as-built drawings, even though the significance may indicate Level II documentation.

HABS Level I measured drawings usually depict existing conditions through the use of a site plan, floor plans, elevations, sections and construction details. HAER Level I measured drawings will frequently depict original conditions where adequate historical material exists, so as to illustrate manufacturing or engineering processes.

Level II documentation differs from Level I by substituting copies of existing drawings, either original or alteration drawings, for recently executed measured drawings. If this is done, the drawings must meet HABS/HAER requirements outlined below. While existing drawings are rarely as suitable as as-built drawings, they are adequate in many cases for documentation purposes. Only when the desirability of having as-built drawings is clear are Level I measured drawings required in addition to existing drawings. If existing drawings are housed in an accessible collection and cared for archivally, their reproduction for HABS/HAER may not be necessary. In other cases, Level I measured drawings are required in the absence of existing drawings.

Level III documentation requires a sketch plan if it helps to explain the structure. The architectural data form should supplement the photographs by explaining what is not readily visible.

Level IV documentation consists of completed HABS/HAER inventory cards. This level of documentation, unlike the other three levels, is rarely considered adequate documentation for the HABS/HAER collections but is undertaken to identify historic resources in a given area prior to additional, more comprehensive documentation.

Standard II: Quality

1. Requirement: HABS and HAER documentation shall be prepared accurately from reliable sources with limitations clearly stated to permit independent verification of information.

2. Criteria: For all levels of documentation, the following quality standards shall be met:

a. Measured drawings: Measured drawings shall be produced from recorded, accurate measurements. Portions of the building that were not accessible for measurement should not be drawn on the measured drawings, but clearly labeled as not accessible or drawn from available construction drawings and other sources and so identified. No part of the measured drawings shall be produced from hypothesis or non-measurement related activities. Documentation Level I measured drawings shall be accompanied by a set of field notebooks in which the measurements were first recorded. Other drawings prepared for Documentation Levels II and III, shall include a statement describing where the original drawings are located.

b. Large-format photographs: Large-format photographs shall clearly depict the appearance of the property and areas of significance of the recorded building, site, structure or object. Each view shall be perspective-corrected and fully captioned.

c. Written history: Written history and description for Documentation Levels I and II shall be based on primary sources to the greatest extent possible. For Levels III and IV, secondary sources may provide adequate information; if not, primary research will be necessary. A frank assessment of the reliability and limitations of sources shall be included. Within the written history, statements shall be footnoted as to their sources, where appropriate. The written data shall include a methodology section specifying name of researcher, data of research, sources searched, and limitations of the project.

3. Test: Inspection of the documentation by HABS/HAER staff.

4. Commentary: The reliability of the HABS/HAER collections depends on documentation of high quality. Quality is not something that can be easily prescribed or quantified, but it derives from a process in which thoroughness and accuracy play a large part. The principle of independent verification HABS/HAER documentation is critical to the HABS/HAER collections.

Standard III: Materials

1. Requirement: HABS and HAER documentation shall be prepared on materials that are readily reproducible for ease of access, durable for long storage, and in standard sizes for ease of handling.

2. Criteria: For all levels of documentation, the following material standards shall be met:

a. Measured Drawings
Readily Reproducible: Ink on translucent material.
Durable: Ink on archivally stable materials.
Standard Sizes: Two sizes: 19″ x 24″ or 24″ x 36″.

b. Large-Format Photographs
Readily Reproducible: Prints shall accompany all negatives.
Durable: Photography must be archivally processed and stored. Negatives are required on safety film only. Resin-coated paper is not accepted. Color

photography is not acceptable.
Standard Sizes: Three sizes: 4" x 5", 5" x 7", 8" x 10".

c. Written History and Description
Readily Reproducible: Clean copy for photocopying.
Durable: Archival bond required.
Standard Sizes: 8½" x 11".

d. Field Records
Readily Reproducible: Field notebooks may be photocopied. Photo identification sheet will accompany 35mm negatives and contact sheets.
Durable: No requirements.
Standard Sizes: Only requirement is that they can be made to fit into a 9½" x 12" archival folding file.

3. Test: Inspection of the documentation by HABS/HAER staff.

4. Commentary: All HABS/HAER records are intended for reproduction; some 20,000 HABS/HAER records are reproduced each year by the Library of Congress. Although field records are not intended for quality reproduction, it is intended that they be used to supplement the formal documentation. The basic durability performance standard for HABS/HAER records is 500 years. Ink on Mylar is believed to meet this standard, while color photography, for example, does not. Field records do not meet this archival standard, but are maintained in the HABS/HAER collections as a courtesy to the collection user.

Standard IV: Presentation

1. Requirement: HABS and HAER documentation shall be clearly and concisely produced.

2. Criteria: For levels of documentation as indicated below, the following standards for presentation will be used:

a. Measured Drawings:
Level I measured drawings will be lettered mechanically (i.e., Leroy or similar) or in a handprinted equivalent style. Adequate dimensions shall be included on all sheets. Level III sketch plans should be neat and orderly.

b. Large-format photographs:
Level I photographs shall include duplicate photographs that include a scale. Level II and III photographs shall include, at a minimum, at least one photograph with a scale, usually of the principal facade.

c. Written history and description:
Data shall be typewritten on bond, following accepted rules of grammar.

3 Test: Inspection of the documentation by HABS/HAER staff.

ARCHITECTURAL AND ENGINEERING DOCUMENTATION PREPARED FOR OTHER PURPOSES

There a preservation planning process is in use, architectural and engineering documentation, like other treatment activities, are undertaken to achieve the goals identified by the preservation planning process. Documentation is deliberately selected as a treatment for properties evaluated as significant, and the development of the documentation program for a property follows from the planning objectives. Documentation efforts focus on the significant characteristics of the property, as defined in the previously completed evaluation. The selection of a level of documentation techniques (measured drawings, photography, etc.) is based on the significance of the property and the management needs for which the documentation is being performed. For example, the kind and level of documentation required to record a historic property for easement purposes may be less detailed than that required as mitigation prior to destruction of the property. In the former case, essential documentation might be limited to the portions of the property controlled by the easement, for example, exterior facades; while in the latter case, significant interior architectural features and non-visible structural details would also be documented.

The principles and content of the HABS/HAER criteria may be used for guidance in creating documentation requirements for other archives. Levels of documentation and the durability and sizes of documentation may vary depending on the intended use and the repository. Accuracy of documentation should be controlled by assessing the reliability of all sources and making that assessment available in the archival record; by describing the limitations of the information available from research and physical examination of the property and by retaining the primary data (field measurements and notebooks) from which the archival record was produced. Usefulness of the documentation products depends on preparing the documentation on durable materials that are able to withstand handling and in sizes that can be stored and reproduced without damage.

APPENDIX B

ADDRESSES OF HABS/HAER AND RELATED ORGANIZATIONS

Historic American Buildings Survey/Historic American Engineering Record
U.S. Department of the Interior
National Park Service
PO Box 37127
Washington, DC 20013-7127

National Register of Historic Places
National Historic Landmarks Program, History Division

can be reached at the same address as HABS/HAER

The American Institute of Architects
1735 New York Avenue, NW
Washington, DC 20006

American Society of Civil Engineers
The American Society of Mechanical Engineers
Institute of Electrical and Electronics Engineers

can be reached at the following address:

345 East 47th Street
New York, NY 10017

Society of Architectural Historians
1232 Pine Street
Philadelphia, PA 19107-5944

Society for Industrial Archeology
Room 5020, National Museum of American History
Smithsonian Institution
Washington, DC 20560

HABS/HAER Collection
Prints and Photographs Division
Library of Congress
Washington, DC 20540

INDEX

References to illustrations are in italics.

G

H

I

N

O

P

Q

R

S

T

U

V

W

X

Y